The Strenuous Decade: China's

Nation-Building Efforts, 1927-1937

Edited with an Introduction

by

Paul K. T. Sih

Director, Center of Asian Studies

St. John's University, New York

A Symposium in Celebration of the

St. John's University Centennial, 1870-1970

ASIA IN THE MODERN WORLD SERIES, NO. 9

Published by the

ST. JOHN'S UNIVERSITY PRESS

under the auspices of the

Center of Asian Studies

Contents

Preface

BY VERY REVEREND JOSEPH T. CAHILL, C.M.

PRESIDENT, ST. JOHN'S UNIVERSITY

THE STORY OF THE DOMINATION of China's mainland by the Communists has long puzzled experts as well as laymen. Indeed, reasons attributed to its cause are varied and even contradictory. One widely alleged reason, for example, ascribes Communist rule to the corruption of the Nationalist Government and inadequate leadership of the Kuomintang, its ruling Party. The question inevitably arises: is this charge true or false? Quite understandably, reliable comprehensive data pertinent to this allegation have been meager and inconclusive and not even available. It is significant to note, however, that, from the founding of the Chinese National Government in 1927 to the outbreak of war against Japan in 1937, the state of political and economic affairs profoundly influenced the course of events preceding the Communist takeover. If the Government and the Party, during the period of 1927-1937, were totally corrupt and inefficient, another question can validly be raised: how could this same Government and this same Party have been able to sustain the eight years of war efforts from 1937 to the final victory over Japan in 1945?

The reality is that the National Government had established a splendid record during the period of 1927-1937.

The reason why this Government failed to continue to operate from 1937 to 1949 as efficiently as before should be found in some grounds other than in the sole and unique accusation of political corruption and inefficiency.

In an effort to provide such a historical study, St. John's University, in its Centennial Year Celebration, sponsored a symposium on modern China with special emphasis on China's nation-building efforts from 1927 to 1937. We were fortunate to have Dr. Paul K. T. Sih, Director of the Center of Asian Studies, to organize the program.

Being a noted Chinese scholar, Dr. Sih was particularly qualified to be in charge of the task. When the National Government was founded in 1927, he completed his secondary education in Shanghai and served as a social worker in the urban and rural areas of the municipality of Soochow. He then pursued the study of law for five years at the Comparative Law School of China, Soochow University (1928-1933), which operated evening courses, and worked during the day first at the Metropolitan Shanghai Chamber of Commerce as research fellow in charge of economic analysis and then at the Head Office of the Bank of China in Shanghai in the field of research and publications.

After he earned his law degree, he went to Italy for advanced studies at the University of Rome. At the same time, he served as attaché in charge of political and economic affairs at the Chinese Embassy there. He earned his doctorate in Political Science in 1935 under Professor Alberto de'Stefani, a world-known economist. Dr. Sih's thesis was a study on *The Financial and Economic Reforms of Post-war Italy.* The Chinese Government later invited his mentor, Professor de'Stefani, to serve as High Adviser to the Government in charge of economic and financial reforms of China.

Professor de'Stefani's work in China was administered by the National Resources Commission. This Commission was entrusted with the industrial and economic development of China. Dr. Sih was made a Technical Counselor of this organization and served with Professor de'Stefani. This assignment provided Dr. Sih with special opportunity for dealing with the most vital problems relative to the economic and industrial development of modern China. He made field trips with Professor de'Stefani throughout the interior of China. With the assistance of Dr. Sih, Professor de'Stefani drafted a set of economic and financial reforms for China for adoption by the Chinese Government. Had the Sino-Japanese hostilities not broken out in 1937, there would have been ample opportunities for carrying out these reform programs.

Dr. Sih's experiences after 1937 with responsible positions in the Ministry of Railways and the Ministry of Communications are even more extensive. After World War II, he served his government as a diplomat until 1949. Since then, he has been teaching in the United States. In 1959 Dr. Sih joined the faculty of St. John's University as Director of the Center of Asian Studies and Professor of History, a position that he holds today. We should like to reiterate, therefore, that with his education background, training and qualifications, particularly during the period of 1927-1937, Dr. Sih was eminently qualified to administer the symposium on modern China. Indeed, this very volume attests to his scholarly merit.

May God bless the efforts of our brother—China.

Introduction

BY PAUL K. T. SIH

THERE ARE MANY CONDITIONS for the modernization of a nation. Among the most essential are political reconstruction and economic development. Without a sound political environment, the people would not enjoy the fruits of economic growth and thus would not be able to sustain the effort required for continued progress. Also, without sufficient economic development, political reform would not inspire the people to make contributions to the building of their nation. The democratic system would lack an adequate foundation.

China began its modernization process in 1894 after the outbreak of the Sino-Japanese War. Realizing the urgent necessity of China's self-strengthening and transformation, Dr. Sun Yat-sen founded the Hsing Chung Hui (Revive China Society) in Honolulu for the restoration of Chinese rule. It was the forerunner of the Kuomintang which, since then, has been the mainstay of China's modernization program. Despite the difficulties and tribulations experienced in this development, the Kuomintang made significant contributions to China's nation-building endeavors.

Its first and foremost contribution was the Revolution of 1911. The Kuomintang overthrew the Manchu regime and founded the Republic of China. However, during the period, 1911-1927, there were scant political accomplishments. Warlords dominated the situation; civil strife was the order of the day; and Yuan Shih-k'ai, President of the young Republic, betrayed his pledge to democratic principles by ignoring the constitution, dissolving the Parliament, and outlawing the Kuomintang. He even went so far as to declare the restoration of a monarchy in 1915. These outrages compelled Dr. Sun to resume revolutionary activities. He established himself at Canton in 1917 with a view to overthrowing the government at Peking which, after Yuan's death in 1916, was ruled by the corrupt Northern warlords. As Dr. Sun could not secure any aid from Western countries, he had to adhere to a policy of alignment with Soviet Russia and the admission of Chinese Communists into the

Kuomintang—a policy which is based on a sincere desire for nationalism; it does not in any way imply acquiescence of Communism.

When Dr. Sun died in 1925, he had not achieved his full political aims. "The work of Revolution," he had stated in his will, "is not yet done." The responsibility for carrying on the revolution and unifying the country fell on his able and faithful disciple, Generalissimo Chiang Kai-shek.

In Chiang's mind, national unity held the highest priority. Without it, he reasoned, there would be no country and no other program would carry meaning. In 1926, accordingly, as Commander-in-Chief of the Revolutionary Army, he began the Northern Expedition. No sooner had the National Revolution achieved success than Generalissimo Chiang recognized the danger of the Communist conspiracy—a conspiracy that would take advantage of the National Revolution and convert it into a social revolution patterned on the Soviet model. Along with the establishment of the National Government in April 1927 at Nanking, Chiang took decisive action and purged the Kuomintang of Communists. Were Dr. Sun alive at the time, he would certainly have followed the same course of action.

The purge of 1927 saved China from the Communist conspiracy for the time being, but it began a series of wars which did not subside until the famous "long march" when the Chinese Communists were driven to the far northwest in 1935. The Communist military strength was now of minor significance.[*]

In the midst of these military campaigns against the Communist insurrections, the young National Government had been confronted with ever-increasing "internal worries" and "external threats." In November 1929, Soviet Russia initiated armed clashes with China along the Manchurian border. In April 1930, war operations were undertaken by the National Government to crush the Yen-Feng joint separatist movement. In September 1931, Japan invaded Manchuria. In November and December 1933, the National Government put down the "People's Government" staged by the Nineteenth Route Army in Fukien. These internal strifes provided Japan with pretext for aggressive attempts. After the puppet regime of "Manchukuo" was founded in 1932, Japan charted an adventurist course by manipulating the separatist movement in North China. In 1936, an "Autonomous Government of the Five

---

[*]The tragic situation of the Communists at that time was well described by Mao himself in the following words: "As a result, all the revolutionary bases were lost except the Shensi-Kansu border area, the Red Army was reduced from 300,000 to a few tens of thousands, the membership of the Chinese Communist Party was reduced from 300,000 to a few tens of thousands, and the Party organizations in Kuomintang areas were almost wiped out." (*Mao Tse-tung: Selected Works.* New York: International Publishers, 1954, Vol. I, p. 193.)

Northern Provinces of China" was created under the guidance and protection of the Japanese Army. Japan's drive for a total conquest of China was apparent. Meanwhile, the Chinese Communists, who had been cornered in the far northwest, promoted the policy of a "United Front" against aggression by the "Fascist" powers—a policy adopted by the Seventh World Congress in Moscow in August 1935. With this policy, the Communists intended to undermine and destroy the National Government and Chiang Kai-shek under the guise of fighting Japan. Not many Chinese were as apprehensive of the Communist plot as they were of the immediate Japanese threat.

Chiang was kidnapped by a Communist-inspired general, Chang Hsueh-liang, in December 1936. After being held for a time, Chiang's life was spared and he was released. His unprecedented prestige and popularity as the undisputed national leader of modern China further increased the already mounting threats of Japanese invasion. In July 1937, Japan attacked China. The war raged for eight years, until V-J Day in 1945.

Such is a brief account of China's "internal worries" and "external threats," particularly from the founding of the National Government in 1927 to the outbreak of war against Japan's invasion in 1937. During this decade, China had few days of peace. The Nationalist Government, under the leadership of Chiang Kai-shek, nevertheless, was able to embark upon a national program of reconstruction with impressive results.

As soon as the National Government had been established in 1927, it spared no effort in negotiating with a score of nations for the abolition of unequal treaties. Political reconstruction was carried out, in a variety of ways, with a view to achieving the new status of a modern government. The Provisional Constitution, with the Five-Power system as the main structure, was promulgated in June 1931, while a draft Permanent Constitution was enacted in May 1936. Laws and regulations for the preparation of local self-government were also enacted. In the economic and financial fields, many meaningful measures were adopted. These included the establishment of a national revenue system and budget, the reform of currency and banking institutions, the development of agricultural economy and increase of farm production by a more effective application of science and technology to cultivation along with sensitive reforms of land tenant system. Modern industry was developed; railroad construction was undertaken with the combined objective of assuring the people's economic life and national security. Education was given a very important place in the total program of reconstruction and modernization even though the entire nation was engulfed in a series of internal and external difficulties.

To say all this is to indicate that this ten-year period, 1927-1937, presents the most strenuous as well as glorious decade of China's nation-building efforts. It deserves a special place in China's modern history. Very little, however, has been written in this regard. Still less is found in the historical works published in Western languages. Had China not engaged itself successfully in this national development during these ten years, would she have been able to sustain eight long years of war against Japan and to fight along with the Allies to total victory? Historians interested in Far Eastern affairs must have posed this question for a long time.

In an attempt to provide an answer to this important problem, St. John's University sponsored a symposium, as part of its Centennial Celebration program, to make a systematic study of China's nation-building efforts during this important period of 1927 to 1937. Organized by the University's Center of Asian Studies, the symposium was held at the deAndreis Gallery, St. Augustine Hall, on the Jamaica campus, from July 14 to July 25, 1969. Twenty prominent American and Chinese scholars were invited to take part as speakers or discussants. Most of them had made direct or indirect contributions to this national program, their personal experiences outweighing any theoretical investigation. In addition, sixty participants selected from teaching faculties and research staffs of leading institutions of higher learning in the United States, Canada, and representative nations of East Asia attended the ten-day session. This volume is a result of that symposium; it provides a political and economic record of China during the strenuous decade, 1927-1937.

Of the years 1927-1937, covered in this volume, the first four years —with the Mukden Incident of 1931 as the line of demarcation—were for the National Government preparation for the last six. These six, the period of Generalissimo Chiang Kai-shek's strong leadership, saw the entry of China, in the midst of internal and external difficulties, into the new era of a modernized society. To the responsibilities and needs of that time, the nation summoned an imaginative effort unique in history and even greater than that made in the preceding four-year period of preparation. All who served in those years had an opportunity to give the best of their ability. Yet an account of the experience, as we read from this book, despite its successes, inevitably leaves a sense of disappointment and frustration, for the achievements fell short of the projected final goal. How often what seemed almost within grasp slipped away. The Marco Polo Bridge Incident of July 7, 1937 destroyed all that had been accomplished in that decade!

The first paper delivered by Dr. Joseph W. Ballantine was concerned with the international setting in which China found itself in the nineteenth and twentieth centuries. He observed that China could be partitioned by the European powers around the close of the nineteenth century. Had it not been for the "Open Door" policy pronounced by the United States, 1899-1900, China's political integrity would hardly have been safeguarded. He noted, in particular, China's foreign relations in the 1920's and 1930's. China had to face the mounting threats of Japanese aggression; she had also to deal with the "Trojan Horse" tactics of Soviet Russia. Britain and the United States could do little about the situation as they were both deeply disturbed by economic depressions at home. The League of Nations could offer only lip service to China during the Mukden crisis in 1931. The international situation of China at the time could hardly have been worse.

As a diplomat in the U. S. Foreign Service in charge of Far Eastern Affairs at the time, Dr. Ballantine reminisced: "On July 7, 1937, Japan launched an all-out attack on China following a minor incident at Marco Polo Bridge near Peiping, provoked and enlarged upon by the Japanese Army. Three weeks later, Premier Konoe announced the establishment of a 'New Order in East Asia.' This Japanese aggressive action not only brought all kinds of nation-building efforts being made by China practically to a standstill, but also provided for Soviet Russia an ideal chance to land a catch in China's troubled waters—an attempt that the Tsarist Empire made as far back as the sixteenth century."

Dr. C. T. Liang was a discussant of Dr. Ballantine's paper. Commenting on the crucial issue regarding war or peace between China and Japan, he put it in this historical prospective: "We are told that it was China's weakness that encouraged Japan's ambition; but we are also told that it was China's strength that begot Japan's aggression. . . . The more improvements China achieves, the quicker the relation between China and Japan approaches its doom."

Another discussant of Dr. Ballantine's paper was Dr. William L. Tung. Based upon his personal experiences as a Chinese diplomat and with his professional teaching background he added a very lively discussion on the efforts that the Chinese Government made with regard to the abolition of unequal treaties. The primary objective of the National Government, upon its birth in 1927, was to achieve national independence and freedom. This could not be done as long as the unequal treaties imposed upon China remained in force. Under the National Government, serious efforts were made for their abolition. "Had it not been for the Japanese invasion of Manchuria (in 1931)," Dr. Tung noted, "China's aspirations in this respect would most likely have been fulfilled before 1937."

The next theme dealt with the political reconstruction of China during the period of 1927-1937. In presenting his paper, Dr. Dison Hsueh-feng Poe singled out the "internal worries" and "external threats" that China experienced in the developing stages. However, for all its trials and tribulations, the Chinese Government was able to make steady progress in:

1) the achievements of gradual national unification,
2) the cultivation of national consciousness,
3) the augmentation of defensive military strength,
4) the embarkation upon tutelage Constitutionalism,
5) the founding of the Five-Power central system,
6) the preparation for local self-government,
7) the launching of judicial and administrative reforms,
8) the attempts at improving popular economic life.

The performance made by the National Government was so impressive that Dr. Poe remarked: "There are two fruitful evidences of this net result or overall balance. One is China's ability to have fought the eight years of resistance war against Japan. The other is the undisputed accomplishments in Taiwan today. Both of these achievements have their historical foundation in the arduous nation-building efforts under review."

In discussing Dr. Poe's work, Professor Franz Michael observed in particular the significant success that the National Government scored in the military order. "The new Chinese Government," he stated, "had to deal with three major military problems: the elimination of warlordism and unification of the country; the defeat of the Communist insurgency and the defense of China against the growing danger of the Japanese attack. The success of these military tasks was of primary importance to defend and guarantee the survival of the nation and of the whole program of modernization of that time."

Indeed, China could not speak of modernization if she were deprived of a central government which was to be in charge of the task. It was precisely for the unification of the country that the National Government had to confront, at one and the same time, these three opposing forces— warlords and Communists within, and Japanese invasion without. These three forces aimed at different objectives, and while they used different methods to achieve these objectives, at times they capitalized on common difficulties to act in collusion, thus undermining the position and strength of the Central Government.* A glimpse of the attached chronology at the end of this volume illustrates this important fact.

---

*For instance, when the National forces were defeating the Communists in September 1931, Japan invaded Manchuria, and as Japan further advanced toward Chinchow in December, the Communists attacked the National forces at Kanchow in Kiangsi. In the midst of these crises, the Communists set up the Central Soviet Republic in Juichin in November as a rival regime, while the separatist elements of the Canton group forced Generalissimo Chiang Kai-shek to resign, thus greatly undermining the power of the central authority to deal with both Japan and the Communists.

Dr. Arthur N. Young, a well-known specialist in public finance, was China's financial adviser for eighteen years (1928-1946). He played an active role in China's financial reform. In his paper, "China's Fiscal Transformation, 1927-1937," Dr. Young discussed at full length his theme under several headings: the fiscal situation before 1927-1928; founding a fiscal system, 1927-1928; the quest for stability-building revenues; expenditures, deficits, and borrowing; and the rehabilitation of credit. He observed, among other things, that in the decades before World War II, the Chinese National Government transformed the finances and began an impressive program of development. This was the more creditable because of extreme difficulty from attempted subversion by warlords and Communists, and Japan's aggression. By 1937, when Japan attacked, the Government had settled $270 million of defaulted Peking debts. Leading foreign bond issues rose greatly and prices were on a 5 per cent basis in London in mid-1937, while internal bonds which earlier had yielded 15 to 25 per cent were on about an 8 per cent basis. Financial reforms cleared the way for foreign credits for development and currency support. Foreign credits granted in 1934-1937 equalled well over $100 million, and others under negotiation were of similar size.

No one is more qualified than Dr. Young to reach such an emphatic conclusion: ". . . by 1937, China's fiscal system was remarkably transformed from the chaotic condition of ten years earlier. The Government was beginning to be able to act effectively. The economy was moving forward strongly. I may quote the *London Economist* of July 24, 1937 (p. 167): 'All observers seem to be agreed that China has been pulling round with remarkable success during the last year or two. The Central Government's authority has been becoming rapidly more effective over an ever wider area. . . . The financial and economic condition of the country has been distinctly improving'."

The discussant of Dr. Young's paper was Dr. Ta-chung Liu. In his comments, Dr. Liu, sharing Dr. Young's views, added: "Starting in 1937, the system was more or less in operation. . . . Burdened heavily with internal and external debts contracted by the now defunct Central Government in Peking and its own continuing deficits, the National Government made several successful efforts to rehabilitate and simplify the debt structure. The successful currency reform in 1935 was a major achievement which contributed significantly to China's ability to resist single-handed the full-scale Japanese invasion for four years, from 1937-1941."

Public finance has a close relationship with currency and banking system. In discussing "Toward Modernization of China's Currency and Banking, 1927-1937," Dr. Chang Kia-ngau provided a comprehensive and scholarly study based primarily on his personal experience. Dr. Chang spent several decades in his banking career and has been respected as a builder of modern banking system in China. He was of the view that after the establishment of the National Government in 1927, politically China was unified and the central authority of the Government was asserted. As a result, the currency and banking systems were reformed, just as had occurred in Germany. After the founding of the German Empire, there evolved the standardization of currency in 1872 and the founding of the Central Bank in 1875. Unfortunately, the political situation in China was far from stable. Civil wars, Communist insurgencies, floods and the military threats of Japanese invasion made it most difficult for an early and effective application of the reforms, notably the institution of a standard uniform dollar and the standardization of subsidizing coins, the termination of the note-issuing rights of provincial and private commercial banks, and the establishment of a single note-issuing authority. However, the National Government, in the midst of enormous difficulties, still was able to carry out gradually the above important reforms toward the modernization of currency and banking institutions. The Central Bank of China began operation in November 1928. The Bank of China was given special duties in the area of foreign financial transactions, while the Bank of Communications was assigned primary responsibility for fostering the growth of Chinese domestic industry. The *tael* system was abolished and the unification of silver currency was achieved in 1933.

Dr. Chang further added that when the Silver Purchase Act was passed in the United States Congress, resulting in a rise in the price of silver on the world market causing an outflow of silver from China, the National Government was ready to change the Silver Standard to Foreign Exchange Standard in November 1935. The exchange rate for the new currency was stable up to the outbreak of the Sino-Japanese War in July 1937. Were it not for the outbreak of the war, the National Government would have been able, within a relatively short period of time, to balance the national budget and bring about a favorable international balance of payments. This would naturally have led China to a position where a modern banking system, sound fiscal policies, and an acceleration of industrial development were imminent.

By the same token, Dr. Sho-chieh Tsiang, discussant of Dr. Chang's paper, observed: "The National Government during the decade of 1927-1937, beset as it was with Communist uprisings, disastrous floods and Japanese encroachment and aggression, still managed to carry out some fundamental reform in the monetary system and to bring about an expansion and strengthening of the bank system. . . . Dr. Chang's conclusion remains quite warranted, namely, that if China had been spared the destructive war forced on her by Japanese aggressions, she would have been well on her way towards developing a sound monetary and banking system as well as rapid industrialization during the decade following 1937."

China is primarily an agricultural society. People's livelihood depends largely upon the progress of agricultural development. In this respect, Dr. John Lossing Buck provided us with a detailed account of his personal experiences covering the agricultural economy of China, 1927-1937, as exemplified by his work at the University of Nanking where he taught and was engaged in research and experimental work throughout those strenuous years. So successful was his work that he could state: "By 1936 . . . the sleeping lion was wide awake; there were enough Chinese in every facet of development that all foreigners could go home and the progress would continue at an accelerating rate!"

In his comments on Dr. Buck's paper, Dr. Franklin L. Ho, also personally involved in the same economic tasks, offered a supplement by providing a meaningful study of two important subjects: (1) agencies engaged in the development of agricultural economy; (2) lines and extent of the development, such as the promotion of rural cooperatives, agricultural cooperative financing, agricultural marketing, and the regulation of land tenure and land taxation. After a detailed discussion of these relevant problems, Dr. Ho remarked: ". . . China was on the road toward a 'take-off' in the development of her agricultural economy during the period from 1927-1937. Had there been no Communist rebellion within and no foreign aggression without, she could have been able to overcome all the traditional resistance to a steady and sustained development of her agricultural economy."

Dr. T. H. Shen is presently Chairman of the Sino-American Joint Commission on Rural Reconstruction (JCRR). To this symposium, he contributed his study on "First Attempts to Transform Chinese Agriculture, 1927-1937." "Among many remarkable accomplishments in the modernization of China's agriculture through the application of science and technology and capital to cultivation during this particular period," Dr. Shen stressed, "a national program was carried out by the Chinese Government in the 1933-1937 period for reducing the imports of cotton, wheat, and rice by increased production, better marketing, and the levying of import duties on foreign commodities. . . . In 1936 and 1937, the imports of rice were much reduced; those of wheat became insignificant for prewar consumption." Evidently, without these improvements it would be difficult for China to sustain the war against Japan, as communications with the outside world were practically cut off and no imports of any agricultural products could be effected.

In his comments on Dr. Shen's paper, Dr. Franklin L. Ho offered his observations with special emphasis on three subjects: (1) research in crop improvement, insect and disease control, fertilizer, soil, animal husbandry, sericulture and agricultural engineering; (2) agricultural extension, and (3) water control and irrigation. Among other things, he pointed out: "Before 1937, a total of thirteen irrigation projects were completed, irrigating a total of more than six million *mou* of land. The most important canals constructed during the period were the Minsheng Canal in Suiyuan completed in 1932; the Kinghui Canal in Shensi completed in 1932; and the Lohui Canal in Shensi completed in 1935." The benefits derived from such irrigation developments were obvious when the discussant again remarked: "In Tinghsien, Hopei province, for instance, the value per *mou* in the middle of the 1930's was CNC $75.00 per irrigated land by wells as compared with CNC $33.00 per non-irrigated; the value of annual crops per *mou* was CNC $13.00 on irrigated land by wells as compared with CNC $5.00 on non-irrigated land."

In dealing with "Industrial Development and Economic Policy of China in 1927-1937," Dr. Yuan-li Wu, presently Deputy Assistant Secretary of the United States Department of Defense for Policy Plans and NSC Affairs, emphasized achievements on the transformation of China from a traditional to a modern economy. Marked progress was made in the realm of industry. In particular, he cited six cases whereby joint public and private ownership of industrial enterprises were operated. Special credit was given to the efforts exercised by the National Government. "In general," as Dr. Wu put it, "Government encouragement was given in the form of (1) exemption from export and raw material taxes, (2) reduction of freight rates by Government owned transport facilities (including notably the railway), (3) cash awards, and (4) monopoly privileges in specified geographical areas for a period of five years."

Likewise, Dr. Chi-ming Hou remarked in his discussion of Dr. Wu's paper: "At any rate, few would deny that the many measures adopted by the National Government were instrumental in providing a helpful environment and essential 'pre-condition' for industrial development, both in the 1930's and later."

Communications, especially railroads, are important instruments for the development of a nation's economy. This is particularly true with China which has a vast expansion of territory and an enormous population. In his paper, "A Decade of Chinese Railroad Construction, 1926-1936," Professor Ling Hung-hsun, a leading railroad expert who spent several decades in railroad construction in China, summed up the achievements in these words: "On the whole, the period between 1926 and 1936 was a very active decade for the construction of railroads in China. During this period, China had built altogether 2,900 miles of trunklines, including 804 miles in the Northeast and 2,080 miles within the Great Wall. In July 1937, when Japan first started invading China, there were about 1,110 miles of railroads under construction. Due to the Japanese invasion, loan contracts for more than 2,240 miles of railroads could not be finalized. At this time, the re-adjustment of old debts was estimated to be in the amount of £40,360,000. If it had not been for the Japanese invasion, the history of China's railroads would have been entirely different." On the other hand, if China had not been making rapid progress in railroad construction, notably in the completion of the Canton-Hankow Railroad in 1936, and, before that, the building and completing of the Hang-Kiang Railroad from 1930-1934, and also the construction of the Chientang Bridge (a combination of highway and railroad bridge) from 1933 to 1937, Japan would not have become so aggrieved and impatient as to launch a total attack on China in July 1937.

Professor of Geography at the University of Pittsburgh, Dr. Chiao-min Hsieh singled out the main characteristics of China's railroads in bringing about important economic and political consequences. While paying tribute to the successful efforts made by the National Government of the Republic of China during the 1926-1936 period in railroad construction, Dr. Hsieh criticized Communist China for the building of two long railroads for the purpose of connecting the mainland with the Soviet Union. One runs from Tsining through Ulan Bator in Outer Mongolia, then on to the Soviet Union; and the other runs between Lanchow and Urumchi via Hami in Sinkiang. In Dr. Hsieh's words, "The Communist Government obviously feels that the political importance of these railroads is greater than their economic value. . . . Moreover, there is at the moment a sand-dune problem confronting the operation of the railroad in these desert areas. This seems to be insoluble by use of present techniques and makes the value of the whole project even more questionable."

Education, it has been said, is the soul of a nation. Without adequate educational foundations, a nation cannot renovate or regenerate itself. This is especially true of China when it had to face the challenge of change and renewal as soon as the National Revolution under the Kuomintang was accomplished in 1927.

Dr. Theodore H. E. Chen, who experienced this critical period of 1927-1937 as dean of the Fukien Christian University, pointed out in his "Education in China, 1927-1937" the remarkable progress that the Chinese National Government achieved in these years. "Chinese education in the decade preceding the outbreak of the Sino-Japanese war," Dr. Chen stated, "was marked by growth, expansion, greater government efforts and better co-ordination. For the first time since the introduction of modern schools, China had a stable government committed to long-range education planning." Again he said, "An over-all review of education during this decade must conclude with genuine gratification over the substantial progress made within a few years, and with high praise for the positive policy of the government to support education, to broaden its scope, to equalize educational opportunity, and to make education an effective instrument of nation-building."

The discussant of Dr. Chen's paper was Dr. Chi-pao Cheng. In his comments, he supplemented the description of efforts made by the Chinese Education Mission to Europe in 1932-1933. Unfortunately, because of the war with Japan in 1937, the meaningful recommendations submitted by the Mission for further educational improvement could not be put into practice.

After considering the above discussions relating to China's international relations in the modern era along with its nation-building efforts in the realm of political reconstruction, fiscal transformations, currency and banking reforms, agricultural production, industrial development, railroad construction, and educational improvement, we realize that although the speakers and discussants presented their views from their respective point of interests, they unanimously reached one and the same conclusion: *During the decade 1927-1937, the Chinese National Government, with the Kuomintang as the ruling party, did a superb task in the nation-building development. In the midst of "internal worries" and "external threats," the Government was able to carry out the national program with efficiency and effectiveness. Policy was sound; leadership was intelligent. Had it not been for the outbreak of the Resistance War against the Japanese invasion in July 1937, China would have been able to attain the status of a new, modern society, whereby the Principles of the Three Peoples would have been fully realized.*

Present-day China, like other countries, can be comprehended only in the light of its past. The nation-building efforts made by the Nationalist Government, particularly in the political and economic fields, bore profound and far-reaching consequences on the years that followed. The specific aims and objectives of the present volume are, it is hoped, made clear by this introduction. The Editor's aim was to persuade scholars available during this ten-day symposium to present the information concerning a period of vital importance to the modernization of China. It was especially desirable that this volume should be the product of international cooperation. But the nationality of cooperating scholars was not, however, a matter of prime importance. What was particularly intended was that each contributor should be outstandingly qualified to handle the subject undertaken. No less desirable was that the portrayal should be realistic rather than sentimental, objective rather than subjective. It is reasonable to infer that these aims have been attained.

To all those who have helped in the production of this work, the Editor wishes to express sincere thanks and gratitude. In a special way, he wishes to thank Very Reverend Joseph T. Cahill, C.M., President of St. John's University, for his sustained trust and kindness in a particularly busy period to write the preface. To Dr. Henry C. Mills, Vice President and Provost; to Dr. Blaise J. Opulente, Administrative Vice President; to Reverend Joseph I. Dirvin, C.M., Vice President for University Relations and Executive Director of the University Centennial Committee; to Dr. Paul T. Medici, Dean of the Graduate School of Arts and Sciences; to Reverend Richard J. Devine, C.M., Dean of the College of Liberal Arts and Sciences, St. John's University, for their unfailing encouragement and suggestions in the formation of the symposium and the final preparation of the manuscript for the Press, the Editor is most grateful. Thanks are due to Dr. Robert D. Barendsen, Specialist for Far Eastern Countries, Comparative Education, in the United States Office of Education (Washington, D.C.), for his participation as a discussant in the session concerning "Education in China." In particular, I am indebted to Dr. Anthony Kubek, Chairman of the Department of History, University of Dallas Station, Texas, for a special lecture on "Chinese-American Relations During World War II" at the conclusion of the symposium. The paper has been published separately in a professional journal.* The chronology of 1927 to 1937 has been prepared with the assistance of Mr. Ho-ping Lo, graduate fellow at the St. John's University Center of Asian Studies.

---

*Issues & Studies, Vol. VI, No. 7 (April, 1970).

CHAPTER I

International Settings:
A Study of Strained Relationships
Between China and Foreign Powers

BY JOSEPH W. BALLANTINE

OR NEARLY A CENTURY after the Napoleonic wars a balance of power had prevailed among the European nations seeking advantage in China. It was in relation to the "hermit" kingdom of Korea that a chain of events was set in motion upsetting this balance.

In 1894 contention between China and Japan for preponderance of influence in the Korean peninsula precipitated a war between them, resulting in China's defeat. Japan thus became dominant in Korea, and in the peace treaty exacted the cession to her of Taiwan; and, in Manchuria, that part of the Liaotung peninsula that commands the sea approaches to Peking and Mukden. At that point Russia entered the scene. As far back as 1580 the Tsarist Empire had begun an advance which, in the course of sixty years, had brought her Cossacks to the Pacific Ocean. Fifty years later relations with China had been stabilized to endure for two centuries. Then, in 1858, the Treaty of Aigun and, two years later, a supplementary treaty brought the area south of the Amur and east of the Ussuri into the Muscovite domain. This latter accretion included the magnificent harbor of Vladivostok. Russian colonists flocked in, and the Russian government began to project a transcontinental railway.

Hardly had the ink become dry on the Sino-Japanese treaty when Russia proceeded with moves to deprive Japan of the fruits on the Asian mainland of her victory. This was effected by persuading Germany and France to associate themselves with her in offering Japan what they euphemistically termed "friendly advice in the interest of the peace of the Far East" to retrocede to China the Liaotung Peninsula Japan had taken from China. Japan was not strong enough to disregard this advice.

1

In 1898, a Russo-Chinese agreement was concluded providing for a twenty-five year lease to Russia, without any material consideration, of the Liaotung Peninsula, including the two important ports, Port Arthur and Dairen, that Japan had been forced to give up to China in 1895. The making of the lease to Russia, it was affirmed, had been prompted by the mutual desire of the Tsar and the Emperor of China to strengthen still further the friendly relations between the two empires and by the wish to ensure the means whereby to show reciprocal support. There was also in the agreement the further meaningless affirmation that "this act of lease in no way violates the sovereign rights of His Majesty, the Emperor of China in the territory affected."

Port Arthur was developed into a naval base and Dairen became the tidewater terminus of a railway to Harbin in north central Manchuria. There is terminated in a junction with a west-east line from the border of Transbaikal Province across Manchuria to Russia's Maritime Province connecting with a line to Vladivostok. All of the Russian-owned lines in Manchuria were comprised in the Chinese-Eastern Railway. Under the railway rights of way that Russia had exacted from China, provision had been made also for Russian administered settlements along the way and for the protection of those settlements by Russian troops. Not satisfied with Manchuria, Russia tried to get a foothold in Korea but was too inept to cope with Japan. Nevertheless Russia's minatory gestures brought on the Russo-Japanese War of 1904-1905.

Russia's leasing of the Dairen-Port Arthur area in Manchuria was a signal for a scramble among other powers for gains in China. Britain obtained a lease of the port of Weihaiwei in Shantung Province across the narrows of the Yellow Sea from Russia's holdings, to be held for the duration of Russia's lease. Britain also took a ninety-nine year lease on some 300 square miles of land contiguous to her colony of Hong Kong. Germany acquired Kiaochow Bay on the south side of Shantung Province. France took Kwangchowwan in Kwangtung Province adjacent to Indochina. Those nations then proceeded to stake out claims for exclusive spheres of influence in the regions adjacent to their leaseholds. Russia claimed all of Manchuria as its sphere; Britain, a good part of the Yangtze Valley; Germany, Shantung Province; Japan, Fukien Province; and France, large areas of three provinces adjacent to Indochina. It began to look as if all China would soon be carved up among the predatory powers.

China at that time was demonstrably unable to withstand the pressure of great power imperialism. Among the circumstances contributing to China's unpreparedness to adjust herself to modern conditions were the fact that the long life of the Chinese system was thought by the

Chinese to have proved its adequacy to meet all exigencies, that in the absence of stimulating challenges over the centuries from competing cultures or rival powers there had set in an ever increasing conservatism, and that China was self-sufficient economically. Added to this there was a complacent glorification of the past. Confucius and other moral leaders had expounded philosophies that tended to perpetuate a patriarchal social order, whose narrowing effects on loyalties were a deterrent to successful large-scale co-operative effort except in such traditional matters as flood control. Chinese intellectual development, moreover, began early to differ markedly from that of the West. In his *Chinese Renaissance* Dr. Hu Shih has pointed out that "at the time when the Greeks were studying plants and animals, mathematics, and tools and mechanics, the Chinese were absorbed with theories of politics and ethics."[1] The absence of a scientific tradition in China helps to account for the country's eclipse by the West after the advent of the Machine Age. It was China's misfortune also that the impact of the Industrial Revolution hit China at a time when the ruling dynasty was in a condition of advanced decay.

When China was confronted by the challenge of the West she lacked effective leadership. She lacked a trained and respected military class. Chinese intellectuals were not generally men of action. Even the more discerning and modern minded among them, who saw the need for making adjustment to the new situation, were powerless to act in the face of a complacent indifference throughout an ignorant, effete, and decadent court. The consequent failure of the Chinese system to withstand the impact of Western civilization had set in motion a process of social and political change. Although the West had thus given China the initial impulse for a change, the restraints that the Western powers and Japan imposed upon full exercise by China of her sovereignty operated to check the process of change.

The impact of Western scientific thought on China produced reactions similar to, but more subdued than, those that the learning of the Greeks and of the Arabs once had upon Western Europe. The foundations of the cultural and political system of China were shaken, and yet to the Chinese their accustomed order was so satisfying that they were reluctant to alter it. These circumstances, together with the vast bulk of the country, its political texture as an agglomeration of numberless practically self-contained village communities, and the low standard of living and high rate of illiteracy among the masses account for the fact that the revolution which began more than a century ago is still going on.

In these circumstances, America in 1899 felt prompted to propose to the governments of Britain, France, Germany, Japan, and Russia formal declaration of an "Open Door" policy with respect to the leased territories and the so-called "spheres of influence" or of "special interest" that these countries were developing in China.

A year later, during the Boxer Uprising, America similarly made a formal declaration of policy of respect for the territorial and administrative integrity of China, since it was reasoned that an independent China was a prerequisite to the preservation of the "Open Door" and to the maintenance of stability in the Far East.

The replies to the notes were somewhat equivocal, the Russian being the most ambiguous of all. Nevertheless the suave tone of these replies apparently were regarded by Secretary of State John Hay as justifying him in announcing that the policy of the "Open Door" had been accepted and that it was the governing policy in China.

United States policy was helpful in achieving settlement of the difficulties between China and the powers arising from the loss of property and foreign lives in the course of the Boxer Uprising. The terms of settlement were contained in the Protocol of Peking, signed September 7, 1901, which, among other things, required China to pay, over a period of years, an indemnity of $333 million. Of this the United States claimed only $25 million, a sum which proved to be more than adequate to indemnify American nationals. In 1908 and 1924, the United States remitted all of the Boxer indemnity payments not allocated to claimants. The Chinese government placed the money, approximately $18 million, in a trust fund for the education of Chinese youths in China and the United States.[2]

Japan's pursuit of a privileged position in China was more extensive than that of any other power. She had become an actor on the continental stage at a time when, by virtue of the Anglo-Japanese Alliance concluded in 1902, her naval security was dependent upon the good will of the British fleet. But the assurance of this protection was dependent also upon adroit statesmanship. Field Marshal and Elder Statesman Yamagata called for a comprehensive defense policy, embodying among other things naval parity with the United States, which was designated as the hypothetical enemy. Two battle fleet construction programs were outlined, one calling for eight battleships and eight battle cruisers, and the second, the reduction of the cruisers by four. Construction lagged for lack of funds.[3]

In 1914 Japan entered World War I on the side of the allies, asserting that it was her duty to do so as Britain's ally. The ally was far from enthusiastic about Japan's decision. Aside from some patrol duties in Asian waters in the common cause, her operations—the takeover from Germany of Kiaochow Bay and the Micronesian islands—were exclusively in her own interest.

The real issues that troubled United States-Japanese relations arose out of Japan's position and attitude toward the Asian continent. It was only natural, under the temptations offered by World War I, that Japan fell into the error of seeking to develop its defensive policy into one of positive and aggressive imperialism at the cost of her weaker neighbors on the mainland of Asia. Early in 1915 Japan secretly presented to China the Twenty-One Demands, which, if accepted in full, would have made China a virtual protectorate of Japan. The Japanese government not only demanded extensive further economic and political rights in Manchuria, Shantung and Inner Mongolia, but also sought exclusive mining and industrial rights in the Yangtze Valley; and she actually insisted upon supervisory control over Chinese social and political institutions, including not only schools and churches but even the government itself. When the United States learned of the Demands, the Secretary of State, in a note of March 13, 1915 to the Japanese Ambassador, called attention to the various international undertakings concerning China, and argued that Japan's demands were inconsistent with its past pronouncements regarding the sovereignty of China. Secretary of State Bryan asserted among other things that the United States could not regard with indifference the assumption of political, military, and economic domination over China by a foreign power. The Secretary concluded his note with a statement that the policy of the United States "is directed to the maintenance of the independence, integrity, and commercial freedom of China and the preservation of legitimate American rights in that republic." Despite these representations Japan forced China, under the pressure of an ultimatum, to agree to revised demands which represented a retreat from the extreme position taken when the original demands were put forth. Thereupon our government notified both Tokyo and Peking that the United States "cannot recognize any agreement or undertaking which has been entered into between the governments of Japan and China impairing the treaty rights of the United States and its citizens in China, the political or territorial integrity of the Republic of China, or the international policy commonly known as the 'Open Door' policy."[4]

As a result of its entrance into World War I, the United States found itself associated with Japan. Their efforts to record a common policy toward China, which had declared war against Germany in 1917, resulted in an exchange of notes known as the Ishii-Lansing Agreement of November 2, 1917. The document contains an affirmation that territorial propinquity creates special relations between countries and that consequently the United States recognizes that Japan has special interests in China. The Japanese made use of this affirmation with the Chinese to discourage their efforts to appeal to the United States for support. The agreement was formally annulled six years later.[5]

Japan's imperialistic elements had always despised and discounted the military capacity of the United States, and Germany's defeat came as a complete surprise to them. This outcome made the Japanese militarists all the more bent on realizing the dreams of their own conception of a "Monroe Doctrine" for East Asia.

In 1918 the Japanese Army saw in the fall of the Tsarist Empire a "golden opportunity" to detach Siberia east of Lake Baikal from Muscovite control and to take over also the Russian sphere of influence in North Manchuria. The Army launched a nation-wide publicity campaign to gain public support for military intervention to achieve those objectives. Japan's business and agrarian interests, concerned over their country's vital dependence upon its trade with the United States, prevailed upon the government to consult the United States before undertaking such a step. The outcome of the consultation was an American counter-proposal for an inter-allied expedition not for the purpose intended, though still hoped for by the Japanese Army, but to give support to anti-Bolshevik Russian elements in their effort to set up in Siberia a regime capable of stemming the Bolshevik tide; and, incidentally, to aid some 50,000 Czech ex-prisoners of war seeking to pass eastward through Siberia to their homeland. The United States likewise had an ulterior motive, though not a selfish one, which was to checkmate the designs of the Japanese Army, which, for its part, still hoped to realize its original purposes. Although it had been agreed upon that the quota of troops to be contributed by any one ally should not exceed 8,000, the Japanese High Command disregarded this commitment subscribed to by the Japanese Foreign Minister and despatched a force nearly ten times as large. One of the principal activities of the Japanese forces was to obstruct the operation of the Russian-owned Chinese Eastern Railway, a function which under inter-allied agreement was the responsibility of a Technical Board, of which Colonel John Stevens, of Panama Canal fame, was chairman.

It was not long before the Japanese military interference had become so flagrant that Ambassador Morris at Tokyo was instructed by Washington to lodge a strong protest and to say that unless this interference was promptly discontinued our government would withdraw its forces from the inter-allied expedition. The interference ceased for a time and then resumed. In 1920 the American government abruptly pulled its forces out of Siberia without giving advance notice either to Ambassador Morris or to the Japanese government.

Following the withdrawal of the American forces from Siberia, Russian partisans, by their guerrilla operations, including a massacre of a 600 man Japanese garrison at Nikolaevsk near the mouth of the Amur river (a long distance away from the agreed upon zone of allied operations), made it so hot for the Japanese that in 1922 they too evacuated Siberia without having accomplished their purposes.

In the meantime, the United States had in 1921 invited China, Japan, and six European powers (France, Italy, Belgium, Netherlands, Portugal, and the United Kingdom) to a conference to discuss limitation of naval armaments and pending political questions pertaining to the Far East arising out of World War I and other questions that had not been disposed of at Versailles or elsewhere. At Washington, Japan with a moderate group in power, which had taken over from the military group after its fiasco in Siberia, agreed in a Five Power Treaty to accept, as a basis for limitation of naval armaments, a ratio in capital ships of three-fifths of the aggregate tonnage allotted each to the United States and the United Kingdom, and all three of these powers engaged themselves not to strengthen the fortifications in their north Pacific island possessions. The Anglo-Japanese Alliance, which had been concluded in 1902 and renewed in 1912 for a second ten-year period, was allowed to lapse and was replaced by a Four Power Treaty, the other two parties being the United States and France, providing for mutual respect for each other's rights in their insular possessions in the Western Pacific area.

In a Nine Power Treaty regarding China, the parties other than China pledged themselves to courses of self restraint regarding that country. Japan also concluded a treaty with China for the retrocession to the latter of Kiaochow Bay, which Japan had occupied in 1914.[6]

With these instruments signed, sealed, and delivered it looked to the American government and people as if, with peace and security in that part of the world thus assured, our country could with ease of mind put the Far East aside as finished business and turn its attention to building up the walls of isolationalism. Unfortunately what was overlooked was that treaties serve no more than to register a meeting of minds for the time being; and, moreover, that Asians, especially the Japanese, view the question of the sanctity of contracts less from a legal point of view than from a standpoint of their own concepts of equity. In 1922 and 1930 we raised our import tariffs on goods important in Japan's export trade, and in 1924 we enacted an immigration law that discriminated against the Japanese as a race, which seriously wounded their susceptibilities. These measures undermined the influence of the moderate Japanese Cabinet and played into the hands of the Japanese Army, which denounced their government for having allowed itself to be betrayed by America. They pointed to our enactments as evidence that the United States was insincere in its professions of international good will and as demonstrating the futility of relying upon international co-operation.

They emphasized that Japan was a "have-not" nation and could survive only by resolute methods. Japan's complaints went unheeded in the United States.

Late in 1929 the New York silk market collapsed. Raw silk was by far the largest source of foreign exchange for Japan. More than 90 per cent of Japan's export of that product normally went to the United States. Acute distress came to prevail through the Japanese countryside, since one third of all Japanese agricultural households in those days, crowded as they were on scant acres, were dependent upon cocoon raising as a secondary occupation to make ends meet. Japan began to convert its economy to meet the new situation by expanding its industries to supply Asian markets. There was a marked drop in the ratio of Japan's American trade to its total trade and a corresponding decline in the importance attached by Japan to keeping American goodwill. When the next significant move was proposed by the Japanese military group, no need was perceived for seeking advanced consultation with the United States.

In the early 1920's Dr. Sun Yat-sen and his followers, who had engineered the successful Republican Revolution in 1911-12 against the monarchy, had their center in Canton. At that time, various so-called warlords, who were for the most part holdovers from the civil service of the imperial regime, were contending among themselves for power.

Dr. Sun was a native of Chungshan District in Kwangtung Province, a region whose people had for generations enjoyed amicable contacts with Western merchants and missionaries. He himself had had a Western education at Hong Kong and in Hawaii, in the course of which he had acquired a medical degree. His chief interest, however, turned to the modernization of his country, politically, economically, and socially. He commanded the loyalty and confidence of his followers and the respect of his foreign friends. The task which he had set for himself and his associates was a formidable one. He lacked funds and an organization experienced along modern lines, one capable of coping with the problems and difficulties that lay in the way of freeing the country of warlordism so that China could be united under a progressive regime. Under the circumstances he had no alternative to appealing to his British and American friends for aid, but his efforts were fruitless; for in those days it would have been impossible to prevail upon their countries' legislatures to appropriate funds for his purposes.

After having appealed in vain for British and American aid in his efforts to unite the country, Sun turned for help to the Soviet government. The late Dr. Hu Shih, in an article in the October 1950 issue of *Foreign Affairs*, observes that it was a most extraordinary opportunity for the Third International to be requested in 1923-24 by Dr. Sun, himself a leader of a revolutionary party, to send political and military experts to China, not only to help reorganize his own party but actually to organize a new army for a new revolution. Dr. Hu Shih adds that it was equally extraordinary for Dr. Sun, in his sincere desire "to bolster the strength of revolutionary elements in the country," to admit Communists as regular members of his own Nationalist Party and even to carry revolutionary propaganda and agitation in the new army.[7]

The basis of Sun's collaboration with the Soviet government was clearly defined in a joint statement by Dr. Sun and A. Joffe, a representative of the Soviet government and the Comintern. The statement reads as follows:

> Dr. Sun holds that the Communist order or even the Soviet system cannot actually be introduced into China because there do not exist here the conditions for the successful establishment of either Communism or Sovietism. This view is entirely shared by Mr. Joffe, who is further of the opinion that China's paramount and most pressing problem is to achieve national unification and attain full national independence, and regarding this task, he has assured Dr. Sun Yat-sen that China has the warmest sympathy of the Russian people and can count on the support of Russia.[8]

This joint statement practically defined the issue of the Nationalist Revolution: it was to achieve national unification by destroying the military power of the separatist warlords, and to attain "full national independence" by abolishing the "unequal treaties" which the foreign powers had imposed upon the Chinese people. It was clear from the very beginning that this latter phase of the Nationalist movement had to be essentially an anti-foreign movement against the imperialist powers. Unwittingly, Dr. Sun's party was being thus guided toward a possible international war.

The Comintern was able to send to China a group of political and military advisers headed by Mikhail Borodin, one of the most astute revolutionary advisers, and General Galen. Borodin soon became the dictator of the Chinese Communist Party and at the same time the most influential man in the new government directing the policy and the strategy of the Revolution. The Whampoa Military Academy was established at Canton in June 1924 with Chiang Kai-shek as its director. The Russian military mission was under Blucher (Galen) who was helping Chiang to train large numbers of new officers to be the nucleus of a new revolutionary army.

Dr. Sun died in March 1925. In June 1926, the Army of the National Revolution, led by Chiang Kai-shek as Commander-in-Chief, launched the Northern Expedition from Canton. The progress of the revolutionary armies was almost an uninterrupted series of victories. The Northern armies were incapable of effectively resisting an inspired army supported by powerful propaganda and organized masses. The cities of Changsha, Hankow, Kiukiang, and Nanchang in the central part of the Yangtze Valley were taken in succession between July and November in 1926. In March, the Chinese city of Shanghai was taken over, but the foreign settlements were too well defended by foreign troops to give way.

In Nanking, a few days later, Communist cadres in the advancing Nationalist forces ran amok, attacking foreigners, looting and defiling residences and consulates, and killing a number of foreign residents. Foreign gunboats stationed in the river fired a barrage to warn against further violence and to guide the fleeing foreigners to escape to the boats. Dr. Hu Shih obesrves that the Nanking incident seems to have been the last of deliberate anti-foreign moves designed to force the foreign powers to resort to armed intervention and thereby to create a situation of a real "imperialistic war"—which Stalin and the Comintern regarded as the necessary "objective condition" for the victory of the revolution. The commanding general responsible for creating the Nanking incident was Cheng Ch'ien, who later joined the Communist regime in Peking.

During the period of collaboration between the Kuomintang (Nationalist Party) and the Communists, the latter was functioning efficiently, and the work of infiltration into the government and especially into the Army was progressing smoothly and successfully. Dr. Hu Shih notes that what was lacking was a real war, a great imperialist war, without which, according to the Stalinist line of thinking, it was difficult to capture the whole of the Russian-influenced Nationalist Army and convert the Nationalist Revolution into another glorious "October Revolution."

The danger of foreign intervention and of a Communist Revolution was averted by the decision of Chiang Kai-shek and the other moderate leaders of the Kuomintang to split with the Communists, end the collaboration, and "purge" the Nationalist Party of the Communists and their sympathizers. The "purge" began on April 12, 1927, first in Shanghai and later in Canton.

After the "split" and the "purge" had been effected in the lower Yangtze Valley, and the National Government had been set up at Nanking, the Kremlin sent a secret message to Borodin in Hankow ordering the Chinese Communists to demand majority control of the Kuomintang, confiscation of land of the land owners, and the formation of a separate Workers' and Peasants' Army. Borodin did not want to present these demands, but Roy, the Indian representative of the Comintern, gave the message to Wang Ching-wei, chairman of the Left Wing Kuomintang Government at Hankow. Even the Left Wing Kuomintang could not tolerate such clear violation of the terms of the collaboration. Borodin and the other Russian advisers were expelled from the Party and ordered to leave China. Eventually the Hankow regime collapsed and was merged with the government at Nanking.

The Chinese Communist Party had been formed in 1921. Its rise, within a space of twenty-eight years from obscurity to ascendancy and finally control of the most populous national society in the civilized world was an amazing feat. How this came about is an illuminating example, on the one hand, of the duplicity and adroitness of international communism in exploiting the weaknesses of its adversaries to extend its influence and domination; and, on the other hand, of unflagging purpose and well planned effort. Communism found in China a national policy whose structure was already tottering from the assaults of Western and Japanese imperialism and a people distraught by the ravages and chaos of internal strife and foreign aggression. In their desperation for relief from their miseries they were clutching at straws, and the specious promises of Marxist-Leninism was to many more alluring than the abstract formulations of Western democracy.

The organization of a Chinese Workers' and Peasants' Red Army was actually ordered by the Kremlin. The order was carried out by those Communist leaders who realized after the 1927 coup that the Party must have an armed force of its own.

The Red Army probably began with less than 10,000 men. In the course of a few years, it grew in numerical strength and in fighting experience. Its mobile units carried on insurrections mainly in the southern provinces. By 1930 the Red Army was said to number about 60,000 men. Toward the end of 1927 the first "Soviet" was set up in Chaling in Hunan Province. The Soviet form was extended to larger areas and early in 1930 a Provisional Soviet Government of Southern Kiangsi was proclaimed. In August 1931 the Executive Committee of the Communist International advised the Chinese Communist Party to establish in some secure region a full-fledged "Central Soviet Government of the Soviet Republic of China" and to carry out a "Bolshevik national policy." Such a "Central Soviet Government of the Republic of China" was set up in December 1931 with its capital at Juichin in Kiangsi Province. Mao Tse-tung was elected Chairman of the Central Soviet Government and Chu Teh Commander of the Army.

Dr. Hu Shih, in his study, calls attention to the very significant fact that the Chinese Communist Party differs from the Communist movement in any country outside Russia in that from the early years of its founding it has possessed a formidable army of its own. He discusses also the strategy and tactics employed by the Chinese Communists with the advice and aid of the Soviet Union. Significant points are: (1) for conquest the party must be fully armed and it must have a strong army of its own; (2) it is not enough to use Russia as a revolutionary base;

(3) Soviet Russia must be made the greatest military power in the world to achieve the revolutionary conquests of adjacent and contiguous territories by sheer overwhelming superiority of military strength; (4) to avoid the appearance of "overt violence" or "revolutionary violence" it is necessary to bring about a "coalition government" with all the "democratic" and "anti-fascist" groups in the country. This latter objective was emphasized by Mao Tse-tung in an encyclical to the comrades in May 1945. "And lastly and above all," it was enjoined, "we must be ready to employ trickery, deceit, law-breaking, and withholding and concealing truth."[9] (There is discernible in the actions of some elements in American radical groups an ominous resemblance to these Communist prescriptions.) In the same program there was a section devoted to the Fundamental Task of Communist strategy and tactics. One of these Fundamental Tasks is for the Communist Party to lead the masses to a direct attack on the bourgeois state whenever the time is considered ripe for this final step in revolution.

The National Government was composed of divergent elements with a consequent inability to achieve cohesion for constructive work. There was a scarcity of men actuated by unselfish motives. There was an inclusion in the government of vicious elements which proved a source of weakness. Failure to carry out a sound economic and fiscal policy and to support any effective administration of the Salt and Customs Services kept the government on the verge of bankruptcy. The civilization of the Chinese people was being shaken by the impact of a radically different machine civilization of the West with resultant disorders. An ancient civilization was breaking up, and it would require many years before the work of constructive agencies (for example, a mass educational movement) would be able to counteract the activities of irresponsible persons to whom a time of disorder presented an opportunity for personal gains at the expense of the community. Such persons were the bandits who roamed over the country in increasing numbers and the horde of minor militarists who, unhampered by guiding principles, combined with and against another with readiness and who, as a rule, left in their wake no tangible evidence of their presence other than further impoverishment of the areas they controlled.

An even greater impediment to the establishment of order and peace in China was the conduct of the Japanese Kwantung Army which was deliberately calculated to overawe the Chinese into submission their program of establishing their overlordship in that country. The Tsinan incident in May 1928 was an early example of the inhuman brutality of the Japanese soldiery. The commander of the Japanese forces there was prevailed upon by two higher Japanese officers (military attachés) to launch a massive attack upon the city in the course of which large numbers of unarmed citizens were killed. The attack had been wholly unprovoked by the Chinese. An eye-witness account of this outrage is given in considerable detail by Dr. Chin-tung Liang, Research Professor of the Center of Asian Studies at St. John's University, New York, who at that time was manager of the Chinese-American Bank of Commerce at Tsinan.[10]

References will be made later in this study to further developments in Japan's program of aggrandizement.

As the tide of Chinese nationalism swept northward in 1928 and 1929 it came into conflict with the rights and privileges of the Soviet Union in Manchuria. In mid 1929 a dispute developed over the Chinese Eastern Railway in Manchuria. The United States immediately took the lead in attempting to achieve a peaceful solution. The efforts of Secretary of State Stimson failed to arrest intermittent armed clashes along the Manchurian border. In mid-November Russian troops invaded Manchuria in force.

Eventually, following direct negotiations, Soviet Russia and China, on December 22, 1929, signed a protocol under which the controversy was settled on the basis of restoring the *status quo ante,* and the Soviet Union retained the special privileges in the Chinese Eastern Railway zone originally acquired by the Tsarist government in the 1890's, but subsequently redefined in the Sino-Soviet Treaties of 1924.[11]

Sun Yat-sen, during his lifetime, had called for a unified China. This idea had not existed under the Manchu regime, where the practice had been to farm out the duties of governing the country to viceroys who acted in the several provinces as the very persons of the emperor, and whose only duty above this was to remit the provincial quotas of tribute rice. Unification was a reversion to semi-feudalism.

Not long after the National Government was established in 1927, serious efforts were made, under the leadership of Chiang Kai-shek, to unify the military system, and to reduce military expenditures for the use of national reconstruction. For this purpose, a Military Reorganization and Disbandment Conference was held in January 1929. On this occasion, Minister of Finance T. V. Soong stated that the nation's finances were disorganized, that there was no real accounting, and that only four of the twenty-two provinces had furnished fairly complete figures of their finances. Several of the sources of revenue had been pledged for the service of loans. Of the total government receipts from June to November 1928 only 55 per cent were derived from revenue while 45 per cent were derived from loans. Revenue estimates for 1929 were $458 million, a substantial part of which was alloted for military expenses.

Military leaders who had participated in the Conference refused to honor and carry out its resolutions, which would provide a real authority to the National Government. They intended to establish a rival regime. Civil war broke out in April 1930 with heavy losses on both sides. In October, after the rebellion had been suppressed, the National Government entered upon a crucial period of reconstruction.

China's internal strength accelerated only Japan's course of aggression. Japanese militarists initiated the Mukden Incident on September 18, 1931. At ten that evening, a bomb exploded on the tracks of the South Manchuria Railway line, a few miles north of Mukden. Its force was not strong enough to derail a train which passed by shortly afterwards. Within three or four days thereafter all of Manchuria south of Changchun was taken over by the Japanese Kwantung Army in a well coordinated plan of action. Notwithstanding the clear evidence that the bombing was the work of the Japanese themselves as a pretext for taking all of South Manchuria, the Japanese authorities insisted from first to last that the Chinese were the culprits. The Chinese military authorities had ordered their troops not to resist, since they lacked the equipment to offer any prospect of self-defense. Other than the order given them, they were wholly unprepared for the Japanese coup.

Diplomatic action by the League of Nations, which was then in session, and by the United States emphasizing Japanese commitments under the Nine Power Treaty and the Kellogg-Briand Pact, were ineffective in bringing Japan to a conference table. Finally Secretary of State Stimson, in identical notes to China and Japan, dated January 7, 1932, declared that "the United States cannot admit the legality of any situation *de facto* nor does it intend to recognize any treaty or agreement entered into between those two governments or agents thereof, which may impair the treaty rights of the United States or its citizens in China, including those which relate to the sovereignty, the independence, or the territorial and administrative integrity of the Republic of China or the international policy commonly known as the 'Open Door' policy, and that it does not intend to recognize any situation, treaty or agreement which may be brought about by means contrary to the covenants and obligations of the Pact of Paris of August 27, 1928 to which treaty both China and Japan as well as the United States are parties."[12]

Secretary of State Stimson stated that "the willingness of the American government to surrender in 1922 in the Nine Power Treaty at the Washington Conference its then commanding lead in battleship construction and to leave its positions in Guam and the Philippines without further fortification was predicated upon, among other things, the self-denying covenants contained in the Nine Power Treaty, which assured the nations of the world not only of equal opportunity for their Eastern trade but also against the military aggrandizement of any other power at the expense of China."[13]

The non-recognition principle enunciated by Secretary Stimson, which was also accepted by the League of Nations, remained the basis of United States policy and was reaffirmed on numerous occasions during the years between the time of its enunciation and American involvement in World War II following the Japanese attack on Pearl Harbor.

The Shanghai incident of January 28, 1932 took its origin in the effectiveness of the boycott of Japanese goods which the Chinese had instituted in June 1931 in retaliation for Japan's course of aggression. Shanghai, on an estuary near the mouth of the Yangtze, was the chief port of China. The Japanese were the most numerous of the foreigners living and doing business there. It was also the center of Britain's China trade, but the United States and France also had large commercial interests. The incident arose out of a clash between Chinese and Japanese residents resulting in the death of one of the Japanese.

On February 7 the first Japanese army forces consisting of a mixed brigade 3,000 strong landed at Wusung and proceeded thence directly to Chapei, fifteen miles away. By February 27, three and half divisions had been landed in the Shanghai area by the Japanese. At the insistence of the British government the French, Italian, and American ambassadors in Japan took joint action in asking that (1) the Japanese warships at Shanghai be moved further down the river to a point where they would not draw fire from the Chinese forces which would endanger the International Settlement and the vessels of other nations at anchor in the river; (2) in the event that further forces were to be sent by the Japanese, arrangements would be made not to land troops in the Settlement but at such points as would not draw fire from the Chinese to the danger of the Settlement or its residents or the vessels lying in the river which belong to other nations. On March 1, the Japanese Foreign Minister replied that "although the Japanese Government has the right to land troops at the International Settlement and to anchor warships at the present position, it desires most earnestly to prevent as far as possible any danger to the settlement or to foreigners and has transmitted the message of the American government to the authorities of the Army and Navy, and will give as favorable consideration to this matter as possible."[14]

In the meantime a communication made by the President of the Council of the League of Nations setting forth certain conditions for the restoration of peaceful conditions in the Shanghai area won immediate acceptance. The text of the Japanese Declaration of the Cessation of Hostilities, signed by General Yoshinari Shirakawa, Chief of the Imperial Japanese Land Forces, March 3, 1932, reads in translation as follows:

The Imperial Japanese Land Forces since their arrival in Shanghai and its vicinity had, in conjunction with the Imperial Naval Forces, made every effort to achieve the objectives of protecting Japanese residents by peaceful means. However, proposals based on such a desire were not, to their regret, acceded to by the Nineteenth Route Army of China and at last hostilities were started.

Chinese forces have now retreated to positions beyond the distance originally requested by the Imperial Forces, and signs are seen of peace, of the Shanghai settlements being recovered and safety of Japanese residents being assured.

I have therefore decided to order the forces to halt for the time being at points actually held and to stop fighting, provided that the Chinese forces will not resort to further hostile actions.[15]

It seems likely in the light of the firmness of the attitude shown by the American, British, and French authorities in the International Settlement and the movement by American and British warships to Shanghai for the protection of their nationals a formal agreement concerning the definitive cessation of hostilities at Shanghai was concluded on May 5.

Looking at the situation in Manchuria, in January 1932, the Japanese occupied Chinchow, a strategic point on the railway connecting Manchuria with Peking. This move made it clear that it was Japan's purpose to control all railways in Manchuria by occupying all important places there and also as a step to move its strategic boundary westward in preparation for a possible clash with the Soviet Union.

Immediately after the Japanese Army had overthrown the Chinese government in Manchuria, the Japanese government began to take a succession of steps to establish the political and economic control of that territory. This was by the forcible creation in February 1932 of an ostensibly independent but actually puppet state controlled by Japan and known as "Manchukuo." By these steps Japan sought first to frustrate the rendering of an adjudication upon the real facts of the situation and, if such adjudication were made, to thwart its enforcement. These successive steps were made the subject of a thorough investigation by the Lytton Commission. Its unanimous report thereon was clear and unanimous. A central government was formed and enacted a "declaration of independence" from China. Henry Pu Yi, the deposed Emperor of the former Manchu Empire in China, was installed as regent on March 9, 1932.

Within ten days after the Assembly of the League of Nations had met to consider China's appeal against this consummation, and the very day after the resolution of non-recognition had been passed, the "puppet Minister for Foreign Affairs" addressed communications to some fifty odd governments announcing the independent state of "Manchukuo" and inviting the establishment of diplomatic relations.

The total Customs revenues from Manchuria and a portion of the salt revenues, prior to the Japanese coup, had belonged to and been forwarded to the National Government at Nanking. All of these revenues were now claimed by the new government of "Manchukuo" and in June 1932 were forcibly seized. Control by the Chinese Government was ended.

The report of the Lytton Commission was signed at Peking, September 4, 1932. It was not made public until it was presented to the Council of the League at Geneva on October 1. At a meeting of the Council of the League on September 24, its President, Mr. De Valera of the Irish Free State, said in part:

> I should be lacking in frankness, both to the Japanese government and to the members of the League as a whole did I not give expression to the regret which I am sure is felt by the generality of the members of the Council that before discussion of the report of the Commission, before even the publication of that reoprt, Japan has not only by recognizing, but also by signing a treaty with what is known as the Manchukuo government, taken steps which cannot but be regarded as calculated to prejudice the settlement of the dispute. For almost a year the Council in its collective capacity, and the individual governments which compose it have scrupulously refrained from uttering any word of judgment on the merits of this grave dispute, on the grounds that a Commission had been set up to investigate the dispute in all of its bearings, and that, until that Commission had reported and its report had been considered by the organs of the League, the whole question to be regarded as subjudice.[16]

On May 23, 1933 the Japanese government forced on China an agreement under which China was obliged not only to accept a *de facto* recognition of "Manchukuo" and Jehol (and this in effect consent to the permanent severance of those territories from China), but also Japan was to extend over the rest of China the system of "co-operation" which the Japanese General Staff was working out in China. It is hardly necessary to emphasize the danger to the Chinese people and the menace to world peace that was involved in these terms. Thus, Chinese retirement along the entire line became continuous. Colonels Itagaki and Ishihara were completely out of government control, and it became necessary to issue an Imperial Ordinance to stop the first drive on Chinchow. It did not take long, however, to obtain permission for the drive.

In January 1934, Japan occupied Shanhaikwan, a pass at the border between China proper and Manchuria. On January 16, a Japanese committee of nineteen presented an amended draft as a basis for conciliation which differed widely from that of the League of Nations. There was at the same time a steady continuance of the Japanese advance toward Peking.

In May, the conclusion of the so-called "Tangku Truce" served to confirm Japan's control of all the railways in Manchuria and Inner Mongolia, except the Chinese Eastern Railway until its sale to China became effective (March 23, 1935). On April 17, the Chinese evacuated Chinwantao, a city adjacent to Shanhaikwan. Early in 1935, the Japanese forced the National Government to withdraw its control of the Peiping area and of the Peiping-Suiyuan Railway. An ultimatum forced the Chinese garrisons in West Jehol to evacuate to the adjacent area of China proper.

The revenues of the Chinese government had become seriously affected by the wholesale Japanese practice of smuggling goods into Chinese-held territory.

During the national crisis caused by Japan's aggression, the Chinese Communists, nevertheless, increased their insurrections. It was necessary for the National Government to pacify the internal situation in order to confront the external invasion. From 1930 to 1934, the National government forces under Chiang Kai-shek carried out a number of military expeditions against the Communist armed forces. By the autumn of 1933, Red districts were being narrowed down to a relatively small area in the border regions between Kiangsi and Fukien provinces. Chiang Kai-shek's strategy was designed to build around the Communist districts a kind of a Great Wall which gradually moved inward. The encirclement and the economic blockade proved so effective that the Reds were forced to try to escape annihilation by retreating westward, then southwestward, then northward, and then northeastward, which ultimately took them into Shensi Province. There they instituted with the toleration of the National government an independent jurisdiction over a small area around the city of Yenan. This retreat, which lasted a whole year and covered about 6,000 miles, has been called the "long march." It is said that at the end of their trek there were less than 20,000 survivors out of the estimated 90,000 who left Kiangsi Province in October 1934.

One of the unexpected results of the "long march" was that the National Government, in following the trail of the Red Army, was able to consolidate its political control over such southwestern provinces as Kweichow, Yunnan, and Szechuan, which had up to then succeeded in maintaining a degree of regional autonomy. The rich province of Szechuan, when it was invaded by the Red Army in 1935, sent a delegation to Nanking for adequate military aid to help the provincial armies combat the Red forces.[17]

The Seventh World Congress held in Moscow from July to August 1935 officially proclaimed the policy of a "United Front" against aggression by the "Fascist" powers. Special attention was paid to China and the

Chinese Communist Party. Four Chinese Communists, including Mao Tse-tung and Chou En-lai, were elected to the Executive Committee of the Comintern. The Party was censured for failure to unite with the leaders of the Nineteenth Route Army who had rebelled against the Nationalist Government and had set up a "People's Government" in Fukien. The quick collapse of the Fukien rebellion enabled the National Government to enforce a more effective blockade against the Communist area in the following year.

The Chinese Communist Party's avowed objective was the overthrowing of the Kuomintang and destruction of its military power. In Communist literature at that time the "United Front" was one of resistance to Japan and opposition to Chiang Kai-shek. The widespread anti-Japanese demonstrations could not fail to affect the psychology of the government troops who were sent to Shensi Province to fight the remnant Red Army. This was also true of the Tungpei (Northeastern) Armies which had retreated from Manchuria after the Japanese invasion and were then under the command of Chang Hsueh-liang. The propaganda slogans against these armies were especially effective: "Go back to your Old Home and Fight the Japanese Devils!"

In the face of the extension of Japanese activities, the United States continued to assert its treaty rights. When a Japanese Foreign Office spokesman (Eiji Amau) issued a statement on April 17, 1934 proclaiming "(1) Japanese political guardianship of China and; (2) special responsibilities in East Asia" and warning the Powers against financial, political, or commercial undertakings prejudicial to Japanese interests in China, the United States quickly replied. In a carefully worded note delivered in Tokyo on April 29, the United States reaffirmed its treaty rights. Secretary of State Hull restated American policy. He said in part: "The relations of the United States with China are governed, as our relations with Japan and our relations with other countries, by the generally accepted principles of international law and the provisions of treaties to which the United States is a party. . . . The American government seeks to be duly considerate of the rights, the obligations and the legitimate interests of other countries, and it expects on the part of other governments due consideration of the rights, obligations and the legitimate interests of the United States. In the opinion of the American people and the American government no nation can, without the assent of the other nations concerned, rightfully endeavour to make conclusive its will in situations where there are involved the rights, the obligations and the legitimate interests of other sovereign states."[18]

When the Japanese puppet state of "Manchukuo" established an official monopoly, the Manchurian Petroleum Company, the United States government, after a number of notes on this subject with Japan had been exchanged, summarized its position in a note to the Japanese government, dated April 15, 1935, as follows:

> The American Government greatly regrets that the Japanese Government has not seen its way clear to use the influence which it possesses through its close and peculiar relations with the present regime in Manchuria to uphold in practice the principle of the Open Door and the fulfillment of the treaty obligations which both the Japanese Government and the authorities in Manchuria have on numerous occasions declared they would maintain.
>
> The American Government is constrained to express its considered view that upon the Japanese Government must rest the ultimate responsibility for injury to American interests resulting from the creation of the petroleum monopoly in Manchuria.[19]

The Japanese plans for expansion in China, as outlined to Japanese news correspondents at Tientsin on October 24, 1935 by Major General Tada, Commander of the Japanese garrison there, called for among other things an "autonomous government" of the five northern provinces of China, Hopei, Chahar, Suiyuan, Shansi, and Shantung, under the guidance of the Japanese Army and detached from the administrative control of the central Chinese government, and for the establishment of a system of exploitation by the Japanese of the region's resources so that it might be brought within the orbit of Japan's economic system. In a statement to the press on December 5, 1935, Secretary Hull reiterated the position of the American government.

By 1936, the Japanese Army had established through intrigue and intimidation "autonomous" regimes in two of those provinces, Hopei and Chahar. Both Peking and Tientsin are located in Hopei. Stiffening Chinese opposition, however, prevented the Japanese from making further progress at that time. On two of their demands, in particular, the Chinese would not budge. These were "Sino-Japanese Economic Cooperation," a euphemism for Japanese control of the key industries and communications in North China, and "Joint Defense against Communism," a formula under which Japan sought the right to station troops at its pleasure in those regions. The Chinese, who had been helplessly watching the progressive dismemberment of the national domain by Japan, were less apprehensive of Communist aggression than of the immediate Japanese threat.

By the summer of 1936, a secret understanding was reached between Communist leaders in North Shensi and Chang Hsueh-liang and his colleagues. Chang, though patriotic, was immature, ambitious and vainglorious. Being also anti-Japanese, he was easily persuaded to lend his support to an anti-Japanese propaganda campaign. It was under these circumstances that the "arrest" of Chiang Kai-shek by Chang Hsueh-liang took place at Sian on December 12, 1936. Chiang had gone there with the full knowledge that he was going into the territory of the conspirators. He actually called at Sian a conference of his highest generals, possibly to convince the conspirators of the futility of attempting a revolt in the face of the overwhelmingly strong position of government forces in the area. For a time, Chiang's life was in real danger. During the fortnight of his captivity, there were persistent demands for his execution or for his public trial. The most reasonable theory for his release was that this was done by orders from Moscow believing that his services in promoting a united front against Japan would be invaluable. Dr. Hu Shih tells us that the Generalissimo left Sian without having to sign any terms and reached home "amidst the really spontaneous rejoicings" of the Chinese people. "But this Puritan Christian," Hu Shih adds, "was won over, probably for the first time in his life by a masterful stroke of strategy. Of all the things that Stalin had ever done, that act came closest to statesmanship."[20]

Chiang's life was saved. Nation-wide joy and acclamation over his personal safety evidenced his increasing prestige and undisputed leadership. This, however, served only to increase Japan's envy which made it practically impossible for any meaningful conciliation. During the years that had followed, the internal politics of Japan were marked by a struggle for ascendency among the various factions within the military group. The nature of the struggle between them may be described as the efforts by a reckless, determined military element committed to expansion by force to impose its will on an irresolute nation through the abuse of power, intrigue, duplicity, and terrorism, This ultra-militarism toward China was manifest as early as 1935 when a leading article appeared in the October issue of a Japanese language review published at Mukden. Entitled "Fundamental Considerations on China and the North Chinese Question," it expressed the belief that the North China Question is not merely a matter of "securing the life line of Japan's national defense"; it represents the application of Japan's fundamental continental policy which provides for the expansion (not necessarily in a territorial sense) to Japan. It further maintains that Japan's basic policy relating to the North China Question is to:

(1) work for the liberation of oppressed peoples,
(2) accord them security of livelihood,
(3) maintain the self-respect of all peoples and their independence,
(4) enable these peoples to co-operate in attaining friendly relations with Japan,
(5) and render possible the establishment of political, economic, and even military relations of inseparability with the Empire.

The article concludes that Japan will use its efforts to make common cause with the Chinese people, first in North China, to promote the security and peace of Japanese residents and the Chinese people. The view is expressed that conditions in North China are favorable to a speedy realization of this aim and that this movement, which had its beginnings with the "Manchuria Incident" of 1931, will be gradually extended from North China southwards, eventually to include all China, and it is anticipated that if the people of North China begin considering the North China question sympathetically they may bring it to the fore at the plenary session of the Central Executive and Supervisory Committees in Nanking next month.[21]

I add here my comments on this article as I reported them to the Department of State on October 28, 1935.

Those who do not appreciate how one-sided and even naive the Japanese can sometimes be in their outlook on foreign affairs and who are unfamiliar with current Japanese comment may not be inclined to take the foregoing observations seriously, but it is believed that they must be taken into account in any appraisal of the moral support which the Empire's present so called "Continental Policy" enjoys among the Japanese public.

In many of its aspects, the present period in Japan has its counterpart in moments in the history of other peoples when a consciousness of national destiny or religious fervor or both spurred them on to a career of conquest and colonization. Although the Japanese as a people have never manifested a zeal for religious proselyting, there is in their nature a strong vein of idealism or sentimentalism. They are capable of concentrating collectively upon a given objective with an intensity of purpose which produces the same effect as religious fanaticism. It is not to be doubted that a large number among the articulate elements are now sincerely convinced that it is their mission as a nation to deliver the Chinese people from the tyranny of warlords and the menace of Communism, and that freed from these the Chinese will eventually see the advantage of joining hands with Japan in an economic alliance which would establish the mutual prosperity of the two nations on a permanent basis.

Japan's attitude toward any disposition on the part of the Chinese to reject this creed is not dissimilar to that which was used generally to prevail in the Occident on religious questions before the advent of the present era of tolerance. So convinced are the Japanese that theirs is the true faith that they ascribe the perversity of Chinese to ignorance, to their being misled by their leaders, and to the malign influence of Western powers. It matters not, therefore, if the Chinese as yet refuse to cooperate, the end seems so desirable to the Japanese that they are determined to go ahead, and they justify any means they may be called upon to employ.

There are not a few Japanese who have made sacrifices to come to

Manchuria for the purpose of serving the ideal of bringing about a new order here. Unfortunately, among the idealists in positions to influence governmental policy and action are many fanatics—men with fixed ideas and narrow vision who insist upon cutting the Manchurian cloth to fit the Japanese pattern and who, oblivious to the differences in racial temperament, conceive of what is good for the Chinese in terms of what has been found good for the Japanese. They are impatient at the non-cooperative attitude of the Chinese, are disposed to adopt inquisitorial methods in seeking out suspects of heresy against the doctrine of the "Kingly Way" and are responsible for a policy of ruthless suppression of the slightest opposition to the present regime.

Another detriment to conciliation with the native population, which must be the basis of any real and permanent stability and progress, is the host of Japanese petty officials, chiefly among the gendarmerie and civilian police, who in their contacts with the Chinese are generally unsympathetic, arrogant, arbitrary, and even brutal. Then too, among the civilian Japanese community, there is an undue proportion of the most lawless elements in Japan: professional thugs, petty swindlers, narcotics peddlers, and other adventurers, who do much to discredit the Empire with the Chinese. Furthermore, there is a disposition among Japanese residents as a whole to regard Manchuria as theirs, having bought it at a heavy sacrifice of blood and treasure, and to expect that their interests must be given preferment over those of the Chinese. The more liberal and fair-minded among the Japanese leaders themselves recognize and deplore the attitude and actions of so many of their countrymen, but so far they have been powerless to counteract it effectively.

It is galling to Chinese pride to witness the rapid tightening by the Japanese of control over the country, but the sensible ones consider it wise to hold their peace over the facetious Japanese assertion that "Manchukuo" was created by the spontaneous will of 30 million people, for fear is the dominating note in the Chinese feeling toward the Japanese. Thus the breach between the two peoples arising from natural antipathies is widening in Manchuria as a result of closer contact.

The thought envisaged by some alarmists that Japan will some day lead the Orient to challenge the supremacy of the Occident is no more than a chimera. It takes more than the possession of a common script and racial similarity to make for mutual understanding and sympathy. The Japanese so far have failed to reveal the moral qualities which are likely to gain the respect of the Chinese people; their methods have rather aroused to the full the remarkable Chinese capacity for opposition through passive non-cooperation and obstructionary tactics.

The prophets of the Japanese "Continental Policy" disclaim any desire for conquest, but it is difficult to conceive of its making headway on account of Chinese opposition except through the gaining by Japan of control of the political machinery in China. The relationship of "inseparability" between "Manchukuo" and Japan exists only through the presence here of the Kwantung Army. Another "Manchukuo" may be created in North China or one embracing all China, and the application of force may not be necessary for this purpose so long as there is presence of force to apply it. In any event, any regime that may be set up in China having relations of "inseparability" with Japan will be established and maintained by the will of Japan and not of the Chinese people.

While a temporary military domination of a part or the whole of China by Japan is by no means a remote possibility, unless in the meantime external factors intervene or the force of the Japanese thrust exhausts itself against the solid wall of Chinese passive resistance, it is unlikely that such an occupation would last long. Even in Manchuria, even apart from its relations with China proper and possible complications with Soviet Russia, it is difficult to conceive of 30,000,000 Chinese remaining permanently under the subjection of another race no more virile and possessing no greater inherent capacity either mental or moral. There have been many instances in history where a people having a temporary advantage, because of superior political cohesion or of better preparedness for war, have been able to gain for a time ascendancy over others, but only races, which are weak in numbers or inferior in stamina or intellect, have been held permanently in subjection. Many observers agree that, man to man, the Chinese is at least the equal of the Japanese in inherent intelligence and decidedly superior in self-reliance. The capacity, which the Japanese have developed for organized and coordinated activity, has given them a temporary advantage. If they are successful in implanting their organization in Manchuria, there is no reason why the Chinese, who form a part of it, will not eventually be able to take a lesson from the Japanese book. While the Chinese are undoubtedly more easy going and less resolute than the Japanese, their desire to rid themselves of Japanese domination may furnish them with the determination to learn well and put it into practice.

Were it not for the blundering methods adopted by the Japanese in their march of progress, arising from a blind disregard of the point of view of others and a disposition to take themselves too seriously, there is no apparent reason why the two peoples should not live side by side harmoniously. In fact, they have much to gain by a closer partnership. But what the Japanese fail to appreciate is that to be successful, the partnership must be on the basis of equality. Admittedly, the Chinese can gain much from emulating the innate orderliness and intensity of purpose of the Japanese; this would enable them to put their national house in order. On the other hand, the Japanese would do well to temper their dourness of character with the urbanity of the Chinese and develop their personality with some of the Chinese individuality.

A harmonious fusion is not likely to result under Japanese hegemony; but dark as the picture now looks for the peace and stability of the Far East, the temporary political domination of Chinese populations by Japan may result in their being able subsequently to assert their self-determination more effectively. When they succeed in doing this, it will mean the discrediting in Japan of the military clique. In this way, the emancipation of both peoples may be brought about.

The eventual adjustment of the two races to one another must inevitably be a long process, which, however, can only be retarded or temporarily suspended by the intervention of third parties. In relation to Japan, such intervention, not necessarily in a miltiary sense, would only serve to stiffen the resolve to go ahead, since the Japanese have a tendency that when confronted with foreign opposition they tended to suppress their internal differences and present a united front. In relation to China, intervention would serve only to confirm the Chinese in their belief in the efficacy of their traditional policy of "controlling barbarians with barbarians." Not until the Chinese realize that their hopes of national salvation lies only in their own efforts, and that national destruction will be the inevitable result of their continuing to shirk their responsibility toward the maintenance of political integrity, will it be possible to expect their regeneration.[22]

In retrospect, it is most unfortunate to note that just at a time when the Chinese, under the National Government, were making sustained progress in a meaningful program of national reconstruction and modernization, even in midst of enormous difficulties, the Japanese ultra-militarist elements dominated Japan's politics. The year was 1937.

On July 7, Japan launched an all-out attack on China following a minor incident at the Marco Polo Bridge provoked and enlarged upon by the Japanese Army. Three weeks later, Premier Konoe announced the establishment of a "New Order in East Asia" (a euphemism of Japanese overlordship throughout that area). This Japanese aggressive action not only brought all kinds of nation-building efforts being made by China practically to a standstill, but also provided for Soviet Russia an ideal chance to land a catch in China's troubled waters—an attempt that the Tsarist Empire made as far back as the sixteenth century.

Comments (1):

BY CHIN-TUNG LIANG

FEEL PRIVILEGED TO BE called upon to make a brief remark on Dr. Ballantine's paper. The task is not easy. Dr. Ballantine is an expert on Chinese and Japanese affairs. He is today one of the few living American officials who served under Franklin D. Roosevelt's administration and who participated in the diplomatic drama with Secretary Hull on the day of the Pearl Harbor disaster at the State Department. To his knowledge and experience of the Far East in general and Sino-Japanese relations in particular, I can hardly add anything new. However, from the historical perspective, I wish to submit a few observations on the Sino-Japanese relations particularly during the 1927-1937 period, and hope that they may serve as a basis for further investigation.

As we are aware, the main purpose of this symposium is to discuss the historical events that occurred in China during the period of 1927-37. I wish to remind the assemblage that the period of 1927-37 under the Nationalist Government at Nanking has been considered the "Golden Decade" of modern Chinese history, as referred to by General Albert C. Wedemeyer in his sworn testimony before the Judiciary Committee of the U.S. Senate, 82nd Congress, 1st Session, September 19, 1951.

During this decade, communications were being improved, the economy was being stabilized and many improvements were being instituted. All of these were essential for strengthening China's ability in resisting Japanese aggression in 1937, tying down millions of Japanese soldiers on the Chinese mainland. This, in turn, helped the United States indirectly during the latter's most difficult time (1941-1942) in fighting a two-front war against Germany in the Atlantic and Japan in the Pacific.

To describe the period of 1927-37 as the golden decade is accurate, perhaps, but only from the Chinese domestic point of view. Looked at from the viewpoint of Sino-Japanese relations, it may possibly be termed the "fateful decade." The Tsinan incident of 1928 was followed by a flare-up of the Mukden in 1931. The Shanghai incident and the establishment of the Manchukuo puppet regime in 1932 were followed by battles from Jehol to Shanhaikwan in 1933. After the Tangku Truce which was dictated by the Japanese, the Kwantung Army again stirred up a series of incidents in North China and Inner Mongolia in 1935-36. Finally, in 1937, war broke out at Marco Polo Bridge which resulted in a fatal tragedy, eventually ruining both China and Japan. Since this tragedy is to no one's liking, one tends to attribute it to *FATE* but for a historian, it may be interpreted otherwise.

In retrospect, I am of the opinion that at least three chances of averting the tragedy did occur in this decade but none of them was being grasped by either side.

The first chance came in 1928, prior to the Tsinan incident. One must remember that up to that incident, Sino-Japanese relations were more intimate than were either Sino-British or Sino-American relations. Shidehara Kijoro, foreign minister of the Wakatsuki cabinet, refused to join the Anglo-American naval bombardment of Nanking in 1927 and Saburi Sadao, the Japanese envoy, made every effort to promote mutual understanding between Japan and China, even at the cost of his life. I have every reason to believe that in the year of 1927-28, if Premier Tanaka were not being influenced by the pressure of Mori Kaku, his vice foreign minister, there would have been no Japanese expeditions to Shangtung and the Tsinan incident would never have occurred. Thus, the whole history of Sino-Japanese relations would have been enirely different.[a] Western writers used to take the anti-Japanese movement in China as the cause of Sino-Japanese conflict; but, in fact, the Tsinan incident was the cause of the conflict and the anti-Japanese movements were merely a retaliation to the incident.

The second chance came at the end of 1931. After the Mukden incident, the Kwantung Army marched southward toward Chinchow. Dr. Wellington Koo, then the Chinese foreign minister, had a plan of making Chinchow a neutral area. This plan was privately advanced through the Conference of the League of Nations at Paris and had the enthusiastic backing of the British. At one time, it appeared very likely to be acceptable to Shidehara. Just at this crucial point, unfortunately, party-strife within the Kuomintang resulted in the Canton's clique's forcing the resignation of Generalissimo Chiang Kai-shek. Dr. Koo's promising plan had to be withdrawn on account of the absence of leadership and of the confusion. In Tokyo, Wakatsuki's cabinet had fallen; Shidehara was gone, and Sino-Japanese relations were rapidly drifting to the point of no return.[b]

The third chance came at the beginning of 1935. At this juncture, the Kwantung Army had two alternative courses open to them: they could either satisfy their ambition by limiting their aggression in Manchuria or they could expand their occupation by invading North China. Choice of the first might have softened or averted the eventual conflict. But as history has witnessed, the second alternative was chosen. Later, Mamoru

Shigemitsu, the Japanese foreign minister during the surrender, regretted this deeply. In his book, *Japan and Her Destiny*, Shigemitsu wrote:

> If again the Government had been able to limit the trouble to the territory outside the Great Wall, I think both the Manchurian affair and the problems of China itself could have been settled by diplomatic machinery.[c]

Taking this account as Japan's destiny, Shigemitsu seems ready to accept the interpretation that the fateful decade does imply. But "fateful decade" and "golden decade" are nothing but semantic terms. They could be different from each other in illustration but common to both in substance depending upon which way they are emphasized. We are told that it was China's weakness that encouraged Japan's ambition; but we are also told that it was China's strength that begot Japan's aggression. To reconcile these two apparently conflicting viewpoints, we may need an explanation. My observation is that improvement vitalized China's strength but at the same time, it undermined Sino-Japanese relations. The more improvements China achieved, the quicker the relation between China and Japan approached its doom. Only in this sense, do the meanings of these two terms—golden decade and fateful decade—coincide.

Comments (2):

BY WILLIAM L. TUNG

THE PERIOD 1927-1937 WAS indeed unique in the history of Republican China, particularly in certain phases of domestic and diplomatic affairs. Immediately after the successful Northern Expedition under the leadership of Chiang Kai-shek, the National Government worked incessantly for the implementation of Dr. Sun Yat-sen's internal and external programs, even though not all of them could be fully carried out partly due to circumstances beyond its control. In his comprehensive paper, Dr. Joseph W. Ballantine has ably reviewed China's foreign relations during that period. His presentation of facts and views is so clear that no further observation on the general subject seems necessary. I wish, however, to call attention to one specific point—that is, China's efforts to terminate unequal treaties.

It is generally known that the Opium War set the precedent for unequal treaties in China. The terms for the restoration of peace as prescribed in the Sino-British Treaty of Nanking, August 29, 1842, were most humiliating. This 1842 pattern was soon followed by the Sino-American and Sino-Franco treaties of 1844. Largely on the ground of applying the most-favored-nation clause, other countries—Russia, Belgium, Germany, Portugal, Denmark, the Netherlands, Spain, Italy, Austria-Hungary, Japan, Peru, Brazil, Mexico, Switzerland, Norway and Sweden—also exacted from China unilateral rights and privileges in the ensuing years. The question might be raised as to what kind of treaties should be considered unequal. On principle, international treaties are concluded on the basis of equality and reciprocity for mutual benefit and convenience of the signatories concerned. Treaties are unequal should their provisions be unilaterally beneficial to one contracting party at the expense of the other. The stipulations in the treaties between China and the aforesaid nations (nineteen in all after the separation of Norway and Sweden) belong to this category.

Unilateral rights and privileges acquired by foreign powers were so extensive that China's territorial integrity and national sovereignty had been vitally affected. The damaging effects included, but were not limited to, the detachment of former dependencies, intrusion on border

regions, cession and lease of territories, establishment of foreign concessions and settlements, opening of ports and inland navigation, stationing of foreign warships and armed forces, exercise of extraterritoriality, restrictions of customs tariff, as well as acquisition of railways and
other economic concessions. Space does not permit detailed description
of their impact on China's domestic development and international status.

To every action, it has been said, there is a reaction. It is quite understandable that, during the course of the Northern Expedition, the Chinese
revolutionists forcibly took over British concessions in Hankow and Kiukiang. Their formal rendition was soon effected by the Sino-British agreements, signed in early 1927. Basically the National Government did not
intend to recover lost rights by unilateral denunciation, but it was
determined to take necessary steps for the total abolition of unequal
treaties. With regard to the means or procedures for the implementation
of this objective, there were fundamental differences between the Nanking and the Peking governments.

For the readjustment or revision of unequal treaties, the Peking government appealed to the Paris Peace Conference in 1919, but the Council
of Four ignored China's request. Although the Washington Conference
of 1921-1922 was receptive to China's proposals, many important items,
including the questions of extraterritoriality and tariff autonomy, were
postponed for future consideration. At both conferences, those participating powers which had common interests in China were inclined to
align themselves for the protection of their vested rights. Because of the
inherent weakness of multilateral approaches according to past experience, the National Government in Nanking decided, from the very
beginning, to resort to bilateral negotiations with the treaty powers.

In June 1928, China had treaty relations with twenty-three nations.
The four new treaties concluded by China with Bolivia, Chile, Finland,
and Persia were reciprocal in nature. Among the original nineteen countries, Germany, Austria, and Russia lost their respective rights and
privileges in China as a result of World War I. Since several unequal
treaties were due to expire, the Nationalist Government proceeded to
negotiate for new treaties on an equal footing. Before the end of the
year, China signed treaties of amity and commerce with Belgium, Denmark, Italy, Portugal, and Spain, all of which agreed to terminate extraterritoriality when the majority of states enjoying that privilege or other
participating states of the Washington Conference should give consent
to its relinquishment. Mexico expressed her readiness to renounce extraterritoriality by an exchange of notes in November of the following year.

Among the remaining powers enjoying extraterritoriality in China,
the United States and Great Britain were pivotal to any conclusive negotiations. While expressing many reservations, they raised no objection to

China's intention to choose January 1, 1930 as the commencement date for the adoption of necessary processes to effect its abolition. Meanwhile, the interested powers accepted the Chinese proposal of reorganizing the Provisional Court at Shanghai on February 17, 1930 as an important step toward the normalization of China's judicial system. Unfortunately, negotiations between the National Government and foreign powers for the abolition of extraterritoriality had to be suspended in 1931, when China was preoccupied with Japan's invasion of Manchuria and subsequent encroachments on Shanghai and North China.

Whereas the foreign powers were reluctant to relinquish extraterritoriality, they complied with China's demand for tariff autonomy. This was accomplished by the National Government not long after its establishment in Nanking. The Sino-American Treaty of July 25, 1928 restored "the principle of complete national tariff autonomy" to China. Other countries—Norway, Belgium, Italy, Denmark, the Netherlands, Portugal, Great Britain, Sweden, France, and Spain—signed similar treaties in the same year. When the Sino-Japanese treaty for that purpose came into force on May 16, 1930 all previous restrictions on China's customs tariff were abolished and the new National Tariff became operative. Considering the importance of tariff autonomy to national revenues and domestic economy and industry, the achievement of the National Government in this respect was most significant.

The war delayed but could not prevent China's efforts to abolish other phases of unequal treaties. In 1941, the National Government resumed negotiations with the United States and Great Britain on the subject. Once China became a major ally of the Western powers after Japan's attack on Pearl Harbor, diplomatic consultations directed toward that end were intensified. Finally, on January 11, 1943, China concluded treaties simultaneously with the United States and Great Britain for the relinquishment of extraterritorial rights and the regulation of related matters. Consequently, all the previously mentioned unilateral rights and privileges were terminated by these treaties. Other countries soon followed suit, and signed new treaties with China on the basis of equality and reciprocity. Thus China's one-century bondage under unequal treaties came to an end.

Although this important task was finished during the war, its groundwork was laid down in the 1930's. Had it not been for the Japanese invasion of Manchuria, China's aspirations in this respect would most likely have been fulfilled before 1937. It is, therefore, only appropriate to conclude that one of the main accomplishments of the National Government during the period 1927-1937 was the negotiations for the abolition of unequal treaties.

CHAPTER II

Political Reconstruction, 1927-1937

BY DISON HSUEH-FENG POE

THE PROCESS OF NATION-BUILDING in modern China just as elsewhere requires continuous, arduous efforts. Of all the phases scheduled for study in this symposium, the most important is doubtless political reconstruction, constituting as it always does, the very basis and condition of all the other works of reconstruction. The most important, being at the same time the most complex and therefore the most difficult, is the most controversial, since political reconstruction involves not merely the relation of historical facts but also the interpretation and evaluation of these facts.

I

Spirit of Objectivity and Criteria for Appraisal

In the study and discussion of our present topic there is one prerequisite: the spirit of objectivity. Without such a spirit, any appraisal would tend to be either willful discrimination or unintentional bias. To maintain strict objectivity, several things are necessary.

First, a uniform standard (that is, a consistent yardstick) should be applied to all nations undergoing political reconstruction. Second, there is a need to examine similar political experiences of other peoples in their nation-building efforts so as to afford comparison and contrast. Third, a legitimate demand is in order for understanding the basic, underlying principles that govern nation-building, albeit they appear to be hidden and elusive. Last and not least, a well-balanced philosophy of history would be helpful—by holding neither "hard determinism" nor "complete libertarianism" but by assuming the libertarian-deterministic stand. Politics and history may operate by invariable laws, but men have a certain amount of freedom in choosing their course of action and in moulding their destiny.

How are we to gauge with objectivity and uniformity the political-reconstruction efforts of modern China from 1927 to 1937? It is submitted here at the outset that we take up two sets of appraisal criteria for our use at the conclusion of this paper.

The first set of criteria is the four ends of the modern state, specifically, the four ends of the state of any period or type. The four ends are: (1) maintenance of domestic order, (2) provision of security against external aggression, (3) administration of justice through the courts, and (4) promotion of popular welfare. In other words, the success or failure depends on whether and how much the nation-building efforts do or do not promote the four common ends of the state: order, security, justice, and welfare.

The second set of criteria that may be warranted is a threefold question concerning China's modernization. Foremost, what are the primary aims to be realized? They are the Three Principles of the People. Secondly, what are the necessary things to be done in order to facilitate the realization of these primary aims? They are three in number: unification, independence and reconstruction. Finally, how are these necessary things to be done—according to the teachings of Dr. Sun Yat-sen, the founder of the Chinese Republic? Unification has to be achieved militarily; independence is to be attained through negotiation; and reconstruction along economic, social and educational lines ought to come gradually, peacefully through legislative reforms.

Aside from the prerequisite spirit of objectivity and the two sets of criteria for appraisal, there is above all the five-element approach to take. The five-element approach is an analytic method with which we may discern more clearly the component ingredients in, and the underlying principles of, politics and history in general, and nation-building in particular.

II

The Five-Element Approach and Nation-Building Precedents

To begin with, politics or the sum total of political affairs, to be rightly understood, calls for a definition. Nowadays politics is usually identified with power struggle. But in reality politics is far much more than mere power struggle. Formerly politics was taken to be confined to matters of the state. Actually politics is found in a church, a union, a school, or a family. The Chinese term for politics is *cheng chih*. According to Dr. Sun, "*cheng* is common affairs; *chih* is management. And management of common affairs is *cheng chih*."[1] This seemingly simple definition is much more meaningful and much more scientific than traditional and current definitions.[2] To elaborate a bit, politics may be defined as organized management of common affairs, with coercive power, through laws and regulations, and involving all sorts of activities varied and conflicting. Suffice it to say, such is politics, the component elements of which we should seek to know so that we may uncover the underlying principles of political reconstruction.

Regarding the five elements of politics, there are four items to be made clear. First, what are the five elements? Second, how are they inter-related? Third, which element is the most important? And fourth, why is the five-element approach taken here? In elucidating these items, illustrations will be drawn from nation-building cases in modern history, such as the successful American Revolution of 1776, the completed Italian *Risorgimento* in 1861, the eventual German unification in 1871, and the establishment of the Turkish Republic in 1923.

First, then, let us analyze politics into five basic component elements. They are: (1) phenomena, (2) ideas, (3) personalities, (4) institutions, and (5) forces.

Political phenomena are facts, incidents, occurrences, movements, situations, and circumstances—either planned or unexpected, and taken to be good or bad, desirable or undesirable. The historic details involved in the oppression of the American colonists by their mother country and their movement for and achievement of independence, and the factors involved in the domination over Italy, Germany, and Turkey by foreign powers and their respective struggles for unification: all these are political phenomena.

Political ideas are notions, beliefs and principles held by individuals, groups, parties or by a whole people. They range from fragmentary phrases, slogans and watchwords to systematic ideologies and myth-complexes, either for or against the whole or part of the existing order, or else championing some sort of utopia. On the positive side, for instance, the writings of men like Locke, Montesquieu, Paine, Mazzini, Fichte, and von Treitschke contributed greatly to the cause of unification, independence and reconstruction.

By political personalities is meant, of course, the relevant individuals, groups, classes or nationalities—either as leaders, rivals, opponents, followers, as well as the general masses. Political personalities, either singly or collectively, have their individuality and uniqueness because of background, training and education, occupation, interest, and beliefs. It is a mistake to assume (as so many thinkers did) that individuals, groups and nations are perfectly alike and can be expected to behave and perform in an identical manner. In all cases of nation-building, leaders like Washington, Cavour, Bismarck, and Kemal are unique and indispensable.

The element of political institutions denotes laws, regulations, usages, and conventions—in a word, systems and procedures either written or unwritten—that prescribe processes, facilitate decisions and transactions, penalize certain behavior, and settle disputes. Political institutions may be timely or outmoded, stationary or changing, operative or decaying. In the study of nation-building cases, political institutions like local self-government (such as the New England town meetings), separation of powers (as embodied in the American constitution), enlightened monarchical rule (in Sardinia and Prussia), and party formation (like the Young Italy, the Young Germany, and the Young Turks) should not be lost sight of.

As to political forces, they are either physical and tangible like weapons, prisons, and troops, or else invisible but nonetheless potent like money power, public opinion, idea-forces, or even geography. Did not Johann Herder of eighteenth century Germany make this appropriate remark: "History is geography set into motion"? Nonetheless, for our purpose, it is sufficient to remember that, in the American, Italian, German, and Turkish nation-building experiences, a combination of forces, economic, social, ideological, and military, played its role and helped bring about the fruitful outcome.

Next, we turn to the interrelationship between the five elements of politics. Here several points in particular need to be presented.

Everything political—from a world war down to a campus riot—has its five elements. To ignore one element or several elements would result in an incomplete picture and, thus, an incorrect understanding. For instance, "government by law" stresses only one element, that of institutions; whereas "government by man" also emphasizes one element, the one other element of personalities. Between "man" and "law," or rather beneath "man" and "law," there is the needed element of force, that of good "tradition." From the brief, random references made above it may be readily seen that in each nation-building case there were inextricably interwoven the five elements of phenomena, ideas, personalities, institutions, and forces.

The same one political matter (whatever it may be) may, viewed from different angles, serve as different elements, and may, given adequate conditions, develop into other elements. This is no juggling of words. It means that political elements are not put, so to speak, in watertight compartments. Take "independence." Viewed as a concept or ideal—as expressed in the American Declaration of 1776, or as entertained in the minds of Fichte and Mazzini—it is an *idea*. But taken as a motivating factor, driving men to action and sacrifice, it is a *force* (an idea-force). And when fully attained, independence is a *phenomenon*, a fact. This divergence in viewpoints and development into some different status applies, too, to constitutionalism. In theory and as an ideal, constitutionalism is a mere *idea*. It must be championed by some leading *personalities*. When embodied in a document, it becomes an *institution*. Only when enforced and workable, it evolves into a *phenomenon*. And, by the same token, if operative constitutionalism actually prevents oppression and promotes welfare, it must have turned itself into a political *force*. The lesson to be drawn from this second kind of interrelationship between the five elements is precisely this: that nation-building must begin as an idea and may, if successful, end as a phenomenon.

There is yet another more subtle and important relationship. The five elements silently and unceasingly interact and re-interact—both horizontally in point of space and vertically in point of time—so as to make history as it is. For example, there may be good laws (namely, *institutions*); yet inept and corrupt officials (namely, *personalities*) may render them ineffective. The form of monarchism may have been discarded, and yet the lingering spirit of monarchism may hamper the smooth working of new democratic institutions. To be more specific, during the American Revolution there were still loyalists and loyalist traditions that were opposed to the cause of independence. The old ideas of separatism and the current sentiments of jealousy were in the way as obstacles; but the phenomenal military successes under the premiership of Cavour and Bismarck swept away these psychological *forces* and brought about the unification of Italy and Germany. One thing must be put in bold relief: only if most of the five elements happen to be dominantly coordinated and cooperative then the desired end, namely the aspired-after *phenomenon*—in this case, nation-building through unification, independence and reconstruction—can be achieved.

This brings up the next issue: which one of the five elements is the most important? In nature, there is no question of priority among the five elements as they are ever present and interwoven. For man there is value and there is priority. Of the five elements the most important is the element of phenomena. This is because man by and large prefers certain phenomena and abhors others: to wit, for order and against chaos; for security and against insecurity; for law and against lawlessness; for life and against death. It is neither the ideas nor the institutions of unification, independence and reconstruction that a nation is after; it is verily the phenomena of unification, independence, and reconstruction. Perhaps a challenge may be made thus: since in the last analysis forces are what bring about phenomena, is not the element of forces the most important? There is some plausibility in this argument. Forces are merely means, however, and there are after all other elements working together. What is more, forces include all sorts, visible and invisible, military as well as pacific. Too often do political leaders of the past and of the present emphasize the tangible, physical forces of coercion and forget the invisible and yet potent forces of persuasion in their attempt to preserve political power.[3]

Finally, the main reasons for taking this five-element approach may now be stated. For one thing, clarity is enhanced by distinguishing the factually mixed but theoretically separable ingredients of any political problem; in this case, the grass roots of nation-building. For another, by examining all the pertinent phases the wholeness or completeness of the problem is furnished. What is more, such an approach throws light on the complexity and difficulty of the problem itself. Above all, it may convince us that it is always beyond the power of any one person, party, or nation, or any combination of persons, parties, or nations to control the course and outcome of human history.[4]

III

Historic Background and Popular Aspirations

Concerning the one decade (1927-1937) of China's nation-building efforts in the realm of political affairs, the first thing to be noted is the background. There are two aspects of this, the long-range and general background and the immediate and particular background. In both aspects the situation was the same, one full of "internal worries and external threats"—to use a very apt classical Chinese phrase. "Internal worries" mean partitions and rebellions, and "external threats" refer to border wars and foreign invasions.

To take the long-range view, China's modernization dates back to the Opium War of 1840-1842. Ever since that military defeat and many other military defeats suffered later the Chinese people began to grope after the ways and measures of nation-building, of making the country "wealthy and strong." But not much was achieved even after the overthrow of the Manchus and the establishment of the Republic in 1912. To the historian and political scientist, China has been caught in the midst of three historic, world-wide, earthquake-like movements that are still shaking up nations the world over, namely: the movements of nationalism, democracy, and socialism.

Looking at the immediate and particular aspect of the background, we must remember the widespread warlordism, the deep frustration of the Chinese people at the Paris Peace Conference, the May Fourth Student Movement, Soviet Russia's reentering the Far Eastern scene, Japan's aggressive designs, and the Northern Expedition. The gigantic task of

China's turning herself into a modern state, unified, independent, and economically reconstructed may best be appreciated if we list side by side in three columns: (a) the facts prevailing on the eve of the Northern Expedition under the Kuomintang (KMT) leadership, (b) the ideals held by the Party and Government leadership, and (c) the arduous nation-building efforts during 1927-1937. The following tabulation is certainly oversimplification; but this oversimplification through the five-element approach may be meaningful and useful.

(a) THE FIVE ELEMENTS IN FACTS PREVAILING	(b) THE FIVE ELEMENTS IN IDEALS HELD	(c) THE FIVE ELEMENTS IN EFFORTS MADE
1. *Phenomena* a. "internal worries" b. "external threats"	1. *Phenomena* a. unification b. independence	1. *Phenomena* achievement of national unification
2. *Ideas* a. breakdown of traditional political myths b. uncritical following of conflicting alien ideologies	2. *Ideas* a. *San-min Chu-i* as the popular ideology b. revitalization of Confucian ethics	2. *Ideas* all in accordance with *San-min Chu-i*
3. *Personalities* a. warlords, politicians and aloof intelligentsia b. corrupt, incompetent, inefficient bureaucrats	3. *Personalities* a. vigorous leadership, a new elite b. selective civil service, censorial control	3. *Personalities* the Party elite; civil service through examination; judicial officers with qualifications, and training
4. *Institutions* a. paper constitution; nominal central authority b. miserable popular economy; sufferings	4. *Institutions* a. constitutional government through three stages b. socialism through gradual legislative change	4. *Institutions* tutelage constitution; preparation for local self-government; economic reforms attempted
5. *Forces* a. separatism and disintegration from within b. aggression and interference from without	5. *Forces* a. a cohesive, unifying national spirit b. strong military strength for defense	5. *Forces* cultivation of national consciousness; augmentation of military strength through army reorganization, etc.

IV

Arduous Political Nation-Building Efforts

Aware of China's distant and immediate background, understanding the popular aspirations of the times, and considering the immensity of her population, the vastness of her territory, and the longevity of her traditional political elements, we should discern that her nation-building, as compared with the nation-building of the Americans, the Italians, the Germans, and the Turks, must necessarily be a hundred times more complex, more difficult. We are now ready to study critically the arduous nation-building efforts of modern China in the realm of political affairs from 1927-1937.

Summarily put, there are altogether eight categories of such arduous efforts. They are the following: (1) the achievement of gradual national unification; (2) the cultivation of national consciousness; (3) the augmentation of military strength for national defense; (4) the embarkation upon tutelage constitutionalism; (5) the founding of the five-power central government system; (6) the preparation for reforms; (7) the launching of judicial and administrative reforms; and (8) the attempts at initiating the improvement of popular economic life. The scope and degree of fruitfulness in these eight categories of efforts certainly varied; but their overall combined success made China sufficiently modernized.

The achievement of gradual national unification

Practically ever since the founding of the Republic in 1912, China remained divided—up till 1927-1928. The central government in Peking was recognized by the foreign powers and thus regarded itself as the legitimate government. This government was popularly known as the Northern government in contradistinction from the Southern government in Canton under the revolutionary leadership of Dr. Sun Yat-sen. Substantially, however, the whole country was partitioned into many more regional spheres of influence under what is now described as warlordism.

On the eve of national unification (1927-1928) China found itself under a weak, unstable, and tottering central government, with the entire domain carved into *de facto* internal spheres of influence. The central government, claiming jurisdiction over the whole land, had control virtually only of Peking. In many ways its orders and decrees hardly reached beyond the gates of the capital. The revolutionary Southern government had nominally, as its basis of operation, two provinces, Kwangtung and Kwangsi. In actuality, there was frequent friction and confrontation between the two provinces, and there was repeated insubordination and conspiracy within Kwangtung. The Northeast, comprising the "Three Eastern Provinces," usually known as Manchuria, was lorded over by Chang Tso-lin. The then apparently most imposing figure was Wu Pei-fu, who was occupying the three strategic provinces in central China—Honan, Hupeh and Hunan. The Southeast, with its five provinces of Kiangsu, Chekiang, Anhwei, Kiangsi, and Fukien, was in the hands of Sun Chuan-fang. The two Northern provinces of Hopei and Shantung were under an illiterate, rude warlord, Chang Chung-chang. Feng Yu-hsiang (the so-called Christian general) happened to be dominating at this juncture the Northwest, the two provinces of Chahar and Suiyuan. The fortress-like province of Shansi had been ever since 1912 the seat of Yen Hsi-shan. Frontier provinces like Yunnan, Kweichow, Szechuan, and Sinkiang had their respective semi-independent warlords. Lastly, the Chinese Communist Party (CCP), now in professed cooperation with the Kuomintang, was by its very nature and under actual direction of Soviet Russia an embryonic *imperium in imperio*.

That such a state of affairs—the phenomenon of disunity—should pose a most formidable task of national unification for the Kuomintang leadership needs no elaboration. This is so especially because, in addition to "internal worries," there were "external threats" from Japan. The revolutionary Southern government, after the reorganization of the Kuomintang in 1924, proceeded with its Northern Expedition on July 9, 1926. By this time the National Government had been set up in Canton on July 1. The northward march under Generalissimo Chiang Kai-shek was so speedily successful that the National Government was established in Nanking on April 18, 1927. The impending ultimate unification was certainly something the Japanese militarists liked least. So they created the May Third (1928) Tsinan Incident, blocking the way and slowing down the last lap of the revolutionary troops' onward march northward. Changing its route, the National Government army eventually reached Peking on June 8, 1928. The American government was the first to render recognition to the Chinese National Government on July 25—one and a half months later. And then on December 29, after several months of confidential negotiation with Nanking's representatives, and spiritually in defiance of Japan, Chang Hsueh-liang of the Northeast (son of Chang Tso-lin) openly acknowledged allegiance to the National Government and hoisted the new national flag. This marked the official national unification of China.

The national unification of 1927-1928 proved soon, however, to be more apparent than real, more symbolic than substantial. "Internal worries" repeatedly reappeared as if to keep pace with "external threats." Omitting lesser crises of insubordination and separatism, we may list ten conspicuous cases of recurrent, intermittent splits, secessions, revolts, and internal wars:

1) The Kwangsi Faction Revolt took place from February to April, 1929.

2) Feng Yu-hsiang attempted an insurrection in May, 1929.

3) The abortive revolts of T'ang Sheng-chih and Shih Yu-shan occurred in October and December, 1929.

4) The Yen-Feng joint separatist movement and war spread through northern, central, and southern China. Severe fighting lasted four months and twelve days from May to September, 1930.

5) In May and June, 1933, Feng Yu-hsiang once more led a separatist movement and headed at Kalgan the so-called "Federated Kuomin Japan-resisting Armies." Meant to be or not, this action was very embarrassing to the National Government in Nanking.

6) For a similar allegation, the "People's Government" was set up in the Fukien province under Li Tsung-jen and Chen Ming-chiu in 1933. This "People's Government" appeared and disappeared within the short span of two months, namely November and December.

7) In the summer of 1936 there happened another revolt by Chen Chi-tang and Li Tsung-jen—for the ostentatious purpose of fighting the Japanese invaders.[5]

8) For two weeks at the close of the year 1936 the unexpected Sian Incident shocked the nation and the world: Chang Hsueh-liang in armed kidnap fashion detained and threatened Generalissimo Chiang—again for the alleged reason of uniting with the Communists and fighting Japan.

9) In January, 1937 Yang Hu-cheng (partner in the Sian coup) led yet another revolt, calling whatever troops under him and his associates the "Federated Anti-Japan and Anti-Chiang Armies." These armies soon melted away.

10) This résumé would be incomplete without mentioning that since 1928 the CCP organized their Red troops and rebelled against the National government.

There was a KMT-CCP coalition from 1924-1927. But it was a *mariage de convenance,* or as the Chinese saying goes, a case of "sleeping on the same bed, but dreaming different dreams." As a Western writer puts it, "The radicalism of the Communists during the Northern expedition inevitably produced a reaction. Merchants, landlords, army officers, and many other groups found themselves menaced; they offered support to conservative leaders in the Kuomintang if they would rid the party of its radical wing."[6] As a matter of fact, it was more than mere radicalism that served as the last straw breaking the camel's back. As is well-known now, it was Stalin's secret telegram—dictating plans and actions for interfering with the Kuomintang policies—conveyed by the Indian M. N. Roy to Wang Ching-wei, the KMT left-wing leader at Wuhan, that caused the final split. From late 1927 to 1934, the Communists started more than two hundred urban and rural uprisings. They established their Chinese Soviet Republic and made Juichin (in Kiangsi) the seat of government, 1931-1934. Having stubbornly resisted several government military campaigns against them, and after the "long march" in the winter months of 1934-1935, the Red Army settled down in Shensi, and Yenan became the Communists' center of authority. By now the CCP had grown from an embryonic to a full-sized *imperium in imperio.*

In a paper like this it is neither possible nor necessary to sketch any details of the above-listed ten episodes of "internal worries." Two observations, nevertheless, are in order. One is about the reasons advanced in the circular telegrams and wordy declarations of those who opposed and fought the National Government. Interestingly enough, and invariably so, the given reasons centered around any one or two, or all three, of these "noble" purposes: to safeguard and promote constitutionalism and democracy; to resist and fight Japanese aggression; and—in the most nebulous term—to save and serve the country.[7] The other observation concerns the ways in which these crises and revolts were dealt with. Two ways were open to the National Government: either political negotiation or military settlement—or, as was usual, a combination of the two. With the exception of dealing with the CCP, the National Government won out in every case.

One related crucial point is to be borne in mind. The "internal worries" came one after the other in the midst of mounting "external threats," and the two almost went hand in hand. Japan attempted to block the Northern Expedition by creating the May Third Incident in 1928. By the Mukden Incident on September 18, 1931, Japan took over the Northeast. On January 28, 1932, the Japanese militarists carried war to Shanghai. On March 1st of the same year the puppet regime of Manchukuo was set up in Manchuria. Japan made further invasion of Jehol from January to May, 1933. And in 1935 Japan was trying to convert the five northern provinces of Hopei, Chahar, Suiyuan, Shansi, and Shantung into an autonomous area. But "external threats" did not come from Japan alone. In a manner more subtle and not less menacing, Soviet Russia, in the name of International Communism, was—through its agents like Borodin and Roy, and by Stalin's personal directives—endeavoring to interfere with China's domestic politics, as indicated above.

Ironically, first the Sian Incident and then half a year later the Marco Polo Bridge Incident served as the last steps toward the eventual united front. However, the open declaration of the CCP, acknowledging its allegiance to the National Government, did not come out until September 22, 1937, two and a half months after the said Marco Polo Bridge Incident. That China managed to achieve unification was unquestionably a creditable achievement.

The cultivation of national consciousness

Military might is not the exclusive factor in bringing about national unification. National consciousness is also indispensable. The awakening of the Chinese people's national spirit started, of course, with the Opium War and its aftermath, and spread with every other military defeat and unequal treaty thereafter. But it was during this decade under our study that China's national consciousness advanced by leaps and bounds. This development in width and depth was cultivated through three channels: through the use of various political symbols, through the vehicle of education, and through the recovery of certain sovereign rights.

National consciousness was primarily accelerated by the use of various political symbols. Take the Last Will of the Republic Founder, Dr. Sun Yat-sen, written on February 20, and signed on March 11, 1925.

> For forty years I have devoted myself to the cause of the People's revolution with but one end in view, the elevation of China to a position of freedom and equality among the nations. My experiences during these forty years have firmly convinced me that to attain this goal we must bring about a thorough awakening of our own people and ally ourselves in a common struggle with those peoples of the world who treat us on the basis of equality.
>
> The work of the Revolution is not yet done. Let all our comrades follow my *Plans for National Reconstruction, Fundamentals of National Reconstruction, Three Principles of the People,* and the Manifesto issued by the First National Convention of our Party, and strive on earnestly for their consummation. Above all, our recent declarations in favour of the convocation of a National Assembly and the abolition of unequal treaties should be carried into effect with the least possible delay. This is my heartfelt charge to you.

According to an American political scientist, Dr. Arthur N. Holcombe of Harvard University, "this is a document which may be most fittingly described as the Declaration of Independence of Revolutionary China."[8]

Then, too, there is the new national anthem, brief, calm, and dignified, penned by Dr. Sun Yat-sen himself.

San Min Chu I
Our aim shall be
To found a free land,
World peace be our stand.
Lead on, comrades,
Vanguards ye are.
Hold fast your aim
By sun and star.
Be earnest and brave
Your country to save.
One heart, one soul,
One mind, one goal.[9]

In bold relief this anthem emphasized the ideals of unification, independence, national liberty, and world peace. Its popularization during these ten years meant a strengthened national consciousness.

There were many other political symbols that served the same purpose and obtained the same result. Such were the national flag, Dr. Sun's ubiquitous portraits, statues and monuments erected in honor of revolutionary martyrs, numerous halls, parks and playgrounds named after the Republic Founder, and the like. All of them contributed to promote a national spirit never before so pervasive and saturating.

National consciousness was also fostered during this decade through the vehicle of education—figuratively speaking along three parallel highways, namely (1) institutional education from elementary to graduate schools, (2) social education in general via all its media, and (3) nation-wide movement in particular to promote literacy among the adults. All these programs were carried out by the government, the Party, and the interested social leaders and groups.

According to the Educational Aims and Practical Policies promulgated in 1929 by the National Government, the propagation of the Three Principles of the People was the overall objective. Here is the explicit stipulation on educational aims:

In accordance with the Three Principles of the People, education in the Republic of China aims at the betterment of popular livelihood, the strengthening of social cohesion, the development of public economy, and the continuation on national life so as to attain the independence of the nation, the realization of the people's political power, and the promotion of the people's livelihood—thereby to help bring about world unity.

As to practical policies, the concrete ways and methods to realize the educational aims, the said document listed eight items. Item One stated thus:

The teaching and learning of the Three Principles of the People in the schools and colleges should be linked with, and unified in, the whole curriculum and all extra-curricular activities: that is, to express the true meaning of the Principle of the People's nationhood through the various lessons and courses on history and geography; to train the application of the Principle of the People's political power through the holding of meetings by students; and to lay the foundation of the Principle of the People's livelihood through the actual practice of different kinds of productive labour. The total objective is to blend together knowledge and morality under the Three Principles of the People so that the result of both earnest belief and arduous practice may be achieved.

Two more items may be cited here. Item Seven declared: "In schools and colleges, as well as in social education, common stress should be put on the development of the citizens' physique. Students in middle schools, professional institutes, and colleges and universities should receive proper military training. The goal of promoting physical education is of course to increase the physical strength of the people; but in particular it is especially to cultivate thereby a healthy spirit and to develop an orderly habit on the part of the people." And Item Three directed the following: "Social education must endeavor to prepare the people for these things: possession of necessary common-sense knowledge of modern urban and rural life; acquirement of abilities to improve home economy; attainment of proper qualifications for citizenship and self-government; formation of the habit of safeguarding public parks and grounds, forests, and other public enterprises; and cultivation of virtues like care of the aged, help to the needy, prevention of disasters, and participation in all forms of mutual aid."[10]

In the spread of new education, and in the cultivation of national consciousness, there was yet another factor very much emphasized: the revitalization of traditional Confucian ethics. As President Chiang Kai-shek put it in his *China's Destiny*:

China's long history is due to her inherent virtues and is at the same time a manifestation of her high culture. As we all know, the fundamentals of Chinese morality are Loyalty, Filial Devotion, Kindness, Love, Faithfulness, Justice, Harmony and Equity, and the principles upon which the Chinese state has been established are Propriety, Righteousness, Integrity, and Honor. Under the permeating influence of these Eight Virtues and Four Cardinal Principles the Chunghua (Chinese) nation has been able to keep its promises and discharge its duties, and in dealing with others, to put itself in their place and thus avoid conflict.[11]

Thus understood, what was taught was not chauvinism but sane nationalism perfectly compatible with internationalism.

In addition, there was the literacy movement for the adult masses. According to estimates, about three-fourths of the population were illiterate. It goes without saying that the acquired ability to read vernacular newspapers and thereby to understand current events, domestic and foreign, could further the spirit of nationalism. To sum up, the educational aims and policies were systematically and energetically striven after by the different units and agencies of both the Party and Government.

National consciousness was sharpened yet in another manner. There was the third channel—through the persistent negotiations and piecemeal successes in terminating unequal treaties. As a matter of fact, the diplomatic movement to rid China of such inequalities was started at the Paris Peace Conference in 1919 and continued at the Washington Conference of 1921-1922. But significant fruitage did not come until the first ten years of the Nationalist regime.

China's long and loud "Rights Recovery" movement sought to terminate the impairment of her sovereignty on the following unilateral, unequal treaty provisions: conventional tariff; extraterritoriality; inland and coastal navigation by foreign ships; the stationing of foreign troops on China's soil; and foreign settlements, concessions, and leased territories.

Historically, the Sino-German Agreement of May 20, 1921 was the first treaty on a basis of equality, recognizing tariff autonomy and ending extraterritoriality. The Sino-Austrian Treaty of Commerce of October 19, 1925 followed suit. Now Germany and Austria were the defeated countries of World War I. It was Soviet Russia that first voluntarily announced in principle in 1919 to terminate the unequal treaties Czarist Russia concluded with Manchu China. Whether it was altogether honest good intention at first or whether it started out to be an attractive bait to win over and then communize China remains a matter of conjecture for historians.

Anyway, with the rapid progress of the Northward Expedition, both the psychology and the handling of the matter of "Rights Recovery" took a sharp turn on the part of China and foreign powers. The termination of unequal treaty stipulations came at long last, though grudgingly and gradually.

For instance, the British concessions at Hankow, Kiukiang, and Chinkiang were returned to China in 1927 and 1929. And there was the return of Weihaiwei by Great Britain in 1930. China's tariff autonomy was recognized by practically all foreign powers during 1928-1929; and Japan and the Netherlands followed suit in the next year. As to extraterritoriality, China announced in December, 1929 a unilateral cancellation, over which the other powers protested. On May 4, 1931 Nanking issued a mandate, declaring the completion of pertinent regulations and thus the exercise of China's full jurisdiction over all aliens by January 1, 1932. The military occupation by Japan of Manchuria made this mandate a dead letter. Finally, a few months after the Pearl Harbor Day, the United States and Great Britain separately concluded treaties with China, terminating their century-old consular jurisdiction in China.

What we are interested in is not the history of the termination of the unequal treaties imposed on China but the painstaking efforts and achievements that most definitely broadened and deepened the self-awareness of the Chinese nation.

The best proof of the highly developed national consciousness through the three channels of political symbols, educational programs, and diplomatic exertions may be found in the spontaneous, nation-wide jubilation over the news release that the Sian Incident was overcome and that Generalissimo Chiang had returned to Nanking. The outcome was taken to be not a matter of personal safety but as something pivotal to the destiny of the entire nation.

The late Dr. Monlin Chiang, scholar and educator, gave this very apt and vivid description. "In the Chih-hsiang Theater at the Tung-an market (in the city of Peiping), where the extras first circulated, waves of applause swept the audience, to the indescribable embarrassment and perplexity of the actors, who were unaware of the happy tidings. In about half an hour the stillness of the gloomy winter evening in Peiping was suddenly broken by the gay sound of firecrackers, while stars of fireworks splashed joyously in the dark sky."[12] This was the universal feature in every town and village that memorable Christmas day, December 25, 1936. Dr. Chiang went on with the following observation:

> The warlords had wrought havoc in the country for a quarter of a century, and people longed for some national leader to rise and sweep away these obstacles to national unity. They had found him in the person of Generalissimo Chiang Kai-shek. His difficulties were enhanced by the double task of dislodging the remnants of the snarling 'tigers' from their lairs in the provinces, on the one hand, and building up adequate forces to resist Japanese invasion on the other. But public opinion was solidly behind him in carrying out his great task.[13]

The augmentation of defensive military strength

It may be challenged whether the augmentation of military strength for national defense should be appropriately listed as one category of political efforts. In other words, is military reorganization a political affair? The answer is emphatically positive, since order and security (the first two ends of a modern state) can never be possible without adequate military might and because military might is also indispensable for national unification. And this is precisely why at the outset of this paper a true definition of the term "politics" was sought.

The triumphant march of the revolutionary troops into Peking (soon renamed Peiping) marked the close of the Northern Expedition. At this juncture there were four Army groups with Chiang Kai-shek (with 420,000 men including the other forces under the control of the State Council), Feng Yu-hsiang (with 220,000 men), Yen Hsi-shan (with 200,000 men), and Li Tsung-jen (with 230,000 men)—all under Generalissimo Chiang, concurrently the commander-in-chief over and above the four Army Group Commanders. Almost immediately after having reached Peking, the high military leaders held a conference. There the government policy was outlined:

"1) The National Government shall have supreme command of the armed forces.

2) Unity of command shall be thus realized:

a) the existing army units shall be reorganized by the central government into a truly national army;

b) all rights of command must be vested in the central government;

c) the system of organization, training and supply shall be standardized; etc."[14]

In a statement to the press at Peking on July 13, 1928, Commander-in-chief Chiang stressed the important points in the government scheme:

"1) to better the quality of the nation's armed forces by reducing the huge, heterogeneous army to a manageable size;

2) to centralize the military administration in the National Government (particularly the aspects of finance, supply and personnel) and to curtail the illegal interception of revenues by the various warlords, then still a prevalent ill in the Chinese financial picture;

3) to improve the standard of living of the common soldier; and

4) to enforce a 'soldier-labor' policy, utilizing demobilized soldiers, as a disciplined and trained labor force for reconstruction plans."[15]

All these items are fundamentals taken for granted in any modern state. But they were in the then China still lofty "ideas," requiring more time and energy and struggle to be translated into actual "phenomena." Indeed, the victorious take-over of Peking merely symbolized the death of warlordism in form, but warlordism in spirit was still very much alive—even among some of the military commanders themselves, who were participating in the said conference. Actually, some suspected that the government proposals of reducing the number of troops and of unifying military affairs were partisan, intriguing designs to lower their own status and potency. So, out of the military conference came nothing fruitful except an empty agreement in principle on certain matters.

In spite of all this, however, military reorganization and modernization did take place bit by bit and step by step. Briefly put, military modernization meant primarily military unification, and military unification meant primarily military centralization or standardization. To a layman, the overall military problem may be succinctly stated. Just as there should be in any well-ordered country one postal service, one customs service, or one system of courts, so there should be one and only one military system. In the midst of untold difficulties four military reforms emerged during this turbulent and yet progressive decade: (1) unified organization, (2) unified management, (3) unified command, and (4) unified training. With unified organization, the number, the composition, and verily the whole system of the armed forces were fixed by law; and no troops of any personal or regional nature were permitted. Through unified management, matters like the budget, finance, payment, and accounting, and also the supply and equipment were turned into the hands of the central government agencies. Under unified command came the centralization of the appointment of officers, the stationing and movement of troops, the assignment of missions, and the like. Unified training included all kinds and levels of military training of petty officers, staff members, and high commanders. The one most noteworthy point is that with such military modernization the military strength of China was greatly increased in ways many and varied.

Of the different military training centers, the Central Military Academy at Nanking is worth mentioning. This was a continuity and a counterpart of the original Whampoa Military Academy at Canton, which brought into being the nucleus of the revolutionary army on its Northern Expedition and also served as the birthplace of many leading generals. Its historic role in helping unify the country and popularize its Director, the then General Chiang, cannot be overemphasized. After the official unification of the country, its successor was set up at Nanking as the Central Military Academy. Here, year by year prior to 1937, three thousand new cadets (all high school graduates) were taken in and given a most rigorous training.

To the whole program of military modernization a number of competent foreign advisers rendered their services. During the KMT-CCP coalition period (1924-1927) it was the Russian military advisers who helped in the Whampoa Military Academy. These Russians were at the same time political agents. With the breakup of that coalition Generalissimo Chiang turned to German experts: first, Colonel Dr. Max Bauer, then Lieutenant Colonel Hermann Kriebel, Lieutenant General

Georg Wetzell, General Hans von Seeckt, and lastly, General Alexander von Falkenhausen. These talented, experienced German military advisers rendered much valuable help. From 1934 to 1936 a Three-Year Plan of rearmament was made; but the Japanese invasion in the beginning of July, 1937 put an end to this program.

As another illustration of China's military modernization during this period, a passing observation may be made on the Conscription Law of June 17, 1933. By a government mandate issued later on February 25, 1935 this conscription law should become effective from March 1, 1936. It was not enforced by that date. Even though its enforcement was repeatedly postponed and even though later during the war of resistance conscription was carried out not altogether in accordance with the letter and spirit of the law, the very fact that there was a law of conscription promulgated in 1933 was a matter of epochal significance. In ancient China there had been crude forms of conscription by law and in practice. But later on centuries of traditional ethical teachings culminated in the nation-wide slogan: "Good iron is not made into nails; good men are not turned into soldiers." There persisted a strong psychology of contempt for as well as fear against militarism. It was something radical and courageous for the legislators to have passed the Law of Conscription in 1933. The people were not yet ready for it. Hence, the delay and postponement in its enforcement. Nonetheless, the passage and promulgation of such a law was indicative of the mode of military modernization.

At the bottom of things, military strength nowhere consists in mere troops, however well trained, equipped, and indoctrinated. Military strength also depends on other related factors such as good communications, sufficient means of transportation, a sound currency, abundant agricultural products, developing industries. Significantly enough, reconstruction in these fields went ahead side by side with military modernization within this span of ten years. All of these things combined to augment modern China's national strength, of which military strength is a share, albeit the lion's share.

After the Marco Polo Bridge Incident on July 7, 1937, Generalissimo Chiang had this to say in his address to the nation:

> From the military point of view we may say that Japan's preparations are complete in all aspects. . . . Now let us look at our own situation. How do we stand? Have we fulfilled the conditions necessary for resisting the enemy? We ourselves can answer that question simply and sadly in one brief sentence: we have made no preparations whatsoever. Not only have we not organized our resources, but we are not even unified in thought and spirit.[16]

What was spoken of here was certainly comparative unreadiness. The eight-year resistance war itself demonstrated unmistakably that there had been considerable augmentation of China's military strength, supported by other muscles and sinews of the whole nation.

The embarkation upon Tutelage Constitutionalism

Now we turn to one important but controversial phase of China's nation-building, which is in its very nature political *par excellence*. This is the embarkation upon Tutelage Constitutionalism—the carrying out of Dr. Sun's teachings of constitutional government through three successive stages, and the adoption and operation of the Provisional Constitution for the Period of Political Tutelage. Here, more than elsewhere, the need of objectivity in spirit, of uniformity in appraisal standards, and of the appeal to underlying principles of politics is all the more urgent.

According to Dr. Sun, democracy could not be obtained overnight; there had to be three stages: (1) the period of military rule (during the revolutionary years), (2) the period of political tutelage (for teaching the people how to exercise their political powers), and then (3) the period of constitutional government (with the full operation of democratic institutions). Political tutelage implied party dictatorship, with the Kuomintang serving as the vanguard of the people. Dr. Sun conceived and preached this idea very early in his revolutionary life. Later it was embodied in his *Fundamentals of National Reconstruction*, dated April 12, 1924.

Here is Article VI of the said *Fundamentals*: "During the period of military operations the area of operations shall be subject to martial law. The military authorities shall use their power to suppress reactionary and counterrevolutionary forces and to propagate the principles of reconstruction so that the people may be enlightened and the country unified." Article VIII describes the second stage: "During the period of political tutelage the Government shall appoint trained men, who have passed the civil service examinations, to assist the people in the local districts (*hsien*) in preparing for local self-government. . . ."[17]

Another passage quoted in Generalissimo Chiang's address to the Omei Military Training Corps on September 15, 1935 makes the meaning even more clear:

During the period of military operations the combined forces of the revolutionary army and the people should be used to root out all old obstacles and bad institutions in order to facilitate the carrying out of all aspects of reconstruction work. In the period of political tutelage the duty and burden of protecting and cultivating the people should be undertaken by our Party so as to lead and instruct them in doing reconstruction works under political tutelage, thereby increasing the people's political knowledge and ability. In this way the people may be enabled to manage by direct participation their own political affairs.[18]

On October 3, 1928 the Central Executive Committee of the Kuomintang adopted the *Essentials of Political Tutelage* to guide the Party and the Government in initiating the period of political tutelage as envisaged by the Party and Republic Founder. This document is important because before the later promulgation in 1931 of the Provisional Constitution for the same purpose there had been Tutelage Constitutionalism, in fact, even not in name. The Preamble of this document, the *Essentials,* reads: "In carrying out the Founding Leader's Three Principles of the People, and in accordance with the principles for the Period of Political Tutelage as stipulated in the *Fundamentals of National Reconstruction,* the Kuomintang of China hereby formulates the following Essentials in order to train the citizens in the exercise of their political powers up till the inauguration of Constitutional Government when popular democracy shall in completeness begin."

The six articles of the *Essentials* are worth quoting because substantially they served as constitutional provisions of the land:

1) The Republic of China shall, during the Period of Political Tutelage, have the Kuomintang National Convention guide the people, on behalf of the People's National Assembly, in the exercise of their political powers.

2) The Kuomintang National Convention shall, at the close of its session, delegate to its Central Executive Committee the exercise of its powers.

3) The people shall be trained gradually to exercise their four political powers of election, recall, initiative, and referendum as prescribed in the Founding Leader's *Fundamentals of National Reconstruction* so that the way to Constitutional Government may be paved.

4) The total possession and separate exercise of the five governing powers shall be delegated to the National Government so as to lay the foundation of a popularly elected government in the Period of Constitutional Government.

5) The guidance and supervision of the National Government in its carrying out important state affairs shall be entrusted to the Central Political Council of the Kuomintang Central Executive Committee.

6) The amendment to and interpretation of the Organic Law of the National Government shall be done in resolution by the Central Political Council of the Kuomintang Central Executive Committee.[19]

It was not without anxiety and struggle that three years later there was adopted the Provisional Constitution for the Period of Political Tutelage, conveniently known in Chinese as the *Yueh-fa,* in the year 1931. Foremost among the objections raised was the contention that Dr. Sun never explicitly taught the need of such a thing. By the same token, however, nor was there any teaching explicit or implicit that there should not be such a fundamental document. Anyway, a split threatened the Party.

It was Hu Han-min, then President of the Legislative Yuan, who led a vigorous opposition to the drafting of a *Yueh-fa* for political tutelage, though himself a loyal supporter of the principle of political tutelage and the need of having a Period of Political Tutelage. He threatened to resign, and eventually did resign. His resignation was followed by that of several other leading party-members. The crisis was somehow and anyhow solved but not without some repercussions, at least in the element of personalities. When the crisis was over, Generalissimo Chiang declared on March 2, 1931 at the National Government weekly Memorial Service: "And of all problems before the People's Convention the question of the institution of *Yueh-fa* (*i.e.*, a Provisional Constitution) to be adopted during the Period of Political Tutelage is of the highest importance, which all comrades have agreed to discuss at the People's Convention. Hu Han-min, President of the Legislative Yuan, however, insists that the People's Convention should not be allowed to discuss the adoption of a Provisional Constitution. In so doing, he will not see that without a Provisional Constitution there could be no security for the lives and property of the people; he will not see that without guarantees to person and property there could be no real unification of the country and an end to civil wars."[20]

The Tutelage *Yueh-Fa* as adopted by the People's Convention and promulgated by the National Government on June 1, 1931 had one preamble and eighty-nine articles in eight chapters. To all intents and purposes, it was a full-fledged modern constitution, containing as it did, a bill of rights and duties of the People, a list of powers belonging to the central government, the composition of the five *Yuan*, a clear demarcation of powers between the central government and local governments, stipulated principles on the people's livelihood and the citizens' education, and finally provisions for interpretation of the *Yueh-fa* and the drafting of a permanent constitution (*Hsien-fa*) for Constitutional Government. There were conceivably some unique features. It contained a special chapter on the essentials of political tutelage in accordance with Dr. Sun's basic teachings. Article 30 stipulated: "During the Period of Political Tutelage, the National Convention of the Kuomintang shall exercise the governing powers of the Central Government on behalf of the National Assembly. During the adjournment of the National Convention of the Party, the Party Central Executive Committee shall exercise the said powers." And by the same token the Party Central Executive Committee was empowered in Article 85 to interpret this Provisional Constitution when necessary.

A brief discussion is in order about the *raison d'être* of "political tutelage." Is there anywhere actual need of, and justification for, such a thing? Is it a theory and device to whitewash naked oligarchy and dictatorship? Or is it—whether one likes it or not—one of the fundamental laws of politics in evolution?

The best approach to the problem is to resort to history. The leaders of the French Revolution in 1789, for example, wanted to bring about democracy overnight by the sheer use of violence and bloodshed—by sending thousands upon thousands of men and women to the guillotine. Violence and bloodshed resulted in a dismal failure. The revolutionaries' successors and their successors' successors failed too. After three *coup d'etats* and nine constitutions and with the establishment of the Third Republic almost a century later did the French people learn how to operate democratic institutions. The American Revolution of 1776 was no exception. For one thing, the American colonists had for a long period learned the art of self-government through institutions like the New England town meetings. For another, the American people had learned under the Articles of Confederation the need of a stronger central though federal government. In each case there was political tutelage—in fact though not in name, at random though not systematically. The British rule over India turned out to be a blessing in disguise. Without that period of political tutelage the Indian people would not have been able to operate the institutions of democracy smoothly and successfully as soon as they did.

Thus viewed, Dr. Sun's principle of political tutelage may be taken as a genuine contribution to modern political science. Any ordinary politician would try to flatter the people by paying unreserved tribute to their political capacity. Dr. Sun was not afraid of telling his own people and the world that, to be able to practice democracy, a people has to go through a period of political tutelage.[21]

In accordance with the stipulation in the *Yueh-fa*, the national legislature did make, and the National Government did promulgate, a draft permanent constitution on May 5, 1936 for the Period of Constitutional Government. By promulgation, the Government was submitting the draft constitution to the people for their study, criticism, and consideration. But before the National Government had time to call the National Assembly for the adoption of the draft supreme law of the land resistance war against Japan broke out. Suffice it to say here, the adoption and operation of the *Yueh-fa*—with whatever shortcomings—was certainly a political achievement of high significance.

The founding of the five-power central system

Another contribution of Dr. Sun to the political reconstruction of modern China, intimately related to his Three Principles of the People, is his unique Five-Power Constitution. The background, theory, institution, and operation of this Five-Power System should be understood.

The background is usually taken to be twofold. On the one hand, there is the Western traditional separation of governmental powers into three branches—for the sake of check-and-balance—namely, the executive, the legislative, and the judicial. It was Montesquieu who first propounded this in his *De l'Esprit des lois* by erroneously observing that there was such a separation of powers in England. About thirty years later the fathers of the American Constitution, more out of need than on the ground of theory, embodied this system in that historic document. With the development of "party government" and through the experience of national crises, there came to be substantial changes in, and diverse criticisms of, the three-power system.

On the other hand, traditional China had its centuries-old imperial system, which, according to Dr. Sun, also entailed a separation of three powers, but naturally of a different kind. As Dr. Sun saw it, imperial China had its long, unwritten constitution. There were three powers: (1) the *imperial* power, combining the executive, legislative, and judicial powers; (2) the *examining* power, for the recruitment of scholar-officials; and (3) the *censorial* power—the power to impeach officials and affairs.[22] In the West, the examining power comes under the executive branch of government, and the censorial power is a part of the legislative power.

As a result of comparative study, Dr. Sun championed his own Five-Power Constitution—that is, to make the five powers co-equal in status, the executive, the legislative, the judicial, the examining, and the censorial; and withal to establish five branches of government. He first formulated this idea about 1893.[23]

The Five-Power theory has been regarded very differently. It is, in the words of Paul M. A. Linebarger, "one of the most disputed points in his (Dr. Sun's) proposal. Some writers see in it nothing more than a crass conjunction of the theory of Montesquieu and the practices of the Chinese Imperial system. His followers are disposed to regard the doctrine ... as the product of intrepid imagination, which succeeded in reconciling the traditional scheme of Chinese things with the requirement of modern self-government."[24] Thus, the one dominant version of this Five-Power theory is that it is a synthesis of Western and Chinese traditions.

Linebarger has his own interpretation. "If, however, a further step is taken, and the Five Powers are associated with Sun Yat-sen's doctrine of the three naturally unequal classes of men, they assume a somewhat less superficial significance."[25] Here he is referring to Dr. Sun's division of men into "three groups: those who know and perceive beforehand, those who know and perceive afterward, and those who do not know and perceive—the discoverers, the promoters, and the practical men."[26]

Linebarger proceeds to explain his viewpoint: "If the rule of the people is placed over the administration by the geniuses, the geniuses must be assured a method of entering the government service. The oligarchy of the intellectuals is to be reconciled with the dictatorship of the majority."[27]

Another version, similar in nature but different in approach, is to juxtapose this Five-Power theory with Dr. Sun's theory of separating "power" with "ability." The people must possess "power"—the four powers of election, recall, initiative, and referendum. The government must possess ability—ability expressed through the five governing powers. Hence the necessity of having the Five-Power parity. Such parity ensures more check-and-balance and at the same time more "ability" to each branch of government.[28]

The late Dr. Wang Chung-hui has yet another keen observation. "What is the Five-Power Constitution? The ordinary answer is this: its uniqueness lies in the organization of government, namely, to have five branches. . . . But this is merely a skin-deep observation. . . . Our Republic Founder's Five-Power Constitution is meant not only to change the form of government but also especially to extend the spirit of democracy. . . . With Dr. Sun the Three Principles of the People are almost always accompanied by the Five-Power Constitution. . . . Without the Five-Power Constitution, the Three Principles of the People would lose their body; and without the Three Principles of the People, the Five-Power Constitution would lose its soul. Therefore, to discern the fundamental significance of the Five-Power Constitution, one has to study the Three Principles of the People, particularly the Principle of People's Power."[29] This penetrating view by Dr. Wang Chung-hui deserves our special attention. While Dr. Wang was a loyal follower of, and a close associate with Dr. Sun Yat-sen (serving as the first Minister of Foreign Affairs under Dr. Sun's Provisional Presidency in 1912), Dr. Sun respected Dr. Wang for his scholarship. As a matter of fact, it was no other than Dr. Wang whom Dr. Sun referred to as the jurist with a Yale doctorate in his 1921 address at Canton on the very topic, *The Five-Power Constitution.*

I wish to venture one more idea: perhaps the theory of fivefold power is also closely associated with the doctrine of Political Tutelage. Even though in Dr. Sun's political thinking the division of government into five branches is permanently needed during the eventual Period of Constitutional Government, it is even more immediately required in the initial Period of Political Tutelage. Political Tutelage is a necessary transition, and everything should be set on the right track. Every candidate to a public office—even an elective office, a representative office—should have passed some sort of examination. Besides, every official or representative, and every act by the government or by a government official may be impeached. Such is Dr. Sun's theory. It is evident that there is an underlying purpose in making the five powers coequal. It is an attempt, a device, to make the government as a whole not only "able" but also rightfully "able," just as the people as a whole should be made not only "powerful" but also rightfully "powerful."

As to the translation of such an "idea" into an "institution," Dr. Sun did have such a plan in 1912. "When I was in charge of the Nanking government (then as the Provisional President of the new Republic)," he recalled, "I at first intended to propose to the Legislative Assembly that the Five-Power Constitution be adopted. Unfortunately a great majority of its members did not understand the theory and system, and so they ignored my proposal while framing the Provisional Constitution."[29] Not until 1923 when Dr. Sun set up his revolutionary headquarters at Canton was there established a censorial branch of government, the first symbolic step in the direction of putting theory into practice. In 1928 the Organic Law of the National Government (drafted by veteran Kuomintang leaders like Wang Chung-hui, Hu Han-min, and Tai Chi-tao) embodied the Five-Power system. And the system was, of course, put into the Tutelage *Yueh-fa* of June 1, 1931.

The Five-Power institution of this decade is typically provided by the said *Yueh-fa* of 1931 and also by the revised Organic Law of the National Government of December 30, 1931. Article 71 of the *Yueh-fa* stipulated: "The National Government shall be composed of five *Yuan*, the Executive *Yuan*, the Legislative *Yuan*, the Judicial *Yuan*, the Examination *Yuan*, and the Control *Yuan*, as well as various Ministries and Commissions." This and other related articles prescribed the general principles. The details of the composition, scope of powers and functions, and inter-relationship of the various *Yuan* were left to the Organic Law.

The said revised Organic Law of December, 1931 provided the following essentials. The National Government was to be composed of one Chairman and 24-37 State Councilors. The State Council was to fulfill functions not pertaining to any individual *Yuan* and to settle matters referred thereto by two or more *Yuan*. Actual executive power was now vested in the Executive *Yuan*. Herein lay a big difference between the Organic Law of October 8, 1928 and the revised Law of December 30, 1931. According to the former the National Government was relatively strong and the Executive *Yuan* relatively weak. According to the latter the position was reversed. The personality that was expected to occupy the chairmanship of the Executive *Yuan* did much to account for this shift.

Each of the five *Yuan* was to have a President, and a Vice President, appointed from among the State Councilors. Parenthetically it may be reiterated that this was the Period of Political Tutelage and that, therefore, all the high-ranking officials of the National Government were nominated by the Kuomintang Central Executive Committee. At the meetings of the Executive *Yuan* (comparable to Western cabinet meetings) important matters like the annual budget, bills to be submitted to the Legislative *Yuan*, amnesties, treaties, declaration of war, and conclusion of peace were to be decided on. The 50-100 Members of the Legislative *Yuan* were to be appointed by the National Government on the recommendation of the President of this *Yuan* for a two-year term, and not permitted to hold concurrently any administrative offices. The Judicial *Yuan* was to be composed of the Ministry of Justice, the Supreme Court, the Administrative Court, and the Commission for Disciplinary Punishment of Officials. The Examination *Yuan*, with its small number of Members, was to have the Examination Commission and the Board of Personnel. With its 29-49 Members, the Control *Yuan* was to have the power of impeachment. As to auditing, there was a special Ministry under the *Yuan* for the exercise of the power. The last-named three *Yuan* could separately send bills to the Legislative *Yuan* on matters within their respective competence.

One significant point should not be overlooked. However much did Dr. Sun teach about the Five-Power Constitution it was about its theory, not about its concrete system. Dr. Wang Chung-hui wrote thus:

> According to my humble opinion, the initial founding of the Five-Power system should be divided into two problems: the ascertainment of its fundamental theory and the proposal of a concrete scheme. In Dr. Sun's teachings only the basic principle is elaborated; as to how to institutionalize this principle, not one word can be found. As I recall, our Republic Founder said, "First of all, the principle itself must be endorsed. As to practice, it may be left to later study. The case should not be first to think out a concrete Five-Power system and then to endorse the principle."[30]

So, the Party and Government leadership should be credited with the gradual working out of the Five-Power central government system.

The revised Organic Law of the National Government of December 30, 1931, just as the earlier and later versions, operated in the main rather smoothly, though not without pointed criticisms, anxious moments, and embarrassing situations all of a fragmentary nature. There is no room here to describe the actual working of the Five-Power system. Maybe it is more meaningful to list some of the more puzzling problems raised then and even now—just to show how many-sided the system is. For instance, which after all should wield the overall, substantial executive power, the National Government or the Executive *Yuan?* To which *Yuan*—the Judicial *Yuan* or the Executive *Yuan*—should the Ministry of Justice belong? Should candidates to elective offices including people's representatives be required to have passed some sort of examination? And should the judges of the courts at different levels be subject to the scrutiny, investigation, and impeachment by Members of the Control Yuan?

A decade is too short a period to test out the soundness of any governmental system. Still, some objective appraisal may be given. Time was when scholars competed in theorizing about the best form of government. Aristotle started and Montesquieu two thousand years later popularized the teaching that there is no *a priori*, intrinsic and absolute "best form of government," and that that form is the best which, suited to the time and place, operates in the fulfillment of governmental functions. Ever since the founding of the Republic in 1912 many imported, imitated forms of government had been tried—the presidential and the cabinet forms, the unitary and the federative types. None had succeeded. The Five-Power system, developed from *idea* to *institution* during this initial period of political reconstruction (1927-1937), did become operative and did take root.

The preparation for local self-government

To be able to operate constitutional democracy, the Chinese people must first learn the art of self-government; and for the Chinese people to learn the art of local self-government, a sufficient period of Political Tutelage is necessary. Such is the profound understanding and firm conviction of Dr. Sun Yat-sen. Thus during this period of our study the most gigantic task is to educate the people in acquiring through actual participation democratic experiences in local affairs. This is all the more important because, as we know, Dr. Sun's ideal is not representative democracy but an approachingly direct democracy by adding recall, initiative, and referendum to mere election.

As referred to above, the National Government should during the Period of Political Tutelage appoint trained men who have passed the required civil service examinations to assist the people in preparation for local self-government. According to Article 8 of *The Fundamentals of National Reconstruction,* preparatory work consists of five items: (1) census taking, (2) land survey, (3) police organizing, (4) road building, and (5) people training in the exercise of their political powers and the performance of their civic duties. Constitutional Government cannot be attained too soon. The same *Fundamentals* stipulates in clear-cut terms in Articles 16 and 23 the necessary conditions. "When all the *hsien* (districts) within any one province shall have attained full self-government, the Period of Constitutional Government shall begin in that province." "When a majority of the provinces shall have reached the Period of Constitutional Government by having well-established local self-government in all *hsien* (districts) there shall be a National Assembly empowered to adopt and promulgate the Constitution."

There was another exclusive document on the matter by Dr. Sun: *Practical Methods for the Introduction of Local Self-government.* Herein six kinds of preparatory work are listed:

(1) taking of census,
(2) setting up of offices,
(3) assessment of land value,
(4) reclamation of land,
(5) building of roads,
(6) establishment of schools.

With these things accomplished, local efforts should be turned to the promotion of cooperative enterprises—agriculture, industries, banking, exchange and the like.

Now we can turn from theory to practice during these ten years of nation-building. In 1928 the Standing Committee of the Central Executive Committee of the Kuomintang decided on a seven-point program; and this program was enforced through the government. The seven-points were: (1) literacy, (2) hygiene, (3) *pao-chia*,[31] (4) reforestation, (5) roads, (6) cooperatives, (7) native-goods. These seven items were the primary working goals of both the local party units and local government agencies. It is interesting to observe that some of these items were timely demands of that particular decade.

In March, 1929 the KMT Third National Convention passed a four-point resolution: (1) to prepare local self-government; (2) to enact laws and regulations for self-government suitable to the locality and for the ultimate realization of the principles of democracy and livelihood, (3) to send well-trained party members by the government to help the local people prepare for self-government, and (4) to take gradual steps in the realization of self-government, with the fulfillment of all necessary conditions and the completion of elections as the final objective." A careful reading of this resolution and program would reveal that there must have been, due to pressure and impatience, some anxiousness for shortening the Period of Political Tutelage.

In February, 1934, the KMT Central Political Council decided and accordingly, the National Government decreed that local self-government was to have three stages: first, preparation; second, initiation; and third, completion. During the first two stages the local magistrate or the municipal mayor was to be appointed by the government; at the second stage the qualified voters of the locality could elect their assemblymen, but up to half of the candidates could be nominated by the magistrate or the mayor. This new policy and the new regulations were made in the face of Japan's mounting aggression. The Party and the Government were then expecting that the program of local self-government might be completed within the period of 1929-1934.

Of course, Dr. Sun's *Fundamentals of National Reconstruction* and *Practical Methods for the Introduction of Local Self-government* remained, as they still remain today—the basic guide for achieving local self-government. On September 15, 1935 Generalissimo Chiang, addressing a military training group on Mount Omei, stressed the same oft-quoted points: the taking of local census, the organizing of a police force, the survey of local land, the development of local communications, the popularization of education, the promotion of cooperatives, and the reclamation of local land.[32] In passing, it may be noted that all local government work, both preparatory and permanent, was conveniently summed up during this period in four watchwords: "management, education, nourishment, and defense."

As local self-government involves two aspects, the institutional as well as the functional, we should take a look at the machinery of local government through which the different functions are performed. At first, Republican China retained the old, traditional three levels in local government, namely provinces, prefectures, and districts. In 1930 a change was made; the two-level system of provinces and districts (or municipalities) was inaugurated. Later on, in some provinces, a certain number of "Administrative Supervisors" were appointed, each to supervise several districts. These offices, however, were not permanent in nature. Again, after 1931, several regional "Political Councils" were set up at places like Peiping, the Southwest, and Hopei-Chahar. They, too, were temporary structures to meet the political and military exigencies of the times. The point is that the two-level system in local government was on the whole maintained in letter and spirit.

The division of powers between the central government and local government was very elastic. It was stipulated in Article 59 of the Tutelage *Yueh-fa* of 1931: "In the division of power between the central and local governments the principle of equilibrium shall be adopted, as stipulated in Article 17 of *The Fundamentals of National Reconstruction*." Actually this Article 17 prescribes such division of power during the Period of Constitutional Government:

> During Constitutional Period political powers shall be distributed between the central and local governments. Affairs of national interest shall be entrusted to the central government and those of local interest shall be entrusted to the local government. There shall be neither undue centralization nor undue decentralization.

The real point is this: what was intended as the guiding principle of division of political authority between the central and local governments for the *Constitutional Period* was now used for the *Tutelage Period.* Article 60 of the *Yueh-fa* provided a very convenient solution:

> The various local governments may, within their respective spheres of authority, make local laws and regulations. Should such local laws and regulations conflict with those laws of the central government, they shall be null and void.

The Provincial Government had an executive council of 7-9 members, appointed by the National Government, one of whom was designated as the chairman. Mostly a provincial government had four departments (civil affairs, finance, education, and reconstruction) headed by members of the provincial council. Besides, there was a secretary general, sometimes also a council member. Occasionally there was added a Provincial Security Forces Headquarters. In such a case the chairman of the Provincial Council was concurrently the commander.

Each district or municipality had its magistrate or mayor, with a secretary and usually four section chiefs of public safety, finance, reconstruction, and education. Peiping became in 1933 the first municipality with an elected municipal assembly of thirty-seven members. As determined by law, such a local assembly had as its functions deliberations on matters like the budget, local legislation, poor relief, educational and cultural affairs. The Assembly's resolutions were to be carried out by the magistrate or mayor, who might request reconsideration on some of the items. If the Assembly should uphold the original resolution by a two-thirds vote and if the local chief executive should still refuse its execution then the matter would be decided by a popular vote.

Inevitably there were obstacles, shortcomings and difficulties both in the operation of local government tasks. The very novelty of the common undertakings, the meagerness of financial and material resources available, the lack of expertise, the deep-rooted psychology of familyism and localism, the want of an adequate public-spiritedness—these and many other factors together with the internal and external conditions of the country as a whole contributed to hinder and hamper the progress of local government and the preparation for local self-government. And yet serious efforts were made, and practical success was scored. Even during the most trying years of war that immediately followed this decade the Party and Government leadership pushed hard and moved ahead this program of promoting local self-government.

On the importance of promoting local self-government there is no one more competent to speak out than General Chang Chun, a veteran statesman in both domestic administration and foreign affairs, who served as Governor of Hupeh (1933-1935) and later of Szechuan (1940-1946) and who contributed much to local government laws and regulations. His discerning observations and instructive directives can be found in his address, "The Role of Local Self-government in Resistance-War and Nation-Building." A short passage is quoted here below:

China is abundant in her human power and material resources but is in lack of solid organizational strength. This lack stems from the long, continuous separatism and local chaos from the establishment of the Republic to the Northward Expedition. . . . Our Party Leader (Generalissimo Chiang) resolved soon after the Incident of July 7, 1937 (the Marco Polo Bridge Incident) to start our Resistance-War and simultaneously to continue our nation-building. Resistance-War is our present chief task, and nation-building is our one ultimate goal. . . . Resistance-War is to sweep away the primary obstacle to our nation-building, and nation-building is to augment our strength in carrying on the Resistance-War. . . . To increase our national power, we must develop our organizational strength so as fully to utilize our human power and material resources. And to develop our organizational strength, we must promote to the utmost our local government reconstruction.[33]

The launching of judicial and administrative reforms

Another aspect of China's political modernization during the ten years under review is the many-sided series of judicial and administrative reforms. True, some portions of these reforms might have appeared to remain at first as mere paper work; but earnest exertions were made, and much translation was rendered from words to deeds.

Of these reforms the most conspicuous were in the judicial field. Chief among them were the promulgation of new codes; the change in the prosecution and trial system; the increase in the number of local courts; the examination, appointment, and training of judges; prison reform, and the implementation of administrative justice.[34] Although there is little need to go into details concerning all these phases of modernization, a few illustrations should be given.

Perhaps the strongest motivation behind the laborious study, draft, passage and promulgation of the new codes, civil, criminal, procedural, and commercial, was to bring harmony to Chinese and Western legal systems so as to convince the foreign powers of the justifiability of speedily terminating their extraterritoriality in China. These said codes were completed mostly from 1928 to 1935. In drawing up these new codes there was the one highest, unifying principle: the embodiment of the Three Principles of the People. For example, the heavier penalty attached to crimes like collaboration with the enemy is based on the Principle of Nationalism. The recognition of equality between the two sexes; the right of daughters to inherit property, equal to that of sons; the granting of freedom of marriage to parties of legal age; the permission of divorce by mutual agreement; the increased punishment for wilful interference in the exercise of the right to vote or in the administration of conscription: these are instances of applying the Principle of Democracy. Again, new provisions like penalty for usury, protection of factory workers, and enhancement of tenant farmers' interests illustrate the embodiment of the Principle of Socialism.[35] Besides these, there were other novel provisions such as furnishing correctional education to juvenile delinquents, affording supervisory protection over insane persons, and granting compulsive medical treatment to persons afflicted with leprosy or venereal diseases.

Admittedly not all of the new provisions worked smoothly right away. Some of them sharply conflicted with traditional ethics and centuries-old customs. Conservative parents disliked the idea of letting their sons and daughters marry of their own will and choice. Brothers of the old type resented their sisters' sharing their erstwhile exclusive rights of inheritance. But then this is a sort of universal phenomenon: a new code anywhere usually takes time to operate smoothly.

The new requirement of higher qualifications for judicial officers was also a significant advancement. Candidates for district courts must now have one of the following qualifications: (1) having passed a required public competitive examination and undergone a prescribed training; (2) having taught at least for two years certain law courses in a public or private college or university; (3) having served as judges or procurators for one year or more; (4) having practiced law for three years or more; or (5) having graduated from a public, or registered private, law college. For higher positions more strict qualifications were stipulated. This new system put an end to the old way, on the part of a number of judges, of securing the appointments through sheer political pull, or even worse, naked money influence.

Under the Examination *Yuan* serious efforts were made, too, for reform and efficiency. The Law of Examination was promulgated on August 1, 1929, with the operative date set at April 1, 1930. Now in accordance with Dr. Sun's teachings, the taking and passing of examinations are required of three types of persons: (1) candidates in popular elections; (2) appointees to public offices; and (3) certified professional specialists and technicians. Apparently the demand for the people's representatives to have some examination taken beforehand is controversial. What about the president of a country, the premier of a cabinet; should they, too, have passed some sort of examination? And what sort of examination? So, the Law of 1929 was rather limited in its application.

There are three categories of examinations: High, Ordinary, and Special. The High Examination held periodically is open to persons with any kind of the following qualifications: (1) graduates of colleges or professional institutes; (2) persons certified, after proper appraisal, to have qualifications equal to the above graduates; (3) persons recognized, after due process, to possess special learning or talent or to have some special publication; and (4) those who have passed the Ordinary Examination for at least four years and in addition have been in the civil service with the "designated" rank for at least three years. It is abundantly clear that the law is lenient, permitting as many types of graduates and civil servants to take the High Examination. The Ordinary Examination is open to high school graduates or persons who are, after appraisal procedure, declared to possess an equivalent qualification. Special Examinations are given in different professions and specialties.

The Ministry of Personnel under the Examination *Yuan* has three main functions to perform. The first is arrangement for appointment so that the successful candidates who have passed the examinations may get proper jobs. The second is the determination of respective ranks of the civil service men, which ranks point to their salary amounts. The third is the rating of personal efficiency. Important as this rating work is, because it forms the basis of salary raising and rank promotion, it is most elusive, difficult, and controversial.

The theory and system of ranking is worth scrutinizing. There are then as now many different ranks. Those who serve as ministers and ambassadors are appointed with the "special" rank; they require no qualifications whatsoever. Their jobs are political in nature. Positions of administrative nature carry with them at the top of the ladder the "selected rank" with its eight grades, in the middle the "recommended" rank with its twelve subdivided grades, and at the bottom the "designated" rank with its sixteen grades. All of these require respectively different qualifications of education, writings, and length of time in service—most minute and exacting. Later, there is the so-called "elective" rank, reserved for a few top-most officials such as the presidents of the five *Yuan*. This hierarchy of ranks in the civil service and the whole officialdom has been very much criticized but it still persists. From 1931 to 1937 inclusive there were 589 successful candidates who passed the High Examinations, and 1244 who passed the Ordinary Examinations. Those who passed the various Special Examinations numbered 2166.[36]

Even though indirectly, and perhaps negatively, the Control *Yuan*—by its Members' individual exercise of their censorial power—did contribute its part to the fostering of reform measures and promotion of administrative efficiency. In old Imperial days the censors had been regarded as "tigers" because they were ferocious in criticizing and attacking officials and affairs. In a way the new censors of this *Yuan* were no less feared as they themselves enjoyed by law certain special immunities and privileges. By the same token, however, some of them, just like some of the old Imperial censors, might readily overstep the proper bounds and misuse their power.

Either prescribed by law or grown up as conventions, the Control *Yuan* from 1931 on had the powers or functions of impeachment, auditing, inspections, and investigation. Still later on, during the war, the "warning power" was by decree given it by the Supreme National Defense Council. From 1931 to 1937 inclusive there were altogether 841 impeachment cases, involving a total number of 1443 officials.[37] It is evident that the Members of the *Yuan* were vigilantly making use of their censorial power. However, for all their contributions to the political system, there was no lack of criticism. It was alleged, for instance, that there was too much lingering spirit of the imperial days: that is to say, ethical conduct and political activity were not demarcated clearly; what was deemed unethical was taken to be what was illegal. Of course, no system particularly at its developmental stage could be entirely perfect. This was particularly true with the exercise of the censorial power which called for a higher degree of dedication and self-sacrifice. Like all other political institutions, there left room for further improvement and continued progress. The overall balance of the system was undoubtedly in the affirmative. The Control *Yuan* through its Members had a very wholesome effect on administrative reforms and administrative efficiency.

For the promotion in particular of administrative efficiency, there was during this decade a significant, articulate, nation-wide movement. To begin with, the form of and terminology in official documents were both simplified. Much superfluous verbiage was excised; clarity and exactitude were aimed at. A wider objective was to reduce unnecessary red tape and paper work. New filing systems were devised, new archive rooms provided, and reference books assembled. On the matter of purchase and supply a series of studies and reforms were ushered in. The main objective was to ensure fair bidding and to eliminate corruption.

At one time the system known as "Centralized Office-work" was taken as a serious reform measure especially in the provincial government. Actually this system, or its basic principle, need not be confined to the provincial level. Any ministry, and any administration, may resort to it. The writer can testify through his own experience that, for instance, a minister or vice minister, by assembling all Department heads (with their secretaries sitting behind) and having the pertinent documents and files ready on hand, could conveniently hold brief discussions and reach appropriate decisions then and there—without having to let documents travel back and forth between the different bureaus and departments of the same ministry. "Concentrated Office-work" like this on one forenoon may suffice for one whole week's paper work. However, administrative efficiency cannot stem from a mere formal "system."

Naturally the problem of administrative efficiency involves all the five elements of politics. It is never a simple affair, and it can never be solved once and for all. In spite of old habits and customs, inertia and indifference, the movement of this decade to promote administrative efficiency did produce a healthy effect and score some fruitful result.

The attempts at improving popular economic life

It is something of much greater significance than hitherto recognized that in Dr. Sun's *Fundamentals of National Reconstruction* the priority order of the Three Principles of the People is (1) the People's Livelihood (Socialism), (2) the People's Power (Democracy), (3) the People's Nationhood (Nationalism)—exactly the very reverse of what appears in his *San-min Chu-i* (where the order is Nationalism, Democracy, and Socialism). This is the relevant Article in the *The Fundamentals:*—

> The first important matter in reconstruction is the People's Livelihood. Thus, regarding the four urgent popular needs of food, clothing, shelter, and movement, the government shall cooperate with the people in the improvement of agriculture so that all may have sufficient food, in the development of the textile industry so that all may have sufficient clothing, in the large-scale building of houses of various types so that all may have comfortable homes, and in the building and improvement of roads and waterways so that all may have convenient movement.[38]

It is to be noted that the precedence of Livelihood over both Power and Nationhood can also be detected by the records and resolutions of the Kuomintang and in the speeches and statements of President Chiang. Such priority recognition is no mere accident. After all, the betterment of the economic life of the general masses should be the ultimate goal of a progressive state; and the solution of this most complex and therefore the most difficult problem must take a long, long time.

The one same goal may be reached by different routes. And the zigzag, up-and-down pathway of gradualism and evolutionism may prove to be the surest short-cut. What appears to be the straight line between two points may, in the improvement of human affairs, especially of popular economic life, turn out to be illusory. Herein lies the fundamental difference between the so-called Scientific Socialism of Karl Marx and the *Min-sheng* Doctrine of Dr. Sun Yat-sen.

While Dr. Sun respected Marx he refuted his materialist philosophy. Marx was to Dr. Sun a pathologist, and not a physiologist. "Marx found only one of the diseases of society; he did not discover the law of social progress. He made class war essential to social progress, the driving force, in fact, of social progress. He made class war the cause and social progress the effect." Pronouncing this as a tragic error, Dr. Sun elaborated his philosophy of man and of human history: life, and life maintenance, is the central force.

Livelihood is the center of government, the center of economics, the center of all historical movements. Just as men misjudged the center of the solar system, so the old socialists mistook material forces for the center of history. . . . We must recognize livelihood as the center of social history.[39]

Is Dr. Sun's Principle of Livelihood Socialism? And is it the same as Communism? Dr. Sun's answer to both of these questions is emphatically *yes* and *no*.

Why not follow the West and speak directly of socialism? Why use the old Chinese term *Min-sheng* in its stead? There is a very significant reason. . . . Western nations have not yet found a solution for the questions involved in it, and a severe dispute is still raging over them. What is more, every country's socialism has different theories and different proposals.

And Dr. Sun took one step further in his elaboration of Livelihood:

The communism which we propose is a communism of the future, not of the present. This communism of the future is a very just proposal, and those who have had property will not suffer by it. When the landowners clearly understand the principle involved in our plan for equalization of land rights, they will not be apprehensive. So in working out our principle of livelihood we cannot use or apply in China the methods of Marx.[40]

Seen in this light, *Min-sheng'ism* has its proper place in the world history of socialism.

In the West there have been, as an up-to-date record, twelve types of socialism that followed in chronological order: (1) "Utopian Socialism" (by Owen, Saint Simon, Fourier, Cabet, etc.); (2) Christian Socialism (by Maurice and Kingsley); (3) "Scientific Socialism" (by Marx and Engels); (4) Anarchism (by Babeuf, Godwin, Proudhon, Bakunin, and others); (5) Syndycalism (by Pelloutier and Sorel); (6) State Socialism (by Blanc, Rodbertus, and Lassale); (7) Labour Unionism; (8) Fabian Socialism (by Shaw, the Webbs, and others); (9) Guild Socialism (by G.D.H. Cole); (10) Revisionism (by Bernstein and Jaures); (11) Sovietism (by Lenin and Stalin); and (12) Democratic Socialism.[41]

The present writer once chose to observe: "What is now termed as Democratic Socialism was stressed and elaborated by our Republic Founder, Dr. Sun Yat-sen, in his San-min Chu-i. . . . He said 'The

methods to carry out the Principle of Livelihood are first, the equalization
of land rights, and second, the regulation of capital.' 'As to the people,
they certainly ought to fulfill their duties of citizenship; failing that, they
would not be qualified as citizens . . . but would become useless idlers
. . . parasites in the community. The government should by law coerce
such idlers to work. . . . If every one becomes a productive element the
society will find itself well-fed and well-clothed.'[42] President Chiang
added in his *Two Supplementary Chapters to the Lectures on the Principle of People's Livelihood*: '. . . The problem of people's livelihood
(*Min-sheng*) included, in addition to food, clothing, housing and means
of travel, other aspects such as national fecundity, social welfare, education, and health and happiness. As Dr. Sun himself has said, it is the aim
of the *Min-sheng* Principle to enable 'the young people to have education, the grown-ups to have jobs, the old people to have the means of
support, and all persons irrespective of age and sex to enjoy security
and comfort.' It is only when 'China has become a country living in
comfort and security' after having carried out various projects for 'the
care of the young, the aged and the sick, the relief of the destitute
stricken with natural calamity, and the satisfaction of manifold other
public needs,' 'the establishment of institutions for the deaf, the dumb
and the disabled and incapacitated to soften the hardships of nature,
and the opening of public parks for the enjoyment of the people in
time of leisure,'—'it is only when all these projects have been carried out
and China has become a comfortable and secure place to live in that the
Min-sheng principle may be said to have been fully realized.'[43] These
quoted passages show unmistakably that Dr. Sun's *Min-sheng Principle*
and the overall *San-min Chu-i* may be best identified as the forerunner
of contemporary Democratic Socialism."[44]

Dr. Sun firmly stood, and the political party he founded, the Kuomintang, has steadily stood, for gradual, legislative, and therefore peaceful means to carry out the Principle of the People's Livelihood. The
following list of six peaceful avenues of approach is suggested as a
summary of Dr. Sun's teachings on this matter: (1) equalization of land
rights; (2) regulation of capital; (3) land-to-the-tiller; (4) establishment
of cooperatives; (5) development of agricultural and industrial enterprises; and (6) social welfare without class war.

It is interesting to observe that in the Tutelage *Yueh-fa* of 1931 there
was a special chapter on "People's Livelihood." The fourteen articles
therein dealt with the many and varied means of realizing the *Min-sheng
Principle*: encouragement and protection to all private productive enterprises; improvement of the peasants' living conditions by reclamation of
waste land, establishment of agricultural banks and cooperatives,
strengthening of public granaries, development of agricultural experi-

mentation and education, and road-building in rural region; opening up of public and private mines; expansion of shipping enterprises both private and public; freedom to choose one's own profession; liberty to make contracts; right to form occupational organizations; cooperation between capital and labor; protection of labor, especially of women and children workers; labor insurance; cooperative enterprises, regulation of the production and sale-prices of the people's daily necessities; prohibi-tion of usury; and appropriate relief to disabled veterans.

Now let us turn from theory and abstract principles to legislation, administrative programs, and actual practice concerning the attempts at the improvement of popular economic life. Naturally we should look at the efforts made to improve in particular the economic conditions of Chinese labor and peasantry.

Regarding labor, there was the Factory Law, promulgated on December 30, 1929, effective from August 1, 1931, and amended on December 30, 1932. This law was quite comprehensive, dealing with the hours of labor, compensation, welfare, health and safety, as well as with employment relations. It prohibited the employment of children under fourteen years of age, but, as a transitional measure, permitted the retention of children above twelve years of age already employed before the law became effective. Boys and girls between 14-16 were to be engaged in light work only. As to general working hours the 8-hour day in principle was stipulated, with up to ten hours permitted under certain prescribed circumstances. On February 26, 1930 the Pao Sheng Cotton Mill of Tientsin was the first to put into practice the 8-hour per day system.[45]

Much attention was given to the improvement of the economic life of the peasants. In December 1929 the National Congress on Agriculture and Economic Life was held. Based on its findings, the Ministry of Agriculture and Mining formulated a comprehensive program. Three months later, after consultation with the Ministries of Education, Railways, Communications, and the Central Commission on Reconstruction, another program was announced. Items ranging from land tenure reform, promotion of cooperatives, irrigation work and river conservancy to control of pests and introduction of new, improved seeds were included.

This leads to the question whether the problem of equalizing land rights was tackled with at all. Yes, it was. In the words of the late Vice President Chen Cheng, under whom, then as Governor of Taiwan, the land reform projects were planned and carried out:

> The policy of land rent reduction had long been one of the planks of the Kuomintang platform. A 25 per cent rent reduction was first introduced in Kwangtung, and then in Hunan, Hupeh, and Chekiang provinces. But owing to a variety of obstacles which prevented the smooth implementa-

tion of the program, no marked result was achieved. In 1930 the central government promulgated the Land Law, which provided among other things that farm rentals should not exceed 37.5 per cent of the total annual yield of the main crop. That was how the program came to be known as a "37.5 per cent rent reduction."[46]

A very useful footnote explains away some confusion. The two terms, 25 per cent rent reduction and 37.5 per cent rent reduction, really mean the same thing. By the former term is meant the taking of one quarter of the total annual yield as the tenant's share and then dividing the remaining three-quarters equally between landlord and tenant. By the latter term is meant the assignment to the landlord of one half of the remaining three-quarters, or 37.5 per cent of the harvest.[47] As mildly described, "internal worries" and "external threats" rendered this part of the Land Law of 1930 practically inoperative.

According to the original scheme of Dr. Sun, the equalization of land rights appears to be simple and easy. The landowner himself is to fix and report to the local government the price of his land. The government is to levy a land tax accordingly. However, the government may anytime when necessary buy back from the landowner according to his own declared value. This is to discourage him from undervaluing his own land so as to pay less tax. After the declaration and registration of the landowners' land prices, whatever increase—the unearned increment—shall revert to the community.[48] The scheme, seemingly simple and by no means impracticable, presupposes a long period of order and peace.

In passing, another serious undertaking is worth mentioning in connection with the desire and device to better the living conditions of the masses. This is the movement to set up different kinds of cooperatives. In his *Practical Methods for the Introduction of Local Self-government*, written between 1919 and 1920, Dr. Sun stressed that

> after the six essential items will have reached a sufficient degree of success new exertion for other matters should be undertaken, for instance, the establishment of cooperatives devoted to agriculture, industry, exchange, banking, insurance, and the like.[49]

According to the late Chen Kuo-fu, the most enthusiastic promoter of the cooperatives, the initial period of 1919-1926 was not promising due to the lack of encouragement from the government, but the second period from 1927 on scored increasing success. The number of cooperatives in the country grew from 2,796 in 1931 to 37,318 in 1936.[50]

In all fairness it must be admitted that out of the eight categories of nation-building efforts there was comparatively little accomplishment in the attempts of improving popular economic life, and that nevertheless arduous efforts so far as possible were made and some foundation was laid.

V

Critical Appraisal and Fruitful Evidences

Of the eight categories of nation-building efforts in the realm of political affairs there are two that have been severely criticized by certain quarters both within and without China, then and now—one as an error and the other as a failure. The one that is stigmatized as an error deals with the matter of Political Tutelage and withal party dictatorship. The other that is regarded as a failure concerns the problem of People's Livelihood. These two points of criticism are worth investigating for two reasons. One is that they seem to furnish the exclusive ground on which to gauge and negate the worth and merit of the National Government and withal the Kuomintang leadership. The other reason is that they actually conflict with and thus cancel each other. Why? The explanation is easy, indeed. If democracy of the Western type were, as if by magic, possible to be transplanted in the then China the operation of democratic institutions would not permit any radical, violent, bloody overthrow of the long entrenched economic system of the people, as impliedly wished by the critics. And if, on the other hand, confiscation and redistribution of land were resorted to by force and through terrorism then there would have to be the most strict type of party dictatorship. The critics appear to be unaware of the ironical inconsistency involved in their two points of criticism. Let us proceed with the investigation of the two points separately.

Political Tutelage is often labeled as undemocratic. The crux of the whole question is that democracy as a political institution has its necessary conditions. To be brief, the people concerned must have (1) considerable experience of local self-government; (2) a prevailing spirit of tolerance and cooperation; (3) a sufficient percentage of literacy; (4) a decent standard of living; and (5) an enlightened, public-spirited bureaucracy. All these five conditions take a long period to come into being.[51]

What is more, even for nations well-advanced in democracy, the actual needs in times of crises do always by themselves call for and bring about modifications in the operation of their democratic institutions. Instances are too numerous. The Emergency Banking Bill that President F. D. Roosevelt sent to the Congress on March 9, 1933 was passed by the House and the Senate within eight hours—without having gone through any committee procedure and with its printing not yet finished during the initial discussion.[52] During World War I, the British government put into prison the eminent philosopher Bertrand Russell; the British War Cabinet was at one time composed of only three members (as against twenty-odd members during peace time); and the British Parliament prolonged its own term repeatedly because the war was still going on. During World War II, the American President, Franklin D. Roosevelt got himself elected for the fourth time—breaking the unwritten constitution of having no president serve for more than two terms. And, by the same token, both the British and American legislatures granted "delegated legislation," namely empowering their respective executive branches to make laws—to issue orders and decrees as laws.[53] Besides, there was "party truce" in both countries.

It is understandingly fitting and proper for China in the midst of "internal worries" and "external threats" during this critical period to practice Political Tutelage. Indeed, Dr. Sun taught this doctrine long before the Kuomintang came into power; surely it was not an afterthought to whitewash the Party's desire to remain in power.

As to one-party dictatorship in general during the contemporary period, the objective approach is not to praise or condemn it but to seek to understand its *raison d'être*. That political power is, or can be, diffused among all the people is a chimera. Political power always and everywhere—according to the theorists of elitism—is in the hands of the few. This is aptly summed up in the "iron law of oligarchy" of Robert Michels, the "circulation of the elite" of Vilfredo Pareto, "the ruling class" of Gaetano Mosca, and "the managerial revolution" of James Burnham.[54] As a matter of fact, nothing is more emphatic than this statement by Lord James Bryce: "There are no forms of government. There is only one form of government. And that form of government is the rule of the few."[55] Professor Arthur N. Holcome puts it differently but means the same thing: "For the rule of the few over the many, no matter what its nature or what its form, has always been and must always be a kind of tyranny."[56]

Understood in the proper historical perspective, party dictatorship is simply a new form of oligarchical rule. Conducive to governmental stability and political order, "one-party dictatorship is most likely a temporary phenomenon during a transitional period"—this is the conclusion of the present writer in "An Analysis of Party-and-Government Relationship in Sixty-three Nations," an article published in 1932.[57] Two recent books suggest similar findings: one by A. S. Banks and R. B. Texter, *A Cross-Polity Survey* (MIT Press, 1963), and the other by S. P. Huntington, *Political Order in Changing Societies* (Yale University Press, 1968). According to S. P. Huntington's tabulation, coups (namely disturbances and upheavals) are found in six out of twenty-six countries (only 25 per cent) with one-party systems, in seven out of sixteen countries (44 per cent) with two-party systems, and in seventeen out of twenty countries (85 per cent) with multiparty systems. Another table shows that of the twenty-three one-party countries nineteen are stable, four are moderately stable, and none is unstable; of the seven two-party countries all are stable; and of the twenty-six multiparty countries eleven are stable, two moderately stable, and thirteen unstable.[58]

Studies and writings like these mentioned above seem to warrant one conclusion: one-party dictatorship is a product of environment (of phenomena as forces) and not a result of the "idea" or will of one person or group of persons. Party dictatorship is intimately associated with Political Tutelage. Professor A. N. Holcombe had a discerning view when he observed: "It is evident that his (Dr. Sun's) distinction between the different stages of the revolutionary process is sound." "The period of tutelage, when it shall have been securely established, will make an undubitable advance. If the dictatorship of the Kuomintang proves durable it is likely to endure a long time."[59]

The next severe criticism that has come about especially since the Communist takeover of China mainland centers on the problem of Popular Livelihood. The charge often made today is that no endeavour was done to better the lot of Chinese peasants, roughly 80 per cent of the population, or that the whole endeavour was a dismal failure. The reverse side of this coin is impliedly what is called peasant revolution.

To adopt a spirit of objectivity, let the five-element approach be resorted to again here, though in a suggestive, oversimplified way. The *idea*, the ideology of *Min-sheng* is, as indicated before, basically different from Marxism and Sovietism. That being so, the *institution*, the process of improving the economic system (through it the economic life of the masses) is evolution, not revolution, and peace, not class war. As to *personalities*, the groups of people the leadership is turning to for immediate support at this juncture is unashamedly the middle class in particular. The chief driving *force*, that which is over above everything else motivating the Kuomintang and the National Government in their commissions and omissions during this period is practically no more than unification of the country and preparation for resisting external aggression. And yet it is an undeniable *phenomenon*, an undeniable fact that serious efforts are being made to realize in some measure the Principle of the People's Livelihood, though with meagre fruitfulness.

Here is a fairminded, appreciative, and at the same time objective understanding of the whole situation:

> If Sun Yat-sen's plan of national reconstruction is to be followed, it is evident that during the period of tutelage the stability of the government should not be jeopardized for the sake of a more rapid rate of economic and social changes which occur, though perhaps slower than may be desirable, are bound to be in the right direction. Political instability means a revision to the military stage of the revolution.[60]

It must be reiterated that *The Chinese Revolution* of Harvard Professor Arthur N. Holcombe, from which the above quotation is taken, was published in 1929.

On June 30, 1933 General Hans von Seeckt presented at Peiping his *Denkschrift fuer Marschall Chiang Kai-shek*. That document began with a very meaningful opening statement:

> The hypothesis of every reorganization of any army is, first of all, peace on the outer borders. That means several years of external peace and a state of political stability. . . . Before these conditions are achieved a successful military reorganization cannot be accomplished. Success cannot be attained while you are in a continual state of war.[61]

And the blunt and yet not untruthful remark made by Mao Tse-tung to Edgar Snow during the early Yenan days, as recorded in the latter's *Red Star over China*, is very revealing, too.

> For a people being deprived of its national freedom, the revolutionary task is not immediate socialism, but the struggle for independence. We cannot even discuss communism if we are robbed of a country in which to practice it.[62]

How many times did Dr. Sun Yat-sen and President Chiang speak of seeking national freedom first and individual freedom afterwards! In this connection, a re-reading of this passage should bring out more meaning than usual:

> Unfortunately during this period, there were some who borrowed the slogan of "democracy" as a screen to cover their feudalistic domination of certain regions and their struggles for power; there were others who borrowed the slogan of "liberty" to cover their reactionary and violent activities; all of these, adding insult to injury, branded the great task of unifying the country as an attempt to set up "absolutism" and "dictatorship," hoping thereby to frustrate the country's unification.[63]

Perhaps it is something stemming from the innermost of human nature that defense of the authorities that be always appears to be more difficult and therefore more seldom than denunciation of them. This is especially true of scholars. The following lines penned by the late Dr. Tsiang Ting-fu, while teaching at National Tsing Hua University, are exceptionally significant:

> Without a unified political power, there can be no good government. . . . In sum, the political history of all countries is divided into two phases: first, the building of a state; and second, the promotion of national welfare by means of the state. Since we have not completed the first phase, it is idle to talk of the second. . . . Our present problem is the existence of our state, not what type of state we should have.[64]

Directly or indirectly against such argumentation as Dr. Tsiang's, the critics of today would readily retort that the desperate suffering peasants are sure to rise and overthrow the regime as they have repeatedly done in the past. But this "peasant revolution" is more a myth than a reality. Dr. Kung-chuan Hsiao has contributed much to making clear the true picture: "The phrase 'peasant revolution' that has gained favor in some quarters may be useful or indispensable to propaganda purposes but it can hardly withstand objective historical analysis." It is true that "the Chinese peasantry (is) an indispensable ingredient of every uprising against local officials or against the existing regime itself." But they are mere pawns in the game.

Economically or psychologically they gained little in the uprisings to which they participated . . . and when their movements succeeded in overthrowing the existing government, those that survived the battles and hardships became the objects of control under the new regime.

The good, honest, simple, and peace-loving Chinese peasants, or the so-called silent majority, are not political and far less ambitious. "One simple desire—the will to live—governed their actions and reactions; one remitting task, cultivating the soil in order to keep alive, engaged their attention and energies."[65] No part of the Chinese population—and for that matter, of any population—more desires unification and order and law than the peasants.

It is now evident that neither the great stress placed on Political Tutelage nor the limited improvement of popular economic life should in any way reduce the merit of all the different nation-building efforts in the political field. The two sets of appraisal standards mentioned at the beginning of this paper may be applied here now.

In the first place, the many and varied arduous efforts did as a whole promote the four common ends of the modern state. In particular, *order* was brought about by national unification, by Political Tutelage, by the Five-Power system, and by preparation for local self-government; *security* was enhanced by the cultivation of national consciousness and the augmentation of military strength; *justice* was modernized through judicial reforms; and *welfare* was given an initial start, however much restricted the result was in the attempts at improving popular economic life.

In the second place, the three items the Chinese Revolutionary leadership was conscious of and striving after were in manifold ways and varying degrees considerably carried out: namely, (1) the initial realization of Dr. Sun's Three Principles as the primary aims; (2) the fruitful exertions for unification, independence and reconstruction as the necessary things to be done; and (3) the respective application of the methods of revolution, negotiation, and gradualism in performing the necessary things.

To sum up, the overall balance of many-sided arduous efforts in political reconstruction and nation-building is, as evidenced by facts and principles, on the side of success. However, it would be ignorance and stupidity to claim that there were no mistakes and shortcomings and that many things could not have been done better. Indeed, most of the Government and Party leaders acknowledged in their public utterances and written statements their dissatisfaction and disappointment. In a critical study like this a few of the could-have-beens may be illustrations. The Party could have tried harder to appeal to, and absorb, more intellectuals. The Government could have selected more men of knowledge, talent and integrity. Both the Party and Government could have taken more disciplinary measures against those at the top posts for disloyalty, insubordination, and misdemeanour. They could have put emphasis more on honest, substantial work and less on ritualistic form and paper reports. Yet, in spite of these and other could-have-beens, the net result of all nation-building efforts, let it be repeated, was the progressive modernization of China.

There are two fruitful evidences of this net result or overall balance. One is China's ability to have fought the eight years of Resistance-War against Japan. The other is the undisputed accomplishments on Taiwan today. Both of these achievements have their historic foundation in the arduous nation-building efforts under review.

In the long, courageous war of resistance, Generalissimo Chiang's iron will—as manifested in the "scorched-earth" policy and the "space-in-exchange-for-time" strategy—was, of course, the deciding factor. There still are other supporting factors: a united front, an awakened national spirit, a stable government, hard-working local administrators, widespread and coordinated Party organs, an appointed but representative People's Political Council, a well-trained army nucleus, and many other factors. All these had their foundation in this decade of political reconstruction.[66] President Chiang himself recognized and recorded this in his *China's Destiny*:

> That we are able to engage in the present protracted war against Japanese aggression is due solely to the strength we are able to draw from the spirit of revolutionary reconstruction.[67]

Furthermore, the same spirit of unity and cooperation, the same Three Principles of the People, the same system of Five-Power central government (with expansion and development, of course), and the same programs of national reconstruction have been continued on Taiwan these twenty years. The successful, expanding local self-government, the fruitful land reform, the rapid industrial and agricultural development, and the general economic betterment of the people, especially of the peasants, on Taiwan all have their firm foundation in the arduous efforts made on the mainland from 1927 to 1937.

A candid reader of this paper may bluntly—and honestly, too—raise the question: why then the loss of China mainland to the Communists? Yes, this is a pertinent question but beyond the scope of the present paper, and beyond the scope of this symposium. May it be suggested in all frankness and seriousness that such a question may best be studied through the five-element approach so that all the relevant *phenomena, ideas, personalities, institutions,* and *forces*—both inside and outside China, and both open and clandestine—may be laid bare and understood in the bringing about of that unfortunate, unexpected event. The United States of America, as "the arsenal of Democracy," helped most in winning the last war but played perhaps a leading role in losing the peace.[68] The National Government of China fought eight long years and won the war against Japan but lost the mainland to the Communists. Both of these events together with their aftermath have been apparently separate and yet substantially parts of one and the same global problem.

Comments:

BY FRANZ MICHAEL

THE BROAD SCOPE OF Dr. Poe's paper makes it necessary to limit myself to underline, stress, and perhaps develop some of the points so ably presented by the speaker. The period under discussion encompasses the crucial years of development under the National Government in which every task of domestic transformation and the defense of Chinese independence against foreign threat were to be handled at once. Basic was the problem of transforming the Chinese social ethics of the past into a value system that could serve a modernized society. Of primary importance was the introduction into China of a modern educational system taken from the West but adapted to a Chinese society.

In retrospect, the intellectual freedom of this system as represented in the educational development looms as perhaps the most important aspect of the government's program; and it is the continuation of that tradition on Taiwan which is of such importance as an alternative to the ever narrowing doctrinal development on the Mainland today. The rapid growth of modern universities, the establishment of the Academia Sinica representative of a Chinese scholarship second to none, were the great accomplishments of that time. This education introduced not only Western thinking but also Western development into the social and economic life. The new position of women which Dr. Poe stressed was based on the equality of education. The freedom of new social relationships and new attitudes introduced by the May Fourth Movement found its organized expression on this educational basis. It also provided the training for the new economy based on the concept of a free enterprise system which developed rapidly in the coastal areas. Chinese enterprise, skill, and diligence have been manifest wherever the opportunity was provided, as demonstrated today in Hong Kong, Singapore, and Taiwan. The pre-war period on the Mainland, with all its problems and dangers, was a time of social and economic growth buoyed by a spirit of optimism. For anyone living in China at the time and traveling a great deal, the economic advance in the countryside as well as in the cities was very apparent.

The framework in which this modernization was to take place was Western law, continental European law, derived originally from the Code Napoleon and taken from the German and Swiss codes via the Japanese example. Over 100 new laws were drawn up and ratified by the Legislative Yuan in the early 1930's to make up the body of codification on which the modern Chinese society was to be based. Laws of procedure and the court system served the application of this law. The Chinese Supreme Court decisions of that time are still a most valuable testimony to the success of this system and still are guides for problems of development elsewhere.

To make this development possible there was the order and security stressed in the four points of Dr. Poe. Basically this was a military task. The new Chinese government had to deal with three major military problems: the elimination of warlordism and unification of the country; the defeat of the Communist insurgency; and the defense of China against the growing danger of the Japanese attack. The success of these military tasks was of primary importance to defend and guarantee the survival of the nation and of the whole program of modernization of that time. These military tasks were to be dealt with in the order of priority mentioned above. Dr. Poe has described the battles with the warlords which continued virtually until the outbreak of the war with Japan in 1937. What is important is that these campaigns against the warlords were uniformly successful and that warlordism as a major threat was eliminated before the war of resistance began. The same was true for the campaigns against the Communist insurgency. By 1937 the Communists had been forced out of the central part of China into a corner in the Northwest where they were greatly reduced in power and importance. But the new Communist opportunity came with the war with Japan. Towards this most serious danger the National Government directed its main preparations; and the war of resistance, lasting through eight years, is testimony to the soundness of the strategy which was adopted to prepare for it. However, the war itself, with its economic suffering aggravated by the isolation in which China found herself during the last years, weakened the moral fiber and gave the Communists the opportunity to profit from the destruction and chaos with their own military victory.

In retrospect, the accomplishments of these short ten years are amazing. A foundation was laid which still may be important for the future. The outcome of the crisis created by the Cultural Revolution on the Mainland is uncertain and the existence of an alternative tradition that was so successful may still count in the years ahead.

CHAPTER III

China's Fiscal Transformation, 1927–1937 *

BY ARTHUR N. YOUNG

OCUS ON THE CHANGE IN CHINA wrought by the Communist take-over on the mainland in 1949 has diverted attention from the major transformation after 1927 when the National Government set up its capital at Nanking. That transformation could not have taken place had not the Nationalists developed solid financial resources instead of the hopelessly small receipts at the disposal of the preceding Peking regimes. No government can operate successfully without a reasonably adequate inflow of money.

Let us look at the fiscal position of the Peking regimes in the years before the Nationalist accession to power in 1927-1928.

I

The Setting: The Fiscal Situation Before 1927-1928

Under the imperial regimes the government's receipts and payments, and the people's fiscal burdens, could not be told in definite figures. Taxes were levied on land, such products as salt and tea, and movement of goods within China and abroad. Payments in money, grain, and silk were sent to Peking as taxes and tribute. But the amounts involved, so far as data can be ascertained, by no means show the burdens on the

---

* A fuller discussion of the matters with which this paper deals is contained in my forthcoming book, *China's Nation-Building Effort, 1927-1937: The Financial and Economic Record,* to be published shortly by The Hoover Institution, Stanford University.

people. Collectors of taxes, as historically in so many countries, were unregulated and uncontrolled. Official posts were commonly bought. To keep them holders had both to see to the welfare of their staff and contribute to immediate superiors, and so on upward to the throne. In the hierarchy, it has been said, an official existed "solely for his own maintenance and that of his fellow-officials, his superiors and his subordinates."[1] Estimates put the general cost of government at all levels at the time of the fall of the empire at something like C$400 (Chinese dollar or *Yuan*) million. But that did not include "any of those delightful exchange operations which alleviate the burden of officials charged with receiving and disbursing official funds."[2]

In the confusion from the revolution of 1911 to 1928 the old financial system largely disintegrated. Budgets were prepared, but, in the words of the *China Year Book, 1928,* "No budget published since the establishment of the Republic has been other than a pious expression of hope that the revenues and expenditures would correspond with the estimates. The figures . . . , therefore, have little value except as showing what the revenue and expenditure of the Central Government might be expected to be, if the country were united, and more or less normal conditions restored." The last such budget before the advent of the Nationalist Government in 1927 was for 1919-1920. It showed revenues of C$490 million, including C$51 million from loans. Expenditures were C$496 million, including C$139 million for War and Navy and C$136 million for Finance, mainly for debt payments.[3]

The Republican regimes at once found themselves without sufficient revenues. Nearly all of the customs receipts were needed for payments on the Boxer Indemnity and loans. The customs had been administered since 1854 by the Sino-foreign service under British leadership, and customs-secured debt payments were duly maintained. The foreign powers showed by a naval demonstration in 1923, when Sun Yat-sen's new Kuomintang regime threatened to seize the Canton customs, that they would not then tolerate that interference with customs revenues.[4] The salt revenue since 1913 had been administered by the Sino-foreign Inspectorate, also under British leadership, as security for foreign loans. But, especially as salt was produced largely in the interior of the country, the salt revenues were subject to seizure by warlords. As a result, the revenue reaching Peking shrank steadily, until by 1927 not enough was received to meet salt-secured loan payments. The warlords likewise seized other revenues belonging to Peking, along with railway receipts.

The Peking regimes, lacking revenues, lived largely on loans until about 1920. But with revenues far short of meeting even the government's basic needs, most of the debt fell into arrears. By 1927 only the customs-secured foreign debt and a small part of the railway debt continued to be duly paid. Most of the internal loans were in default.

Hardly anyone would lend any longer to governments with such poor credit. Payments to the staff of government organs and other expenses fell into arrears, except for agencies with a cash flow such as railways and telegraphs. There was no central bank to act as the government's fiscal agent. Customs funds and such salt revenue as reached Peking were placed in foreign banks.

In 1926 Finance Minister Wellington Koo, who held the post briefly, gave an account of his stewardship. When he took office he said, ". . . the Treasury was empty and all sources of revenue were exhausted," while ". . . telegrams and letters pressing for funds were pouring in every day." Minister Koo set a precedent by giving a public accounting. When three and a half months ended on October 1, total receipts reached the munificent total of C$3,521,000. All of that came from loans from Chinese banks, except C$1,462,000 which came from customs and salt revenues. All but C$27,000 was spent—more than two-thirds for the military.[5]

The governments at Peking could be only impotent with revenues of but a few millions yearly, while warlords in the provinces consumed the rest of such revenues as existed. In 1927-1928 the government's writ hardly ran beyond Peking's walls and the adjoining area which the warlord ruler of the day controlled. The frequently changing central governments could not speak for China as a whole, although recognized by foreign states in default of a better alternative. It came to be said that China was not a nation but a geographic expression. "China and chaos have become synonymous terms," said Sir John Jordan, long-time British Minister to China. The Peking governments were caught in a vicious circle. They could not strengthen themselves because of lack of revenues. And they could not develop revenues because of lack of authority.

The Nationalists got a head start in fiscal matters by developing considerable revenues in South China before embarking on the Northern Expedition which led to conquest of the Yangtze Valley area in the spring of 1927 and overthrow of the Peking regime in mid-1928. Also they had a central bank at Canton. These constructive developments were largely the work of the youthful American-trained Tse-vung Soong (T. V. Soong).

II

Founding a Fiscal System, 1927-1928

In the spring of 1927 the Nationalists' Northern Expedition reached the Yangtze River, taking over the Shanghai-Nanking area which was China's economic heart. In April they set up the capital at Nanking. But it was not until June 1928 that they captured Peking, establishing them-selves in nominal control of China. Peking was renamed Peiping, or "Northern Peace."

When the new government took over nation-wide authority in 1928 China was unified only in name. Only the lower Yangtze region was solidly controlled. Elsewhere the degree of control varied, and in many areas was only nominal. In Manchuria the "Young Marshal" Chăng Hsueh-liang had raised the national flag, but expected to remain mostly free of control by Nanking. The Kwangsi leaders held the Peiping-Tientsin area. Marshals Feng Yu-hsiang and Yen Hsi-shan had moved arsenal machinery inland in the northwest and threatened revolt. In the west and southwest the warlords were practically independent. Control of the Hankow and Canton areas was uncertain. In Kiangsi the Com-munists were holing up and plotting to take over China.

The regional rulers sought substantial military independence and control of local government, and some of them hoped to displace Chiang Kai-shek at the top. With such ambitions they wanted to hang on to the local revenues. That posed a major fiscal problem for Nanking. The aspiration of a strong, independent, and progressing China as visualized by Sun Yat-sen could only be realized through a strong central govern-ment drawing revenues from most of the chief productive parts of China. Extension of political control had to go hand in hand with extension of control of revenues. Thus the financial history of the prewar decade cannot be viewed apart from political and military events.

Promptly after taking the Shanghai area, and without waiting to complete the Northern Expedition, the Nationalists moved to strengthen their financial resources. They had the benefit of the larger part of the 2½ and 5 per cent customs surtaxes, which were being collected even though the powers had not agreed to a new general tariff. But current revenue was far from adequate to finance the Northern Expedition. So the new regime prevailed upon the Shanghai bankers to issue as of May 1, 1927, a loan of C\$30 million secured on the customs surtaxes at Shanghai. To give effect to the security, the pledged revenues were paid over to a commission composed of representatives of banking inter-ests and public bodies. That procedure strengthened confidence in the loan, and a considerable market for bonds developed.

Promptly after the capture of Peking the new government acted to formulate an economic and financial program. Soong, as Minister of Finance, addressed the National Economic Conference which met at Nanking in June 1928, days after completion of the Northern Expedition:

> Now that the war is over, we shall have to raise enormous funds to rehabilitate the country, to restore peace and order, to disband the surplus troops, to restore the dilapidated railways, to care for famine-stricken areas

which have served as the battlefield. In this work of rehabilitation, the people must have a voice. . . . We have called together responsible nonpolitical persons . . . to guide us. This is, so far as I know, the first conference of its nature to be held in China.

In addressing the Financial Conference which met in July, composed of national and provincial officials concerned with finance, Soong said:

> Without coming to a definite understanding with the military authorities to let taxation alone, without arranging with the provincial authorities to give a free hand to the Ministry of Finance in the control of national revenue, and finally without knowing what our actual total income is, all talk of unifying China is idle.[6]

The conferences concluded that control of expenditure, and especially of military outlay, was of vital importance. As to revenues, the central government should have the customs; taxes on salt, tobacco and wine, and mining; stamp dues; revenue from government properties and enterprises; and *likin* (the tax on inland movement of goods, which was to be promptly abolished). The provinces were to have the land tax, formerly a national revenue, and miscellaneous business taxes and licenses. The conferences called for recognition in principle of obligations of the former regimes, and settlement of debts in arrears. The leaders, with national responsibility, saw the need to alter the policy of the first Kuomintang Congress in 1924 which held that China should not repay foreign loans that were "contracted by an irresponsible government, such as the Peking government, to maintain the power of the warlords."[7] The conferences also called for creation of a Central Bank, which could serve as the government's fiscal agent.

The Central Executive Committee of the Kuomintang, at a plenary session in August, substantially adopted the recommendations of the conferences.

The greatest immediate potential for higher revenue was in raising rates of import duty. Since the middle of the nineteenth century rates were held to a nominal 5 per cent. But the greed of the powers, in seeking nearly free markets for their exports, held rates which were mostly specific at an even lower level. Thus the tariff of 1858 stayed in effect for more than forty years until the need for more revenue to pay the heavy cost of the Boxer Indemnity forced a revision. The Washington Conference of 1921-1922 agreed that China should have more revenue from the tariff. Rates were to be raised at once to an effective 5 per cent. A Tariff Conference was to meet to arrange a general 2½ per cent surtax, and a 5 per cent surtax on certain luxuries. At the Tariff Conference of 1925-1926 China asked for full tariff autonomy. Plans for a revised tariff were agreed in principle, but were stalled by the instability of governments at Peking. Meanwhile the 2½ and 5 per cent surtaxes began to be levied, first by the Nationalists at Canton and then at ports controlled by Peking, although the foreign powers had not consented.

One of the first acts of the Nationalists after taking over at Peking in mid-1928 was to seek full tariff autonomy through formal agreement of the powers. The break-through came in July by the signing with the United States of a brief treaty on tariff autonomy. The treaty was signed on July 25, and of course involved American recognition of the new government. Agreements were made with the other powers, and the new tariff took effect February 1, 1929. The rates were substantially those informally agreed at the Tariff Conference in 1926.

The enforcement of higher tariff rates was of great fiscal benefit to the government. From average yearly revenues of C$121 million in 1924-1928, customs revenue rose to C$244 million in 1929, C$290 million in 1930, and C$385 million in 1931.[8] Part of the larger figures reflected depreciation of silver during the depression; but a large real gain of revenue resulted, because internal prices in China rose much less than silver fell.

Besides building up the yield of customs, the new government moved promptly to develop the internal revenues, the single most important of these being revenue from salt. After 1920 the provincial authorities detained more and more salt revenue. By 1927, although about C$60 million was still collected by the Salt administration, only about C$3 million reached the central government. In two-thirds of the districts Inspectorate functions had been disturbed, with some offices taken over and Inspectorate offices suspended or closed. Payment of salt-secured loans fell into arrears.

Minister Soong fully realized the importance of restoring the Salt administration as an effective revenue organ under the central government, and also of restoring loan service. On September 25, 1928, he issued a statement that the government "is anxious to maintain the national credit even before complete unification of finance has been achieved, and before the entire Salt revenue has become centralized under the Ministry of Finance." Each salt district was to remit a monthly quota to provide a yearly total of C$10 million for debt service. That would cover a year's current obligations. There was no provision for dealing with arrears.

Nationalistic opposition to the Salt administration developed. Foreigners were taking the leading part in its operation. Collections were deposited in foreign banks, with collection costs and debt payments deducted and the balance remitted to the government. But in the disorders of the 'twenties that system had broken down. On November 16,

1928, Soong announced that he was taking steps to make the administration "an effective part of the National Government under the exclusive control of the Ministry of Finance." The Ministry would take "full responsibility for . . . loan service." The new arrangements departed from the terms of the Reorganization Loan of 1913. But the infringement was only nominal, because since 1917 that loan under its terms had been paid from customs revenue. The other salt-secured loans called for no special arrangements concerning the handling of salt revenue. The British, French, and Japanese governments objected to the "unilateral action." Soong's action was a concession to strong nationalistic elements in the government and public. Without some such action he would have found it hard to find support for maintaining Sino-foreign collaboration in collection of salt and customs revenues and recognizing in principle the old Peking debts. The success of Soong's new arrangements in restoring debt service took the edge off the protests.

The National Government moved promptly to reform and develop internal revenues other than from salt. It "fell heir to a motley collection of taxes, surtaxes and miscellaneous imposts which were levied without any pretense at system by innumerable bureaux all over the country."[9] There were more than 130 national tax offices in Shanghai alone at the time of the Nationalist takeover. For the first time China had a government with a coherent tax policy on modern lines. As Finance Minister Soong said early in 1929:

> Now, we believe that our policy is inherently sound and that if applied equitably and honestly, it will result in an increase of revenues, while at the same time, trade will be relieved of vexatious impediments. Briefly stated, our policy requires: first, taxation at the source; second, evenness of taxation; third, a simplified system and consolidation of taxes on the same commodity; fourth, the elimination of leakage; fifth, strict accountancy.

To accomplish that policy Soong sought "efficient, honest administrators who will fearlessly do their jobs," and he brought new and younger men into the Ministry.[10]

An early break-through was the arrangement Soong made in January 1928 for foreign tobacco-manufacturing companies to pay specified taxes. Previously they paid no taxes to the central government in view of the old treaties giving them extraterritoriality ("extrality"). Likewise, Chinese companies produced free of tax in the international settlements. Provincial and local authorities imposed a great variety of taxes on tobacco. The settlements became centers of huge smuggling operations. Soong and the companies agreed that after paying the specified national taxes on rolled tobacco these would be their only taxes, and that the government would reimburse them if they had to pay further taxes in specified areas under government control. These areas first included only the lower Yangtze provinces and Fukien, but in 1929 were extended to the rest of central China, Hopei, Kwangtung, and Kwangsi. Since the government did not have full control in all these areas, some collections were retained. These arrangements were not easy to make. To get around the treaty difficulties the government exempted from tax one case of cigarettes and one of cigars each month at each foreign factory. For the producers the *quid pro quo* was freedom from the arbitrary exactions and bribery that had impeded their operations.

Also before completion of the Northern Expedition the new government moved to reform the stamp tax. It had been collected by tax farming, the collector contracting to take a fixed amount of stamps for a given region or a particular kind of business. Often the tax farmers did not insist upon actual attaching of the stamps, since they turned over regular revenue to higher authorities. In November 1927 the government began enforcing use of uniform stamps sold at post offices, and added cosmetics to the list of taxed items along with documents, even though the revenue did not necessarily come to the central government as yet. Likewise, agreements were made to apply the tax to Chinese in the foreign settlements. A beginning was made to end the tax farming system. But abolishment was to take some time. Furthermore, the government in July 1927 committed itself to eventual abolition of *likin*. That tax was collected on transit of goods at about 700 barriers along the main trade routes. Originally a tax of a tenth of one per cent, it had been created by the imperial government in the 1850's to raise revenue for putting down the Taiping rebellion. But, with time, rates up to 10 per cent or more were common. The tax applied mostly to necessities, was burdensome, and gave rise to much corruption.

Spectacular results followed the moves to build a revenue system. In the fiscal year ended June 30, 1929, the first after the takeover at Peiping, national revenue totaled C$334 million. That contrasted strongly with the few millions previously available to Peking. And the people and producers were beginning to benefit from the improvement of the financial system and its administration.

Although revenues grew rapidly, receipts were not enough to cover the costs of ongoing govenmental operations, especially in the military field. After mid-1928 military operations continued with little interruption. First was the liquidation of the remnants of Peking's troops. Next was to deal with threats to the central government both from the remaining warlords and Communists and from dissidents within. Data presented to the Economic and Financial Conferences showed that the military establishment, as it existed in the summer of 1928, would cost at least C$360 million yearly. This sum greatly exceeded total revenue expected to be available after debt payments. The recommendation was to reduce the armies, cut costs to C$192 million, and to raise a loan for disbandment. Disbanded troops were to be used temporarily on public works. Unhappily the reduced figure quickly became unrealistic. Soon the Kwangsi leaders revolted, and other revolts followed in 1929—the most serious being that of Marshal Feng Yu-hsiang in the northwest. Heavy military costs proved to be a continuing serious burden.

Finally, creation of the Central Bank of China in the fall of 1928 facilitated financial management and paved the way for notable improvement of fiscal administration.

III

The Quest for Stability: Building Revenues

The prewar decade was stormy, both as to internal and external affairs. Revolts of warlords and dissidents were endemic until mid-1936. The Communists holed up in Kiangsi Province in central China until driven to the far northwest in 1935. In September 1931 Japan began the seizure of Manchuria, followed by encroachment in north China. Military expenses thus continued large throughout and making ends meet was not easy under these conditions. The government was firmly resolved not to rely upon paper money financing. It had to raise money in hard silver up to the currency reform of 1935, and thereafter in a convertible currency held firmly at par.

Although the new tariff took effect February 1, 1929, China had not attained full tariff autonomy. Japan agreed to that tariff, but before conceding autonomy sought assurance of continued favorable rates, abolition of *likin*, and agreement to settle debts in arrears. Negotiations began in 1930 and were concluded in May. China agreed not to raise rates on certain cotton goods, fishery products, and wheat flour for three years, and on a number of other items for one year. China also declared her intention to end *likin* on October 10, 1930, and to abolish other similar charges as soon as possible. Also China undertook to set aside C$5 million yearly from customs revenue for debt settlements, and to convene a conference of representatives of creditors on or before October 1, 1930 to discuss debts in arrears. Since the powers other than Japan had already agreed to full tariff autonomy, agreement with Japan completed the process. This was an important step toward ending the nineteenth century servitudes known as the unequal treaties.

Although the National Government's control of customs revenue became internationally recognized, there was a struggle to maintain the integrity of revenues under central control. The first step was to procure abolition of the special bureaus created to collect the surtax. Soong accomplished this after a struggle with some of the local authorities that had been enjoying this revenue. Several times—in Tientsin in 1930, Canton in 1931, and Foochow in 1934—rebellious military and political leaders seized the customs revenue. This was partly for themselves and partly to deprive Nanking of means of thwarting them. The government was able to recover the right of collection, although after some lapse of time. More serious was Japan's seizure of the Manchurian customs revenue which began in 1932. In the case of each seizure there was recognition of responsibility to contribute in some measure to the cost of debt service, but in practice this proved mostly verbal. In the case of Manchuria no way could be found to receive debt payments without implying recognition of the puppet regime of "Manchukuo."

China's first use of newly won customs autonomy was to collect import duties on a gold basis from February 1, 1930. Fluctuations in silver exchange had long been a fiscal problem for China. The slump in silver from 1873 had roughly doubled by 1895 the cost of acquiring foreign exchange. The fiscal difficulty first became serious after China had to contract the large loans of 1895-1898 to indemnify Japan after defeat in 1894. Import duties were largely specific in terms of silver, but payments on foreign debts were in terms of gold. And the burden became much heavier when China had to pay the Boxer Indemnity after 1900. In 1896 and again in 1900-1901, China sought permission to collect duties on a gold basis according to plans prepared by Sir Robert Hart as Inspector General of Customs. But the powers refused this wise proposal. Finally in 1902 they agreed to revised rates in terms of silver, after unseemly higgling about favorable rates on exports to China.

In 1928 silver began a drop which carried by 1932 to the lowest ever prices of silver. The value of the Chinese silver dollar fell from around US$0.45 to about US$0.20. In 1929 the Ministry of Finance proposed collecting duties on a gold basis, influenced by observation in France during the 'twenties of a somewhat similar measure during the inflation there. The plan was adopted in January 1930. It was effective February 1, a year after the former revised tariff whose rates China had agreed with Britain not to raise for a year. Import duties were thereupon collected in terms of the Customs Gold Unit (CGU) valued at US$0.40. Banks and importers were enabled to establish CGU accounts at the Central Bank on which they could draw for duty payments. That Bank covered the liability in gold and foreign currencies. Buyers of CGU could pay in silver but the Bank set rates favorable to payment in sterling or dollars. It thus obtained increasing balances abroad, as payments for most purchases of CGU were made in foreign currencies.

Collection of duties on a gold basis was a reform of first importance. It protected the government to a large extent from the slump in silver. It assured maintaining foreign debt payments, despite the difficulties during the depression that forced default in so many other countries. The larger revenue in local currency automatically resulting from the fall of silver was invaluable to the government while incurring the heavy costs of putting down revolts of warlords. *Finance and Commerce* of Shanghai stated on July 22, 1931 that "it would probably be no exaggeration to say . . . that . . . the collection of the revenue in the form of gold units saved the country from financial disaster."

Moreover, the Central Bank derived important benefits. Until early 1930 that Bank had no balances or correspondents abroad. The CGU system showed the need for these arrangements. The Bank established balances in London and New York. It became an important factor in the exchange market, handling foreign business matters for the government, and building up substantial reserves in London and New York. It gained valuable experience in exchange operations, establishing prestige at home and abroad. By 1935, the year of the currency reform, the Central Bank was able to take charge of maintaining stable rates of exchange.

The government did not hesitate to use actively the freedom to set new rates of duty. Most changes were increases, as the urgent need for revenue continued without interruption. The shift of import duties to a gold basis was devised so that rates were raised but slightly in terms of the gold value of imports. But the cost in terms of silver rose steadily as silver slumped until the latter part of 1932. The first increase of rates, at the beginning of 1931, affected 57 per cent of the rates. The most important increases were on matches, chinaware, sugar, cement, glass, soap, cosmetics, artificial silk, and woolen goods. This tariff was primarily for revenue but also had elements of protection. The increase was partly to compensate for removal of a variety of old obstacles to trade, namely *likin,* coast trade duties, transit dues, and "native customs" levied on movement of imported goods away from the immediate area of treaty ports. The government, however, imposed in 1931 "interport duties." These duties were levied at low rates, mostly about 2 to 3 per cent on native goods moved between treaty ports for consumption in China.

After 1931 considerable further increases of import duty took place. A revision in the summer of 1932 affected mainly luxuries, and was designed to add to revenue following Japanese seizure of the Manchurian customshouses. In May 1933 rates were raised, especially on Japanese goods, following expiration of the rates bound in 1930. Further protection was introduced, especially on textiles. One unfortunate increase affected sugar. Some members of the Tariff Commission along with the foreign advisers had urged lower duties on sugar as well as on other items, for revenue reasons, but this counsel did not prevail. The result was large-scale smuggling of sugar, especially from Formosa, creation of a sugar monopoly in Canton which engaged in official smuggling, and consequent loss of revenue.

Japan strongly objected to the rates of 1933, although these were not discriminatory, and accompanied the protests with aggressive pressure in north China. While not openly recognizing the pressure, the government issued a revision in the summer of 1934, reducing some rates important to Japan and raising others on such items as kerosene, gasoline, wool and woolen goods, chemicals, machinery. The changes were generally considered unfavorable by Western trading interests.

China thus moved in a few years from a low to a high level of duties. Before 1929 revenue was about 4 per cent of the value of imports. The level rose to about 10 per cent in 1930, 15 per cent in 1931 and 1932, 20 per cent in 1933, and over 25 per cent in 1934-1937. The rising proportions, however, partly reflected lesser demand for imports during the depression. Rates were productive of revenue, though not maximizing it. Yield grew from C$134 million in 1928 to a peak of C$388 million in 1931, and stayed over C$300 million in the following years despite disturbed economic and political conditions. About five-sixths of the revenue came from import duties, and the rest from export duties and the minor duties on inland trade.

High duties, besides producing revenue, gave rise to grave problems. Smuggling had not been important under the pre-1929 rates, but now it grew apace. Hong Kong was practically a free trade area, and smuggling to south China was easy. Also the Japanese colony of Formosa was a convenient base, and "puff-puff" boats plied from there to the mainland. The government negotiated with Hong Kong to combat smuggling, but strong vested smuggling interests in South China blocked the making of an effective agreement. There was even smuggling by official organs, especially Navy and Salt authorities. Officially protected smuggling ended in South China only in 1936, when the central government finally established firm control.

The most serious smuggling and evasion took place in north China in 1935 after the Japanese created the puppet "East Hopei Autonomous Government." Contraband goods were openly landed, and a smuggler offered to bring in "anything you want, anything except, perhaps, an elephant."[11] Smuggled goods flooded the northern part of China, legitimate trade was throttled, and loss of revenue ran to millions monthly. The Japanese motive was partly to bring pressure for a puppet region in north China. Partly also it was a protest against high rates on Japanese imports. China and the friendly powers protested, but to little avail.

China set up land barriers which had some effect, but bad conditions continued until Japan seized North China in mid-1937.

The unhappiness of Japan's business interests with China's tariff policy merged with the expansionist ideas of the militarists who wanted to control all of China. China's tariff policy thus became one of the factors contributing to the all-out fighting that followed the incident at the Marco Polo Bridge on the Double Seventh of 1937.

China agreed, when contracting the 1898 loan, that the Customs administration "shall remain as at present constituted during the currency of this loan," which was until 1943 (Article 6). Also in 1898 China agreed that the Inspector General of Customs should always be British so long as British trade with China exceeded that of any other nation. By 1929 the trade of the United Kingdom with China was much less than China's trade with the United States or Japan; but trade with the British Empire, notably including that with Hong Kong, still predominated.

The First Kuomintang Congress called for ending "foreigners' management of customs dues." T. V. Soong thus summarized in 1933 grievances which the government and nationalistic elements harbored vis-a-vis the Customs at the time of the Nationalists' advent to power:

> It was said that the Customs had become an *imperium in imperio;* that it was an adjunct of Legation Street; that the word of the Inspector-General had become law in national finances . . . that the Customs funds were deposited in foreign banking institutions, and had served merely to build up their credit to the neglect of Chinese banks; and that the higher ranks of the Service were exclusively occupied by foreigners and were not open to Chinese.[12]

In addition, it was often charged that costs of collection were unduly high. These costs were around 10 per cent before 1929, but fell to 6 or 7 per cent when revenue grew. As higher rates encouraged smuggling the Customs had to develop an expensive preventive service and costs again became about 10 per cent. The Customs paid its people well and gave good value in return.

The Nationalists, with the responsibility of ruling China and with moderates in control, recognized China's legal obligation and also that it was in China's interest to maintain and support the venerable Inspectorate of Customs. Soong took action to remedy the grievances but with due regard to China's commitments. He integrated the Inspectorate into the Finance Ministry. He ended the discrimination against Chinese attaining the higher ranks (previously no Chinese had held the rank of Commissioner of Customs). Foreigners were to be added to the staff only for technical reasons and with Ministry approval. By 1937 about a third of the commissioners were Chinese.

Also the Customs was relieved of various extraneous functions performed because China lacked the means of performing them. For years foreign banks had been depositories of customs funds and, with the Customs, administered debt service. From March 1, 1932, revenues were concentrated in the Central Bank. After the CGU system became effective the government had large receipts in foreign currencies, and it became advantageous to use these currencies to pay debt service directly through the Central Bank instead of buying them in the exchange market. The right to do this was clear under some agreements, but under others the foreign banks questioned the right. To settle the controversy the government compromised by paying to these banks an extra 8th per cent of the amounts due.

Thus the policy was to make changes in the set-up of the Customs by evolution rather than by infringing agreements. It is significant that in 1937 when Finance Minister H. H. Kung was seeking loans in London he appeared ready to agree to extend the customs arrangements during the life of a further loan. But no firm commitment was made, the projected loan being dropped in view of the outbreak of hostilities.[13]

The salt tax, although burdensome, had proved a productive national revenue, especially in the years following the creation of the Salt Inspectorate in 1913. The government in 1928 had no choice but to develop and improve the salt administration. The system inherited by the Nationalists was complex. There were close to a thousand offices and sub-offices spread over China. The authority of the Inspectorate varied from place to place. The rate structure also varied, with numerous surtaxes and fees. The variations promoted smuggling from low cost to high cost areas, and smuggling was carried out on a large scale with producers, merchants, guards, and officials often in collusion. Depots and works to control salt at the source were inadequate. There were ingenious ways to defraud the revenue, as by unstandardized measures and adulteration by adding sand. Those transporting salt by boat, cart, or on animals often sold as they went. Organized banditry and piracy also preyed on the salt trade. F. A. Cleveland, Associate Chief Inspector, called the old system "an inheritance from past bargaining between corrupt officials and groups of organized exploiters of the salt trade—a remaining complexity of interlocking and conflicting monopolies granted by officials to merchants in exchange for ready cash." The beneficiaries "have gained an economic, social or political status or influence which has protected the system."[14]

The new government's immediate problem was to gain control of the producing areas. Minister Soong in his first annual report for fiscal 1929 reported considerable progress. Control had extended throughout the Yangtze Valley, into Shantung, Hopei, and the southwest. The

Ministry strove for "uniformity of the rate of taxation and methods of collection, to consolidate the various surtaxes under the sole control of the Salt Inspectorate, to abolish the old system of farming out taxes, to institute better control of the preventive service, and to extend the depot system so that revenue can be collected at the source." By the fall of 1929, said Soong, 60 per cent of collections went to the central government.[15] The progress continued despite interruptions by civil wars, and by 1937 most of the revenue was under central control—although at the cost of turning over some revenue to provincial authorities. The Ministry preferred to do this by subsidies, so that it would benefit from improvements in administration.

The Inspectorate with Ministry support struggled against abuses. The new *picul* of 50 kilograms, 110.23 pounds, was made the standard measure. The Inspectorate worked for quality inspection, improvement of salt depots and works, ending of monopolies, freedom of trade, consolidation of taxes and surtaxes, uniform and lower rates of tax, and taxation at the source. Formerly salt often had been heaped up with little supervision by guards. The Inspectorate built depots and other works at places of production to bring about better control. Soong took great interest in developing revenue guards to combat smuggling, and purged many undesirable elements from revenue personnel.

One cause of difficulty was the dual system whereby the government maintained a separate bureau, with Salt Commissioners in the districts, to oversee nominally the Inspectorate. All too often the commissioners were involved in abuses and smuggling. In 1932 Soong merged the two organizations at the top, and locally so far as he had control. The reform could be extended to the Canton area only in 1936, and had not been enforced in Shansi and Yunnan by mid-1937. In Kwangtung, collections increased 40 per cent in the year after abolition of the Commissioner's office.[16]

The deeply entrenched abuses could not easily be eradicated. But throughout the prewar decade progress was steady. Revenue collected by the Salt administration grew from C$60 million in 1927 and C$54 million in 1928 to C$218 million in 1936. Yields by calendar years were (millions of C$): 1929, 85; 1930, 130; 1931, 155; 1932, 145[17]; 1933, 159; 1934, 176; 1935, 184; 1936, 218; 1937, 213.

The changes in the Inspectorate in 1928, described above, were deemed necessary by Soong to remove the implication of a foreign-controlled receivership for China's finances. The infringement of the 1913 loan agreement did not in practice hurt holders of the 1913 loan, which under its terms had been paid from customs revenue since 1917, and the foreign protests were not insistent. The growth of salt revenue after 1928 and restoration of payments on the salt-secured loans of 1908 and 1912 were followed by approximate doubling of the prices of the bonds in London within about five years.

The Associate Chief Inspector had always been British since Sir Richard Dane and his Chinese colleague Chang Hu had reorganized the Salt service beginning in 1913. In February 1931 Soong named an American, Frederick A. Cleveland, as Associate Chief Inspector. He had had an extensive career in public administration and accounting and was better qualified than his predecessor. Although there was no agreement that an Englishman should always hold the post, some British publicists called the appointment a "breach of faith." Besides Cleveland's superior qualifications, the government felt it desirable to name an American. An Englishman, Sir Frederick Maze, held the Customs post, and relations between China and the United States were becoming closer. Cleveland justified his appointment by effecting improvements in administration and procedures. Upon his retirement in 1935 Oliver C. Lockhart, who had served since 1929 as Financial Adviser with special reference to taxation, succeeded him and continued with measures to strengthen the administration.

The Sino-foreign system resulted in more effective operation than a wholly Chinese organization could have provided under existing conditions. Chinese officers, if there were enough with training and ability, could match the technical competence of the foreign staff, and of course would have much deeper knowledge of conditions. On the other hand, the foreign staff could much better resist pressures from the salt trade and from civil and military officials for action contrary to the public interest. The cooperative efforts of the Sino-foreign staff resulted in great improvement.

Rising nationalism had a much greater effect in changing the salt revenue arrangements than in the case of the Customs. Under the old set-up the foreign co-chief and district officers took the lead in management. But some of the more active Chinese members of the organization began during the 'thirties to try to reverse the position. They did this more by indirection than overtly. The Chinese chief officer began taking up certain matters directly with the Finance Ministry without participation of his foreign colleague. And in the districts various Chinese officers also began acting alone in dealing with producers and merchants. The smooth working of the Sino-foreign cooperative arrangements depended upon personalities at the different levels. Friction easily developed. Lockhart appreciated the need to take account of rising nationalism, but took the position that in China's best interests the changes should come by evolution rather than by undermining the agreements and the position of the foreign staff. Good faith was involved because settlements of defaulted foreign loans had involved emphasis upon the Sino-foreign arrangements.

In July 1936 the Legislative Yuan adopted an Organic Law for the Salt administration, to become effective April 1, 1937. The law reflected the nationalistic trend and contained indications that the prerogatives of the foreign personnel were being diminished. The organization was called Directorate General instead of Inspectorate General, and the Chinese title suggested reduction in status. Translations read that the' Associate Director General was to "assist" the Director General, and there were corresponding clauses regarding the foreign district officers.

The time was inappropriate for such a change. With Japan becoming more and more aggressive in the north, China badly needed the support of the Western powers. China was also actively negotiating settlement of debts in arrears, in some of which salt revenue security was being held out as an inducement to acceptance of reduced rates of interest and cancellation of some or all of the arrears of interest.

The representatives of the bondholders asked for an interpretation of the new law. Minister Kung replied that "in our interpretation and implementation of this law the foreign associate officials continue to have joint responsibility as to essential functions and thus no material change in the established practice is being introduced." Instructions in the above sense were issued to the district offices. But the position of the foreign staff was in fact impaired. The Chinese officers came to feel that in view of the law they had the upper hand. Many of the foreign staff resigned.

The desire to get rid of foreign constraint, regardless of any loss of efficiency, is understandable in view of rising nationalism. Nationalistic views overrode the importance of regard for agreements, whether stated or implied. The Chinese staff were becoming more and more effective. Also the often stricter ideas of the foreign staff and suppression of long-standing abuses made enemies. The prewar trend of nationalism continued, and during the war the Sino-foreign administration gradually disintegrated.[18]

Development of internal taxation, besides taxes on salt, was logically based upon taxing a few commodities of wide consumption and ending exactions that unduly hampered production and trade. Soong's progressive ideas, mentioned above, were reinforced in 1929 by the recommendations of the Kemmerer Commission. Its *Report on Revenue Policy* urged concentration on improving existing sources rather than experimenting with untried taxes. The report began on page 1 with the recognition that "taxes are a contribution to the expense of maintaining essential public services" was mostly lacking, both by the public and "in practical ways by public servants themselves." Realization that taxes are "not a mere 'one-sided' compulsory exaction of wealth by the government (or, it maybe, by officials, largely for their private and personal benefit), must be gradually built up through the devotion of public funds to useful public purposes." The report recommended taxes on matches and cement, and a plan to revise the stamp tax. It also urged avoiding multiple taxes on the same item, and doing away with such burdensome taxes as *likin,* native customs, and coast trade duties.

The government was in general accord with these recommendations. The commodities chosen for taxation, in addition to rolled tobacco as already described, were cotton yarn, flour, matches, cement, flue-cured leaf tobacco, foreign-style wine and liquor, beer, alcohol, and mineral products. Administration was entrusted to special organizations which were soon consolidated into the Internal Revenue Administration. Forward-looking men were recruited. Payment of taxes was evidenced by affixing stamps when practicable, or by issuing receipts and permits to accompany shipments. Arrangements were made with the Shanghai International Settlement for inspection in factories. These arrangements put on a more equal footing taxpayers in the Settlement and the rest of China. Regional offices of the Administration were created. Also the two offices in charge of the old wine and tobacco tax and the stamp tax were merged.

The Internal Revenue Administration was a wholly Chinese body which developed a large degree of efficiency under its director, Tse Tsok-kai. It was respected as one of the best-working branches of the government. The reforms were extended throughout the country as the government gradually extended its control. Some compromises with regional rulers were necessary in the form of retentions of some revenue or subsidies. Lockhart as Financial Adviser with special reference to taxation participated in devising the tax measures and their working, and contributed importantly to their success. He continued his work on taxation concurrently, after becoming co-chief of the Salt administration in 1935.

Abolition of *likin* was decreed in January 1930, and made effective as of January 1, 1931. *Likin* had given rise to extortion and squeeze, and was "the fountain-head of political corruption."[19] The allocation of revenues in 1928 had made *likin* a national revenue, when giving the land tax to the provinces. But the provinces did little to improve the land tax, and continued to receive as of 1930 much of the C$80 to C$100 million of *likin* revenue. Success of the abolition exceeded the general expectation. It proceeded gradually with extension of government control. In January 1934 American Minister Johnson reported that "abolition has been almost complete" in government-controlled areas.[20] At the time of decreeing abolition the government also ended transit and coast trade dues. Native customs duties, which were on junk-borne trade, were ended in two stages as of January 1 and June 1, 1931. The duties and dues thus ended yielded about C$20 million annually. Early in 1931 to replace the lost revenue, the government added excise taxes on cotton yarn, flour, and cement. Besides subsidizing provinces about C$20 million yearly, provincial business taxes, to be planned and operated under central supervision, were also authorized.

The ending of the various taxes on movement of goods was most constructive. Besides freeing the movement of goods by cutting red tape and ending delays, the government relieved the people of the burden of supporting a host of officials who often made large irregular exactions.

Because revenue came almost wholly from indirect taxes—tariff, salt, and excises—the system was regressive and had little regard for ability to pay. An obvious remedy was an income tax, if practicable. An income tax decreed in 1914, which became effective in 1921, was a dead letter. Its yield in 1921 was C$10,311.69. The Kemmerer Commission in 1929 recommended against adopting an income tax, although it favored it when conditions made it feasible. Lockhart later made similar recommendations.

In 1936 the government adopted an income tax law, with moderate and progressive rates. It was first made effective October 1, 1936 on income of public officials and from government bonds, and made fully effective January 1, 1937. It would then apply also to (a) "profit-seeking business enterprises," with rates from 3 to 10 per cent; (b) "people practicing free professions, and those engaged in other profitable vocations"; and (c) interest on corporate bonds, stock dividends, and interest on bank deposits. There was a complicated formula for taxing profits, based upon return on capital. Both collection at the source and declared returns were specified.

It was clear to experienced persons that such a tax could not work successfully with general application and throughout the country. Public administration had greatly improved since 1928, and the Internal Revenue Administration was working well; but the success of an income tax depended upon even more than having competent administrators, and not enough were available. There was need both for general practice of accounting with proper standards, and for public acceptance of the idea of such a tax, as well as confidence that it would be fairly and fully enforced. The public, especially after the misgovernment of the 'twenties, held to the notion that wealth and profits should be concealed from government.

Moreover, the law had serious defects. Wages as low as C$30 per month and income from capital as low as C$2,000 were taxable. Income from urban and rural real estate was not taxed. Many of those charged with operating the law tried faithfully to make it work, but the task was impossible. The practicable result was that the tax applied mostly to salaries of officials and income from government bonds and bank deposits. The yield in the first year was only C$7 million. During the war the yield was only about 3 to 4 per cent of non-borrowed receipts.

The measures above described brought about a large growth of revenue, as shown in Table 1. From the first full fiscal year, which ended June 30, 1929, total revenue grew from C$334 million to C$870 million in 1936-1937. The growth was even more striking because C$50 million or more of customs and salt revenue yearly was lost after Japan's seizure of Manchuria in 1931. Revenue distribution is shown in Table 2. Details are shown in Table 3 appended hereto. The customs was much the largest single source, providing over half for a number of years until other revenues grew faster. Salt provided roughly a fourth of the revenue after 1929. Other internal taxes grew from 11 to 22 per cent in the period. Because heavy debt payments were charged on the customs, free revenue available to the government in the latter years came in roughly equal parts from customs, salt, and the other internal taxes.

Table 1. Expenditure, revenue, and deficit, 1929-1937 (in millions of C$)

Year ending June 30	Expenditure, excluding balances at end of the period	Revenue, non-borrowed, excluding balances at beginning of the period[a]	Deficit covered by borrowing	
			Amount	Percentage of expenditure
1929	434	334	100	23.0
1930	585	484	101	17.3
1931	775	558	217	28.0
1932	749	619	130	17.4
1933	699	614	86	12.3
1934	836	689	147	17.6
1935	941	745	196	20.8
1936	1,073	817	256	23.8
1937	1,167	870	297	25.4

Source: Finance Ministry, for 1929-1935 from published reports, and for 1935-1937 from unpublished data stated to be final.

[a] For fiscal years before 1934-1935 costs of revenue collection were shown as deductions from revenue. Thereafter they were shown as expenditures, as explained in the Ministry's Report for 1934-1935, p.16n. These costs are here treated as expenditures.

Table 2. *Distribution of revenues, 1929-1937 (millions of C$)*

	Customs	Salt	Other taxes	Miscellaneous
1929	53.5%	9.0%	11.0%	26.5%
1930	57.0	25.2	11.0	6.8
1931	56.1	26.9	12.2	4.8
1932	59.8	23.2	16.5	0.6
1933	53.1	25.8	15.9	5.2
1934	51.3	25.7	19.	4.1
1935	47.3	22.4	17.3	12.9
1936	33.3	22.6	20.4	23.7
1937	43.4	22.7	22.2	11.7

Source: See Table 1.

As of 1936-1937 the total yearly revenue in China proper comprised C$870 million for the central government, plus approximately C$534 million for the provinces and C$190 million for the *hsiens*. The total was about C$1,594 million. Assuming for purposes of calculation a population of 500 million, the tax burden averaged a little over C$3 per capita. In absolute terms that would not seem heavy. But it bore unduly upon those least able to support it, while many well-to-do paid no direct taxes and were burdened but slightly by customs duties and excises. The public sector was not large, being only perhaps 5 per cent of total gross national product. Extensive enlargement of the public sector to provide needed infra-structure would have required drawing much more revenue from agriculture, as the Communists were to do later.

IV

Expenditures, Deficits, and Borrowing

Despite the strong growth of revenues, heavy expenditures led to deficits in each fiscal period. Total expenditures increased from C$434 million in 1928-29 to C$1,167 million in 1936-1937 (excluding changes in balances). Yearly totals of revenues, expenditures, and deficits are shown in Table 1, and details in Table 3 appended hereto. Borrowing covered roughly a fifth of total expenditures in the prewar decade.

When the Nationalists took over the government there was no real system of budgets, accounts, and fiscal control, as already mentioned.

Soong in his report for 1928-1929 urged a proper budget, without which "all thorough-going financial plans are rendered impossible" (p. 9). He took the first step in mid-1929 by circulating to all branches of government forms for estimating receipts and expenditures. These were to be returned to the Finance Ministry for scrutiny, to the Central Political Council for approval, and to the Bureau of Audit for enforcement. Nearly all the offices complied, except in areas outside central control. The Finance Ministry adopted, as of January 1, 1931, a comprehensive accounting system, making use of recommendations of the Kemmerer Commission. In 1931 the Directorate General of Budgets, Accounts, and Statistics was created as an independent office. It did not prepare basic records of transactions, but used the data of the Finance Ministry. Full and accurate reports could not always be prepared because of disturbed conditions in various areas. And lack of fiscal control of the military was a continuing weakness. But the reports prepared by the Ministry showed reasonably well the government's receipts and payments, not including transactions of the Ministries of Railways and Communications which were handled apart from the Finance Ministry.

Overall budget control was inadequate for the reasons indicated. Expenditures exceeded the budgets in five of the nine years from 1929-1937. The Executive Yuan did not feel bound by the budget in emergencies. Until 1935 budgets were not promulgated in time. But the system was improving, and by 1937 real budgeting was becoming feasible subject to willingness of the military leaders to accept it.

In presenting and analyzing the fiscal data I use those materials prepared contemporaneously by the Finance Ministry. Unfortunately differing sets of data exist, especially the figures issued by the Directorate General of Budgets, Accounts, and Statistics and a later set published by the Ministry in 1943.[21] The contemporaneous Ministry figures were published in the *Annual Reports* in English and Chinese covering the period from July 1, 1928 through June 30, 1935. No reports were published for the next two years to June 30, 1937, but I received at the time figures stated to be final, which are included in the Tables herein.

Some writers, notably D. S. Paauw,[22] have seen nefarious motives in the failure to publish figures for 1935-1937, and in the conflicts between Directorate and Ministry figures for fiscal years 1934 and 1935. The real explanation of failure to publish the figures for 1935-1937 is simple. I was charged with preparing the reports, although Ministers Soong and Kung made changes to make them their own. I was absent for eight months from just after the close of fiscal 1936, partly on leave and partly to negotiate debt settlements in the United States. Upon returning I began preparation of the 1936 report. But soon after my return Kung went to London to attend the coronation, remaining until after the close of fiscal 1937, when hostilities began in July. There was never any thought of omitting reports, which were viewed as both a responsibility to the public and a chance to publicize progress.

The Directorate did not prepare original reports, but rather used Ministry figures in issuing them. There are wide differences in the two sets of data for fiscal 1935 in particular. But the total of the two sets of figures for the four fiscal years ended June 30, 1937, do not greatly differ. The differences can be explained by differences in accounting methods. When the Directorate figures for fiscal 1935 appeared I urged that only a single set of official figures be used, to avoid confusion. But the recommendation was not heeded.

The Ministry's figures issued in 1943 contained some obvious mistakes, e.g., stating customs revenue in fiscal 1937 as C$636 million while the Inspectorate General of Customs' contemporaneous figure was C$379 million. Most other figures are of the same order of size as contemporaneous Ministry figures, except that figures of receipts and payments for debt transactions are much larger. These figures seem to include gross turnover instead of net figures, and also to include in some form the unissued balance of the 1936 consolidation plan. The item of total expenditure of C$1,894 million in fiscal 1937 is highly misleading. Apparently the method used in 1943 was recognized as misleading, because the Ministry abandoned it in presenting the wartime financial statistics in the *Public Finance Yearbook, 1948* (Section III, pp. 98-101). Unfortunately the lack of published Ministry figures for 1935-1937 comparable with preceding data misled some postwar writers on China's inflation, who have used as the prewar base the figure of C$1,894 million of expenditures, whereas the figure comparable with wartime expenditures was C$1,167 million (excluding ending balances).[23] Although quantitative conclusions are distorted, fortunately the general conclusions of these writers are not much affected.

Questions have also been raised as to the completeness of the accounts. These relate particularly to the latter part of the decade, when the government was planning an extensive program of economic and military development. The charge is that hundreds of millions of concealed expenditures were made and to be made outside the budget with financing by inflation.[24]

Minister Kung announced in mid-1937 that a capital budget of C$400 million was planned for the coming fiscal year over and above the general budget. That was to be financed by loans whose service would be included in the general budget, which was to be balanced. Apparently that capital budget was part of a three-year program launched during 1936, providing for expenditure of C$1,034 million for economic and strategic development. That program was not made public, but I received a copy confidentially. The proposed costs included C$555 million for railways, C$37 million for highways, C$69 million for water conservancy, C$175 million for heavy industry, and C$198 million for armaments.

This program called for relatively little expenditure to be concealed and not included in the general budget. The large item for railways was to be financed from railway revenues, with the Finance Ministry temporarily guaranteeing payments on certain internal loans. The items for highways and water conservancy were in the general budget. Part at least of the strategic items was included in the general budget for military affairs. Some strategic items were financed through the barter agreement with Germany, as to which I had little information. There certainly was some concealment of strategic spending, in view of strained relations with Japan. Concealment of certain items was authorized under Article 45 of the Budget Law.[25] But in my judgment the amount of items not in the railway program and the general budget, concealed for strategic reasons, was at the most a few per cent of the total expenditures. That judgment is based upon both my present analysis and my recollection of the flow of current information at the time and access to Central Bank accounts.

There were defects and delays in some reporting of receipts and payments and many reports of the military were in global figures. But the contemporary figures of receipts and payments shown in the tables herein are in my judgment the best available and reflect reasonably well the true situation.

The biggest item of expenditure was military, caused by efforts to cope with internal disturbances and trouble with Japan. Next in size came debt payments, which grew as borrowing increased to cover deficits. Military and debt payments were 84 per cent of the total in 1928-1929, and in 1929-1937 never fell much below two-thirds.

The attempt to limit military outlay to C$192 million yearly pursuant to the Disbandment Conference of 1929 soon broke down. Later in that year the government had to put down the revolts of the Kwangsi leaders and Marshal Feng Yu-hsiang. Other revolts continued sporadically until 1936. The most serious threat was by the Communists. It took several costly campaigns to drive them out of Kiangsi Province south of the Yangtze. Their retreat in 1935 was their famous "long march" to the far northwest, mostly through areas where the inefficient armies of local warlords could not contain the determined Communist remnants. By 1935 there was substantial internal peace in the most important areas, although it was only in mid-1936 that the dissidents in

South China were definitely dislodged. But as internal conditions improved Japan encroached more and more, giving rise to heavy costs for military preparations.

Finance Minister Soong struggled hard for better control of military outlay. He saw clearly that the constant drain of military costs prevented proper allocations for economic development, education, and public health. In offering his resignation on June 11, 1932, he asked: "Have not banditry and communism thriven on political, military and economic maladjustments, and will they not respond better to a systematic, if unspectacular, combination of politico-military-economic treatment?"

In these conditions it was hard to find money for education, culture, and economic development. Yet considerable sums were made available. These were shown separately only in the accounts for fiscal years 1934-1937, as follows (millions of C$):

	1934	1935	1936	1937
Education and culture	13	32	37	42
Reconstruction (development)	7	26	88	54
Capital for government banks and other public enterprises		74	33	29
Total	20	132	158	125

Other items were provision of capital for the Central Bank in 1928, C$20 million; and payments for such purposes as education and development from remitted Boxer Indemnity funds, mostly American and British, which totaled roughly C$100 million during the decade. Altogether outlay for these purposes in the decade was about an eighth of total expenditure. In addition the railways and telecommunications operated autonomously, and provided from their cash flow considerable sums for development.

Because of the shortness of revenues the government was fortunate in being able to borrow locally to cover deficits. Borrowing abroad was out of the question in view of Peking's defaulted loan issues, apart from the fact that foreign lending hardly existed during the depression. The government hoped to create conditions favorable to foreign loans, which were needed for development. Although capital in China was relatively scarce the growth of modern-type banking provided increasing resources to the banks. Shanghai was a rich and growing metropolis where the country's financial resources were centered.

Borrowing for general purposes was as follows (millions of C$):

Fiscal year ended June 30		Fiscal year ended June 30	
1927	30	1933	20
1928	106	1934	254
1929	163	1935	220
1930	114	1936	360
1931	350	1937	nil
1932	190		—
		Total	1,807

Other borrowing, for special purposes, comprised C$45 million to redeem banknotes issued by the leftist regime at Hankow in 1927-1928; C$115 million and C$120 million respectively for financial rehabilitation of Szechuan and Kwangtung Provinces; C$132 million for railways; and a total of about C$30 million for electric utilities, water conservancy, and silk industry improvement.

Internal and international emergencies hurt confidence, and in most of the decade only short-term issues were acceptable in the local market. The larger part of these consisted of Treasury Notes, whose interest and principal were paid monthly. Loans were mostly negotiated with the Shanghai banks. Sometimes they advanced funds against issues as collateral, and sold the bonds as the market could absorb them to repay advances. Also at times banks bought bonds from the government.

Although interest rates on internal issues in much of the decade were 8 to 9.6 per cent, market yields were much higher. Yields on government issues were mostly in the range of 15 to 20 per cent in 1927-1933, except that following Japan's invasion of Manchuria rates rose to 25 per cent and more. In these conditions the government realized loan proceeds at a large discount. Indications are that in 1927-1933 only 60 to 75 per cent of face value was realized. In the later years of the decade the situation was better. Average yields fell to 11.6 per cent in 1936, and 8.7 per cent in June 1937, with rates under 8 per cent on the eve of Japan's attack in July.[26]

Repayment of the full face value in near-term installments of bonds issued at large discounts caused a drain that absorbed a growing part of available revenues. Thus there was a vicious cycle. Since spending could not be drastically cut, it became only a matter of time until the government would be unable to meet current debt payments and further borrowing would become impossible. That situation led to the debt reorganizations of 1932 and 1936.

In December 1931, Chiang and Soong resigned to allow the Canton dissidents the chance they coveted to take charge of the government.

Earlier in 1931 the Canton group had set up a rival "government" in South China and seized the customs; but the differences had been patched up after the Manchuria incident that began in September. Chiang and Soong were convinced that the Canton group would fail, and that the former leaders could soon return with greater authority and more national unity. After the Manchuria incident the bond market was demoralized and fresh borrowing was impossible. At the same time heavy payments on outstanding issues absorbed most of the revenues, which in turn were reduced by the crisis. The Canton group could not cope with the situation and there was talk of a moratorium. That raised a great out-cry from the bankers and other bondholders who had put hundreds of millions into the bonds. The Shanghai Stock Exchange had to close. The crisis was compounded late in January when serious fighting broke out at Shanghai, with Japanese bombing of the densely populated Chinese city. Meanwhile on January 21, Chiang and Soong returned to power. It was in the nick of time, because delay would have made the situation much harder to repair.

Shortly after I arrived in China early in 1929 I concluded that the process of issuing at a discount loans payable at par in a few years could only end in default or a negotiated reorganization of the debt structure. Interest payments seemed manageable in view of revenue growth. I hoped that conditions would improve so that negotiated refunding with payments spread over a longer period would become feasible. Minister Soong at once grasped the situation when it was set forth in figures. I prepared a succession of refunding plans adapted to the changing situation. When Soong and Chiang resigned they had in mind that adoption of such a plan might be feasible after their return. The collapse of confidence, and the grave situation accompanying Japan's attack, provided the opportunity.

As of January 1932 scheduled payments on internal debt were about C$200 million, of which about three-fourths was for debt retirement. Negotiations with representatives of the bondholders led to agreement on a plan to cut payments roughly in half. Interest was set at a uniform 6 per cent, and schedules of payment lengthened. Thus about C$100 million yearly was saved, enabling the government to carry on without further loan issues in 1932. The public received the plan well. During 1932 bond prices greatly improved. Soong said in his report covering the period:

It should be a matter of satisfaction . . . that since February 1932, for the first time in the 21 years of the Republic, the Government has been able to balance its budget at a time of world economic depression when practically every government has large deficits and when, in addition to the depression, the Government has had to confront the colossal burden of the 1931 floods, the slump of silver, the Japanese seizure of revenue in Manchuria and the attack on Shanghai.[27]

In October 1933 Soong resigned as Finance Minister. He was succeeded by his brother-in-law, H. H. Kung, who held the post for more than ten years. Kung retained most of the experienced personnel of the Ministry, but he faced great difficulties. The impact of the depression on China was delayed because, with the slump in silver, general prices were steady or rising until the winter of 1931-1932. But then deflation began in China as silver's value rose, influenced by the beginning of world-wide recovery and aggravated by the American silver-buying policy. The rising foreign exchange value of China's currency was accompanied by a severe drop of internal prices, business failures, and unemployment. Meanwhile there was heavy fighting with the Communists until they were driven from central China in 1935. Also Japan kept encroaching in the north. Besides large military costs the government had to spend large sums to rescue banks and firms hard hit by the depression.

Deficits began again in 1933 and continued to grow, giving rise to increasing loan issues. Although the term of the issues was somewhat longer than before, payments for debt retirement were still heavy. Loans still had to be marketed at a discount. Revenues slumped as the depression continued. In the second half of 1935 customs receipts fell short of covering debt payments, especially because of heavy costs of debt retirement. Although military outlay to combat subversion decreased with defeat of the Communists, it was felt necessary to build more strength in view of Japan's growing aggression in the north.

As the gap between revenues and payments grew, it became clear in the latter part of 1935 that another reorganization of the internal debt would be necessary. It became specially important to bring about substantial fiscal balance in view of the currency reform of November 1935. Maintenance of confidence required assuring the public that the government could carry out the policy announced at the time of that reform, namely, to attain budgetary balance within 18 months, and "avoid inflation."

In December 1935, the Ministry of Finance recommended consolidating the thirty-eight internal issues, except for a few with special characteristics, into five groups according to nearness of maturity. The new maturities of the five groups should be of increasing length. The interest rates of 6 per cent should remain unchanged.

The government substantially adopted the plan which, after negotiations with the Bondholders' Association, took the form of a proposal by them embodying agreement with the government. As of February 1, 1936, a 6 per cent Consolidation Loan was issued in five series, with maturities of twelve, fifteen, eighteen, twenty-one, and twenty-four years. The old loans were classified in groups according to nearness of maturities. The new issues were to be retired by drawings each half year. In addition, the plan authorized a new 24-year loan, the 25th Year Recovery Loan of C$360 million.

The consolidation reduced debt payments by about C$85 million yearly. That saving was important in a budget of about C$1 billion, and contributed importantly toward fulfillment of the promise of balancing the budget within eighteen months. The consolidation greatly simplified the debt structure. The exchange of securities was duly completed within a few months. The market generally recognized the need for the consolidation, although regretting a readjustment under pressure. Confidence slowly grew and bond prices rose, especially in the first half of 1937. By mid-year the bonds were on about an 8 per cent basis, an unprecedented figure in China, and contrasted with yields of 15 to 20 per cent and more in earlier periods. The government had no need to issue further loans for general purposes in 1936 and the first half of 1937. Pressure on the market was relieved. A further factor was demand for bonds, resulting from the arrangement after the currency reform whereby private banks could obtain bank notes from the government banks by tendering 60 per cent in silver, which was nationalized under the reform, and 40 per cent in bonds.

Besides borrowing from the public there were advances to government from the Central Bank and other banks. There was considerable turnover of advances and repayments. The net total of advances from 1928 to mid-1937 was C$525 million, of which about 85 per cent was from the Central Bank.

The only foreign borrowing included in the general accounts was about US$17 million in 1933-1935, the proceeds of the American Cotton and Wheat Loan of 1933. That money was used wholly for purposes of development. The Flood Relief Loan of 1931 of US$9 million was used to buy wheat which was used mostly in kind for work relief and famine relief, and accounted for through the National Flood Relief Commission. The Railway Ministry, whose transactions were separate from the general budget, issued, with the cooperation of the Finance Ministry, loans of C$132 million for rehabilitation and extension of railways, as mentioned. Also, as discussed in the next Section, substantial foreign credits were obtained in 1934-1937, largely for railways, and others were under negotiation in mid-1937. Had not war supervened, China's development would have benefited from quite substantial foreign resources.

V

The Rehabilitation of Credit

China's debt situation when the Nationalists took over reflected the troubles of the preceding generation. China had assumed obligations equivalent to about US$667 million to pay indemnity: first to Japan after defeat in 1894-1895; and in 1901 to pay the Boxer Indemnity. Beginning about the turn of the century large loans were contracted in Europe for railways. After the fall of the empire in 1911, the new regimes lacked revenues and borrowed wherever they could to make ends meet. As conditions got worse nearly all the loans except those secured on the customs went into default.

The debt structure in 1928, after hundreds of borrowing transactions, was probably the most complicated in the world. Early in 1929 when I came to China I found it hard to get full and accurate data about the debts. As security the government had pledged customs, salt, and other revenues and also railway and telecommunications revenues and properties. The equivalent of debt being paid in 1928 was US$418 million, and of debt in arrears US$475 million of principal plus large arrears of interest. A debt burden of about US$2 per capita does not look heavy. But in the 'twenties debt service took nearly all the customs revenue. In the Nationalists' first fiscal year which ended June 30, 1928, payments for debt service were C$160 million, or nearly half the non-borrowed receipts of C$334 million.

In 1928 the new government recognized its obligation as a successor to assume Peking's debts. But settlement of debts in arrears raised issues of great difficulty and complexity. Besides perplexing technical questions settlement depended upon the state of the finances, which was precarious in view of internal difficulties and, from the fall of 1931, Japan's encroachments.

A general settlement with creditors of the Western powers and Japan was the solution preferred both by them and China. This was discussed in detail at and after the Peking Conference of 1925-1926 which dealt with increase of customs revenue. Much progress was made in informal talks. But negotiations foundered because there was no Chinese government with solid financial resources that could assume realistic obligations for the future.

After the Nationalists took over they and the foreign powers contemplated a general settlement. It was important to China to restore her credit, especially because the government sought foreign capital for rehabilitation and development. And bondholders suffered because even the customs-secured issues sold at low prices to yield 7 to 11 per cent in 1927-1928, while bonds in arrears sold in the 20's or 30's or even lower. But a settlement had to be within China's reasonable capacity. It was neither in her interest nor in that of the creditors to make a settlement that would result in a fiscal breakdown.

Because of uncertainties caused by warlord revolts it was some time before the government was in position to take up the debt situation comprehensively. Meanwhile creditors criticized the government for pledging the best revenues for new internal loans while old debt secured thereon was left in arrears. The answer clearly was that the government needed the borrowing for self-preservation; that it had undertaken to settle the defaults as soon as practicable; and that without the loans the government could not prevent reversion to the previous chaos, with small chance of settling the old debts.

Japan was the most active of the governments pushing the debt issue in 1928-1930. As a condition of Japan's agreeing to tariff autonomy, China promised to hold a general debt conference by the fall of 1930. China also agreed to set aside C$5 million yearly as a first step toward debt settlement. Pending the conference there were negotiations between the two governments. Japan's ideas were in line with what I had been recommending: increase of the C$5 million as customs revenue grew and as old debts were paid off—there was a sharp drop in payments after 1940; and consideration of a large consolidation loan, to be distributed by agreement among the creditors. These proposals were in line with what was tentatively agreed at Peking. The idea of a general settlement was promising. But it had to be recognized that it would not be easy to determine what claims would be included, especially the treatment of the Nishihara loans. These loans, made for political purposes by Japanese interests to the An-fu Clique at about the end of World War I, were a bone of contention. The Nationalists in the Canton period had strongly objected to these loans, which were in support of a regime that wanted to suppress Sun Yat-sen's movement.

At the conference which met at Nanking November 15, 1930, China made tentative proposals for a general settlement. The plan contemplated increasing payments from customs and railway revenues to retire the debts over thirty years, and an agreement as to distribution of payments among the creditors. The conferees undertook to consult their governments. Extensive negotiations between China and Japan followed. But events made a general settlement impossible. In the spring of 1931 came a Canton revolt leading to seizure of customs in South China. In the summer came the very serious floods in Central China. And in September Japan marched into Manchuria.

The failure of efforts for a general debt settlement reflected the gradual breakdown of the cooperation envisaged at the Washington Conference of 1921-1922. That breakdown was not the intended policy of the powers, but rather a divergence of interests. A basic factor was that Japan refused to see that having different policies for Manchuria and the rest of China would bring a grave clash with China and also involve the Western powers.

Thus from 1931 piece-meal settlements became the only feasible way for China to restore her credit. A beginning was made in 1928 when Soong, as already mentioned, restored payments on the salt-secured foreign loans. That arrangement was elaborated in 1929, under a plan adopted on my proposal to provide for orderly payment of the arrears. In 1933-1935 the government settled a number of debts especially relating to railways and telecommunications with Japanese and Western creditors. But besides floating debt a number of public loan issues remained in arrears. These reflected most harmfully on China's credit.

Persisting internal political difficulties, the deepening deflation accompanying the rise in silver, large deficits, and friction with Japan continued to interfere with action on the old debts. It was only after the successful adoption of the currency reform of November 1935 that the government felt that it could begin a program of debt settlement. Adoption of the reform made the financial and economic outlook much brighter, and also made more clear the importance of access to private foreign credit for currency support. At that time such support was not available either from friendly governments or international financial institutions.

The government realized that piece-meal settlements would lead inevitably to the charge of discrimination, as well as involving the risk that early settlements would set a pattern which other creditors might not like but which could not easily be changed. But no other alternative was feasible. In 1933-1934, at the instruction of the Ministry of Finance, I made detailed studies of the chief loans in arrears, and the terms of settlements that I felt would be fair and within China's capacity. Also I prepared drafts of offers with some room for negotiation, but not too far from the terms desired. It proved gratifying that the eventual settlements were close to the terms drafted in 1933-1934.

The first loan taken up, shortly after the currency reform, was the Tientsin-Pukow Railway issue of £6.15 million, underwritten in 1908-1910 by British and German interests. That was the senior loan with a contingent claim on customs. After extended negotiations a settlement was announced in February 1936. Interest was to be 2½ per cent per annum for the first three years, and then at the regular rate of 5 per cent. Four-fifths of the interest arrears would be cancelled and non-interest-bearing scrip issued for the remainder. The loan would be retired during thirty years out of the railway's revenues, but interest payments would be guaranteed by the customs.

A few weeks before the settlement was concluded on the Tientsin-Pukow issue the government made a proposal in similar terms regarding the Hukuang Railway Loan of 1911 of £6.56 million, issued by American, British, and German interests. That loan also had a contingent claim on customs, although less senior. We felt on the Chinese side that the settlement should be substantially like that sought for the Tientsin-Pukow issue. During the negotiations the British and Germans agreed with that idea. But the difficulties of piece-meal settlements appeared when the American Foreign Bondholders Protective Council, with apparent French support, argued for better terms. China stood firm, and the Americans finally acquiesced but only after delay of more than a year. The British negotiators and the British government with an interest in both loans felt, I think correctly, that the Council was wrong in deeming the Hukuang Loan deserving of better treatment than the Tientsin-Pukow.

After a start was made in piece-meal negotiations, other debts were taken up. Altogether debt in arrears equivalent to about US$270 million was settled by mid-1937. Only about 10 per cent of the total debt then remained unsettled. Negotiations under way or contemplated in 1937 would probably have completed settlement of debts in arrears had not the war supervened. The 10 per cent did not include the Nishihara loans, which had to remain in abeyance in view of Japan's seizure of Manchuria and encroachments in North China.

The results of the settlements were shown in a rise in quotations of the foreign loans. In mid-1937 these sold at London on about a 5 per cent basis, which was better than the position of Japanese loans.

Beginning in 1934 foreign investors took a growing part in providing funds, first for railway extension and rehabilitation of existing lines, and also for development of a variety of industries. Foreign governmental agencies participated in underwriting part of the risks of some credits. The Germans were the first to extend such credits. A barter agreement was made with China under which credits for industrial and military purposes equalled a sum of the order of US$40 million as of mid-1937.[28] Soon British, French, Belgian, and Czechoslovak interests granted credits. American interests were slower to participate, but began in a small way in 1937. Altogether railway credits granted in 1934-1937 were equivalent to about US$40 million. Further credits for railway purposes granted by Belgian, British, French, and German interests, but whose use was prevented by the war, were equivalent to about US$80 million. In mid-1937 other railway credits by British and French interests, equivalent to about US$35 million, were under negotiation or contemplated. Also a British credit of £20 million to be used in installments for currency support and refunding internal debt was near to conclusion in July 1937. At that time Finance Minister Kung, after negotiating for the aforementioned credits in Europe, visited the United States. He found a favorable climate for American financial support through the Export-Import Bank. But unhappily all such plans had to be dropped when the hostilities begun on the Double Seventh at the Marco Polo Bridge escalated into full-scale war.

Total debt in mid-1937 was equivalent to US$1,260 million, compared with US$893 million in 1928.[29] The largest factor in the increase was growth of internal debt from the equivalent of US$95 million to US$682 million. Most of that borrowing was for deficits, but a sum of the order of a fifth was for constructive ends such as capital of the Central Bank, reform of the currencies of Szechuan and South China, and railway extension. Since the comparison of 1928 and 1937 is in dollars, the drop in the exchange value of Chinese currency from about US$0.47 in mid-1928 to US$0.30 in 1937 tends to minimize the large increase of internal debt in the decade. As to foreign currency debt, the comparison involves several factors. Much foreign debt was retired during the decade. There was also new borrowing in foreign currencies, as already mentioned. The foreign currency debt was largely in sterling, whose dollar value did not differ much in 1937 from that of 1928.

VI

Appraisal: The Prospect in Mid-1937

There is striking contrast between Wellington Koo's pathetic report of 1926, showing less than two million Chinese dollars of non-borrowed revenue during his three and a half months' tenure as Finance Minister, and the situation a decade later when revenue was approaching yearly yield of a billion. There were both plus and minus factors which call for appraisal.

As to revenues, full tariff autonomy was achieved. Rates were raised to triple the revenue. Miscellaneous obstructive levies collected by the Customs on internal trade were abolished. Regional efforts to seize the customs were thwarted, except as to the "Manchukuo" puppets. The Customs service was integrated into the Finance Ministry and many Chinese raised to senior posts. Collection of import duties on a gold basis preserved and increased the real yield, greatly strengthening the position of customs-secured loans and the finances generally. The Salt revenue service was rehabilitated with great increase of receipts by the central government. That service also was integrated into the Ministry.

The improved situation permitted restoration of service of salt-secured loans. Many reforms were made in administration of salt revenue. Excise taxation was simplified by concentration of taxes on a few items of wide consumption. The Internal Revenue Administration worked effectively as an all-Chinese service. Numerous obstructive taxes were ended, notably *likin*.

Yet the revenue system had serious weaknesses. It was inelastic and when revenue needs grew a common recourse was to raise rates. Various tariff rates were raised beyond the point of maximum return. That aggravated smuggling and became one of the factors leading to Japanese encroachment in North China. The system was regressive. The salt taxes and the excises burdened items of wide consumption and bore relatively lightly on the well-to-do. The income tax of 1936 was defective and premature, the conditions of reasonable success being absent.

A major defect was failure to reform and develop taxes on rural and urban land. Agriculture engaged more than three-fourths of the people and produced about 60 per cent of the national product. A reformed land tax along with land reform should have been a prime aim, both for fiscal reasons and for greater social justice. Execution of such measures would have taken years. But there was no serious beginning and little effect was given to laws and pronouncements for these reforms. Here there is a strong contrast with Japan's action after the Meiji Restoration. A firm program of land tax reform provided dependable revenues which were a major factor in enabling Japan to modernize so well. China's division of revenues in 1928 assigned land tax to the provinces. But they did little to develop what could have become their major fiscal resource. Instead they relied too much upon fiscal aid from Nanking, which also was a drain on national revenues. The central government was unable to balance its revenues and payments by relying upon indirect taxes. When the war came, revenues from the coastal and more modernized areas were quickly decimated. It became much harder to control wartime inflation.

A reformed tax on rural and urban land was clearly the most practicable important way to make the system as a whole more equitable. Unhappily a desire to accomplish that aim was not potent in ruling circles either nationally or in the provinces. Landholding and business and military elements were averse to accepting higher taxation, and were unaware of the disastrous consequences of failure to do so. These elements held the important political power.

Expenditures were dominated by military outlay, to put down revolting warlords, regional dissidents, Communists, and for national defense. This heavy expenditure involving large borrowing has been criticized as wasteful, unproductive, and a drain on the savings accumulated in the banks. The failure of the Nationalists to achieve better control of the military and reform the grave abuses of the army system was a major defect. There was reliance on veteran leaders of the early days, even when they were inefficient and corrupt, because they were deemed loyal. Moreover the government felt obliged to subsidize various provincial and local authorities and/or let them retain some national revenues. Partly that was to supplement inadequate local revenues. And partly it was a price to keep them in the fold, which at times partook of blackmail. Often the government had little room to maneuver. Force could not always be used or threatened. And public opinion became more and more averse to frequent use of internal force, especially as Japan's threat grew.

This is not the place to appraise the turns of policy and action in dealing with dissidents, nor do I have the data to attempt to do so. At the time and in the light of information then available, I felt that in principle the government was right in countering force with force. The government had set itself the task of building a strong and unified China. Since leaders usually wish to keep on leading, the government's survival was a priority. Granting the need for internal order as a precondition of progress, it is hard to argue that necessary costs of creating and maintaining order were unproductive, even though rising taxes and the drain of borrowing funds which the public accumulated in the banks reduced in the short run the money available for economic and cultural activities. In any event, by 1937 the government had mostly overcome forcible internal resistance to its claim to rule. Most regional centers, notably Szechuan and Canton, were in the fold.

Heavy military outlay was the chief cause of deficits and borrowing. Debt payments ranged between 25 and 40 per cent of total expenditure. Rising debt payments in particular, which revenues could not continue to meet, forced the internal debt reorganizations of 1932 and 1936. The first of these was forced by the Japanese seizure of Manchuria followed by the attack at Shanghai. The second was forced by the deflation, aggravated by the American silver-buying, and the need to take drastic action to buttress the currency reform of 1935. These reorganizations saved respectively about C$100 million and C$85 million yearly. Both were followed in a reasonable time by higher quotations of domestic loans. These reorganizations can be regarded as a substitute for default, which would have been disastrous, and for inflation which the government to its credit firmly resolved to resist.

All too little money was available for constructive purposes. Yet it was a considerable accomplishment to provide for these purposes something like an eighth of the budget totals during the decade, plus further sums from the cash flow of railways and telecommunications.

The purposes for which growing allocations were made included education, agricultural improvements, flood and famine relief, restoration and extension of railways and telecommunications, roads, civil airports, port works, water conservancy and river improvements, support of banks during the deflation, and capital for the Central Bank. The government was committed to development, a major tenet of Sun Yat-sen. Progress of rehabilitation and development in the decade, with government encouragement, was substantial. Thus in 1927-1936 compounded rates of growth were 9.4 per cent for electric power, 8.4 to 17.1 per cent for modern-type communications with air communication growing spectacularly from nothing, 5.6 per cent for industry, and 15.9 per cent for bank deposits (with relatively little inflation).[30]

Development of larger and dependable revenues laid the basis for borrowing internally, without which the new government could not have survived. The handling of deficits by Ministers Soong and Kung showed great resourcefulness under enormous difficulties. Evidence of this is found in the drop of yields on government loans from the range of 15 to 20 per cent and more in the first years to an average of about 11 per cent in the first half of 1937 and about 8 per cent in June.

Rehabilitation of the external debt presented most difficult problems, since the new government inherited a situation in which half, besides large arrears of interest, was in default. The settlement of debts equivalent in principal amount to about US$270 million, or well over 80 per cent of the total foreign debt in arrears, with negotiations begun or planned as to the rest, was a notable feat—especially during the years of depression while defaults were endemic all over the world. Evidence of progress is found in the improvement of yields on leading bonds in the London market to around 5 per cent in 1937. Evidence also is found in the readiness of foreign interests to grant credit to China on a large scale in the latter years of the decade.

The decade saw much progress in public administration. In 1927-1928 competent and experienced administrators were in short supply. In the field of taxation Chinese were moving to higher posts in the Customs and Salt administrations, and the Internal Revenue Service was becoming a respected all-Chinese organization. The Finance Ministry was becoming an integrated administration with improving personnel. The Central Bank became a new and vitally important part of the governmental machinery, as an effective fiscal agent handling receipts and payments and managing loans. Formerly public funds were put in a variety of banks, including foreign banks, and service of foreign loans was handled by them without competition to get the best rates of exchange. Collection of import duties on a gold basis was managed so that the Central Bank received payments mostly in foreign currencies. That avoided the need to buy exchange in the market, and an important incidental advantage was to give the Central Bank experience in currency operations that stood it in good stead when in 1935 the time came to operate a managed currency at stable rates of exchange. The Central Bank also was able to handle foreign purchases and miscellaneous payments abroad for the government. Although many of the operations mentioned were routine, policy matters were often involved. Growth of administrative experience was enabling China to recover by evolution the right to function in more and more fields as a modern-type government should, without the limiting restrictions that were unpalatable to a sovereign country.

The government planned a civil service system, for which rudiments existed in the revenue services along with the tradition of selection by examination. But accomplishments were mostly on paper by 1937. Abolition of the old practice of "squeeze" was part of the government's policy. Much progress was made in curtailing that system, and I feel that progress to that end was greater than in many less developed countries where I have had experience. Yet the old ideas were hard to eradicate, and much of the system remained. Over-staffing with many poorly paid officials was all too common, instead of a lesser number adequately paid and held to proper standards of performance. And despite progress in the civil sector there was far too little progress in control of military finances. There the system of lump-sum payments to top officers gave rise to such abuses as padded payrolls by retaining dead men or deserters on the rolls, and inadequate pay to individual men.

Traditional distrust of government was not conducive to psychological support of government and especially of tax policies. With too much of each tax dollar going for uses which did not specifically and obviously benefit tax-payers, and with inequitable distribution of taxes, it was hard to gain broad support for fiscal policies. Many sincere and loyal men in the government were working to improve conditions. Yet too many used their office for personal advantage, sometimes subtly but sometimes crudely, especially the military.

What was the prospect in mid-1937, had there been no major war, for maintaining fiscal stability for the future? That question is specially important because nationalization of silver and substitution of a fiduciary currency from November 1935 opened the door for possible over-expansion of credit by the government banks to the government and/or the public. The government pledged at the time of the currency reform to balance the budget within eighteen months and avoid inflation.

The budget for fiscal 1938 published in June 1937 stipulated a balance at C$1,001 million. The country was at peace internally; economic recovery was proceeding; a feeling of optimism was in the air;

and the Japanese elections in the spring suggested, although falsely as it proved, a moderation of Japan's policy toward China.

On the revenue side the raising of C$1,001 million seemed within reach. But the problem was with expenditures. There was a strong urge both to promote economic growth and to strengthen China's military posture. Loans equivalent to scores of millions of American dollars were in the works, and the Chinese currency costs of using them would have been substantial. Also there were indications that Minister Kung had the idea, which he frequently stressed during the war, that existence of large reserves in gold and foreign currency could permit monetary expansion without inflation.[31] A further problem was the arrangement made with the private banks at the time of the currency reform, whereby they could obtain banknotes from the government banks by tendering 60 per cent in silver and 40 per cent in government bonds. That arrangement was proving very profitable to the banks, and led to considerable expansion of currency. The arrangement was to end in November 1937. But the pressure to continue it made its ending doubtful, adding a further risk to eventual stability.

Departure from stability did not seem imminent in mid-1937. The balance of payments was favorable and monetary reserves abroad were large (US$379 million equivalent) and increasing. Although prices in China were rising, price recovery was taking place in the rest of the world. Loans to finance internal costs might have been absorbed largely by the public. Nevertheless, for the future there was definite risk that China like so many other countries, including those with advanced economies, would over-expand the money supply and in time jeopardize stability of the currency.

Despite the risks that lay ahead it was clear that by 1937 China's fiscal system was remarkably transformed from the chaotic condition of ten years earlier. The government was beginning to be able to act effectively. The economy was moving forward strongly. I quote the London *Economist* of July 24, 1937 (p. 167):

> All observers seem to be agreed that China has been pulling round with remarkable success during the last year or two. The Central Government's authority has been becoming rapidly more effective over an ever wider area. . . . The financial and economic condition of the country has been distinctly improving.

But although the government was the strongest in generations, it had not developed the fiscal structure to a strength that could withstand the strain that began when Japan's attack at the Marco Polo Bridge on July 7, 1937 forced the country into more than eight years of bitter warfare.

TABLE 3   *Receipts and expenditure, July 1, 1928 to June 30, 1937 (millions of C$)*[a]

Receipts (years ending June 30)

	1929	1930	1931	1932	1933	1934	1935	1936	1937
Revenue									
Customs	179	276	313	370	326	352	353	272	379
Salt	30	122	150	144	158	177	167	184	197
Consolidated taxes									
Rolled tobacco	28[b]	37	46	62	54	71	68	89	110
Cotton yarn			2	17	15	18	16	23	23
Flour	2	4	4	6	6	6	5	6	5
Matches			1	3	4	5	9	10	10
Cement				1	1	2	3	3	5
Cured tobacco						4	4	4	5
Tobacco and wine tax	4	7	9	8	10	13	11	15	15
Stamp tax	3	5	6	5	5	8	7	10	9
Income tax									7
Mining tax					3	2	4	4	4
Banknote tax					5	2	2	2	2
Collections by provincial governments	77[c]	11	4					2	2
Government property receipts						3	2	9	3
Government enterprise receipts[d]				1	20	18	61	67	13
Government administrative receipts						3	11	12	8
Profit on government business enterprises[d]		1	1	2	2	2	1	10	9
Miscellaneous	12	21	25	15	5	4	21	78[e]	68
	334	484	561	633	614	689	745	801	870
Refunded revenues (−), and recovery from suspense (+)		−1	−3	−14		−1		+16	
	334	484	558	619	614	689	745	817	870

	1929	1930	1931	1932	1933	1934	1935	1936	1937
Proceeds from borrowing									
Domestic bonds and treasury notes	69	91	193	125	26	80	164	148	223
Bank loans and overdrafts	32	10	24	5	86	91	36[f]	128	113
Cotton-wheat loan of 1933						8	25		
Cash balance at beginning of fiscal year:									
Customs and Salt services						26	40	73	45[g]
Depositories						2	19	17	
Total	434	585	775	749	726	896	1,031	1,182	1,251

Expenditure (years ending June 30)

	1929	1930	1931	1932	1933	1934	1935	1936	1937
Party	4	5	5	4	5	6	6	8	7
Civil expenses									
National Government Council	4	2	.2	2	2	3			
Executive Yuan and subsidiary organs	22	30	30	23	36	2			
Legislative Yuan and subsidiary organs	0.5	1	1	0.6	1	2			
Supervisory Yuan and subsidiary organs	0.4	0.6	1	0.8	1	2			
Judicial Yuan and subsidiary organs	0.5	0.4	0.1			1			
Examination Yuan and subsidiary organs	0.2	0.6	1	0.6	1	1			
Other civil establishments			5	2	3	5			
National Government Council and subsidiary organs						4	16	15	18
Interior						10	5	13	13
Foreign affairs							9	11	10
Financial		45	60	66	55	72	69	67	64
Educational and cultural						13	32	37	42
Judicial							4	4	3
Industrial						2	7	7	3
Communications						5	7	6	5
Mongolian and Tibetan affairs						2	2	3	2
Reconstruction						7	26	88	54

Capital for government banks	20								
Capital for other government enterprises							74		
Subsidies, provincial and local	4	6	19	23	29	26	55	33	29
Subsidies, other	1	1	0.3	0.4	2	6	1	99	86
Transfers to local authorities from the Salt Revenue Inspectorate		36	48	48	37	23			
Transfers to Special Funds from the Salt Revenue Inspectorate									
Compensation and awards			1	1	1	1	2	2	3
Famine relief	10		2	2	2	4	1		
Miscellaneous	1		1		2				
Military expenses, current fiscal year	147	245	312	255	262	327	330	390	521
Military expenses, previous fiscal years			49	49	59	46	58		
Military expenses, disbursed directly by provinces	62								
Miscellaneous	1		1						
Debt service									
Loans	121	159	241	239	170	203	141	186	192
Domestic bonds							62	62	63
Foreign loans							30	5	7
Bank loans and overdraft									
Indemnity	39	41	49	31	40	42	32	36	38
Debt readjustment fund							5	5	5
Refund of principal and interest on bonds and notes held by Treasury							−32		
Net additions to reserves and suspense items, less refunds	7	2		−7		22	1	−4	
Cash balance at end of fiscal year:									
Customs and Salt services						26	40	73	65
Depositories						2	19	17	45
									83e
Total	434	585	775	749	726	896	1,031	1,182	1,251

Comments:

BY TA-CHUNG LIU

D R. YOUNG'S PAPER presents a concise and balanced description and analysis of the fiscal system and policies of the Republic of China during 1927-1937. After the death of Yuan Shih-k'ai and prior to the capture of Peiping by the Northern Expedition Armies of the National Government, there was no national fiscal system to speak about. The authority of the so-called central government in Peking, dominated by a succession of warlords who held power for short durations, extended hardly beyond the gates of the capital. The main sources of funds of the central government had been foreign and domestic loans.

After the National Government was established in Nanking in 1927, important steps were taken toward the development of a national fiscal system. During this process of transformation of China's fiscal and financial system from a disintegrated chaos to a relatively modern scheme, Dr. Arthur N. Young played a constructive and important role as an adviser to the National Government.

In spite of the tremendous internal and external difficulties which continued to harass the new national authority, impressive achievements were accomplished. Negotiation with the United States for tariff autonomy was successfully concluded in 1928, and most countries had to fall in line afterwards. New and higher tariff rates became effective in February 1929. A more difficult negotiation on tariff autonomy was concluded in 1930 with Japan. The administration of the salt tax (an important source of revenue), originally largely in the hand of foreigners, became an integral part of the Ministry of Finance in 1928. Foreign tobacco-manufacturing companies began to pay specific taxes. The Central Bank was established in 1928. By 1929, national revenue amounted to 334 million Yuan (Chinese dollars), as compared with the few millions available to the government in Peking in 1926.

Efforts continued after 1930 to build a revenue system. In order to counter the long term decline and short run fluctuations in the price of silver in terms of gold, import duties were collected on a gold basis. With autonomy now gained, duties on imports were raised a number of times from 1931 to 1937, both for the purposes of increasing revenue and according some measures of protection to domestic industries. Various special agencies responsible for the collection of different types

of internal revenue were consolidated into the Internal Revenue Administration, staffed wholly by Chinese civil servants, many of whom had
modern training. A number of the recommendations made by the Kemmerer Commission were adopted. Excises were imposed on a few commodities, such as rolled and flue-cured tobacco, cotton yarn, flour,
matches, cement, foreign-style wine, beer, and mineral products. Some
of these taxes were highly regressive, but they gradually replaced the
notorious and corrupt *likin* system which hampered domestic movements of goods. An income tax law was adopted in 1936 which, however,
succeeded only in taxing civil servants. Revenue of the Central Government increased by 160 per cent from 334 million in 1929 to 870 million
yuan in 1937.

Starting in 1931, the National Government began to develop a
budgetary system; by 1937, the system was more or less in operation.
In preparation for the large-scale war with Japan and internal pacifica-
tion, military spending led all other expenditures. Given the circumstances then prevailing, this undesirable situation could hardly have been
avoided. During 1934-37, outlay for education and economic development amounted to about 13 per cent of the total expenditure. In spite
of the rapid increase in government revenue, the share of government
deficits in the total expenditure increased from 12 per cent in 1933 to
25 per cent in 1937. Burdened heavily with internal and external debts
contracted by the now defunct central government in Peking and its
own continuing deficits, the National Government made several successful efforts to rehabilitate and simplify the debt structure. The successful currency reform in 1935 was a major achievement which contributed
significantly to China's ability to resist single-handed the full-scale
Japanese invasion for four years from 1937 to 1941.

Dr. Young came to China early in 1929 as a member of the Kemmerer
Commission, after resigning as the Economic Adviser of the U. S. Department of State. He stayed in China after the Commission's work ended to
become an adviser to the Chinese government. A great deal of the
reform measures outlined in Dr. Young's paper was based upon his recommendations. Among other contributions, the collection of import duties
in gold units and the simplification of the debt structure were formulated
by Dr. Young. He was also assigned to Washington to help the National
government during the Second World War in the negotiation with the
United States for financial and other assistance to China's war effort. This
discussant had the pleasure of meeting Dr. Young at that time in Washington and his services were widely known to be most valuable to the
Chinese Government.

As Dr. Young has pointed out, in spite of the improvements which
took place in the fiscal system during 1927-1937, many weaknesses
remained. The tax system was inelastic and regressive. No major effort

was made to reform taxation on land. Military considerations overrode all other factors, and these resulted in continuous deficits in the budget. In view of the forthcoming Japanese invasion and domestic rebellions during that period, it is doubtful, however, whether a great deal could have been done to reduce military expenditures.

If one must criticize Dr. Young's excellent paper, the following points could be made.

(1) As Dr. Young was aware, the expenditures of the Ministries of Communications and Railways were not included in the budget. The figures on economic development given by Dr. Young, therefore, do not include investment in transportation and communications. Investment in these sectors of economy, however, represented a large share of capital formation during this period. Data on these expenditures are available in several sources. The inclusion of these data would have given a more complete picture of economic development during the decade.

(2) Except in one paragraph following the presentation of Tables 1 and 2, there is relatively little discussion in Dr. Young's paper of the relation of government revenue and expenditure to the entire economy. The proportions of the revenue and expenditure of the Central Government in the national product during 1931-1936 are presented in Table I.

Since prices fell very significantly from 1931 to 1934, Dr. Young's data on revenue and expenditure are converted to constant 1931 Yuan on the basis of Liu's GNP deflator.[a] It is seen that both revenue and expenditure increased much faster in real terms (1931 prices) than indicated by Dr. Young's original data in current prices. The success of the transformation of the fiscal system, when measured in real terms, was therefore greater than when expressed in current prices.

The proportion of central government revenue in GNP increased from 1.43 per cent in 1931 to 2.87 per cent in 1936; however, that of the expenditure in GNP increased almost as rapidly during the same period from 1.99 per cent to 3.77 per cent. The result was, of course, that central government deficits increased also. However, government deficits were never more than one per cent of the gross national product during 1931-36. If this had been a more peaceful period, it would not have been difficult either to increase tax revenue for financing economic development[b] or to wipe out the deficits.

In order to see the total weight of government revenue and expenditure in the national product, data on the budgets of provincial and local governments are required. Dr. Young gave the data for 1936-37; but figures for the earlier years are necessary to observe the trend.

The two points discussed above may have been covered in Dr. Young's forthcoming volume on *China's Nation-Building Effort, 1927-1937: The Financial and Economic Record*. All of us are eagerly looking forward to this new volume.

TABLE I

The Gross National Product and the Revenue and Expenditure of the Central Government

(In constant 1931 Yuan and per cent)

	Revenue[1] (Billions of 1931 Yuan)	Expenditure[1] (Billions of 1931 Yuan)	Deficit[1] (Billions of 1931 Yuan)	GNP[2] (Billions of 1931 Yuan)	Percentage in GNP Revenue (%)	Percentage in GNP Expenditures (%)	Deficits (%)
1931	0.558	0.775	0.217	38.9	1.43	1.99	0.56
1932	0.799	0.966	0.167	40.9	1.95	2.36	0.41
1933	0.904	1.029	0.125	39.3	2.30	2.62	0.32
1934	1.094	1.327	0.233	37.3	2.93	3.56	0.63
1935	1.168	1.475	0.307	40.9	2.86	3.61	0.75
1936	1.184	1.555	0.371	41.3	2.87	3.77	0.90

[1] The basic data are taken from Table 1 of Dr. Young's paper. His figures are then deflated by the GNP deflator in Liu's monograph, cited in footnote 2 below, so that the data given in Table I are in constant 1931 prices. The deflators (1931 = 100) are as follows: 1931, 100; 1932, 77.5; 1933, 67.9; 1934, 63.0; 1935, 63.8; 1936, 69.0.

[2] Liu Ta-chung *China's National Income, 1931-36*, The Brookings Institution, 1949.

CHAPTER IV

Toward Modernization of China's Currency and Banking, 1927–1937

BY CHANG KIA-NGAU

THE USE OF MONEY and the art of banking has a long history in China. Metal coins of gold, silver, and copper made their appearance in the fifth century B.C. Bills of exchange were employed in the tenth century A.D. and by the twelfth century, the use of paper currency had been established. As early as the eleventh century, the government established institutions to provide loans to farmers and to regulate interest rates. Marco Polo remarked favorably in his writings on the art of banking and the highly developed commercial practises based on money and credit in China.

Despite its early and promising origins, the money and banking system of China did not keep pace with developments in Europe during the eighteenth and nineteenth centuries. Geographical barriers and the isolationist policy of the Manchu dynasty kept the Chinese ignorant of the new commercial and banking practises in the West. The self-sufficient agrarian economy of China provided little incentive for the promotion of standardization of currency and expansion of banking. In addition, the lack of adequate systems of communication and transportation and the virtual autonomy of local political entities made the creation of a national organization (e.g. a central bank) nearly impossible.

During the eighteenth and nineteenth centuries, copper coins and silver bullion were the primary exchange mediums. Silver bullion was calculated in terms of the *tael*, which consisted of approximately 530 grains of so-called "standard silver"—.935 fine. A variety of foreign silver dollars, imported in the course of foreign trade with the West, were also used; and beginning in 1889, provincial mints issued silver dollars and fractional silver and copper coins. The defects of this currency system

129

for transactions purposes were numerous: (1) the grains of silver per *tael* varied from city to city; (2) provincial coinage practices were not uniform; (3) the relationship between the *tael* and subsidiary coins was not standard; and finally (4) lax administrative practices permitted debasement and counterfeiting of currency. Complaints from the foreign merchants led to an article in the MacKay Treaty of Commerce and Navigation with Great Britain in 1902 which stipulated that China would take the necessary steps to provide for a uniform national coinage. The attempt of the Manchu regime in 1870 to establish the "Dragon" dollar as the standard unit of exchange with fixed relationships to fractional currency failed due to the debility of the dynasty.

China's banking institutions also reflected the nation's isolation and agrarian economy. At the end of the nineteenth century, the "native banks" retained the same character as when they were first instituted— in the twelfth century. The three kinds of native banks were (1) money changers (*ch'ien p'u*), (2) money lenders (*ch'ien-chuang*), and (3) remittance banks (*p'iao-hao*). Of these banks, the money lenders in the treaty ports and the remittance banks were the most important. The money lenders acted as intermediaries between traders in the interior and foreign merchants. The remittance banks were initiated and operated solely by men from Shansi province and were often called "Shansi Banks." These banks were established throughout China; they undertook the remittance of central and provincial government funds and sent government officials' income to their families. The weakness of the native banks stemmed from limitations on their size, capital, and geographic range. This was the result of family and partner ownership, inefficient banking practices, and a loan system secured solely by personal credit. Many of the native banks were free to issue notes redeemable in silver *taels* or in copper coins.

From 1896 onward, provincial government banks began to mushroom. They operated much like the native banks. Because of a lack of central supervision, some of the paper notes issued by the native and provincial banks depreciated or became irredeemable.

The banks of foreign treaty powers began to operate under the shields of extraterritorial rights in treaty ports from the end of the 1840's. They enjoyed the rights of issuing notes, accepting any type of deposit, and acting as custodians of custom revenues pledged for Chinese foreign debt services. Because they were able to operate free of government interference, the treaty port foreign banks gained the confidence of the wealthy Chinese. The banks' deposits and note issues increased and their influence began to penetrate into the interior.

In imitation of foreign banks, three modern Chinese banks were established around the turn of the century. In 1896, the Imperial Bank of China, a private bank, came into existence. It was patterned after the British Hong Kong and Shanghai Banking Corporation. The Government granted the Imperial Bank the right to issue notes, to handle government funds, and to be under government supervision. In 1904, the government-sponsored Hu-Pu (Board of Finance) Bank, intended to be the central bank, was set up by the Board of Finance on the model of the Bank of Japan. This predecessor of the Bank of China was chartered to issue notes, to act as the agent of the Treasury, and to handle the coinage of national currencies. In 1908, the Bank of Communications was established by the Board of Posts and Communications. This bank was intended to facilitate financing of Chinese industry and was patterned after Japan's Industrial Bank. The Bank of Communications, however, was given the same rights as the Hu-Pu Bank. Since the remittance business of the Shansi banks was taken over by the government banks, the Shansi banks declined while the other native banks were left unaffected.

Following the promulgation of a banking act in 1908 governing the establishment of private banks, three more private commercial banks were set up. Like the Imperial Bank of China, they also enjoyed the right of issuing notes.

China's entry into modern banking was not auspicious. Though the government banks were entrusted with different tasks, the assignment of complete banking powers to both negated the central banking concept. There was no supervision over the provincial, private, and native banks. Many of the early note issues of the provincial and native banks depreciated rapidly and were soon worthless.

I

The Condition of Currency and Banking Before 1927-1928

After the establishment of the Republic in 1912, there was hope that a thorough-going reform of currency and banking would take place. The emergence of new leadership in the field of government finance augured favorably for reform. The hope was shattered, however, by President Yuan Shih-k'ai's monarchical aspirations and by his declaration of a moratorium on the redemption of bank notes and withdrawal of deposits from the two government banks. This move, quite naturally, shook people's confidence in the new Chinese banks. Yuan Shih-k'ai's death in 1916 was followed by a long period of warlordism and concomitantly a fractionalization of governmental authority. During this period, there was very little improvement in currency and banking stemming from the policy and leadership of the central government. Instead, however, Chinese banking leaders took the initiative and promoted measures to bring China's money and banking practices up to modern standards.

Currency

Under the administration of Liang Chi-chao, as Minister of Finance, the National Coinage Act was enacted in 1914. The Act called for the standardization of the dollar, the abolition of the *tael*, and the adoption of the silver standard. Liang was convinced that the gold standard was preferable, but that its establishment would be greatly facilitated when currency uniformity was achieved. The first step taken under the new act was the establishment of a central mint at Tientsin to mint the new "Yuan Shih-k'ai" dollars. Because uniformity standards were rigidly observed, because the two government banks cooperated in exchanging old dollars and silver bullion for the new dollars, and due to the increasing demand for currency by merchant's trading in the interior, the new dollars were initially quite popular and soon became widely accepted.

These favorable developments were soon negated by the instability of the government. Because of this instability, the confidence of the foreign banks, the merchants, and the people in the ability of the government to maintain a standard of value was shaken. The foreign banks and the native banks, which were more powerful than the government and the modern Chinese banks, preferred to continue the use of the *tael* as a unit of account. By so doing, they forced the entire country into a dualistic monetary system with new dollars, as well as old, being expressed in terms of *taels*. The deleterious effects of the continued use of *taels* were more pronounced because of the seasonal nature of the Chinese agricultural system. As an example, the merchants who went into the interior to bring tea and silk to the ports had to borrow great quantities of dollars to pay the peasants. Repayment on the dollar loans were stipulated in terms of *taels*. Since all merchants went into the interior at the same time, there naturally arose an excess demand for dollars, thus increasing its price in terms of *taels*. When the merchants returned, sold their goods in the port, and went to repay their loans, there was an excess demand for *taels*, thus increasing the price of *taels*. Merchants were therefore forced to borrow when *taels* were cheap and repay when they were dear. In 1919, the *tael*/dollar rate fluctuated from 74.06 Shanghai *taels* per 100.00 dollars to 72.92 *taels* per 100.00 dollars. Also, due to this dualistic currency situation, merchants had to open two accounts—one in *taels* and the other in dollars. Banks in turn had to keep two kinds of reserves. In addition, no interest was paid by the native and foreign banks on dollar accounts nor could banks earn interest on their dollar reserves. This entailed not only inconvenience to the merchants and banks, but also a waste of their capital funds.

The new dollar was further weakened by the eclipse of the central government's power after 1919. The provincial mints became more independent of the central mint and issued dollars without regard to the needs of the economy. The effect was such an excess supply of money that the dollar value dropped below the mint rate of 72.50 Shanghai *taels* per 100.00 dollars. In the period 1921-26, the high monthly average never exceeded 72.78 *taels* and was as low as 71.66 *taels* per 100.00 dollars. This resulted in a loss to those holding dollars and created anxiety over the future of the dollar as a store of value.

The National Coinage Act of 1914 stipulated that the token subsidiary coins should also be standardized and that the decimal system be instituted. This provision was never implemented. The subsidiary coins, silver and copper, also continued to be expressed in terms of *taels*. The central mint began to produce new subsidiary coins in 1916 and attempted to enforce the decimal system in the region around Tientsin. The attempt was soon abandoned. At the end of the First World War, metal prices dropped and this, together with improvements in transportation, increased Chinese metal imports. This situation tempted the provincial mints to augment their profits by increasing production of both silver and copper coins. Initially, they observed the stipulated fineness of 70 per cent silver and 30 per cent copper for 20-cent and 10-cent silver coins and 95 per cent copper, 4 per cent tin, and 1 per cent lead for copper coins. Before long, however, these coins were debased. Their fineness varied according to the mint which issued them. There were thirty kinds of silver coins in Shanghai in 1926. The most inferior 20-cent silver coins contained only 67.3 per cent silver in 1920 and 51.7 per cent silver in 1921, while the copper content of copper coins fell to about 70 per cent. Token coinage standards were naturally weakened by debasement, variety, and the counterfeiting which the first two factors prompted. By far the most serious impediment to standardization of coinage, however, was the extensive over-supply of coins from the provincial mints. They flooded the market, thereby causing the value to drop rapidly. At the time of the promulgation of the Act, the ratio between the dollar and 10-cent silver coins averaged up to 12.87. In 1926, the high monthly average was nineteen 10-cent coins to the dollar. In the same period, the number of copper coins needed to constitute a dollar, rose from 130 to 265.

Inevitably the retail prices of daily necessities rose as the value of copper coins fell. This created a serious social problem. The Shanghai Chamber of Commerce requested the two government banks in Shanghai to issue subsidiary coin notes which could be used as a means of pay-

ment and store of value within the Shanghai Settlement. They began
to issue these notes at the end of 1926. Many other port cities requested
the local authorities to prohibit the importation of debased coins. The
provinces which minted coins banned the importation of other provinces'
coins. This disordered and confused situation was worsened by the subsidiary notes issued by provincial banks. These paper notes were backed
mainly by small coins, silver and copper. Out of twenty provinces, only
six had notes which circulated at face value; some became totally
irredeemable.

Along with the attempt to standardize the national coinage, the
government acted to withdraw provincial paper notes. In 1915, an act
governing the issuance of paper notes was promulgated. It stipulated
that (1) any banking institution which had the right of note issue under
special government permission was allowed to continue issuing notes
until the expiration of its charter, (2) any banking institution which did
not have special permission was required to limit its monthly issue to an
amount which was the average of the latest three months, (3) a bank
without special permission must withdraw its notes within a period fixed
by the Ministry of Finance, (4) notes issued must be backed by 50 per
cent cash and 50 per cent bonds and commercial papers. But owing to
the political disturbance, government measures to withdraw provincial
notes were successful only in Kwangtung province and soon discontinued. Provisions for controlling notes issued never became effective.
Despite subsequent frequent admonitions by the central government,
little heed was paid by the warlords.

As the wave of internal war rose, the warlords relied upon printing
paper notes to defray their military expenses. They made up the declining value of notes by printing more notes. The amount of issue rose
from 163 million dollars in 1914 to 500 million dollars in 1926. This flood
of money was largely responsible for an increase in the Shanghai price
index by 71 per cent between February 1913 and October 1926.[1] At first,
the inferior silver and copper coins had driven the better ones out of
circulation. Now the depreciated paper notes drove out the metal coins.

Fortunately, the two government banks, Bank of China and Bank of
Communications, made efforts to uphold the credit of their note issues.
This constituted a counter force against the deluge of depreciated provincial notes. There were five distinct measures which were taken by
the government banks to insure that their note issues were honored and
dispersed. First, by refusing to obey Yuan Shih-k'ai's moratorium order
on cash payment of deposits and bank notes, the Shanghai Branch of
the Bank of China inspired the people's confidence in its note issues.
The Shanghai Branch of the Bank of Communications followed the
order but soon resumed cash payment. Second, the two government

banks made efforts to completely withdraw the irredeemable notes of their branches in the vicinity of Peking. These branches had submitted to the moratorium order, but at the same time, they were forced to lend large sums of depreciated money to the government. The withdrawal, which took four years to accomplish, was achieved as the government retired its debt by issuing bonds. Third, the two government banks concentrated their issue of notes and kept their cash reserves in port cities such as Shanghai and Tientsin where they were free of the warlords' interference. Fourth, in order to induce modern commercial banks and native banks to forfeit their right to issue notes, the Shanghai Branch of the Bank of China instituted a system in 1915 whereby the modern banks were allowed to use notes of the Bank of China. This system was further extended to native banks in 1924. The modern and native banks could draw up to a certain limit upon paying 60 per cent of the value in cash and 40 per cent in securities. To inspire confidence in this scheme, the modern and native banks were invited to participate in regular examinations of the Bank of China's note reserve structure. Fifth, the Shanghai Branch of the Bank of China concluded an agreement with pawn shops, silk, tea, and salt merchants. They would use Bank of China notes as partial payment of their purchases from producers. The bank, in return, extended various commercial privileges not open to non-participants in the agreement. The amount of notes issued by the Bank of China increased from 46,437,000 dollars in 1916 to 159,001,000 dollars in 1927 and that of the Bank of Communications from 21,297,000 dollars to 65,096,000 dollars in the same period. The notes of five modern commercial banks in circulation in 1927 amounted to about 37,000,000 dollars. These three categories of notes constituted the backbone of Chinese paper currency.

The foreign banknotes circulating in China was mainly those issued by the British banks in Hong Kong, French banks in Indo-China, and Japanese banks in Dairen. They penetrated into the neighboring areas of China: Kwangtung province, Yunnan province, and South Manchuria. The amount of foreign banknotes issued by their branches in the port settlements of Shanghai, Tientsin and Hankow was relatively small. Since the expansion of notes issued by the two government banks and modern commercial banks, the latter category of foreign banknotes lost its traditional importance. In 1927, notes issued by foreign banks in the port cities amounted to only about 5 million dollars.

The above developments clearly show that issue of banknotes in the treaty port cities and Peking, the primary financial centers, tended to be concentrated in the two government banks. On its face, the concentration of note issuing power in the two government banks was a favorable step toward currency unification. Offsetting this, however, was

popular feeling that if the govenment banks were each allowed to issue
their own notes, then provincial banks should also be allowed to do so.
This had the effect of delaying unification of paper currency.

Banking

The growth of banking from the birth of the Republic was made
possible by the stability and independence of the management of the
two government banks and by the entrepreneurical spirit displayed by
leaders of both the government and private banks. The independence
of the government banks was guaranteed by new charters issued by the
government. The Bank of China obtained its charter in 1917. The charter
embodied the traditional spirit of the Bank of England and the Bank of
Japan in the following respects: (1) the election of directors by the
shareholders, not appointment by the government, (2) long tenure of
the chief executives, (3) close cooperation with the Treasury but not
submission to it, and (4) the governor and vice-governor were to be
appointed by the government from among the directors and with the
same tenure as the directors. It further stipulated that both government
and private shares in the bank's capital were to enjoy the same rights
without discrimination.

This charter aroused the enthusiasm of bankers, industrialists and
the wealthy class, and raised private shares in the Bank of China from
3,643,300 dollars to 7,279,800 dollars in 1917. The government's shares
in the same year amounted to 5 million dollars for a total capitalization
of 12,279,800 dollars. By 1927, private shares had increased to 15 million dollars, thus giving the bank a total capital of 20 million dollars
on the eve of the Nationalist government. Another measure of the Bank's
growth was the increase in its deposits. They increased from 148,695,000
dollars in 1917 to 330,497,000 dollars in 1927, an increase of 122 per cent.
Despite several attempts by members of the An-fu party in the legislative body to modify the charter in favor of more government control
over the bank, the bank was able to maintain its traditional independence. This was due in large measure to strong public opinion
favoring the bank. This favorable sentiment had been engendered by
the bank authorities' firm emphasis on the integrity of its officials, the
efficiency of its operations, and a policy of service to the people.

The Bank of Communications' government/private capitalization
ratio of 60 per cent/40 per cent was reaffirmed by its new charter in
1914. Its directors were elected by the shareholders, but unlike the Bank
of China, its president and vice-president were also elected. Its traditional favored position was undoubtedly strengthened by the continued
independence of the Bank of China. Its progress was also striking—its

deposits amounted to 158,311,000 dollars in 1927 as against 38,536,000 dollars in 1917.

Due to the overlapping of their governmental functions, there was at times a waste of financial resources by the two government banks. Overall, however, the strength of these two banks stimulated growth of commercial banks and the increased financing of trade and industry.

In addition to the two government banks, commercial banking was spurred by the change from the Manchu monarchy to the Republic. It aroused public enthusiasm for adoption of Western institutions, political and economic. It also served to stimulate the initiative of the students of economics and finance who had studied abroad. These students foresaw the inability of native banks to meet the demands generated by the changing economic conditions under the new Republic and they wanted to establish foreign type financial institutions in China. Meanwhile, China benefitted by the First World War. A lack of imports encouraged domestic industry, crop conditions were favorable and a period of prosperity ensued. The development of modern private banks made steady progress. According to the *China's Bankers Handbook* (1927), there were fifty-seven modern banks by 1927; of this number forty-eight were private commercial banks, with about 80 million dollars of capital subscribed. In addition, two jointly-owned banks, a Sino-Japanese (The Exchange Bank of China) with a capital of 5 million *Yen* and a Sino-American bank (The Bank of Commerce, China) with a capital of 7.5 million U.S. dollars, were set up. These banks, however, despite being more heavily capitalized than the Chinese modern commercial banks, were not able to establish themselves in the Chinese or foreign community. The Chinese who entered into arrangements with the Japanese and Americans were ex-government officials interested in short-term returns, not in developing viable businesses. Relations between the Chinese and foreign partners lacked the cohesiveness necessary for successful banking operations. Further, the Chinese public, particularly in this era of emergent nationalism, favored their own banks over those that involved foreigners.

Out of total deposits of 360 million dollars held by the forty-eight modern commercial banks, 80 per cent was held by ten banks. These leading banks were the National Commercial Bank, Kincheng Banking Corporation, Yien Yieh Commercial Bank, China and South Sea Bank, Shanghai Commercial and Savings Bank, Ningpo Commercial and Savings Bank, Continental Bank, Chekiang Industrial Bank, Four Banks Joint Savings Society, and the National Industrial Bank of China. Their operations reflected all of the modern commercial practices—making loans backed by warehouse receipts, accepting trade bills accompanied by documents issued by railroads or steamship lines, accepting savings, opening of silver dollar accounts on which interest was paid, using checks, conducting foreign exchange operations, and establishing branch offices. In carrying out these operations, the banks utilized modern accounting systems. Few of these practices had been employed by the native banks. At the same time, the few Chinese banks provided better service to its Chinese customers than the foreign banks who were hampered by the language barrier and an incomplete understanding of the customer's mentality. Therefore, more and more business flowed from native and foreign banks into the Chinese commercial banks in the port cities.

The banking situation in these cities underwent a great change. The small commercial banks jammed in the port cities and Peking were squeezed by the big banks on one side and the native banks on the other as they were unable to provide facilities and services that could be offered by the other two institutions. To attract business, the small banks had to resort to bad banking practices. They paid higher interest in order to compete for deposits; this forced them to seek high yield, and concomitantly high risk investments for their funds. Some banks made loans to the Peking government which was in financial straits and willing to pay high interest; or they bought high interest government bonds which were sold at discount prices. Other banks made loans to customers of low credit standing or speculated on industrial stocks. This misutilization of resources stood uncorrected because of a lack of proper government supervision or indirect control from a central bank.

Meanwhile, there was a growing geographic concentration of the banking system in the port cities and the government capital. The government banks kept their reserves almost exclusively in the major port cities. Among the forty-eight modern commercial banks, one third had their headquarters in Shanghai and another third were operated from Tientsin and Peking. The internal struggles between the warlords prompted their movements of capital to the port cities for security. This greatly weakened the credit system in the interior. The unbalance between the development of banking in the major cities and in the interior aggravated the deterioration of the rural economy brought about by increasing internal warfare. Agriculture played a predominate role in the economic growth of the country. More than 80 per cent of the national product and from 70 to 80 per cent of exported goods originated on the land.

While the modern commercial banks were growing in number and strength, the native banks found that their position was deteriorating. Traditionally, their position rested upon their ability to issue native bank orders in *taels,* their closer contact with merchants, the close ties between native banks in the port cities and the interior, simpler procedures and low overhead expenses. This foundation of banking influence was undermined by the larger capitalization and better services of the modern banks. In addition, the modern banks, through their branches, established close ties with native banks in the interior. By opening *tael* accounts in the native banks, the modern banks were able to furnish their patrons with native bank orders.

Though the number of native banks changed little from year to year, their individual strength diminished as they did not have the financial facilities to cope with the demands of the growing industrial and trade sectors. The total resources of the native banks in the main industry and trade centers, such as Shanghai, Tientsin and Hankow, amounted to about 11.1 million dollars or only 25 per cent of the resources of the ten leading banks. Native bank resources in other cities were negligible.

Further deterioration of the strength of native banks in Tientsin and Hankow was occasioned by outbreaks of civil war in the vicinity and the resulting destruction of agricultural production and trade. The diminution of native banks' strength had an adverse impact on the supply of commercial credits inasmuch as the modern banks were not able to service all of the former customers of the native banks. The modern banks were not in a position to grant credits on personal credit, and many merchants were unaccustomed to dealing with modern financial institutions.

The foreign banks in China suffered a rapid series of catastrophies which served to weaken the confidence of the Chinese business community and wealthy class in foreign banks. The Deutsch-Asiatic Bank in China was taken over by the Chinese government in 1914 upon declaration of war against Germany; shortage of funds caused suspension of the Banque-Industrialle de Chine in 1921; and the Russo-Asiatic Bank was liquidated after the Bolshevik revolution. On the other hand, the American and Japanese banks grew in number and activities as a result of increases in trade and investments. The British banks, led by the Hong Kong and Shanghai Banking Corporation, were able to maintain their dominant position among the foreign banks in China. There were twenty foreign banks which were considered to be of greatest importance. They were branches or subsidiaries of large foreign · institutions and conducted complete banking operations. There were four British, three American, six Japanese, two Dutch banks and one each for France, Germany, Belgium, Italy and Soviet Russia. Each treaty power had its own financial institutions to look after its national interests. In addition, there were forty-two foreign banks organized by local interests or specializing in certain fields of business, among which twenty-five belonged to Japan and were located in Manchuria.

The foreign banks were an obstacle to efforts for unifying the currency, establishing a Central Bank and adoption of the gold standard. The foreign banks continued to use silver bullion as a means of payment and monopolized the foreign exchange business. Payment for imports, foreign debt service, exports proceeds, and overseas Chinese remittances were handled almost entirely by the foreign banks. In addition, the Hong Kong and Shanghai Banking Corporation held a major share of customs and salt revenue. This revenue served as security for the payment of principal and interest on foreign loans which had been made to the government. Small additional shares were held by the Banque de L'Indochine and Yokohama Specie Bank.

In concluding this description of the currency and banking system prior to 1927-28, it is well to summarize the problems and deficiencies of the earlier period in order to bring into sharper focus the measures undertaken during the "nation-building" era. With respect to currency, the most important issue was the institution of a standard uniform dollar and the standardization of subsidiary coins. To accomplish this goal, it would be necessary to abolish the *tael*, terminate the note issuing rights of provincial and private commercial banks, and establish a single note issuing authority. In the field of banking, the major concern was the establishment of a central bank, which of course entailed a redefinition of the roles of the two existing government banks. The lack of effective banking in the interior seriously hampered rural economic development and the extension of government and commercial bank branches into the interior was of prime importance. To further encourage industrial development, it would be necessary to implement the use of commercial bills and rediscounting of these bills by a central bank. Government supervision of all commercial banks, domestic and foreign, was a further step needed for an effective banking policy. Finally, the practice of depositing government revenues with the foreign banks and the foreign monopoly in foreign exchange would have to be terminated.

II

The National Government's Role in
Developing Chinese Banking, 1928

Following the unification of the whole country and the establishment of the National Government in Nanking, the Ministry of Finance set about the task of founding a state central bank. It was first decided that the bank would be named the Central Bank of China. This name was closely associated with Dr. Sun Yat-sen. He had set up a Central Bank of China in Canton in 1924.

Initially, the financial authorities weighed the merits of establishing a new bank or converting the Bank of China into the Central Bank. When I[2] was approached on this question, I advanced the opinion that the disadvantages of making the Bank of China the state central bank were greater than the advantages to be gained from utilizing an existing institution. To change the name "Bank of China" would shake the people's confidence in the bank, a confidence which had been built up slowly over many years. To those not conversant in financial affairs, a change in name would forbode a change in policy and in the bank's stability and could affect the immediate financial needs of the new government. Furthermore, the Bank of China had begun to acquire recognition and good credit standing in international banking circles, a necessary ingredient in developing the foreign exchange business. To alter its existing structure and tie the Bank to the fledgling National Government would affect the Bank of China's standing. I further proposed that since China's economic heritage was more closely identical to Japan's rather than the Western nations that the Japanese central banking group system be adopted. This proposal was accepted by the Minister of Finance, T. V. Soong. The charter of the Central Bank of China and the revised charter of the Bank of China and Bank of Communications were promulgated on October 15, 1928, October 26, 1928, and November 16, 1928, respectively.

In his report to the Party National Congress in 1929, Minister Soong outlined the functions of the new state bank and the revised duties of the two existing government banks:

> To maintain the currency and oversee movements of the money market it was necessary to establish a state bank, the Central Bank of China. This bank will be responsible for executing these duties and, at the same time, for laying down a foundation for the whole banking system. The Bank of China is assigned responsibility for development of the foreign exchange business in order to restore the loss in influence China has long suffered in international financial circles. In view of the importance of promoting industry, the Bank of Communications is assigned responsibility for industrial finance.

Central Bank of China

The capital of the Central Bank of China was fixed at C$ (Chinese dollar or *yuan*) 20 million and paid up by the government. The articles of the charter provided that in case an increase of capital was desired, public subscription would be accepted, but only up to 49 per cent of total capitalization. The bank was given special rights: issue of banknotes, minting and distribution of coins, depository and fiscal agent of the Treasury and agent of the Government in floating and servicing domestic and foreign loans. It was also authorized to transact general banking business including the acceptance of all kinds of deposits; the Ministry of Finance put off the idea of a bankers' bank until conditions were more favorable. The Bank was not allowed to make unsecured loans, loans on real estate, merchandize or bonds, or on stocks and debentures of any corporation, nor was the bank allowed to purchase securities or direct interests in industrial and commercial undertakings. The governor and deputy governor were to be appointed by the Government from the nine directors who were also appointed. Three directors were chosen as representatives of industrial, commercial, and banking interests. The charter further stipulated that the head office of the bank was to be established in Shanghai, the banking center of China, rather than the government capital, Nanking. It appeared that the financial authorities felt that the Central Bank's success hinged on its identification with the modern banking institutions in Shanghai. Further, the Central Bank's duties required that it exert influence over the money markets in that region of the lower Yangtze River. The initial policy regulations of the Bank were modeled after the Bank of China and stipulated that the reserve for notes issued should be open to public examination, and that the number of notes issued and the amount of reserves kept should be published every ten days. This measure appeared to be aimed at preventing possible excessive issue of notes caused by financing the government budget deficit.

The Central Bank began operation in November 1928 with the appointment of the Minister of Finance to serve concurrently as governor of the bank. Only four months after its opening, a run on the bank took place stemming from nonacceptance of its notes by money exchange shops. The shops reacted to the news of the struggle between the Government and a number of generals in Hunan province. It was expected that the first reaction of the public to Central Bank notes in a time of political disturbance would be unfavorable. But because the credibility of adequate notes reserves was maintained by the arrangement of the 60 per cent cash reserve on notes and the open examination of notes issue and reserves, the run only lasted three days and only a small number of notes were withdrawn. This experience proved beneficial as favorable public opinion enabled the bank to withstand several subsequent political turmoils of a graver nature. Henceforth, the bank made steady progress. By 1934, total notes issued amounted to C$86,048,617 and total deposits were C$272,592,827 and by the end of that year, there were thirty-three branches in ten provinces (Kiangsu, Chekiang, Anhwei, Kiangsi, Hupeh, Honan, Hopei, Shantung, Fukien, and Kansu). In addition to this growth, the Bank played a key role as the depository and fiscal agent of the Treasury. Where possible, all government agencies carried on their official transactions through the Central Bank. By 1934, 70 per cent of the Bank's deposits originated from government institutions. Further, the bank collected, and was the depository for, all government revenues. In 1933, this revenue amounted to C$442,235,000.

Bank of China

The revised charter of the Bank of China gave it special duties in the area of foreign financial transactions. The new charter made no fundamental changes in the organization of the bank, except in the composition of the Board of Directors. Three of the fifteen directors and one of the three supervisors were to be appointed by the Ministry of Finance. The Board elected five managing directors who elected the General Manager and from whom a Chairman of the Board was to be designated by the Ministry of Finance. In the previous charter, the Ministry of Finance cast its votes for election of directors and supervisors as private shareholders. The previous government's share of C$5 million had been sold to private interests; the new government replenished this sum and enlarged the Bank's capital to C$25 million. The Bank functioned as: (1) the government agency for floating loans abroad and servicing the payment of principal and interest, (2) the depository and fiscal agency of the government abroad, (3) the financial agency for the development of foreign trade and (4) the depository for Treasury funds in areas not covered by the Central Bank. The Bank of China was allowed to continue issuing notes with the government's special permission. Meanwhile, the Bank informed the Ministry of Finance that it intended to relinquish this right in the interests of unifying the currency, provided that the debts owed by the previous and present governments could be liquidated.

In developing the foreign exchange business, the Bank of China started off with a weak foundation. The Bank held only about one million sterling in Chinese Government Gold Bonds bought during the First World War and only the Hong Kong Branch of the Bank had personnel trained in foreign exchange operations. Now the Bank set upon the task of extending its foreign exchange activities by (1) providing services to the recipients of overseas remittances in Hong Kong, Swatow, Canton, and Amoy, and, at the same time, appointing overseas Chinese banks in Singapore, Bangkok, Manila as its agencies to obtain remittances, (2) establishing its own agencies in London, Osaka, Singapore, and New York and designating correspondents in other major cities of the world, (3) inviting a foreign exchange expert from Darmstadter and National Bank, Berlin, to assist in organizing a Foreign Exchange Department and training personnel, (4) obtaining an expert in accounting from Midland Bank, London, to assist in reforming the accounting system in order to improve the working efficiency of both domestic and foreign operations.

The total amount of foreign exchange transactions in 1932, 1933, and 1934, as reported in the Bank's annual report was C$161 million, C$956 million, and C$989 million respectively. Taking the 1933 devaluation of U.S. dollars into account, the increase in foreign exchange transactions from 1932 to 1934 was four-fold. Due to the concentration of foreign trade in foreign firms, however, the Bank of China obtained very little foreign exchange from trade. Therefore, the Bank had to utilize its resources in domestic trade and industry. After the loss of Manchuria in 1931 and consequent reduction of China's exports by one-third, the Bank intensified its assistance to domestic exporting and import competing industries in the hope of improving the adverse balance of payments. Between 1928 and 1934, due to the change of emphasis from note issue to deposits, the former increased only 14 per cent from C$179,304,026 to C$204,713,465, while the latter increased by 42 per cent, from C$387,688,787 to C$546,693,902.

Bank of Communications

The revised charter of the Bank of Communications gave it primary responsibility for fostering the growth of Chinese domestic industry. To achieve this purpose the bank was entrusted with the following functions: (1) issuing and servicing debentures of public industrial organizations, (2) acting as the fiscal agency of public transportation and communications enterprises, (3) finding methods to promote and develop industry, and (4) handling Treasury transactions in areas where the Central Bank was not yet established. The Bank was allowed to continue issuing notes with the Government's special permission. The Ministry of Finance contributed C$2 million in order to augment the original capital of C$8 million held by private interests. The procedures for election of directors and the general manager and the designation of the Chairman of the Board was similar to that of the Bank of China.

After the re-organization, the Bank attempted to carry out its responsibility by increasing its financing of industry. But due to the lack of internal peace, Japanese aggression in Manchuria, Communist ravages in the regions south of the Yangtze, and disastrous floods affecting ten provinces in 1932, most domestic industries were in a perilous situation. Under these circumstances, the Bank could hardly make comprehensive plans for industrial financing and was compelled to confine its activities to setting up more warehouses and making loans secured by merchandise. Between 1928 and 1934, the amount of notes issued increased by 65 per cent, from C$68,076,114 to C$112,512,472. However, deposits increased only by 16 per cent, from C$150,944,448 to C$253,210,314.

The establishment of the Central Bank of China and the redirection of the Bank of China and Bank of Communications were but the first steps in the development of a sound banking system. Historical experience has shown that achievement of this goal is a long evolutionary process. Although the Japanese experience differed, the political and economic development of Japanese banking is instructive in this regard. The government of Japan followed a very cautious policy with respect to the expansion of notes issued by the Bank of Japan. In the period of rapid economic growth in the nineteenth century, the government placed strict limits on the number of notes which could be issued with security backing. Even during the Russo-Japanese War (1904-05), the Bank's advances to the government were small compared to the size of its assets. The effect of this cautious policy was that the value of money was maintained and confidence in the Bank remained strong. The Yokohama Specie Bank and the Industrial Bank likewise expanded their financing at a pace compatible with the growth of trade and industry. The Yokohama Specie Bank (established in 1880) took thirty years of painstaking effort in channeling imports and exports to Japanese firms to build their level of foreign trade financing in 100 million *Yen*.[3] The Industrial Bank (established in 1902) attained a level of industrial financing of 40 million *Yen* after ten years.[4] On the basis of the Japanese experience, it was to be expected that the Bank of China and Bank of Communications would have to depend on general traditional banking business in the early stage of banking history. The demand for their full time entry into their specialized fields was still undeveloped. Hence, competition with the government bank would continue for a time.

Modern Commercial Banks

The Chinese government's realistic policy toward the central banking group was also applied to private banks. When the central government was established, the Ministry of Finance intended to set up a bank supervisory office in Shanghai. Realizing the difficulty of executing its authority in foreign settlements, however, this proposal for close supervision was dropped and the private banks were required only to register with and send annual reports to the Ministry. This *laissez-faire* policy resulted in a rapid increase of new commercial banks, from forty-eight in 1927 to 110 in 1931. The deposits of these banks grew to more than half those of the central banking group and the range and quality of their services also expanded.

III

The Strength and Stability of Chinese Banking
Under the Silver Standards, 1927-1934

Under the silver standard, the financial strength of the banks depended on their holdings of silver reserves and their stability was contingent on the liquidity of their assets. This was particularly true in
China where the initial reaction of the people to any type of instability
was to hoard precious metals. At the beginning of the new regime,
several factors emerged which were favorable to the growth of Chinese
banking. They were, first, the hopeful prospect of political unity and
stability; and, second, the realistic policy of the authorities in dealing
with financial matters. Bonds issued by the previous government were
recognized, the continuity of Bank of China and Bank of Communications was maintained, and the notes reserves of the Central Bank of
China were opened to public examination. Next, a spirit of national
self-reliance in financial and economic matters emerged. This, in turn,
stimulated the officials of the central banking group and private bank
leaders and reestablished the confidence of the people in Chinese banks.
Finally, the abolition of the *tael* meant that native and foreign banks
which had dealt in *taels* almost exclusively were at a disadvantage with
respect to the modern banks. The abolition of the *tael* also facilitated the
extension of the use of the dollar and increased dollar deposits of the
modern banks thereby giving them a further advantage. Between 1927
and 1934, the notes issue of the central banking group almost doubled
and deposits increased by more than 70 per cent (see Tables A and B).

Growth was also reflected in the number of commercial banks which
were newly established. In 1927, there were fifty-seven; in 1934, there
were 138. There was also a trend toward increasing concentration among
the larger banks; the ten leading banks held nearly one half of the total
commercial deposits (see Table C and the last column of Table B).
Economies of scale enabled them to provide more services and departments, such as savings, trust, foreign exchange, and travel, for their
customers.

The strength of all Chinese banks increased greatly; the quantity of
silver stocks held by Chinese banks in Shanghai in 1934 was twenty
times that of 1913 and three and one half times that of 1926. The rise
in the silver stocks of Chinese banks was particularly important compared with foreign banks' silver holdings. In 1921, the Chinese holdings
were less than half of foreign holdings; from 1926 onward, the Chinese
holdings were at least equal to or greater than foreign holdings (see
Table D). Although the foreign banks held an edge in terms of foreign

exchange, the Chinese banks were able to compete with them in terms of silver holdings.

The stability of Chinese banks was subjected to an acid test in early 1932 when, as mentioned above, the Japanese were engaged in a bitter battle outside Shanghai. The Chinese Chamber of Commerce requested all business organizations to stop operations for three days; this was quickly extended for another three days. At this time, the banking community was concerned about a run on the banks when they re-opened. The Bank of China took the lead in favoring early resumption of operations despite the continuing battle. All of the banks reopened on February 4; unexpectedly, there was no run on notes and deposits. For the purpose of further consolidating the position of Chinese banks to meet the present and future contingencies, the Joint Reserve Board of Shanghai Bankers' Association was established. Twenty-six banks subscribed a reserve fund of 70 million Shanghai *taels.* Joint reserve notes were issued for circulation in the market in lieu of cash, joint treasury certificates were used as security reserves for banknote issues, and security certificates were accepted as loan security between members of the Board. A similar joint reserve board was established by the Shanghai Native Banks' Association with seventy native banks, each contributing a minimum reserve of 200,000 Shanghai *taels.* Some deposited over one million *taels* each. Their total reserve exceeded 37 million *taels.* In Tientsin, twenty modern banks and thirty-seven native banks combined to contribute to a joint reserve amounting to C$5 milion. A similar reserve fund was established in Hangchow. As a result of these arrangements, current panic was averted and the prospects for future stability were increased.

Because of the Japanese aggression in Manchuria occurring at this time, the government revenue decreased greatly. A general reduction in tax receipts also resulted from a disastrous flood and the Shanghai hostilities. The result was that the government's ability to meet the monthly loan service on domestic bonds (C$16 million on a total out-standing balance of C$753 million) was endangered. The Ministry of Finance indicated that a moratorium on bonds' service might be imposed for a short period. Such action, however, according to banking leaders, would destroy the frail credit standing of the new regime and block the prospects for issuing bonds in the future, upon which the government depended heavily. Moreover, as more than 30 per cent of the outstanding loans were held by the banks, a further drop in the bond price would mean serious difficulties for small banks. In discussions between the Ministry and banking leaders, a scheme was worked out whereby the integrity of the bond issue would be maintained and the stability of the money market preserved. On February 24, 1932, the government announced a plan which reduced the interest on the bond and lengthened the repayment period. This had the effect of reducing monthly loan services by one-half. The government pledged its strict adherence to the plan regardless of future financial problems. When the stock exchange reopened on May 1, the bond price was stabilized at the level existing before hostilities. It was generally felt at the time that without the respect which the leading banks commanded from the public, the bond market would have collapsed. In the previous year, between September and December, the bond price had already fallen 31 per cent.

In spite of the growing strength of big banks, and the stability of the money market attained by the concerted action of the modern and native banks, signs of weakness began to appear in the banking community in 1934. Depressed economic conditions and a silver drain contributed heavily to the closing of eight small commercial banks in 1934. In addition, four native banks were suspended. During the first months of 1935, a wave of panic arose among the native banks, with strong implications for commercial banks and the banking community as a whole.

TABLE A

Notes Issuing*

Year	Central Bank[1]	Bank of China[1]	Bank of Communi- cations[1]	Total	Commercial Banks[2]
1927	—	159.0	65.1	224.1	
1928	11.7	172.3	68.0	252.0	
1929	15.4	197.7	60.2	273.3	
1930	22.7	203.8	82.9	309.4	
1931	25.2	191.7	81.1	298.0	
1932	40.0	184.4	82.4	206.8	
1933	71.1	183.7	83.1	337.9	
1934	86.1	204.7	112.5	403.3	143.4

*Unit: Million Dollars

[1] Source: Annual Reports of each bank.

[2] Source: Annual Reports of each bank which issue was submitted to public examination.

National Industrial Bank of China	33.6
Agricultural and Industrial Bank of China	6.2
Land Bank of China	7.1
National Commercial Bank	9.2
Four Banks Joint Treasury (The Yien Yieh, Kincheng, Continental China and South Sea Banks)	44.7
Commercial Bank of China	24.3
Ningpo Commercial and Savings Bank	18.3
Total	143.4

TABLE B

Deposits*

Year	Total of[1] Modern Banks(A)	Central Bank[2]	Bank of Communica- tions[2]	Bank of China	Total of Central Banking Group(B)	Commercial and Local Banks(A-B)
1927	1,052.9	——	158.3	330.5	488.8	564.1
1928	1,216.5	15.5	150.9	387.7	538.6	677.9
1929	1,434.3	49.8	160.5	438.1	598.6	835.7
1930	1,773.4	76.2	174.7	535.5	710.2	1,063.2
1931	2,067.3	90.6	190.3	608.2	798.5	1,268.8
1932	2,363.8	168.5	212.1	476.3	688.4	1,675.4
1933	2,876.6	227.2	239.9	549.3	789.2	2,087.4
1934	3,302.6	249.5	286.7	546.7	833.4	2,469.2

* Unit: Million Dollars.

[1] Source: *Economic History of Republic,* p. 509, published by *Bankers' Weekly,* Shanghai, 1947.

[2] Source: Annual Reports of each bank.

TABLE C

Deposits of Ten Big Commercial Banks

	1927*
National Commercial Bank	44,244,464
Kincheng Banking Corporation	42,426,308
Yien Yieh Commercial Bank	40,763,667
China and South Sea Bank	33,791,436
Shanghai Commercial and Savings Bank	31,329,199
Ningpo Commercial & Savings Bank	29,311,743
Continental Bank	25,989,419
Chekiang Industrial Bank	25,265,204
Four Banks Joint Savings Society	23,466,900
National Industrial Bank of China	17,746,971
	1934**
Shanghai Commercial & Savings Bank	158,159,145
Kincheng Banking Corporation	132,775,376
Continental Bank	116,071,333
China and South Sea Bank	96,531,964
Yien Yieh Commercial Bank	96,411,988
Four Banks Joint Savings Society	90,530,283
National Commercial Bank	88,086,094
Ningpo Commercial Bank	67,390,632
National Industrial Bank of China	61,338,142
Chekiang Industrial Bank	53,723,846

*An Analysis of the Accounts of the Principal Chinese Banks, 1921-31, published by the Research Department, Bank of China, 1933.

**China's Bankers Yearbook, 1935.

TABLE D

Silver Stocks of Chinese and
Foreign Banks in Shanghai*

Year	Chinese Banks	Foreign Banks	Total
1913	12,249	62,111	70,391
1921	21,313	48,950	70,263
1926	73,494	73,859	147,353
1929	144,196	96,064	240,260
1931	179,305	86,883	266,188
1932	253,289	185,050	438,339
1933	271,786	275,660	547,446
1934 (May)	254,775	258,777	534,997

*Unit: Thousand Dollars
Source: *Yokohama Specie Bank Report, 1913-1933* quoted in Takahashi Ka-
   mekichi's *China's Economic Collapse and Japan*, pp. 322-3.
   Bankers' Weekly, 1934, Vol. 18, p. 82.

IV

Unification of Silver Currency, 1933

The National Coinage Law of 1914, promulgated under the administration of Liang Chi-chao as Minister of Finance, contained in it a plan
for abolishing the *tael*. There was, however, a lapse of fourteen years
between this plan and the emergence of a government strong enough
to actuate it. During the course of those fourteen years, many voices
had been raised in favor of abolishing the *tael* system. Among the most
powerful were the Shanghai Chamber of Commerce, organized by
foreign merchants, and the Shanghai Chinese Bankers' Association. The
Shanghai Chamber of Commerce adopted a resolution in 1919 appealing
to the Chinese government to abolish the *tael*, to unify the coinage
system, to establish a central mint in Shanghai, and to institute free
coinage of silver dollars. This measure was supported by the Hong Kong
and Shanghai Banking Corporation, but no action was taken. In 1921,
the Shanghai Chinese Bankers' Association signed a loan agreement with
the Ministry of Finance to finance construction of a Shanghai mint.
Attached to the agreement was a proposal that a special committee be
organized for the purpose of studying the problem of abolishing the
tael. This committee was to be composed of members of the Chinese
Bankers' Association, Foreign Bankers' Association, and the Inspector-

General of Chinese Maritime Customs. Because of the continuing political disturbances, the consequent weakness of the government, and delay in the construction of the mint caused by bad management, support for abolishing the *tael* withered and the proposal lay dormant.

On the other hand, it was more than a matter of governmental inertia which was responsible for the continued use of the *tael*. The Chinese public, particularly the native banks, clung to the *tael* system because they had very little confidence in the government's currency management ability and because they considered the bullion standard a safeguard against debased silver coins and depreciated paper currency. Additionally, the *tael* system was supported by the foreign banks who found profitable advantages in the dual currency situation. Finally, the government held an inadequate supply of silver to institute a system based on silver dollars.

The *tael* system itself was composed of the real *tael* and fiduciary *tael*. The real *tael* defined the value of a quantity of silver of a certain weight and fineness considered standard in a particular market. This standard, however, differed from city to city. The fiduciary *tael* was a unit of account only which defined the value of silver of a certain weight and fineness. The value of the fiduciary *tael* also differed from city to city, and traditionally differed from the real *tael*. Essentially, the fiduciary *tael* was a device used to economize on silver. To illustrate the variety: one real Shanghai *tael* was defined as 565.65 grains of .935 fine silver. One fiduciary Shanghai *tael* defined the same weight of silver as .9167 fine. One real Tientsin *tael* defined 622.21 grains of .987 fine silver. One fiduciary Tientsin *tael* defined the same weight of silver as .980 fine.

From the time that the National Government was established in 1927 until the Silver Standard Dollar Coinage Law of 1933, several factors emerged which greatly facilitated the abolition of the *tael*.

First, the economic condition of the rural economy declined markedly. The fall in agricultural production was caused by continued internal wars, floods, and drought, and this together with the deteriorated conditions of transport facilities drastically reduced rural sales to the port cities. Consequently, imports into the interior exceeded its exports and caused a drain of silver bullion and silver dollars from the interior to the port cities. The quantity of silver in circulation in the interior was further reduced by the deluge of provincial paper notes which drove silver into hoardings or into banks in the port cities. As a result, the real silver *tael* gradually disappeared in the markets of the interior cities. The value of the fiduciary *tael* in the interior dropped heavily in relation to the fiduciary *tael* of port cities and consequently the former lost its usefulness. The *tael* system in many interior cities vanished without official note, but in some cities its abolition was publicly announced. As early as 1925, the Swatow Money Exchange Banks' Association decided to call in all notes issued in terms of *taels*. Then in March 1929, the Canton Native Bankers' Association resolved to cease dealing in *taels* and in September 1930, a local government order in Chungking abolished the *tael* system there.

The second factor which caused a decline in the use of the *tael* was the rapid increase in the quantity of silver dollars in circulation. In 1918, according to a Finance Ministry estimate, there were 250 million silver dollars in circulation. In fifteen years, the number of silver dollars had increased nearly six times. By March 1933, the Ministry estimated that 1,400 million silver dollars were in circulation. This increase is partially explained by a rise in transactions demand for money as the rural interior was gradually brought into the market economy and as the economy, as a whole, grew. Part of the increase is also attributable to the demand for silver dollars as reserves for note issues of the banks. The quantity of silver dollars for this purpose is estimated to have been about 200 million; the total number of silver dollars in circulation in 1933 was, therefore, about 1,600 million. The silver which was coined in terms of *taels* amounted to 153 million Shanghai *taels* (about 200 million dollars). The quantity of silver dollars in circulation was clearly much greater than that of *taels*. This factor assured that there would be minimal disruption when the *tael* was abolished and the dollar made the sole currency.

The third factor which facilitated the abolition of the *tael* was the decline of the dollar's value in terms of the *tael*. This development was desirable because it created an opportunity for the operation of Gresham's Law, that is, where a diversity of monies exists, the higher valued currencies will be driven out of circulation by the lower valued one. The decline of the dollar's value with respect to the *tael* was due primarily to unstable military conditions around Shanghai in early 1932. Because the value of the dollar in Shanghai traditionally reflected conditions prevailing in most of the country, it was considered the standard value for all other money markets. The value of the dollar in Shanghai was dependent on (1) the quantity of dollar stocks there, (2) the demand for dollars by merchants in the interior for purchases of seasonal harvests, (3) the demand for dollars by exporters in Shanghai to pay wholesalers, and (4) the interest rates on *tael* loans (higher rates caused a drop in the market value of dollars in terms of *taels*).

On January 28, 1932, there was a brief, but bitter battle between the Chinese and Japanese on the outskirts of the Shanghai Settlement. The battle had three principle effects: (1) it paralyzed the Shanghai money market, (2) it created a great deal of uncertainty in the Shanghai bankers with respect to the security of their outstanding credits, and (3) it cut off the large flow of credit emanating from Shanghai. This was particularly disastrous as the date of the battle coincided with the end of the Chinese year—the time when debt settlement between the native banks in the interior and those in Shanghai were to take place. When conditions normalized, the Shanghai native banks demanded settlement in cash; they were not willing to extend credit lines further. This resulted in a sharp increase in the quantity of silver dollars in Shanghai. The rapidly deteriorating situation in the interior, however, meant that the demand for dollars by merchants and traders was dropping markedly. This increase in the supply of dollars, coupled with a decrease in the demand for them, led to a drop in the dollar value from about 73 *taels* to 100 dollars in the period 1928-31; and to 69.95 *taels* to 100 dollars in April 1932. By the end of 1932, the rate was restored to about 71.4 *taels* to 100 dollars, but there was no prospect of achieving the previously prevailing rate.

In mid-1932, the Ministry of Finance appointed a study group composed of representatives of different public bodies, both foreign and Chinese, to express their views on currency reform. On March 4, 1933, the Ministry of Finance announced its decision and the following four steps were taken:

1) The enactment of the Silver Standard Dollar Coinage Law on March 8, 1933. The Law defined the standard gross weight of the new unit at 26.6971 grams (412 grains troy) with 88 per cent fineness (*i.e.*, 23.493448 grams of pure silver). Free coinage was allowed with a 2.25 per cent mint charge. The old dollars, whose weight and fineness corresponded closely to the original government specifications, were permitted to circulate at par with the new dollar for a limited period. The reason given by the Ministry of Finance for reducing the silver content of the dollar from 89 per cent to 88 per cent (90 per cent fineness defined in the National Coinage Law of 1914, but immediately changed to 89 per cent by a government order) was to facilitate the circulation of the new dollar, not to make a profit. According to its survey, the majority of old dollars in circulation weighed 26.8641 grams and contained 88.8 parts of pure silver.

2) The establishment of a fixed conversion rate between the new dollar and the Shanghai *tael*. The Finance Ministry order stated that as the new dollar contained 23.493448 grams of pure silver and one Shanghai *tael* contained 33.599 grams of silver, the conversion rate, including a 2.25 percent minting charge, should be 71.5 Shanghai *taels* for 100 new dollars.

3) The institution of the new dollar as the sole unit of account. The Shanghai Chamber of Commerce, Shanghai Bankers' Association, and

Native Bankers' Association were ordered to use the dollar as the unit of account both in quoting prices and in conducting transactions from March 10, 1933 on; and other cities were ordered to follow this practice beginning April 5. Any contract or transaction from those dates onward made in terms of *taels* were to be considered illegal and invalid.

4) The organization of a single central mint. The Shanghai mint was named as the Central mint and all others were ordered to cease operation. The Shanghai mint had been ready to operate before the order abolishing the *tael* was announced and was able to start minting the new dollar immediately. The mint had an average daily capacity of 150,000 pieces of the new standard dollar (Sun Yat-sen Dollar). An examination committee, composed of representatives of both the Chinese and foreign banking community, was installed. On July 1, 1933, the new dollar began to circulate.

The above measures were carried out smoothly. Both Chinese and foreign banks changed the unit of account from *tael* to dollars beginning April 4, 1933. The silver shops which made the silver sycee (one real *tael*) and public assay offices which were in charge of verifying the fineness of the sycee were all closed in September of the same year. In December 1933, the government ordered all Chinese banks to hand over their silver sycee holdings to the government banks in exchange for new dollars or silver bars (equivalent to 1,000 dollars) made by the mint. Thus the abolition of the *tael* was almost completed by the end of 1933. The omission of subsidiary silver coins from regulation under the Silver Standard Dollar Law was purposeful. The Ministry of Finance felt that the problem of subsidiary silver coins should be dealt after the unification of silver dollars had been completed. Nevertheless, to prevent the continued minting of debased coins, a government order was issued to the Customs stating that any small silver coins which contained less silver than the government stipulated should be confiscated.

V

Governmental Control of the
Central Banking Group, March-April 1935

Upon assuming the position of Finance Minister in November 1933, H. H. Kung confronted three major problems: (1) an increasing deficit in the government's budget, (2) a drain of financial resources from servicing the bond issues, and (3) an outflow of silver caused by the United States' increase in the price of silver. These problems brought about a classical deflationary situation—falling prices, depressed demand, low output levels, bank shortage of liquidity. The Finance Minister felt that cutting the budget would incur the disfavor of the government leader and all other executive branches. Further reorganization of loan services was prohibited by the pledge of the previous Finance Minister not to change their arrangements. At the same time, Kung was hard pressed by requests of industrial and banking firms for financial help. In an effort to seek a solution to these problems, he resorted to credit expansion of the central banking group. This was attempted by increasing the capital of the Central Bank of China and establishing governmental control of the Bank of China and Bank of Communications. In his proposal to the Political Committee of the Central Executive Committee of the Kuomintang on March 30, 1934, the Minister of Finance stated his reason for increasing the government's capital in three banks for issuing bonds amounting to C$100 million.

"In view of the precarious situation of the tight money market the government and the business community had hoped that the three government banks could have expanded credits to relieve it. But their resources were so limited that they could not afford to extend any assistance to the money market and, therefore, it was necessary to increase their capital in order to augment their strength. . . . For this purpose the Ministry proposed to issue bonds to the value of C$100 million. . . . This bond issue would only serve as an addition to their reserves so that bonds would not be sold on the market and would not affect the price of existing bonds."

Increase in the capital of the Central Bank of China

On April 17, 1935, the Ministry of Finance proposed an increase in the capital of the Central Bank of China from C$20 million to C$100 million. The Cabinet readily approved. Among the important changes were the following: (1) The head office of the Bank would be located in the capital, Nanking, instead of Shanghai; (2) private capital would not exceed 40 per cent of total capital (49 per cent was stipulated in the previous charter); (3) preference in capital subscription would be given to banking firms. Subscription by Chinese citizens was to be allowed only when subscription by banking firms had reached 30 per cent.

Second reorganization of the Bank of China and Bank of Communications

On March 30, 1935, the Bank of China was ordered by the Ministry of Finance to accept the Ministry's order to increase the government's capital from C$5 million to C$20 million; and to increase total capital from C$25 million to C$40 million. The Bank acquiesced. The Bank of Communications was ordered to increase the government's capital from

C$1 million to C$12 million; and to increase total capital from C$10 million to C$20 million. In this manner, the government gained complete control of these two banks.

The government's addition to the note reserves of the Bank of China and Bank of Communications was inadequate to enable them to provide more credits to the business community. The Banks found it extremely difficult to increase their note issue for three reasons. (1) Bank regulations required that 60 per cent of notes issued be backed by cash. (2) The government added only bonds to the Bank's reserves. (3) At the same time, the public was turning in notes for high priced silver which served as reserves. A major effect of the reorganization was that the business and banking communities became apprehensive of the change in the government's policy toward privately owned enterprises, a feeling that was heightened by a sudden change in the top management of the Bank of China made possible by the new policy.

In a further effort to relieve the credit shortage of business and banking firms, the government announced a new measure for credit expansion. In June-July 1935, the Ministry of Finance provided the native banks with C$25 million in government bonds and provided industrial and commercial firms with C$20 million in treasury notes. When a native bank needed credits beyond the security it had available, it took its securities to government-appointed Supervisory Committee. If they approved, the Committee would provide the difference in government bonds. The native bank could then take its securities and bonds to specified banks and receive equivalent value in credits. The procedure was similar for industrial and commercial firms needing loans, though treasury notes were used instead of bonds.

VI

Change from the Silver Standard to
Foreign Exchange Standard, November 1935

Fifteen months after the abolishment of the *tael*, the Silver Purchase Act was passed by the U.S. Congress. Its enactment caused a rise in the price of silver on the world market, and produced several serious effects on Chinese currency. People, for example, were encouraged to sell silver for gold. Note holders were induced to cash their notes to obtain silver. Silver holdings were drained from interior to the port cities for export, and it became profitable to melt down the new dollar. As a result, the credit base of the whole nation was shaken because of loss of its silver reserve. Money became scarce. Commodity prices fell. The government, furthermore, had no time to demonstrate its ability to maintain the credit of the new dollar, nor to dispel public suspicion about the possibility of excessive issues of notes after the abolishment of the *tael*. The problems concerning the withdrawal of provincial banknotes and the unification of subsidiary silver and copper coins were difficult to deal with.

There were also serious effects on custom revenue, import trade, and commodity prices. The custom duty on imports was changed from silver to gold in 1930 with the introduction of the so-called Custom Gold Unit because a sudden drop in the price of silver led to the reduction of custom revenue pledged for foreign and domestic loan services. However, following the Silver Purchase Act, the rise in the price of silver reduced the silver proceeds of revenue in terms of Custom Gold Units and affected the loan services of already weakened domestic bonds.

The high price of silver meant that China could pay less to buy the same imports than before; and, therefore, imports would be encouraged. This would destroy China's infant domestic industry and depress the prices of Chinese products. Yet, in November 1935, circumstances forced the government to make a drastic change from the silver standard to a foreign exchange standard.

The new plan provided that:

1) The banknotes issued by the Central Bank of China, the Bank of China, and the Bank of Communications would be the nation's legal tender, the Chinese National Currency (CNC).

2) The use of silver for currency purposes was prohibited. The public was ordered to surrender to the government-appointed Currency Reserve Board, or to its agent bank, all monetary silver in their possession in exchange for legal tender notes.

3) The Central Bank of China was directed to buy and sell foreign exchange at current rates without any limitation. The first official rates were set at:

For one Chinese dollar (CNC):

	U.S. Dollars	British Pounds Sterling
Buying	0.295	1 shilling 2⅜ pence
Selling	0.300	1 shilling 2⅝ pence

The rate was set in the following manner. World silver prices were 2s/0.4375d for one pure ounce. The silver content of the CNC was pegged at 0.8816 ounce. On this basis, the exchange rate should have been about 2s/2.68d. The CNC was devalued, however, in order to maintain a margin which would protect it against fluctuations in the silver market. It had the further effect of encouraging exports and raising the domestic price level which had recently been depressed.

There existed a number of elements favorable to the successful execution of the plan: (1) a strong public patriotic spirit, engendered by Japanese aggression, contributed to the support of the government's action, (2) the habit of using banknotes had been fully developed during the last twenty years, and (3) a large number of silver stocks in China were already concentrated in the hands of the banks. In addition, the British banks, following the British government's order, announced their support of the plan. This move had an important impact on public acceptance of a paper legal tender. By the middle of 1936, about C$308 million in silver was surrendered by the people. Foreign banks and the Chinese banks also handed over to the government their silver holdings. These amounted to more than C$800 million. As a result of the successful execution of the November 1935 plan, China's long cherished aspiration of converting to a foreign exchange standard internationally and paper currency domestically was fulfilled.

It cannot be denied that the currency reform was generated by the pressure of circumstances and there was no sufficient time to prepare an adequate foundation. Important prerequisites for currency reform were lacking: a balanced domestic budget, a favorable balance of payments, adequate foreign reserves, and an independent central reserve bank. Sir Frederick Leith-Ross, the official British adviser to the Chinese government and key draftsman of the plan, saw these defects and made two proposals: (1) The Central Bank of China should be reorganized as a Central Reserve Bank, with a majority share of capital subscribed by commercial banks and private citizens and with a minority share by the government. The purpose was to separate the Central Bank from the Ministry of Finance and give it independent status. (2) The government should make fiscal improvements with the aim of attaining a balanced budget. This was to reduce the government's dependence on deficit financing through note issue. The Minister of Finance accepted the proposals. He pledged to recognize the Central Bank in the manner indicated, and declared the Ministry would endeavor to bring the budget into balance within eighteen months. The anxiety felt by the business community over the weak foundation of the currency reform was temporarily relieved. Meanwhile, the devaluation of Chinese currency initiated favorable movements in exports and imports. Comparing the closing months of 1935 with earlier months of the same year and the previous year, the improvement can be readily noted (in million of Chinese dollars):

	Imports		Exports	
	1934	1935	1934	1935
September	77.5	54.4	41.7	45.9
October	79.0	61.2	42.7	48.4
November	83.5	72.4	49.8	60.2
December	72.0	65.2	43.6	70.6

This was followed by a bumper harvest in 1935 which reduced imports of agricultural products and further improved the trade balance.

Maintenance of Stable Exchange Rates

The Chinese people who had little knowledge of the workings of a managed currency system based their acceptance of it on the CNC's convertibility for foreign exchange at a stable rate. Fortunately, as mentioned above, 1936 produced a bumper crop thereby reducing the grain and flour imports from C$136 million in 1935 to CNC $49 million in 1936.[5] Exports of cotton fiber increased from C$97 million to CNC $113 million in 1936. As a result, the unfavorable trade balance was reduced from C$343 million in 1935 to CNC $236 million in 1936, and to CNC $115 million in 1937. Overseas remittances were estimated to have increased from C$280 million in 1935 to CNC $320 million in 1936, and to CNC $450 million in 1937, mainly due to the rise of foreign exchange rates. An equally important contribution to the maintenance of exchange rate stability was the Silver Purchase Agreement of May 14, 1936 between the United States and China. The U. S. government agreed to purchase 75 million ounces of silver at the price of U.S. $0.45 per ounce; and, in addition, to give the Chinese credit of U.S. $20 million. By May 1937, the total proceeds of silver sales amounted to about U.S. $270 million. Though there were a few speculative activities late in 1935, and in May and December of 1936, the exchange rate for the new currency was stable up to the outbreak of the Sino-Japanese War in July 1937.

The Impact on Chinese Banking

The change from silver to a foreign exchange standard had an important impact on Chinese banking in five respects. First, the right of note issue by private banks was withdrawn. The private banks were required to withdraw their notes in exchange for the notes of the central banking group within a prescribed period. Second, the notes issued by the provincial banks had to be withdrawn because they were not exchangeable for foreign exchange and therefore not legal tender. Third,

the notes issued by foreign banks, which had previously been reduced
to an insignificant amount, were completely eliminated. Fourth, foreign
exchange was concentrated in the hands of the Central Banking Group,
thereby breaking the monopoly of the foreign banks. Fifth, the commercial banks recovered from the depressed conditions caused by the
effects of the 1934-35 deflation and began to prosper as a result of the
rise of prices generated by the monetary change.

Inflationary Trends

This period witnessed a rapid increase in issue of notes, an increase
which was facilitated by the removal under the new currency standard
of the obligation to back up new issue with holdings of silver. The
government banks were frequently enjoined to make advances to the
Treasury on the security of new bond issues pending their sale to the
public because the bond market was increasingly depressed. Consequently, between November 1935 and the middle of 1937, the note issues
of the four government banks increased from CNC $453 million to
CNC $1,477 million. Only about half of the increase represented notes
issued in exchange for silver

Date	Notes in Circulation, CNC
November 1935	453 million
December 1935	673 million
June 1936	948 million
December 1936	1,331 million
June 1937	1,477 million[6]

Through this period, the financial authorities tended to make light of
the increases in the quantity of notes.

VII

The Expansion of Banking Operations in Rural
Financing Since 1933

The Chinese peasants had long depended on the individual money
lender, the merchant, and the pawnshops for the supply of rural credits
and had in the process suffered the heavy burden of usury. In the
1920's, the China International Famine Relief Commission began to
promote the establishment of rural credit co-operative societies and
invited educational organizations to undertake the task with funds sup-

plied by the Commission. Nanking University was the first to take up this task with the creation of a rural credit cooperative society in the suburbs of Nanking in 1922. In time a number of other cooperative societies were established, and the increasing need for Commission funds led to an agreement with the Shanghai Commercial and Savings Bank in 1931. The Bank agreed to supply a small amount of credits at low interest rates. Earlier, the provincial governments began to establish their own farmer's banks. In 1927, the Kiangsu provincial government set up the Kiangsu Farmers Bank. This was followed in 1928 by the establishment in Chekiang Province of farmer's banks in the provincial capital and outlying counties. These banks were constituted as separate entities under the direction and control of the provincial government.

None of these efforts, however, were large enough to make any material changes in the conditions of the peasants. From 1931 onward, the Chinese peasants were subjected to additional disasters. Devastating floods covered more than ten provinces, the price of agricultural products fell due to the dumping of foreign products, the shortage of credits was compounded by a drain of silver from the rural areas to the treaty ports, and Communist activity curtailed production.

In April 1933, the headquarters of the National Army for the campaign against the Communists established the Four Provinces Agricultural Bank (Honan, Hupeh, Anhwei and Kiangsi) in Hankow with branches in each province. The capital was subscribed by the army headquarters and the four provinces. The Bank's purpose was to rehabilitate the rural economy and to relieve the distress of the peasants in the areas which had been overrun by the Communists. Banknotes issued were circulated in the four provinces. At the end of 1934, credits granted by the Bank amounted to more than C$11 million. The Bank was reorganized in June 1935 as "The Farmers Bank of China" and was put on an equal footing with the Bank of China and Bank of Communications. The charter of the Farmers Bank stipulated: (1) the capital was fixed at C$10 million; one quarter was to be subscribed by the National Government and the remainder by provincial governments and private individuals; (2) the Bank would handle short and medium term loans to farmers for improvements and purchases of agricultural implements; (3) the Bank was authorized to issue bonds up to five times its capital or up to the total amount of its outstanding loans; (4) the right of note issue was granted with a fixed limit at C$100 million; (5) the President of the Bank was to be appointed by the Government upon proposal of the Chairman of the Board and the directors of the Board were elected by the shareholders. In February 1936, the Bank was authorized by the Central Government to take over the note issuing privileges of provincial and commercial banks; and in February 1937, the Ministry of

Finance issued an order recognizing its banknotes as legal tender. Thus, the Farmers Bank of China became a full member of the Central Banking Group. At the end of 1936, the paid-up capital amounted to CNC $7.5 million. Note issues increased to CNC $162 million and deposits to CNC $155 million while rural credits were only about CNC $15 million. The controlling power was in the hands of the Ministry of Finance under the direction of the government leader, a legacy of previous control by the Army Headquarters.

Two modern banks, the Bank of China and Shanghai Commercial and Savings Bank, made efforts to expand rural credits beginning in 1933.

The measures taken by the Bank of China were (1) an increase in loans against agricultural products held in the Bank's warehouses, (2) small loans to the peasants, some against the security of products and some on personal credit, with interest rates as low as one per cent per month, (3) loans to co-operative societies, partly through credit worthy institutions such as the Tsouping Agricultural Improvement Committee in Shangtung, the Tinghsien People's Improvement Committee in Hopei, and the China International Famine Relief Commission and partly through the Bank's directly guided cooperative societies. Total agricultural loans increased from CNC $21 million in 1933 to CNC $43 million in 1936. Of this total, loans to co-operative societies amounted to CNC $8 million and small loans to the peasants amounted to CNC $1 million. The latter two items should be considered as the only rural credits which favored the small landholder.

The Shanghai Commercial and Savings Bank set up a special department in 1933 called Rural Cooperative Credit Department; the following, year its title was changed to the Department of Agriculture. Three kinds of agricultural loans were granted: (1) loans to the producing and marketing co-operatives, (2) warehouse loans which were made on the security of products kept in the bank's warehouse, (3) loans to credit co-operatives. The bank placed emphasis on the production and marketing of cotton because of the steady demand from cotton mills; for wheat, tobacco leaves, and sugar cane only production credits were granted. Warehouse loans were limited to the few warehouses set up in the rural area of Kiangsu province. The number of loans on credit to the co-operative societies was small, amounting to only 3 per cent of the total, because of the expense involved in handling such loans. Though there were about 900 co-operative societies and warehouses involved, the total of agricultural loans reached only CNC $6 million in 1935. After the establishment of the Farmers Bank of China, the savings bank's activities in rural financing were reduced. In 1935, the Government made further efforts to implement the expansion of rural credit by requiring one-fifth of all banks' savings deposit to be invested in agriculture. This measure prompted the banks which accepted savings deposits to organize a consortium for rural financing. In the middle of 1936, the Ministry of Industry established the Agricultural Credit Administration for the purpose of channelling the commercial banks's savings funds allocated to investment in agriculture. Initial arrangements were made with thirty banks, which accepted savings deposits, that one per cent of the savings would be handed over to the Administration for rural financing. The total amount was CNC $6 million. Thus the main sources of rural financing from the Central financial institutions totalled about CNC $36 million.

From provincial sources, the total rural credits are estimated to have amounted to CNC $22 million.[7]

The total of all rural credits was approximately CNC $58 million. These efforts in rural financing provided a good start in attacking the problem. The results realized further impressed upon the government the importance and need of a fully developed banking system in the interior.

VIII

Perspective

From the above discussion, it seems clear that China's currency and banking system had made progress due to the initiative of the Government with the support of the banking community and due to enlightened response to events which forced changes in the system. The change to the foreign exchange standard spelled the demise of provincial banknotes which had long been a serious obstacle to the unification on paper currency. Provincial banknotes suffered a natural death because they were unable to be redeemed in foreign exchange and therefore could not be considered legal tender. The Kwangtung Provincial Bank had the largest issue of provincial banknotes, about C$250 million worth. These notes were withdrawn from circulation with the Government's financial assistance. Other provincial banks with smaller issues were able to call in their notes without great difficulty. For the first time in Chinese history, all note issuing power was consolidated in the hands of the Central Government. The Government was in the unique position of being able to issue a single, universal paper currency. At the same time, the Government succeeded in introducing for universal circulation fractional nickel coins to replace the small silver coins whose fineness varied from province to province. The currency reform of

November 1935 provided for the manufacture of pure nickel coins in denominations five, ten and twenty cents. These coins were first produced in January 1936 by the Shanghai Mint. The nickel coins were uniform in design, fineness, and weight; and, consequently, became very popular. As a result of the withdrawal of provincial notes and the extension of sound fractional coinage, the unification of currency was completed.

The Government now had a firm foundation upon which to build a policy of currency and credit management. Following the advice of experts, a Draft Law was proposed to convert the Central Bank of China to the Central Reserve Bank of China. The Draft Law was adopted by the Political Committee of the Central Executive Committee of the Kuomintang in March 1937 and referred to the Legislative Yuan (Assembly) for enactment. The Draft Law provided that the Central Reserve Bank would be capitalized at CNC $100 million. The one million shares were divided into four classes: 400,000 A shares subscribed by the Government; 50,000 B Shares subscribed by provincial and municipal Government; 350,000 C shares subscribed by Chinese banks, and 200,000 D shares for public subscription.

The new functions of the Central Reserve Bank were (1) to centralize the legal reserves of the various banks, (2) to develop the financial market, (3) to improve the credit system, (4) to facilitate the utilization of the capital of the various commercial banks, (5) to readjust national currency and credit, and (6) to provide adequate flexibility to stabilize the exchange value of the national dollar.

The other functions of the Central Bank, such as issuing legal tender notes, serving as agent of the National Treasury and agent for the issue of Government bonds, both domestic and foreign, remained the same. Administratively, there was to be an eleven-man Board of Directors; five were to be appointed by the Government and three each were to be elected from among class B and C shareholders. The governor and vice governor were to be elected from among the directors. Approval of this Draft Law would have logically led the Government to reconsider its 1935 action with respect to the Bank of China and Bank of Communications. It was foreseeable that a Government policy based on the new Draft Law and the fulfillment of the functions of the Bank of China, Bank of Communications, and Farmers Bank of China would have resulted in a sound, coordinated central banking system. The control of money and credit, the stabilization of the exchange value of the new national dollar, and the financing of industry, commerce, and agriculture would have been established. Unfortunately, the institution of a coordinated central banking group failed to be accomplished because of a dispute over the relative shares of the government and private investors and preoccupation with Japanese aggression. It was generally recognized that in the long run stability of new currency was dependent on the continued inflow of foreign capital.

The prospect for foreign capital flows from trade and aid seemed bright because China had now identified her monetary system with that of industrial nations, and the fluctuations in the prices of gold and silver symptomatic of the previous monetary system were eliminated. Moreover, the threat of the Axis powers, particularly Japan, induced the Western powers to adopt a more sympathetic outlook toward China's economic and financial reconstruction. In response to the Ministry of Railway's reorganization of defaulted foreign railway loans and its plan to double existing railroad mileage, the British indicated their readiness in 1937 to give China sterling credits of 10 million pounds, and the French and Belgian indicated a willingness to provide similar types of support.

Unquestionably, the crucial problem was the large budget deficit of the Government which would intensify the existing inflation and impede necessary investments into industry and agriculture. This problem was compounded by the second reorganization of domestic loan services in February 1936, and the subsequent weakening of the domestic bonds market. By January 1936, the outstanding balance of domestic loans reached CNC $1,460 million with annual loans services of CNC $126 million. At the same time, a new issue of CNC $340 million was added. It was estimated that two-thirds of the new issue was absorbed by banks either for investment or against note reserves, thus indicating that the bond market had reached the saturation point. It was apparent that had it not been for the menace of Japanese aggression, the Government would have been able to cut expenditures and reduce the budget deficit. Events within and outside China led her to a position where a modern banking system, sound fiscal policies, a progressive trade policy, and the stabilization of the new currency were imminent. The full fruits of this aspect of the nation-building effort would have been reaped but for the advent of the Sino-Japanese War.

Comments:

BY SHO-CHIEH TSIANG

I feel very privileged in being invited to be the discussant of Dr. K. N. Chang's paper, which is particularly remarkable in being a first hand account of the history of Chinese currency and banking rendered by a veteran who played a most prominent part himself in the making of this history.

As pointed out in Dr. Chang's paper, the art of banking and the use of paper money and bank drafts had a much earlier start in China than in Western Europe; however, like in so many other things, by the close of the nineteenth century, China was far behind the Western world in matters of banking and finance. The ancient empire of China seemed to have been in a somnolent slumber, Rip-van-Winkle-like, for over a thousand years, when the western nations began to bang on her doors demanding trade.

Her monetary system was indeed in a primitive mess, when the western nations woke her up. There was no uniform coinage system in the empire. Silver bullion was the chief unit of account and medium of exchange. Yet the unit of weight for the measurement of bullion (the *tael*) was not uniformly defined over the empire, but varied from city to city. Nor were the silver ingots used in circulation of uniform fineness. Copper coins of various sizes, weights, and alloys were used as subsidiary coins, but the relationship between the *tael* and copper coins was naturally not standardized. It varied not only between cities but also over time of minting in each city. The native banks in operation were as primitive as they were centuries ago.

Such was the state of the Chinese monetary and banking system when China was first confronted with western traders. The superiority of modern banking methods introduced into the port cities by the Westerners and the convenience of a uniform coinage system was obvious enough to the more enlightened. The need for modernization was clearly recognized by new business leaders like Dr. Chang himself. Unfortunately, just at that time, the country was plunging into great political tumult. First, the corrupt Manchu Dynasty was overthrown by the rising tides of nationalist revolution. Then, the newly established republic was brutally disrupted by the unscrupulous Yuan Shih-k'ai, who tried to install himself as the new emperor. Although his monarchial attempt proved ephemeral, his selfish ambition set a bad example for all the warlords and resulted in continuous internecine civil wars up to the establishment of the National Government in 1927.

Yet in spite of the incessant civil wars and utterly unstable government, considerable strides had been made in the development of modern banking even during this period of turmoil. In this advancement, our speaker today, Dr. Chang himself, played a most important leading role. We need not go into details of this period, which precedes the one we are concerned with. Suffice it to say that the Bank of China was the undisputed leader of modern Chinese banks during that period, and Dr. Chang was for most of the time its general manager and undisputed guiding spirit. Under his leadership, modern Chinese banks, sheltered from civil wars as they were in the safety haven of foreign settlements in port cities, gradually surpassed the foreign banks in those cities both in deposits and note-issue.

In a sense, however, the expansion of Chinese banking in port cities under the shelter of foreign authorities was partly at the expense of the rest of the country; for it involved the drain of capital and funds from the interior and an unbalanced concentration of money in the port cities. This situation could not be remedied so long as the rest of the country was constantly threatened by civil wars. Furthermore, the dependence of Chinese banks upon the shelter provided by foreign settlements in China also implied that the hold exercised by foreign banks over the Chinese financial market could not really be broken so long as this dependence continued. In particular, foreign exchange operation still remained a monopoly of foreign banks; for in those days China's foreign trade was mainly in the hands of foreign firms and consequently the proceeds of China's export went mostly into foreign banks. These foreign banks continued to use *tael* as the unit of account and means of payment, as they had no confidence in the silver dollars and subsidiary coins coined by the succession of unstable central governments and warlord-controlled local governments in China. Thus there was still no uniform currency system in China when the National Government was established in 1927. This unsatisfactory state of affairs was gradually ameliorated after the establishment of the National Government which managed to unify the war-torn country.

Dr. Chang's paper gave us a broad account of the development of the monetary and banking system during the period 1927-1937, the essential features of which may be categorized under the following topics:

(1) The establishment of a Central Bank.

(2) The designation of the Bank of China as a foreign exchange bank and the breaking of the virtual monopoly of foreign banks over foreign exchange operations.

(3) The unification of the currency of the country and the abolition of the use of *tael*.

(4) The change from silver standard to a foreign exchange standard and the concentration of silver stocks in the hand of the Central Bank.

(5) Extension of modern banking services to the interior of China.

It would help us to grasp the gist of the developments during this period, if we review them under the above topics.

(1) The establishment of a Central Bank.

There is no question that the Central Bank of China which the National Government set up in 1928 fell, at first, far short of the ideal of a bankers' bank. This was due largely to the political difficulties with which the new government was confronted. Since all the powerful foreign banks were located in the foreign concessions, they were entirely outside the jurisdiction of the Chinese government. It was not feasible to require every bank to keep as reserves a given proportion of their own deposits in the form of deposits at the new central bank. Nor was the Central Bank able to concentrate foreign exchange reserves of the country in its hand. For as already noted, the foreign trade of China was at that time handled mainly by foreign firms, and foreign exchange transactions were almost the monopoly of foreign banks. These shortcomings were gradually improved, however, particularly after the changeover to a foreign exchange standard, which concentrated the silver holdings of all banks in the hand of the Central Bank.

(2) The breaking of the monopoly of foreign banks over foreign exchange transactions.

When the Bank of China was designated as a foreign exchange bank in 1928, it had hardly any experience in foreign exchange operations to draw upon. Realizing that it could obtain very little foreign exchanges from export trade then handled mostly by foreign firms, it undertook first to capture the inward remittances of overseas Chinese by providing services to the recipients of such remittances residing in China, and establishing agencies in various localities of the world where there were large concentrations of overseas Chinese. It also engaged in fostering export industries with loans and promoting their exports.

With such imaginative measures, the Bank of China quickly built up its foreign exchange operations from hardly anything outside of its Hong Kong branch to CN$161 million in 1932 and CN$989 million in 1934, a truly remarkable rate of increase. Thus the virtual monopoly in foreign exchange business enjoyed by foreign banks was at least partially broken.

(3) The abolition of the use of *tael* and the adoption of a new standardized silver dollar was accomplished smoothly in 1933. Later the debased and non-uniform silver and copper subsidiary coins minted by various provincial governments were also abolished and substituted by standardized subsidiary coins minted by the central mint.

(4) The changeover from a silver standard to a foreign exchange standard in Nov. 1935 was in a sense forced upon the Chinese government. When in 1934 the U.S. government engaged in a large scale purchase of silver as an expansionary policy to combat domestic depression, the price of silver rose sharply on the world market. It exerted powerful impacts upon the Chinese economy in two different ways. First, the rise in the world price of silver implied an automatic appreciation of the Chinese currency which was based upon silver; but it brought difficulties to China's export trade and encouraged imports, thus widening trade deficits. Second, the rise in the price of silver in terms of gold encouraged people to sell silver abroad for gold. Holders of Chinese banknotes were induced to convert their notes into silver dollars for melting and selling to the U.S. These twin impacts caused a heavy drain of silver from China and created a severe deflationary pressure upon industry and commerce.

Consequently, upon the recommendation of a British adviser, Sir Frederick Leith-Ross, the government abandoned the silver standard, and adopted a foreign exchange standard. The circulation of silver dollars was banned and only notes issued by the three government banks were recognized as legal tender. The public and commercial banks were ordered to surrender to the government all monetary silver in their possession in exchange for legal tender notes. The Central Bank of China was to buy and sell sterling exchanges without limit at a devalued rate (one shilling 2⅜ pence buying and one shilling 2⅝ pence selling).

This monetary reform was not an unmixed blessing to China. On the beneficial side, the devaluation of the Chinese dollar revived the export trade, and the suspension of the circulation of the silver dollars stopped the outflow of silver; hence, the forced contraction of the money supply. Prosperity was soon restored to Chinese industries. Moreover, through the cooperation of the British government, the powerful British banks in China supported this reform and surrendered their silver holdings to the Chinese Central Bank. Thus the Central Bank had come a long step closer to the role of a real Central Reserve Bank.

On the negative side, however, the suspension of the convertibility of currency notes into silver dollars removed an effective constraint upon note issue. Once this constrain was removed, the Chinese government was unable to resist the temptation of availing itself of the new ease in monetary expansion to finance urgent preparation against the increasing Japanese aggression. However, viewed in historical perspective, even this was certainly not an entirely negative score, as, without recourse to inflationary finance, it is hardly conceivable that the desperate war effort against Japanese military aggression could have been sustained for eight long years. The monetary reform of 1935 must, therefore, be regarded as a most important preparatory step for the impending war against Japanese aggression.

(5) Dr. Chang did not, however, devote much space to a description of the extension of banking service to the interior of China. Actually after unification of the country by the National Government, banks based on port cities such as Shanghai and Tientsin began to establish branches in the cities of the interior and to extend an increasing amount of credits to industries and agriculture as reconstruction or export promotion measures. Again in this movement, the Bank of China, under Dr. Chang's leadership, was in the lead. Regrettably, his paper does not give some statistics on the branches and new banks opened during this period in contrast to preceding period in the rest of China, and the deposits and loans granted by those branches and new banks to industry, commerce, and agriculture of the interior.

Thus we may observe that the National Government during the decade of 1927 to 1937, beset as it was with Communist uprisings, disastrous floods, and Japanese encroachment and aggression, still managed to carry out some fundamental reforms in monetary system and to bring about an expansion and strengthening of the banking system as well as considerable general economic development. It is true that some puzzling mistakes in policies might have been committed, as Dr. Chang has candidly pointed out, repeated tamperings with government debt services that weakened public confidence in government bonds, and the recourse to expansion of note-issue to finance government expenditures before all other fiscal alternatives had been exhausted. Nevertheless, Dr. Chang's conclusion remains quite warranted, namely, that if China had been spared the destructive war forced on her by Japanese aggression, she would have been well on her way towards developing a sound monetary and banking system as well as developing industrialization during the decade following 1937.

CHAPTER V

The Agricultural Economy of China, 1927–1937, As Exemplified by the Work At the University of Nanking

BY JOHN LOSSING BUCK

OR CENTURIES, FARMS IN CHINA consisted of parcels of farm land owned by farmers, or partially owned and the remaining land rented from other owners and tenant farmers who rented all their land from either resident, or absentee landlords. The heads of the farm family managed these farms with their own labor and that of family members; with exchanged labor of neighbors and relatives, with hired day laborers during busy seasons, and a small proportion having large family farms with hired year laborers.

Implements were hand tools, such as hoes and sickles, and animal propelled equipment, including plows and harrows, two and three row grain drills, and stone rollers for threshing and for packing soil. For transportation, carts were used in North China and boats in the canalized area in the Rice Region of South China. In South China, the Rice Region, "dragon" pumps, propelled by man or animal power, were used for irrigating rice. The Diesel engine for pumping water was the chief modern type of equipment in use beginning with the 1920's and increasing gradually during 1927-37. Even electric motors for pumping the Tseshuyen Power plant at Wuhsi, Kiangsu Province.

L. F. Chen, an engineer, estimates that 200,000 units of various sizes of Diesel engines were manufactured by the year 1937. For the year July 1936-June 1937, the quantity manufactured were about 30,000 units of which some 10-20 per cent were used for irrigation and the remainder for lighting, industrial, and commercial uses. By 1937, there were approximately 500 electric motor driven pumps used along the Grand Canal between Wuhsi and Changchow with power supplied by the Tseshuyen Power plant at Wuhsi, Kiangsu Province.

In general, the farm work was well done and weeding was thorough. Joint ownership of tools, equipment and labor animals was a common practice.

Farmers marketed their main products, such as wheat, rice, and cotton through local dealers, who in turn sold some of the produce locally and the remainder to wholesale merchants in the large cities. There were no farmers' cooperative marketing organizations until introduced in the mid-1920's.

This traditional system of farming was altered by the Communist Regime, 1950-1958, into collectives, first in small cooperatives, then into large Producers Associations where farmers' land, animals, and equipment were confiscated for use by the Associations. In 1958 these Associations were amalgamated into communes as large as a county. It was after the failure of these large county communes in 1958-59 that the production unit was changed to teams of some 20-30 families. Members of the teams were paid in terms of work units, thus reducing farmers to a status of laborers, even below that of a tenant who formerly managed his own business. The accounting unit was assigned to the brigade, consisting of 20-30 teams. It was responsible for the collection of produce as taxes and the supplying of improved seeds, fertilizers, insecticides, and equipment, when available, to the teams. With the exception of an increase in mechanical pumping for irrigation and the use of tractors and equipment on a small percentage of the farm area, tools and equipment, man and animal labor are still of the traditional type.

I

Education Research and Instruction

The development of modern economic aspects in the traditional agriculture of China began with instruction, research and extension in Agricultural Economics at the University of Nanking, Nanking, in 1920 and in the broad field of Economics at Nankai University, Tientsin, first by the University Committee on Social and Economic Research, January 1929 and later in 1931 by the Nankai Institute of Economics under the direction of Dr. Franklin L. Ho.

Training of college students in agricultural economics and rural sociology began at the College of Agriculture and Forestry, University of Nanking, in February 1920, upon the request of Dean Reisner for my appointment to the College staff. Previously, I had gained four years of experience with Chinese methods of farming in the Wheat Region, Anhwei Province, as an agriculturist with the American Presbyterian Mission at Nanhsuchow, Anhwei.

The University of Nanking had been established in 1910 as an outgrowth of middle schools operated by various Mission Boards. The College of Agriculture and Forestry was organized in 1913 with Joseph Bailie as Dean. He was joined by John H. Reisner, supported by the American Presbyterian Board of Missions, in October 1914, to assist in the teaching of students. This first class of eight students had been chosen by Bailie for their willingness to do manual work in aiding settlement of famine refugees and planting forest trees on the foothills and slopes of Purple Mountain. (Prospective students who did not meet this "willingness" test were not accepted for entrance into the College.) They were graduated in 1918. Outstanding in ability and in their eagerness to improve farming, several of them became faculty members of the College.

Registration of the College of Agriculture by the Ministry of Education at Peking was recorded in 1922 after an investigation by a special committee. Forestry was not recognized because the committee considered it to be understaffed.

After two years of teaching at Nanking, based on American text books and four years experience in the Wheat Region, I concluded that farm management and other aspects of agricultural economics and rural sociology could not be taught effectively without data pertinent to the operation of Chinese farms and related social conditions. The President of the University was approached to offer credit to qualified students during their summer vacation for collection of farm management data from farmers in the students' home communities by means of carefully prepared farm business and rural social survey schedules. Fortunately, President A. J. Bowen and the Registrar, Guy Sarvis, agreed that the experience for the students would be worthy of University credit for a summer's work of not less than one hundred farm survey schedules properly completed. Many items in the schedule could be cross-checked and, therefore, neither farmers nor students could be successful in cheating. Three students were elected to undertake surveys during the summer of 1922. The survey data obtained from 102 farms in three villages near Wuhu, Anhwei by Tao Yuen-chiao were analysed first and published in two parts, the first in a semi-popular form to interest the general public.[1]

The analysis of the field data from these 102 farms revealed that the principle of "economy of size" for family farms held true for farms near Wuhu, Anhwei in China, as it did for the many similar earlier farm studies in the United States of America. For instance, it was discovered that on large family farms compared with small farms, human labor was twice as efficient, animal labor was almost three times as efficient, and equipment about twice as efficient. This study indicated that reliable data could be obtained from farmers by trained students. Therefore, summer surveys by students were continued.

In the summer of 1923, five students obtained farm survey data from their home communities. The excellent survey of 150 farms in Yenshan county, Chihli Province (later Hopei), by Tsui Yu-tsuin was analyzed in great detail with the assistance of P. H. Hwa, a 1920 graduate, who supervised Chinese clerks proficient in the use of the abacus. The analysis and interpretation was published in June 1926, under the title *An Economic and Social Survey of 150 farms, Yenshan county, Chihli Province, China.*[2] This publication, as well as the previous two for 102 farms near Wuhu, provided instruction material for students.

By late 1925, nine other similar surveys were completed, seven by students for University credit and two by employed assistants, making a total of 2,866 farms in seventeen localities of seven provinces. While the analysis of the Yenshan data was in process it was decided that the data from the seventeen localities, nine in the Wheat Region of North China and eight in the Rice Region of East Central China, should be presented by averages for each locality, for each Region, and the average for all localities. This involved a tremendous amount of statistical calculations by local clerks experienced in the use of the abacus. Fortunately, unused American famine funds had been allocated to the University of Nanking, College of Agriculture and Forestry, primarily for crop improvement, a very small portion of which were made available for the computations.

The manuscript was completed in 1928 under the title *Chinese Farm Economy* for the farm business of 2,866 farms consisting of 8,500 hectares of farm land, a capital investment of five million dollars (Chinese currency) and a farm population of 17,000 persons. The analysis includes chapters on The Farm Family and Population, Food Consumption, and Standard of Living.

Late in 1928, the manuscript was shown to Dr. J. B. Conliffe, Secretary of the International Research Committee of the Institute of Pacific Relations, New York, who was visiting Nanking, together with L. T. Chen, Executive Secretary of the China Council of the Institute of Pacific Relations. Conliffe's reaction was "This ought to be published." L. T. Chen agreed. Chen gained the approval of the China Council of the Institute of Pacific Relations. Funds from the Institute of Pacific Relations, New York, were allocated to the University of Nanking for its publication with the title of "Chinese Farm Economy" under the auspices of the University of Nanking and the China Council of Institute of Pacific Relations.[3] Its publication in 1930 created considerable public interest in farm problems and encouraged more students to major in Agricultural Economics.

During the period, September 1921 to July 1927, the Chinese staff of the Agricultural Economics Department consisted of the following individuals:

P. H. Hwa, as Associate, a 1920 graduate of the College, who was transferred from the extension work in the College to the Department in September 1921. He assisted me in two classes, and, beginning in the autumn of 1922, Hwa supervised the statistical clerks in analysis of the increasing amount of farm survey data.

The second associate was Paul C. Hsu, a 1918 graduate from the first class of the College of Agriculture. He had received a scholarship from the Episcopal mission at Kaifeng and had returned there after graduation to teach in the middle school. He joined the College in September 1922 on a half-time basis to the Department; and beginning September 1923 on a full-time basis in Rural Organization. Hsu began organizing Farmers' Cooperative Societies in September 1922, and was in charge of developing such societies.

The third and fourth appointments as Associates immediately after their graduation were W. Y. Swen, on January 20, 1924, for Farm Management, and C. M. Chiao for Rural Sociology in June 1924. These two men were among fourteen scholarship students to the College from Shansi Provincial Government where Governor Yen Hsi-shan was interested in developing agriculture. Both participated with instruction and undertook special field studies. During my furlough in 1924-25, Hsu was Acting Head of the Department and Hsu, Swen and Chiao taught all the courses of instruction.

During the period 1924-28 these three associates, in addition to teaching, engaged in field research studies to determine important aspects of farm economy, including population and nutrition. Reference to several of these important studies are recorded as follows:

Chiao: (1) "A Survey of Farm Tenancy," described in a section of this paper on Farm Tenancy and Ownership.

(2) "The Composition and Growth of Population." A survey of 4,216 farm families in eleven areas of eight counties, four provinces.[4] The data indicated a growth rate of doubling the population every seventy years as compared with sixty-five years for the population study in *Land Utilization in China*, Chapter 13, where data for 1929-1933 were obtained from 38,256 families in 101 areas of seventeen provinces.

(3) "Farmers' Standard of Living." A survey of 2,390 farm families in thirteen areas of eight provinces.[5] A significant but unexpected discovery was that the farmer sells and purchases to a larger extent than generally realized.

Hsu and Swen: "Cost of Growing and Marketing Peanuts for the year 1925."[6]

The export of peanuts had been increasing to such an extent that the crop area devoted to peanuts by the Chinese farmer increased from 4 per cent in 1900 to 32 per cent in 1924. The reasons given by farmers were higher net returns from other crops, peanuts being better adapted to sandy soils and high land than other crops, having a high resistance to winds and floods and being a good legume crop in the rotation of crops, as well as being an excellent food.

This survey proves that the Chinese farmers alter traditional methods when they can clearly see the advantages. Another proof is the increased production of eggs in East Central China in the 1920's for export by processing firms in Shanghai. Instead of an average of some four to five hens per farm, farmers increased the number to seven, eight or nine. In 1925, while on furlough in USA, I told a group of farmers that there were only about four hens per farm in China. They asked "Where do all eggs come from?" The reply was simple. "There are over 60 million farms in China."

Hsu: *Farm Credit Survey*

(1) The summary below is a quotation from the *Annual Report for 1926-27 of the College of Agriculture and Forestry,* University of Nanking, Bulletin Volume seven, Number nine, pp. 23-24.

A detailed study of credit conditions has been made in three rural districts and among a total of 486 farmers. Five types of credit loans in the form of cash or grain, land mortgage, pawn shop credit, Yao Hwei (a loan society) and shop credit. Large, medium, and small size farms were included in the study and all made loans of some kind. The amount of credit per farmer for the three places was quite variable, being $43 for Chuchow, Anhwei, $144 for Shwenhwachen, Kiangsu, and $292 for Yienchiawei, Kiangsu. Of the total farmers 38 per cent made short term loans for productive purposes and 80 per cent for non-productive purposes. From 60 to 75 per cent of the farmers in the three places borrowed for the purpose of purchasing food. From 11 to 41 per cent borrowed for such purposes as funerals, weddings, and New Year holiday expenses. Loans made for productive purposes were chiefly for labor, fertilizer and land improvement. The seasonal distribution of loans shows that the proportion was greatest in winter, being 25 per cent in January and 23 per cent in February, and was lowest in August, 5 per cent.

The average rate of interest for these loans in the three places is 34.8 per cent per annum. The highest rate was 96.6 and the lowest 18 per cent per annum. The latter is offered by a modern rural cooperative credit society organized by this department. The average period of short term credit is six and one half months and that of long term is 4.1 years. The longest period found was six years.

(2) "A Marketing Survey at Nanhsuchow (Suhsien), Anhwei."[7] It was discovered that the local middle men and not the farmer were responsible for most of the adulteration of farm products, although otherwise they were performing an important function.

The following are the visiting professors to the Department of Agricultural Economics who gave their services gratis:

Dr. Walter F. Wilcox, Cornell University, September 1930, two weeks of lectures on "Population."

Dr. Edgar Sydenstricker, April 1930, Director of Research, Milbank Fund, U.S.A., two weeks of lectures on "Population and Statistical Methods;" and consultation with C. M. Chiao on the Population Survey.

Professor R. H. Tawney, 1930-31, London School of Economics, a semester's course on Agrarian History in Europe and England. Tawney resided in my residence and completed his book, *Land and Labor in China*, which he had started at Nankai.

Dr. Warren S. Thompson, of Scripp's Foundation for the Study of Population Problems, October 1930 to April 1931. Lectures for two weeks and initiating an Experimental Vital Statistics Project with C. M. Chiao of the Department and funds from his Foundation.

Dr. Robert Pendleton, 1931-1933, lectures on "Soil Survey of the National Geological Survey, Peking"; "Training of Regional Investigators in Soils." The personal assistance of T. H. Shao of the Department to Professor Shaw and Dr. Pendleton in the initial stages of soil investigations was instrumental in their success.

Dr. H. Zorner, 1934, lectures and seminars on Russian Agricultural Collectives. These lectures for two weeks created great interest on the part of students, faculty, and even some outsiders.

Dr. Frank A. Notestein, 1934-36, Director, Milbank Memorial Fund, U.S.A. Machine tabulation (in U.S.A.) of C. M. Chiao's Population Data. (Sydenstricker, the former director, had died.)

Ogden T. King, M.S., University of California, a student from Cornell for a survey of Economics of Farm Implements in China for his Ph.D. thesis with the aid of Hong-shen Pan.

Dr. James Thorp, Spring 1934-Spring 1936, National Geological Survey, Peking, in cooperation of the Survey with the Department. Field trips on soils with staff members and author of "Soils," a Chapter in *Land Utilization in China*, written at the University of Nanking.

Dr. J. Hanson-lowe, on fellowship from the China Universities Committee generously wrote the Chapter on "Topography" in *Land Utilization in China.*

B. Burgoyne Chapman, of Australia, while in Nanking for several years, wrote the Chapter on "Climate," gratis.

Dr. David Weeks, Professor of Agricultural Economics, University of California, Spring 1932. His services were loaned by the University with other expenses paid by the Department. He advised on the Land Utilization Project and gave a series of lectures to students.

In the early summer of 1935 the Ministry of Education in Nanking granted permission for the Department of Agricultural Economics to grant Master Degrees. By July 1945 seventeen students had received their Master Degrees.

The number of student credit hours in the Department of Agricultural Economics, from 1920 to 1942, was 15,732. Students majoring in Agricultural Economics and graduating numbered 294 by July 1945.[8] In 1941 each student graduating had offers for some six positions.

Non-collegiate instruction by the Department amounted to 15,252 student credit hours as follows:[9] "Staff members have participated in giving the following training: The Rural Leaders' Training School of the College of Agriculture and Forestry, University of Nanking, a two years' course which was begun in 1924 and is still being carried on; in 1933, the Cotton Industrial Cooperative Training class with forty-nine students under the auspices of the National Economic Council; the Agricultural Economics Training class with forty-nine students under the auspices of the National Economic Council; the Agricultural Economics Training class in 1935 with eighty students, under the auspices of the Farm Credit Bureau; Rural Cooperative Training classes in cooperation with the National Christian Council, for periods of three weeks each summer, with student registrations of forty, fifty, ninety-four and seventy-three for the years 1936-1939; three courses in the Szechuan Rural Cooperative Training School in 1937 with 500 students, under the auspices of the Szechuan Provincial Cooperative Commission; and the Industrial Cooperative Training Class in 1939 with sixteen students, under the auspices of the Chinese Industrial Cooperatives.

"The Department frequently, upon invitation from other outside institutions, has given single lectures on such subjects as Rural Organizations, Rural Finance, Prices, Marketing, and Land Problems. More recently, lectures have been given to the Agricultural Extension Training Class established by the Bureau of Agricultural Improvement of the Szechuan Provincial Government, to the Cooperative Business Training Class established by the Szechuan Cooperative Bank and the Farmers' Bank of China and to the Field Workers' Training Class established by the Szechuan Food Control Commission."

II

Modern Farmers' Organizations

Regulations for Rural Cooperative Credit Societies to be financed with funds from The China International Famine Relief Commission of Peking were adopted at a special meeting in June 1922, called by J. B. Tayler, Chief of the Committee on Credit and Economic Improvement of the Commission. From the University of Nanking, Dean Reisner and I were invited to attend the meeting and contribute to the formulation of feasible regulations. Immediately after their approval by the Commission, Paul C. Hsu of the Department of Agricultural Economics, organized the first modern farmers' cooperative credit society in China in September 1923. It was financed by a loan of $1,000 from the Commission. This society was just outside the Feng Run Gate of Nanking. The loan was for building a public privy along a street in Nanking from which the farmers obtained fertilizer for their market gardening. The second credit society organized by Hsu was in the Gung Village near Hwaiyuan, Anhwei, just south of the Hwai River in 1924, also with funds from the Commission. However, most of the credit societies organized with funds from the Commission were in North China. Information on these societies may be found in the annual reports of the Commission.

The success with these first societies resulted in grants of funds for new societies. During the academic year 1925-26 Hsu organized fourteen societies with the aid of a $5,000 (Chinese currency) grant from the University of Nanking for loans to Cooperative Credit Societies. In 1932 the National Christian Council entrusted the Department with a fund of $47,522 for promoting cooperative organization in villages with Christian work near Nanking, which had suffered losses from the Great Flood of the Yangtze River in 1931.

The first farmers' cooperative marketing society in China was organized by Paul C. Hsu at Wukiang, Anhwei (about 20 miles from Nanking) in 1926. The Extension Department of the College of Agriculture and Forestry had successfully introduced the American Acala variety of cotton with a longer staple than Chinese varieties. Because local merchants would not pay a higher price for it, Hsu was requested by me to go to Wuhsi, Kiangsu, to obtain the cooperation of a modern cotton mill to purchase the cotton. The mill owner agreed to buy the cotton at a higher price than that paid for Chinese cotton, resulting in a net profit of six Chinese dollars per picul to the farmers. This success caused the local merchants to raise their price but not high enough to deter the cooperative to continue shipping to the mill. This type of cotton required new equipment, such as the American type of gin and a baler to reduce costs and loss in shipment. To accomplish this the cooperative required a loan of $1,000.

K. P. Chen, General Manager for the Shanghai Commercial and Savings Bank, was approached by Dean Reisner, Hsu and I for the $1,000 loan. Chen was hesitant to make the loan for fear the farmers would not repay it. He requested a guarantee from three faculty members. Dean Reisner, Hsu, and I signed for repayment of the loan. After the farmers sold their improved cotton to a mill at Wuhsi, the loan was repaid by the cooperatives. K. P. Chen was so impressed that his bank prepared to extend loans directly to cooperatives. Government and other banks followed with organization of cooperatives and loans.

Beginning in 1932, the Shanghai Commercial and Savings Bank distributed cotton seeds of the American Acala variety in the famine stricken area of Shensi Province, near Sian. The organization and financing of societies by the Bank began in summer of 1933 and ended in 1941 during the Sino-Japanese War. By 1935 there were twenty-six cooperatives. The total amount of loans by the Bank to cooperatives in Shensi, for the period 1934 to 1941 totalled $9,830,000 Chinese currency. Most of the loans were for cooperative irrigation projects. K. P. Chen being a compassionate person, the plight of farmers in this famine stricken area near Sian moved him to give as much aid as possible. I was in the area in 1934, enroute to the Northwest, and observed the farm villages with nothing but crumbling soil-tamped walls remaining. In severe famines farmers have to sell everything to buy food and then to migrate.

In 1932, Paul C. Hsu received his M. S. degree from Cornell in Rural Cooperation, and he continued to devote most of his time to organization and supervision of cooperatives. Because of the additional need of well-trained cooperative organizers, K. P. Chen, in 1934, granted $60,000 (Chinese currency) for two professional chairs in the Department of Agricultural Economics, University of Nanking for two experienced cooperative experts from abroad to assist in the training of leaders in cooperative organization. One was C. F. Strickland of England, who had extensive experience with cooperatives in India; the other, Dr. W. M. Stevens of the United States, in business management of cooperatives. A grant of $3,000 was also given for student scholarships. These two men were followed by Dr. Glenn W. Hedlund, of Cornell University, for teaching and advising on cooperative organization.

In the same year, the Shanghai Commercial and Savings Bank also earmarked $390,000 (Chinese currency) for loans to cooperatives at Wukiang by the Department of Agricultural Economics. By this time, cotton production of the Acala variety, its ginning and bailing and marketing had become big business from the first small quantity of Acala cotton seeds introduced to farmers in 1921 by the College of Agriculture and Forestry, University of Nanking.

In 1934, Paul Hsu resigned to head the cooperative work of the Bank of Communications. By that time he had organized forty-eight Cooperative Credit Societies and two cotton marketing societies. Hwei-chien Li, a February 1932 graduate of the Department of Agricultural Economics who had been working with Hsu, became the Department's leader in organizing cooperatives. By 1935 the Department of Agricultural Economics had organized 113 credit and marketing societies with a membership of 2,916 farmers. After the Department of Agricultural Economics moved to Chengtu, Szechuan in late 1938, Li with a fund from the Szechuan Cooperative Bank of $400,000 organized 140 Registered Credit Societies with a membership of 6,697 farmers.

The first cooperative legislation of a government in China was promulgated by the Kiangsu Provincial Government in 1928 as the "Provisional Cooperative Legislation for Rural Cooperatives in Kiangsu Province." The original draft of the legislation was prepared by Paul C. Hsu at the request of the Planning Committee of the Kiangsu Provincial Farmers' Bank. By request of the Bank, Paul C. Hsu was loaned for about six months to assist in training of cooperative organizers and in bank loan operations. Dean T. S. Kuo of the College of Agriculture and Forestry, University of Nanking, who was so interested in rural credit that he concurrently became Director of the Bank in order to guide this new type of banking.

After the Four Provinces Agricultural Bank was organized in 1933, one of its important activities was cooperative credit loans to farmers in the four provinces formerly under Communist control.

At the end of 1945 there were 150,000 cooperative Societies organized during the period of 1937-1945.[10] By provinces, the largest number was for Szechuan amounting to about 23,000 cooperatives. The purposes of all loans in percentages were 80.2 for agricultural production, 8.2 for credit, 3.0 for supplies, 2.7 for marketing, general 2.6, industrial production 2.5, consumption 0.7 for utilities.

The first Farmers Agricultural Association was organized by C. M. Chiao at Wukiang, Anhwei where the College of Agriculture and Forestry, University of Nanking, was extending the cultivation of the American variety of Acala cotton. The purpose of the organization was to make it easier for farmers to obtain assistance from Government and private institutions which were developing services for farmers. Farms were so small that extension workers could not work effectively with so many individual farmers. Previous attempts in organizing farmers had failed. The extension organizer of the College of Agriculture and Forestry at Wukiang was a former preacher who had graduated from the College of Agriculture two year course at Nanking. It was with his help that six farmers' Associations were organized at Wukiang and Hsiangchwan, Anhwei, with a total membership of 4,000 farmers. The fee for membership was fifty cents. In the third year these associations employed and paid the salary of this extension organizer. Later the associations had a lawsuit with the Magistrate of Wukiang *hsien* and won. The organization of Farmers' Associations continued by Chiao in other areas, and eventually there were so many in the countryside that the National Government enacted appropriate legislation. Associations multiplied rapidly. Chiao emphasized that they were a basic organization for farmers to improve their farming and to maintain a position of dignity in society. As at Wukiang, these Associations also developed local primary schools and even health clinics. It was at Wukiang that the farmers were so well organized in Associations and Cooperatives that they were able to prevent interference by the Japanese Army.

III

Farm Tenancy and Ownership

The proportion of farmers who are owners, part owners and tenants has been both the object of estimates and also of actual counts in a few specific studies. Estimates were obtained by the following organizations: the Peking Ministry of Agriculture in 1919 for eighteen provinces; the National Agricultural Research Bureau in 1935 by its Crop Reporters in 891 *hsien* of twenty-two provinces; and the Summary Report of the National Land Survey Committee of the National Economic Council of the National Government in Nanking (probably about 1933); and actual counts by the Department of Agricultural Economics, Nanking for 16,786 farms in twenty-two provinces (the *Land Utilization in China Survey, 1929-31*). The average of these data from the four sources indicate 54 per cent of all farmers as owners, 24 per cent as part owners, and 22 per cent as tenants.

The average for 2,866 farms in the *Chinese Farm Economy* (Surveys for the years 1921-1924) is 63 per cent for owners, 17 per cent for part owners and 20 per cent for tenants. These averages were not included in above averages of four sources because only seven provinces are represented. Moreover, nine localities were in North China where tenancy is less prevalent than in South China with a representation of only eight localities.

In Chapter V on "Farm Ownership and Tenancy" in *Chinese Farm*

Economy, a detailed farm business analysis is presented for 501 tenant farms. Included in this analysis is a method of determining a fair rent for the tenant to pay the landlord from all farm receipts in the same proportion as farm expenses (cash and non cash) are incurred by the tenant and the landlord. However, this method is too complicated to be used by the tenant farmer. A new calculation from tables 5 and 6 on expenses and receipts indicate that the landlords are receiving an average of 9.5 per cent on their capital investment chiefly land. The degree to which this return to the landlord may be judged as fair is the 10 per cent return on bank fixed deposits.

Government decrees fixing a percentage of rent reduction were impractical because of the great variations in local practices. For instance, in Suhsien, Anhwei of North China, the tenants underpaid landlords by 1.7 per cent of the farm receipts. In Kiangning *hsien* at Shwenhwachen, ten miles from Nanking, landlords were wealthy from businesses elsewhere and they held the land and the large well-built residences by officials for prestige purposes. Tenants in this area were fortunate because a fair rent in terms of value of land would have required an increase of 39.8 per cent in rent payment.

Therefore, it may be concluded that any legislation stipulating per cent reduction in rents would not meet the problem in a realistic manner. The most simple stipulation would be payment of rent at a certain percentage of the land value. The 1946 amendment to the Land Law of the National Government stipulated 8 per cent of the land value as maximum rent.

At the time the Revolutionary armies were pressing northward to oust the provincial Military Governors in the mid 1920's; interest in the rent reduction legislation increased. Chekiang Province enforced a 25 per cent reduction. This influenced some of the landlords in Kiangsu Province, for fear of similar rent reduction, to sell their land and invest the proceeds in industries of the big cities, particularly Shanghai. Various attempts were made by leaders of Land Reform to obtain Government recognition and legislative action on Land Reform. By 1930 a Land Law was promulgated.

The Chinese Association of Land Economics was formally inaugurated in January 1933, with Tseng Hsiao as Director. It grew in membership to 500 members and twenty-seven affiliated groups by the time of the Japanese attack in summer of 1937. The Association published a Weekly and a Monthly in the mid-1930's until the summer of 1937.

A Cadastral Survey and Registration of Land was promoted by the Association and some progress was made. The Generalissimo even issued an edict for all owners to register all their land or risk the forfeiting of their unregistered land. This did have some effect.

An important example is Kiangning *hsien,* where an experimental *Hsien* Government was inaugurated in 1935, or 1936, at Shwenhwachen rather than retain the *hsien* government headquarters at Nanking. The new *hsien* government enforced the edict to register all land with the result that a large increase in the amount of land was registered; so great, in fact, that the taxes on land were reduced to a significant amount.

The Land Law of 1930 was amended in 1946. It was specific on rents, stating that they should not exceed 8 per cent of the land value. It also provided for Landlord-Tenant Purchase projects. An extremely successful project was developed at Pei-peh, near Chungking. Western news reporters travelled to Yenan, Shansi to see the progress there in rural organization, but I have never seen or heard of a reporter writing up this successful project only a few miles from Chungking.

In 1940, the China Research Institute of Land Economic was established at Chungking for research and training. It is still a vital institution in Taiwan. In fact, the efforts to bring about Land Reform on the Mainland enabled the participants to introduce quickly and effectively Land Reform in Taiwan. Tseng Hsiao is head of the Institute and was the leader on the Mainland in promoting Land Reform.[11] The first chapter of his recent book describes efforts to obtain land reform on the mainland, during the mid-1920's until 1949. The remaining chapters of his book describe the successful Land Reform in Taiwan.

The early study of *Farm Tenancy in the Counties of Quisan and Nantung of Kiangsu Province and Suhsien, Anhwei Province, China* (1924) by C. M. Chiao, Department of Agricultural Economics, University of Nanking, created a great deal of interest and demand for the publication. It was the first published study with pertinent information on the economics of tenure. For instance, the interest on investment of landlords from three qualities of land reveal greater returns to the landlord from medium and poor land than from good land.

	Good	Medium	Poor
Quinsan	10.6	12.6	13.4
Nantung	4.2	4.6	4.6
Suhsien	9.2	12.5	15.0

(*Proverb:* In East Kiangsu Province "Every time a tenant moves three are made poor, the tenant, the landlord and land.")

The chief problems in the tenancy system vary by regions, but the common ones are created by a lack of understanding that tenancy is a partnership of the landlord and tenant rather than a system of gouging by the landlord with excessive rents and cheating by the

tenant in various ways, such as hiding some of the grain at the time
the landlord collects his share of crops.

I summarized research and other studies on farm tenancy under
the title "Farm Tenancy in China" in *Economic Facts*, No. 33 and 34,
June and July 1944, pp. 469-487, Department of Agricultural Economics,
University of Nanking.[12] A reprint containing the two articles was also
issued by the Department under the same title.

The following topics were also included: conditions causing tenancy
and landlordship, length of tenure, considerations affecting types of
renting systems, tenant prisons, a form of serfdom, double ownership
of land (the soil owned by one person and the surface by another
person) and attitudes of landlords and tenants. Comparative data
from various sources on important aspects of tenancy were presented
in tables with ample discussion. A list of references to twenty-seven
studies is included. Seven were government publications chiefly statistics on amount of tenancy. Eight were University of Nanking student theses, three by other organizations or individuals, and nine by
the Department of Agricultural Economics.

IV

Land Utilization in China

At the time of a visit by J. B. Condliffe and L. T. Chen to the
Department of Agricultural Economics, University of Nanking, in late
1928, and after approving of the publication of *Chinese Farm Economy*,
Condliffe pulled from his pocket a proposed project for a study of
land utilization in China to be undertaken in Washington, D. C.
I suggested it would appear more realistic to have it conducted in
China. He replied, "If you wish, submit a project." This was done
with a thorough outline of method and content. The prospectus was
first submitted to the China Council of the Institute of Pacific Relations. After it was approved by the Council's Research Committee, of
which Dr. Franklin L. Ho was Chairman, it was forwarded to the
New York office of the Institute of Pacific Relations. In turn it was
submitted to the Social Science Research Council of New York, which
gave its approval. Basically, the proposed research comprised an
appraisal of the natural factors affecting both the type and success of
land use, other factors determining the type of land use and factors
responsible for the degree of success in use of land. Special funds were
provided for me by the Institute of Pacific Relations for a four-month
visit during 1928-29 to institutions and individuals in the United
States who had done research in land utilization.

My visit was helpful, not only for information gained, but also in selecting personnel from the United States to assist in the project. For instance, Dr. Charles Shaw, a Soils Expert at the University of California, was granted a leave of absence February-June 1930 to assist in training of the Land Utilization regional investigators in the recognition of different soils which affect types of farming. Concurrently, he made extensive field surveys in East and North China and wrote a preliminary paper on "The Soils of China." The bulletin was published for the University of Nanking and the China Institute of Pacific Relations by the Geological Survey of China. A second very important contribution by Dr. Shaw was a memorandum recommending the establishment of a Soil Survey organization in the Geological Survey. It was submitted to the China Foundation for the Promotion of Culture and Education. The Foundation approved the project and agreed to finance it if the Geological Survey should accept the proposal.[13] The Geological Survey did accept it and invited Dr. Robert L. Pendleton, formerly with Soil Survey in India and then the College of Agriculture, Philippines. He was followed by James Thorp of the USDA Soil Survey. Dr. W. H. Wong, Director of the Geological Survey, maintained cooperation with the Land Utilization Survey in permitting these two men to train the regional investigators in recognition of soils and in analyzing the soil samples. He also agreed to the writing of the Chapter on "Soils by Thorp" at the University of Nanking for the Land Utilization in China project.

The selection of capable Regional Investigators was the foundation of the study.

Twelve College graduates of the Department of Agricultural Economics native to various agricultural areas were selected to obtain data from types of farming areas representative of larger areas.

The selection of Regional Investigators was made on the basis of their training and experience, nativity to regions where sample surveys were to be made, and, of course, speaking the same local language. Their task was to find local men as enumerators and train them in the use of the schedules. Most of them were graduates of middle schools and could speak the same dialect as that of the farmers to be interviewed. Personnel of local mission stations and several Provincial Governments were of great assistance in finding qualified persons.

Three of the Regional Investigators were selected from the large graduation class of 1930, namely, Ming-liang Li, Hong-shen Pan and Wei-chi Sui-tsao. The other investigators were the following:

W. Y. Swen and C. M. Chiao, on the staff of the Department and having six years of experience.

R. T. Tsui, a 1925 graduate, who had been with the American Presbyterian Mission in Chihli Province (later Hopei) in rural work, and who, as a student, made the excellent survey at Yenshan.

Teh-hsing Shao, a 1921 graduate, with his first two years as a member of the 1918 class, had been with the College since graduation, in extension work and later was Farm Superintendent of the College Experiment Station and the Vegetable and Nursery Gardens. He was very familiar with farmers and their psychology and an excellent person for survey work.

W. Y. Yang, a 1927 graduate who had been engaged in agricultural work with the American Board Mission in Shansi, who also became a staff member of the Department of Agricultural Economics.

Lien-ken Yin, a 1929 graduate, who in 1940 succeeded C. M. Chiao as Head of the Department.

Rwen-tao Liu, a 1925 graduate, who also joined the Department as a member. His previous experience was in Chekiang Province.

Sing-I Chang, B. S., Iowa and M. S., Cornell (1926) a staff member of the Department, August 1927-1930 and in 1931-32 for the Survey. He was native of Kansu Province which enabled him to survey the northwestern part of the Spring Wheat Area.

In most cases the Regional Investigators checked the schedules obtained each day. However, in some instances this was impossible and in one case the local man's schedules had to be destroyed because of inaccuracies. In another situation, the local enumerator was attacked by a Communist group just as he had completed the surveys. He escaped, but with the loss of completed schedules and his baggage.

Schedules were tabulated as rapidly as received by the Department. In 1931 there were sixty-two clerks tabulating the data chiefly with abacuses. The number increased to over 100 during the peak of tabulation.

The task of summarizing the large amount of data in a meaningful and accurate manner was almost formidable. After determining the subject matters to be tabulated, work sheets had to be prepared for statistical clerks. Dr. Stanley S. Warren (Ph.D., Cornell 1931), Agricultural Economist and an expert in Statistical Methods, accepted an invitation for a year, 1931 to 1932, to come to Nanking to assist in the directing of the tabulations and for training the staff in Land Utilization and Statistical Analysis. He was followed by Dr. A. B. Lewis (Ph.D., Cornell 1933), Agricultural Economist, for the period October 1933 to June 1936. Dr. Warren continued assistance in analysis of the Land Utilization data, taught courses in Elementary Statistics and Prices, did research on Prices and on Silver and the Chinese Price Level. He also organized the publication of *Economic Facts* beginning with the September 1936 edition, a monthly in English and Chinese, containing research studies of the Department's faculty and advanced students.

I made several observation trips to areas he had not previously visited. One of these was with the Soil Survey team, headed by James Thorp, Soil Scientist for the Geological Survey in Peking. The group also included Brian Low, Economic Geographer, a New Zealander for the Land Utilization project, and Shao Teh-hsing who was the chief leader on Soils for the Regional Investigators. This trip was by rail from Nanking to Sianfu and then by open truck to Lanchow, Kansu, crossing the boundary between Winter Wheat and Spring Wheat about half way. Then to Sinning (Tsinghai), and to Hwanyuan, the last *hsien* with agriculture. A short distance west the boundary between agriculture and grasslands was crossed before reaching a camp of nomad Tibetans, overlooking Lake Kokonor.

Boundaries of the two Agricultural Regions, Rice and Wheat, and those of the Eight Agricultural Areas were determined by observation and by tabulated data from the Survey schedules and other sources. The data collected made it possible to outline two major regions, the Wheat Region in the North and the Rice Region in the South. The Wheat Region was subdivided into the Spring Wheat Area, the Winter Wheat-Millet Area, and the Winter Wheat-Kaoliang Area. The Rice Region was subdivided into the Rice-Tea Area, the Szechuan Rice Area, the Double Cropping Rice Area, and the Southwestern Rice Area. The boundaries of the two regions and the eight agricultural areas cross provincial boundaries, and provide a better understanding of Chinese agriculture by classifying like with like, such as proportions of cultivated areas and areas in various crops. Agricultural data have greater meaning from an agricultural viewpoint when thus classified than when classified by provinces.

Agricultural Survey schedules were used for information by *hsien*, from actual data from *hsien* government records, and by obtaining estimates of local knowledgeable persons.

The Survey, in addition to land utilization, included two other special surveys, one on farm population with funds from the Milbank Foundation sponsored by Edgar Sydenstricker; and another on nutrition of farm families with a small fund from Leland Stanford Food Research Institute sponsored by Dr. Carl Alsberg. Both of these sponsors, when they learned of the Land Utilization Study, were anxious to have information obtained on these two topics.

The tabulation of data from the surveys to indicate relationship between production, population, standard of living and nutrition was a tremendous task but had the help of over 100 clerks with abacuses. Finally, in 1937, the findings were published in three volumes: A summary and interpretation by regions and areas as Land Utilization in

China, a Statistical Volume with averages for 100 farms for each locality arranged under names of provinces for each agricultural area, averages for the Wheat Region and the Rice Region and the averages for all localities. The Atlas Volume was also published with all data that could be presented geographically and for which Brian Low was chiefly responsible.

Funds from the Institute of Pacific Relations were insufficient for the publication of the Statistical and Atlas volumes. Through the good offices of Dr. H. H. Kung, Minister of Finance, the National Economic Council and the Bank of China supplied funds for the printing of the Statistical and Atlas volumes.

One of the very important aspects of the Land Utilization Survey was the estimate of unregistered land not reported in official statistics. The Regional Investigators queried three different knowledgeable persons in all localities visited on how much cultivated land was unreported in official statistics. The average of these estimates indicated that the official land records should be increased by the factor of 1.337. The average of all the highest estimate indicated an increase by the factor of 1.425. The factor of 1.337 was used in food and agriculture in Communist China[14] to correct the amount of land before the advent of Communist government. The Communists in their official statistics of 1949-1958 began their series with an increased amount of land over the 65.8 million hectares used by the National Agricultural Research Bureau to compute production for twenty-two provinces in 1931-37.

Including Manchuria, Jehol and Sinkiang the official amount in 1931-37 would be about 83 million hectares. If this is increased by the factor of 1.337 the amount of cultivated area would be 108 million hectares. The factor of 1.425 would indicate 115 million hectares for Mainland China. The highest Communist estimate was for the year 1956 at 112 million hectares of cultivated land.[15] The average for the period 1949-1958 amounted to 107 million hectares.

V

Economic Depression in China

In the summer of 1933 a Hongkong newspaper contained an item reporting that the United' States economic depression had reached China. At Shanghai, newspapers were referring to the economic deterioration of rural villages. I suggested to Dr. A. B. Lewis, who had just joined the Department of Agricultural Economics, to study the problem and ascertain the cause.

Dr. Lewis with L. L. Chang, a 1929 graduate of the Department and a staff member who had been collecting information on farm prices, discovered the cause of the problem and reported their findings in a research bulletin of the Department, entitled *Silver and the Chinese Price Level*.[16] Their analysis of price data for farm products at the farm, wholesale prices and prices of import and export commodities revealed a decline beginning in mid-1931 and continuing drastically for over two years.

On the other hand, the purchasing power of silver, the base for the Chinese currency,, was rising during the same period. Thus, because of the rising value of silver the Chinese dollar was worth more than previously and it took fewer dollars to buy farm and industrial products hence the decline in farm and wholesale prices.

After publication of the bulletin on *Silver and the Chinese Price Level*, Dr. Leonard S. Hsu, a sociologist at Yenching University, who was at that time counselor of the Ministry of Industry, was impressed with the gravity of the depression. He immediately attempted to persuade the Ministry of Finance to appoint a government committee to study the problem and present a report on the subject. The Ministry of Finance was not interested, and objected to outsiders meddling in currency matters. However, the Ministry of Industry approved the idea, and appointed a Committee for the Study of Silver Values and Commodity Prices with Dr. Leonard S. Hsu as Chairman and the following members: Dr. Y. C. Koo, Ch'en Chung-sheng, Chen Ping-ch'uan, T'ang Ching-po, Ardron Bayard Lewis, Chang Lu-luan, and John Lossing Buck. The Committee requested A. B. Lewis and L. L. Chang to undertake the necessary research for the Committee. When the manuscript was completed and approved by the Committee[17] it was shown to certain members of the Ministry of Finance, who exhibited no interest, except to remark, "What business has the Committee in delving into matters pertaining to Chinese currency?"

The manuscript was also presented to Dr. H. H. Kung, Minister of Finance, and to Generalissimo Chiang. Later, at one o'clock in the night, Leonard S. Hsu received a phone call asking him to be present at Minister Kung's office at seven o'clock that morning, November 3, 1935. A decision was made to issue a decree that the Chinese currency would no longer be redeemed in silver beginning November 4, 1935. Thus China went off the silver standard, but kept the currency at a constant rate with the English pound which was not at that time tied to silver or any other metal. The Chinese price level immediately rose and returned to a pre-depression level. This resulted in a return to normal farm production and business operations, a kind of golden economic age, soon terminated, unfortunately, by the outbreak of the Sino-

Japanese War in mid-1937, which forced the evacuation of government, industries, schools and colleges to West China. Because its sources of revenue were largely cut off, the government was forced to print money to pay its bills, and the currency depreciated. In December 1939 the currency was pegged at twenty Chinese dollars to one U.S. dollar, but it continued to lose value drastically during the war, because of use of the printing press to finance the resistance to further Japanese encroachment, until dollar bills were practically worthless.

VI

Calamity Surveys and the Department's Publications

I was in Nanking during the great flood of 1931 which seriously affected some 4,242,200 farm families in the Yangtze River Flood Plain and in the Hwai River Flood Plain. As a result of a small sample to test a schedule to be used for a survey of flood damage, T. V. Soong, Director of the National Flood Relief Commission requested the Department of Agricultural Economics, under my direction, to survey the losses, and, for which funds were granted. This required a temporary transfer of some of the Land Utilization Regional Investigators to collect the necessary data to assess the damage.[18]

After the withdrawal of the Japanese troops, magistrates of seven *hsien* affected by the fighting requested relief funds from the National Government. T. V. Soong, Minister of Finance, requested the Department of Agricultural Economics to survey the losses suffered by farmers. Schedules were completed quickly by the Department, several Regional Investigators went to Shanghai and trained volunteer students from Soochow and Shanghai Baptist College in one evening for the survey. From the time of the request until completion of the Report in English and Chinese only three and one-half weeks had elapsed. The Report was a confidential one, but so little damage was discovered that Minister Soong refused any relief.

After the Communists were driven from the four provinces of Honan, Kiangsi, Hupeh and Anhwei by Nationalist forces, Four Provinces Agricultural Bank of China, established in 1933, was given a directive by Generalissimo Chiang to make an Economic Survey of the four provinces as a basis for bank loans and other assistance. The Bank turned to the Department of Agricultural Economics to undertake the Survey with funds provided by the Bank. This was in early 1934 when the Land Utilization Investigator had just finished their work. Some of them were immediately transferred to this Survey under the direction of Professor W. Y. Swen. The summary reports were issued in Chinese and published by the Bank. *Economic Facts*, No. 3, Nov. 1936, pp. 141-151 of the Department carried a summary of the Land Classification Surveys by R. T. Tsui (For a list of new personnel of the Department of Agricultural Economics, University of Nanking, from August 1927 to 1937, see note 19).

The Department of Agricultural Economics, University of Nanking published the following books:

Chinese Farm Economy, 476 pp.; (also translated in Chinese);

Land Utilization in China, 404 pp.; (also translated in Chinese);

Land Utilization in China-Statistics (bilingual), 473 pp.;

Land Utilization in China—Atlas (bilingual), 146 pp.;

Farm Management (a textbook for use in China) by Dr. W. M. Curtis and J. L. Buck (translated also), 156 pp.

Bulletins and papers were published in public periodicals and in *Economic Facts* (chiefly of research nature).[20] The number published under each subject matter are listed as follows:
Agricultural Development, thirteen; Calamity Survey, four; Cost of Production, twenty-four; Farm Implements and Labor Animals, seven; Farm Management, twenty-three; Land Tenure, eleven; Land Utilization and Classification, eight; Population, Standard of Living and Nutrition, fourteen; Prices and Currency, eighty-five; Rural Organization Sociology and Extension, twenty-eight; Statistics of Agriculture, three; Unclassified, nine; total pages, 229.

The three Calamity Surveys indicate that the Department of Agricultural Economics was staffed with a sufficient number of competent agricultural economists, statisticians, and clerks with experience in collecting information, processing it, and submitting reports to undertake almost any project. In other words, the Department had become "Economic in Size."

           * * *

This sketch of China's agricultural economy, 1927-1937, does not include all the development aspects by the National Government, the Provinces, and the *Hsien*, or by all the non-government institutions and organizations. Some are not recorded, or are unavailable, or were omitted. For instance, the International Committee for Famine Relief in the 1920's and 1930's executed a policy of relief in return for labor of refugees on building roads and on construction of irrigation projects. This policy was also one of the National Flood Relief Commission where during the rebuilding of dykes after the 1931 Flood refugees were given food in return for their labor expended in the repairing of dykes.

By 1936, I remarked: "The sleeping lion was wide awake; there were enough Chinese in every facet of development so that all foreigners could go home and the progress would continue at accelerating rate."

Comments:

BY FRANKLIN L. HO

Dr. Buck has presented an authoritative paper on the agricultural economy of China from 1927 to 1937. A master on the subject in pre-communist modern China, Dr. Buck writes from his own experiences in teaching, research and demonstration in agricultural economy during a period he literally lived through in China. I feel a deep sense of incompetence indeed to comment on a paper such as that of Dr. Buck's.

However, Dr. Buck's paper is a sectorial presentation of China's agricultural economy—a record of his personal experiences and observation. As a supplement to Dr. Buck's paper, I propose to offer a brief aggregate account of the development of China's agricultural economy from 1927 to 1937.

Agricultural economy refers, usually, to such subjects as land tenure system, agricultural credit and marketing, land taxation, and so forth. The development of these subjects is of prime importance in the development of agriculture as a whole. They should proceed or, at least, keep pace with the development of the technique of agriculture. This has been well demonstrated from the experience of agricultural development in Western Europe. The reconstruction of the legal fabric of land tenure in Great Britain, for instance, preceded the modernization of productive technology

I: Agencies engaged in the development of agricultural economy.

To begin with, I shall briefly mention some of the government agencies both at the national level and at the local level engaged in the work on the development of agricultural economy in China from 1927 to 1937. I shall not mention any of the private agencies, some of which have already been covered in Dr. Buck's paper. It may be stated, however, that private agencies, though important, were fewer in number and more restricted in scope than government agencies. According to a survey conducted in 1934, of the 691 agencies engaged in the development of agricultural economy in China, private agencies accounted for 109 (16 per cent of the total). Of the remaining 582 agencies all of which were governmental, sixty-two were national, 352 were provincial and 124 were local.

The most important national government agencies in the development of China's agricultural economy from 1927 to 1937 were: (1) The tional Economic Council; and (3) the relevant departments and sub- Rural Rehabilitation Commission of the Executive Yuan; (2) The Na- ordinated organizations of several ministries of the Executive Yuan.

The Rural Rehabilitation Commission was established in May, 1933 with the President of the Executive Yuan as Chairman and the Director of the Political Department of the Yuan as Executive Secretary. The function of the Commission was two-fold: (1) to conduct studies on agricultural-economic problems and make recommendations to the government for action; and (2) to serve as an agency to coordinate and promote the work undertaken by all the public and private agencies directed toward the economic aspects of agricultural development. Although the Commission was active for less than two years, it did a great deal to make the country conscious of the importance of the subject and the serious problems inherent in it. The studies published by the Commission which provided factual basis for policy making include those on marketing of rice, wheat, cotton, silk, tea, etc.; those on land surcharges, the land tenure system and agricultural credit. In addition, the Commission was instrumental in expanding the National Bureau of Agricultural Research, creating the Rice and Wheat Improvement Institutes and Marketing Bureau for Grain, and in launching an extensive program of relief and cooperation in the provinces of Hopei and Chahar. Other activities of the Commission included sponsoring a national cooperative conference, recommending for the establishment of a national system of agricultural extension and promoting a program of land tax reform which dealt in particular with the surcharges levied on land.

The National Economic Council opened a preparatory office early in October 1931, and was formally organized in November 1933. In structure, the Council had eight administrative bodies, namely: the Bureau of Roads, the Bureau of Hydraulic Engineering, the Bureau of Agriculture, the Central Field Health Station, the Kiangsi Office, the Northwest Office, the Cotton Commission, and the Sericulture Commission. In function, it placed emphasis on the economic aspects of the agricultural development with particular reference to land tenure, land taxation, agricultural credit, and marketing. Foreign advisors sent to China through the League of Nations, such as the Salter Mission to Chekiang, made special reference to the gravity of the agricultural economic problems and the need for reform in their recommendations.

In the early 1930's, several of the ministries of the Executive Yuan of the National government had sub-divisions whose functions were centered in agricultural economic development. The Ministry of Industries had a Department of Agriculture and Forestry and that of Cooperatives. In addition, it had such subordinate organizations as the National Bureau of Agricultural Research, the Rice and Wheat Improvement Institute, the Agricultural Extension Committee, and the Agricultural Credit Administration. The Ministry of Interior performed two special functions during the 1930's which contributed to the economic aspects of agricultural development. It established a number of experimental *hsien* and provided in-service training for *hsien* magistrates with emphasis on the economic needs and problems of the peasants. Mention should also be made of the increased emphasis in the 1930's on programs dealing with mass education sponsored by the Ministry of Education and the rural health programs sponsored by the National Health Administration—both problems had immediate bearing on the development of agricultural economy. The Legislative Yuan also became more active during the 1930's in the passage of laws relating to the economic aspects of the agricultural development. The most important pieces of this type of legislation were the Land Law of June 30, 1930; the Forestry Law of September 15, 1932; and the Cooperative Societies Law of February 1, 1933.

A number of provinces had agencies dealing with agricultural economic development. As early as 1917-1918, the government of Shansi Province established the Bureau of Village Administration to promote and supervise political, economic, and social activities at the village level with special emphasis on village industries, organization of cooperatives, and the development of irrigation and aforestation. In 1935, the provincial government under the leadership of Yen Hsi-shan proposed a program of village ownership of land as a solution to the agrarian economic problem.

In Kiangsi during the early 1930's several technical organizations were created to deal with the development of agricultural economy. Among these were the Provincial Institute of Agriculture and the Provincial Cooperative Commission. Suiyuan, Hunan, Hupeh, Kwangsi, Kiangsu, and Chekiang were other provinces which had interesting agricultural economic development programs during the 1930's.

There were also significant developments of agricultural economy during the 1930's at the *hsien* (county) level. On August 16, 1933 the Ministry of Interior ordered the establishment of experimental *hsien* under the jurisdiction of the provincial government. By 1937, fourteen experimental *hsiens* had been established in ten provinces, namely: Kiangsu, Chekiang, Shantung, Hopei, Yunnan, Kweichow, Hunan, Hupeh, Shansi and Chahar. The activities of the experimental *hsien* included crop improvement, cooperative credit and marketing, reforms in land taxation, census taking, promotion of rural industries, and construction of irrigation. The more notable experimental *hsiens* were Kiangning in Kiangsu, Lanchi in Chekiang, Tsouping and Hotseh in Shantung, and Tinghsien in Hopei.

II: *Lines and extent of the development.*

In discussing the agricultural economic development of pre-communist modern China during the decade of 1927-1937, the promotion of rural cooperatives should be mentioned first. China's rural population is loosely organized and very vulnerable to exploitation. In order to break the age-old stronghold of various oppressing groups, the agrarian population should first of all be organized into basic units. This would tend to create in them a temper of mutual confidence, a sense of common problems and needs and a habit of collective action. All in all, such organization would greatly increase their ability to receive and to select discriminatingly assistance offered them from outside sources.

The significant development of agricultural cooperative movement in pre-Communist modern China may be divided into three stages. During the first stage, from 1919 to 1927, the movement was confined for the most part to Hopei Province in North China under the auspices of the China International Famine Relief Commission (CIFRC). During the second stage, after the establishment of the National government in Nanking, various provincial governments, particularly those of Kiangsu and Chekiang, played a leading role. CIFRC was also active in that it made available to the provincial governments the benefits of techniques and experiences acquired during the Commission's work in Hopei. The third stage, beginning in January 1934 after the promulgation of the Law on Cooperative Societies by the Legislative Yuan, signalized the legal recognition of the movement by the National government. Shortly thereafter, the Law was put into effect and a special department was organized in the Ministry of Industries of the Executive Yuan. In this way the promotion of the cooperative movement became a national policy equipped with the necessary administrative machinery.

The functional structure of cooperative societies in China is illuminating. In the early 1930's, cooperative credit societies accounted for over four-fifths of all cooperatives, with producers' cooperatives making a poor second. One reason for this is, of course, the scarcity of credit and capital in rural China. Cooperative societies in China are not the result of a spontaneous growth. Instead, they tended to be the creatures of a policy imposed from above on the masses in that they were dependent on other institutions for organizational as well as financial assistances. For instance, of the societies existing in 1935, 82 per cent had been organized by *hsien* and provincial governments, 7 per cent by the CIFRC, 1 per cent by banks and the rest by social and educational institutions. With regard to financing in Hopei, for instance, where the cooperative movement was carefully fostered by the CIFRC, loans constituted a very large proportion of the total working capital. The proportion which loans formed to the total working capital ranged from a high of 83 per cent in 1924 to a low of 49 per cent in 1933. Savings and deposits constituted only 3 per cent of the total working capital in 1925, but this figure increased to 15 per cent in 1930 and 28 per cent in 1933. This trend was very encouraging. In Hopei, as of 1933, the ratio of share capital to loans was one to 2.7. However, conditions elsewhere were less bright. In Kiangsu and Chekiang, as of 1933, the ratio of share capital to bank loans was one to six and one to nine respectively.

The development of agricultural cooperative societies in pre-communist modern China was, *quantitatively*, remarkable. From two societies in 1919 it increased to 584 in 1927, the end of the first stage; then it increased to 5,335 in 1933, the end of the second stage; by 1937 it reached the figure of 46,983.

Qualitatively, however, the development of agricultural cooperatives in pre-communist modern China was not equally commendable. The function of a cooperative credit society is two-fold: that of encouraging savings and that of granting loans on easy terms of interest and repayment. The savings function is to facilitate the fulfillment of the credit function. After 1928, the national policy of China aimed at fostering the cooperative credit movement resulted in a numerical growth of credit cooperatives so rapid that it became actually unhealthy. It is futile to introduce any new form of economic organization at a rate which the existing society finds it impossible to assimilate and the promoting and directing agencies difficult to administer. Due to this, the formation of credit cooperative societies after 1928 tended mostly to be for the purpose of obtaining the privilege of borrowing from banks in the name of the society. The net result is not the cultivation of the habit of self-help through savings but rather one of dependence upon outside agencies for free help by borrowing. An organization which is a cooperative credit society in name becomes a cooperative borrowing society in fact. This tendency in the development literally negates the basis of a cooperative credit institution whose function is primarily to save in order to be able to borrow.

A second line of development of agricultural economy during the period under consideration is agricultural cooperative financing. Throughout the period from the earlier 1920's on, banks in China showed a growing interest in agricultural cooperative financing. In 1921, the CIFRC entered into an agreement with the Shanghai Commercial and Savings Bank regarding the extension of loans to cooperative credit societies recognized the CIFRC. In time, especially after 1927, other banks such as the Bank of China and the Kingcheng Banking Corporation followed suit. In an attempt to coordinate the loan policy of the banks involved, a joint banking syndicate was formed in 1934 by five banks, namely: the Shanghai Commercial and Savings Bank, the Bank of Communications, the National Commercial Bank, the Kingcheng Banking Corporation and the Four Provinces' Agricultural Bank. At a later stage, five more banks joined this syndicate. In May 1936 a common fund of CNC$ 2.5 million was subscribed to and an allocation of territory for banking purpose was agreed upon by the members of the syndicate.

A forward step was taken in September 1936 toward further coordination and rationalization and more progressive policy when the Agricultural Credit Administration (Nung-pen Chü) was established under the auspices and direction of the Ministry of Industries of the Executive Yuan. The Agricultural Credit Administration, or Nung-pen Chü, was entrusted with the functions of regulating agricultural production and facilitating the flow of agricultural capital in order to promote economic development of agricultural China. The capital of the Administration consisted of CNC$ 30 million provided by the National government and an equal amount of "participating capital" to be subscribed by commercial banks in proportion to the savings deposits of each bank at the time of subscription. The Administration, as one of its policies, undertook to promote the establishment of a system of cooperative banks, known as Cooperative Treasuries, owned and managed by the members of the agricultural cooperative credit societies. The Cooperative Treasuries were to form the basic structure for agricultural cooperative financing in rural China. A *hsien* cooperative treasury could be established with a minimum capital of CNC$ 100,000 jointly subscribed by the *hsien* cooperative credit societies and the *hsien* association of rural cooperatives. Any deficiency in this minimum subscription was to be made up by the Agricultural Credit Administration as the promoting and directing agency. The Agricultural Credit Administration was to withdraw its investment proportionately as the investment of the cooperative credit societies increased; representation in the management of the treasury was to be adjusted accordingly until the entire capital fund of the treasury was owned and managed by representatives of the *hsien* cooperative credit societies. Provincial cooperative treasuries could also be established by the provincial association of agricultural cooperatives under the promotion of the Agricultural Credit Administration. In a similar way, a national cooperative treasury was to be established. In brief, the Agricultural Credit Administration envisaged an agricultural credit system consisting of (a) the village credit cooperative society as the basic credit distributor, (b) the *hsien* cooperative treasurer as the basic banking unit, (c) the provincial cooperative treasury as the co-ordinating financing agency at the provincial level, and (d) the national cooperative treasury as the central agricultural credit institution.

As of 1935, banks either independently or jointly were financing one-half of the cooperative credit societies in the country; CIFRC financed about 16 per cent of them either directly or through the banks; the remaining societies were financed by government funds.

The Institute of Research in Social Sciences of Academia Sinica made a study of the uses to which agricultural loans extended by banks and other sources through agricultural credit cooperatives in 1939 was put. The loans amounted to CNC$ 129 million or fourth-fifths of all agricultural cooperative loans made during the year. About 40 per cent were used for purposes of consumption and debt payment, 30 per cent for providing circulating capital on the farm, and 30 per cent for providing fixed capital on the farm.

The extent of agricultural cooperative financing was impressive when viewed vertically, that is, from year to year. When the CIFRC started the cooperative credit work in Hopei in the earlier 1920's, the amount extended was only CNC$ 3,290.00 for the first year. By 1936, the total agricultural cooperative loans extended by banks and other sources amounted to more than $38 million. However, when viewed horizontally for the country as a whole, the amount loaned in terms of China's needs is insignificant. For the period from 1933-1936 the credit distributed by agricultural credit cooperatives represented only 1 per cent of the total agricultural credit extended and it was granted to only 5 per cent of the farmers borrowing. The bulk of agricultural credit in China continued to be supplied by traditional sources such as individual money lenders, pawnshops, merchants, and *huis* without any effective legal regulation with regard to rate of interest and terms of repayment.

A third line of development of agricultural economy during the decade from 1927 to 1937 is the regulation and promotion of agricultural marketing. An attempt was made in several directions toward the regulation and promotion of agricultural marketing by the National government, but on the whole little was accomplished in an effective way. In 1930, the government organized a Bureau of Standard Weights and Measures and adopted the metric system of weights and measures. However, the system was never effectively enforced. Another step was taken in 1934 when the government organized the Central Anti-Adulteration Bureau under the Cotton Control Commission of the National Economic Council. The work was carried out effectively for three years but was interrupted by the outbreak of the Sino-Japanese War in 1937. In 1937, the government set up a Wheat Inspection Service with offices in the wheat producing regions, but the Service was immediately suspended with the outbreak of the Sino-Japanese War.

The Agricultural Credit Administration and some of the banks, especially the Kiangsu Farmers' Bank, undertook to establish a network of warehouses to facilitate agricultural marketing. From 1936 to 1939, the Agricultural Credit Administration established seventy-seven warehouses in the rural districts in interior China. From 1929 to 1936, the Kiangsu Farmers' Bank had a network of over 300 warehouses in the province of Kiangsu. In addition, the Bank undertook to act as the agent of the peasants in the marketing of their agricultural products.

The few feeble attempts to improve agricultural marketing in China during the period amply illustrate the gravity of the problem of exploitation of the peasantry by the middlemen in the marketing of their products. In 1933 and 1934, both CIFRC and Nankai Institute of Economics undertook to assist in the organization of cooperative marketing of cotton in Hopei Province. The benefits derived by the cotton producers in the reduction of marketing cost through cooperative effort were impressive. Cooperative marketing eliminates the profit of middlemen which amounted in 1934 to almost 10 per cent of the sale price and about 50 per cent of the cost of marketing through traditional channels. While the cost of marketing through traditional channels amounted in 1934 to as much as CNC$ 7.60 per picul in Hopei, it was reduced by cooperative action to CNC$ 1.97 per picul under the supervision of CIFRC and to CNC$ 2.19 under the supervision of Nankai. In addition, the quality of cotton was improved in cooperative marketing through the elimination of adulteration resulting in a higher sale price. In the case of Hopei cotton in 1934, the price of cotton sold through cooperatives was on the average more than 8 per cent higher than the price of cotton sold commercially.

Failure to do more for the regulation and promotion of agricultural marketing in China during the period under consideration was due to several factors among which may be mentioned the enormous difficulties, socially and politically, in the organization and the inadequacy of social over-head capital in the country, particularly transportation.

Lastly, we may discuss briefly the two topics of land tenure and land taxation during the period from 1927 to 1937. The land policy of the Nationalist Regime in China was based theoretically on the principle of "Land to the Tiller." During the period under consideration, however, with the exception of some sporadic attempts at rent reduction and the demonstration of "Tenant Land Purchase" projects in a few isolated regions, the government did not go beyond the promulgation of the Land Law of 1930 and some later amendments to this law.

The Land Law of 1930 and its later amendments established a number of broad and highly commendable principles upon which a sound national land policy could have been formulated. The Law and its amendments provided for (a) equal rights for all people to own land; (b) equalization of taxes on the basis of land values; (c) the promotion of land ownership by the tiller; (d) the limitation of large land holdings; (e) the progressive land taxation of land holding; (f) the protection of owner farmers; (g) the protection of farm tenants with regard to security of tenure, freedom in the matter of choosing the crops to be cultivated, compensation for farm improvements, prohibition of rent deposits, advance rent payments and all other implicit rent payments, registration of leases with the government, and the setting of fair rents (defined as a rent not exceeding 8 per cent of the value of the land); (h) the encouragement of farms of economic size and the consolidation of farm land; (i) taxation of the unearned increment in land value; and (j) compensation for land expropriated.

A comprehensive survey of land is imperative if land reform under the Law of 1930 were to be effected. Attempts to conduct a land survey in China started in 1934. During the period from 1934 to 1946 only 2.7 per cent of the total area of the country was surveyed. In Chekiang which was considered a "model" province for political, social, and economic development in the earlier 1930's, only about 17 per cent of the land was surveyed.

Early in October 1926 the Central Executive Committee of the Kuomintang formulated the policy of "Rent reduction by 25 per cent" as part of the Party's land policy. This meant that the prevailing rents which amounted to about 50 per cent of the main crop yield was to be reduced by 25 per cent to 37.5 per cent of the main crop yield. Attempts were made to enforce this policy in a number of provinces at various times: Kwangtung in 1927, Hunan in 1928, Kwangsi in 1928, Chekiang from•1927 to 1932, Hupeh from 1941 to 1943, and Szechuan and Kweichow in 1949. All did not go beyond the promulgation of regulations pertaining to the reduction of rent except Chekiang and Hupeh. In Chekiang and Hupeh, rent reduction was enforced for a period of time apparently with good results, but due to opposition of landowners it was suspended. The work on rent reduction started in Chekiang in 1927, but it was suspended in 1932 as a consequence of opposition from landowners which took the form of refusals and delays in payment of land tax to the government. During the period when rent reduction was enforced in Chekiang, the price of land fell by 30 per cent to 40 per cent. In contrast, the price of permanent tenure rose by 66 per cent due to the increasing tendency among holders of permanent tenure to sublet their land to small cultivators. In 1941, Chen Cheng, Governor of Hupeh, actively enforced the policy of rent reduction. Upon his departure from Hupeh as governor in 1943, the program of rent reduction was suspended.

Tenant Land Project was conducted by the Chinese government in a number of regions in 1940's. In particular, the project instituted in Pei-peh near Chungking and in Lung-yeh, Fukien, had good results. However, both projects were only experimental and demonstrative.

The Chinese government was aware all along of the burden of taxation on the peasantry. In the early 1930's an attempt was made to abolish exhorbitant taxes and to reduce the surcharges on land taxes. The net result of the attempt was insignificant. The number of taxes abolished during the period from 1934 to 1936 totalled about 6,000 items involving a reduction in revenue estimated at CNC$ 59 million or about CNC$ 0.15 per capita.

✱ ✱ ✱ ✱ ✱ ✱

From the above discussion it may be said, in conclusion, that China was on the road toward a "take-off" in the development of her agricultural economy during the decade from 1927 to 1937. Had there been no communist rebellion within and no foreign aggression without, she could have been able to overcome all the traditional resistances to a steady and sustained development of her agricultural economy.

CHAPTER VI

First Attempts to
Transform Chinese Agriculture,
1927–1937

BY T. H. SHEN

HINESE AGRICULTURE, WHICH HAD DEVELOPED by the slow accumulation of experience over the centuries, did not change much until the introduction of modern scientific ideas and techniques into farming in the late 1920's and the early 1930's. This was made possible through education and research carried out in agricultural schools, experiment stations, and research institutes. But the change did not come about all of a sudden. It was a slow and arduous process. When it finally came in the mid-thirties, Chinese agriculture was about to enter into a new era of unprecedented development. Unfortunately, the Sino-Japanese War intervened and the process that had been going on for a decade was interrupted. All that the Chinese agriculturists could do during the eight years of war from 1937 to 1945 was to maintain a steady supply of food for the people in the unoccupied areas. Not until the political and military situation had been stabilized in the province of Taiwan in the early fifties, following the Communist seizure of power on the mainland, could Chinese agricultural scientists and technicians who had made their way to the free side of the Iron Curtain once more take up their useful work of transforming Chinese agriculture by starting from where they had left off over a dozen years before.

In this paper our attention will be focused on the first attempts made by Chinese agriculturists to modernize their country's agriculture. At the time of their initial efforts, Chinese agriculture was what it had been for thousands of years. The task of modernizing it proved the importance of investing wisely in both human and material resources. It began with the establishment of two modern-type schools, one in Chekiang and another in Kiangsu, to teach sericulture and farming towards the closing years of the Manchu dynasty. With the founding of the republic in 1912, the National Agricultural College came into being by taking over the Agricultural Department of the Imperial Peking University. But the College undertook no research aside from teaching. Most of its teachers were Japanese-returned students, who translated Japanese textbooks into Chinese for use in their classes.

The idea of a land grant college devoted equally to teaching, research, and extension, new to China, was initiated in the 1920's by two scholars from Cornell University, John H. Reisner and Tsou Ping-wen (鄒秉文). The former headed the College of Agriculture of the University of Nanking, a missionary institution, and the latter, the College of Agriculture of the Southeast University (which has come to be known as the National Central University since 1927). Both colleges started as departments but were later raised to collegiate status. They offered undergraduate courses and did some research and extension, though on a relatively small scale. Other national universities established in the different provinces followed the pattern of the National Central University in Nanking, but their research and extension services were primarily intended as aids to teaching. Therefore, they exerted little practical effect on the national economy.

In spite of the long history of agriculture in China, imports of rice, wheat, and cotton were increasing throughout the 1920's and the early 1930's owing to the limitations of traditional farming coupled with lack of adequate communication facilities and concentration of population and industry along the fringes of coastal cities, as well as frequent occurrences of droughts and floods.

As a measure to arrest this trend toward increasing imports of farm products, the Chinese Ministry of Industry established in Nanking in 1932 the National Agricultural Research Bureau (NARB), which began with a fine comprehensive program of research and extension services. Three years later, two other bureaus, one for rice and wheat improvement and the other for cotton improvement, were created; and the three of them worked in close cooperation with one another. In order to standardize the quality of farm products, three inspection services, one for cotton, one for wheat, and a third for rice, were set up in different marketing centers of the country. As a result of the effective work done in the fields of research and extension by the three bureaus just mentioned, rice, wheat, and cotton production was greatly increased by 1936-1937. Consequently, imports of rice were much reduced, those of wheat became insignificant, and cotton production was nearly sufficient to meet the country's needs. To simplify administrative control and promote greater efficiency, as well as for the sake of economy with the expansion of the war with Japan, the Rice and Wheat Improvement

Bureau and the Cotton Improvement Bureau were abolished and their duties and personnel transferred to NARB in 1938.

Aside from improvements in agricultural technology, the development of irrigation, flood control, communications, and agricultural cooperatives in the late 1920's and early 1930's had also played an important part in helping to increase agricultural production and cut down food and cotton imports in 1936 and 1937. It should be noted in this connection that all the progress made in this period was achieved by the Chinese themselves without the benefit of foreign economic assistance, as has been the case in the postwar years. Some of the experiences gained by the Chinese during the 1927-1937 period may not be without interest to those engaged in developing the agriculture of their own countries. Unfortunately, the Japanese invasion of China in 1937 caused nation-wide havoc and disrupted the useful work thus begun. Otherwise, if given another fifteen or twenty years of peace and social stability, the agricultural development on the Chinese mainland could have been just as successful as is the rural development program that has been carried out on Taiwan in the 1950's and 1960's.

However, even during the eight years of war with Japan, the National Agricultural Research Bureau still managed to make significant contributions to self-sufficiency in food and cotton. When the Sino-American Joint Commission on Rural Reconstruction (JCRR) was established in 1948, NARB rendered valuable assistance to it in terms of technical personnel and expert advice. With the fall of the mainland in 1949, JCRR transferred its headquarters to Taiwan, where it continued and intensified its program of rural reconstruction. It succeeded in boosting farm productivity, carrying out a series of land reform measures, reorganizing farmers' associations, promoting family planning, and developing agricultural technical cooperation with a number of countries in Asia and Africa.

I

Traditional Agriculture

While agricultural practices in China have been gradually developed through trial and error by the farmers themselves, Chinese writers have recorded the agricultural knowledge of their times over the centuries. The earliest book which contained sections on farming was a collection of essays written by the close associates of Lü Pu-wei (呂不韋), Prime Minister of the Kingdom of Chin, but credited to him and made public in 239 B. C. Entitled *Lü Shih Chun Chiu* (呂氏春秋) or

Lü's Spring and Autumn, the work devoted the major portion of its last chapter to a discussion of the importance of agriculture, farming practices, soil fertility, the proper size of fields and crop planting, the correct time for land preparation, and planting in relation to time of harvesting and the quality of crops.

As agriculture provides food, fiber, and fuel for the people, ancient emperors in China would perform a ceremonial plowing every spring to show the people at large that their rulers were willing to share with them the hardships of tilling the soil. Similarly, the empress would raise silkworms and do weaving to set an example to the country's womenfolk. Of the four social classes into which the people in China were generally divided up to modern times, farmers ranked only second to the scholars and took precedence over the artisans and merchants.

A second and more comprehensive work on agriculture was written by Chia Ssu-hsieh (賈思勰) of the fifth century A. D. Divided into ten chapters, Chia's *Chi Min Yao Shu* (齊民要術) or *Essential Methods of Governing the People,* went into greater detail on how to till the soil and raise crops as well as other aspects of making a living.

The most comprehensive work on agriculture that has come down to us from former times is Hsu Kuang-chi's (徐光啓) posthumous *Nung Cheng Chuan Shu* (農政全書) or *A Complete Treatise on Agriculture*[1]. Compiled by the author during the years 1625-1628, the manuscripts were edited by Chen Tzu-lung (陳子龍) after Hsu's death. The book was printed by two local officials and presented to the throne by one of Hsu's grandsons in 1643. It is an important compendium on agricultural science, on the basis of which a similar work, *Shou Shih Tung Kao* (授時通考) or *A Comprehensive Study on Farming,* was compiled by imperial order in 1742.

All these works were essentially descriptions of the agricultural practices and customs as gradually developed over the centuries under the population pressure on land in old Cathay, where the conditions were entirely different from comparatively newer countries like the United States with fewer people and broad virgin lands.

For thousands of years Chinese farmers raised crops without fallow and adopted labor intensive culture to increase crop yields. However, the per unit yield of land did not show any appreciable decrease, a fact which was palpable proof that the soil fertility had not been exhausted. Though no chemical fertilizers were ever used before the twentieth century, the Chinese farmers still were able to maintain soil fertility through an ingenious practice of soil management. Unlike their American or European fellow-farmers, they carefully saved all human and animal manure, all the straw and wood ash in their homes, the mud from ponds, canals, and rivers and applied them to their fields. They were adept in crop rotation and generally included one legume crop such as beans, peas, peanuts, or clover, in their conventional cropping pattern in order to improve soil fertility.

To increase crop yield per unit of land, the Chinese farmers usually grew two crops on the same piece of land every year or three crops in two years. Early maturity is the most important characteristic of Chinese crop varieties. The native varieties are always superior in early maturing in any comparison between Chinese varieties of wheat, cotton, rice, barley, corn, sorghum, soybeans, millet, sweet potatoes, and vegetables and introduced varieties of the same crops from foreign countries.

The essential features of traditional Chinese agriculture have been vividly described by F. H. King in his *Farmers of Forty Centuries* published almost sixty years ago.

II

Initial Period of Agricultural Education, 1897-1911

Major changes in agriculture have often been associated with social and political changes in the country. As China suffered a series of military defeats at the hands of the Western powers and Japan in the nineteenth century, the then ruling Manchu court gradually came to realize the need for adopting Western methods and reforms. One of the things it did was to establish institutions for agricultural education. The first such school was the Sericulture Institute set up on the scenic Western Lake in Hangchow, Chekiang in 1897. With Provincial Prefect Lin Ti-chen (林迪臣) as principal and Kiang King-sheng (江金生), who had studied sericulture in France, as dean, the Institute invited a few Japanese to teach their methods of growing mulberry trees and raising silkworms. The students, who came from different provinces on the recommendation of the provincial governments, were mostly children of high government officials and some of them had not seen silkworms before. To teach the boys the essentials of sericulture, they were provided with a mulberry orchard and a laboratory where they could practise what they had learned in the classroom. After graduation, they returned to their native provinces to teach and introduce new methods of sericulture to others.

Chang Chien (張謇), a leading industrialist, educator, and social reformer in the first quarter of the present century, established an agricultural school in his native city of Nantung, Kiangsu, in 1910. The school curriculum included courses on sericulture as well as general courses on farming and practical field work.

As to the Manchu court itself, it also took the initiative in setting up the Imperial Peking University with agriculture as one of its seven departments in 1898. The students were selected from the various provinces and most of the agricultural teachers were Japanese who lectured in Japanese (with the assistance of a Chinese interpreter) and used Japanese specimens to illustrate principles and theories. Under such an arrangement, their teaching was far removed from actual conditions in China and had little to do with Chinese agriculture.

A few years later (1906) the Central Agricultural Experiment Station situated just outside the West Gate of Peking was established. It acquired a number of foreign plants and grew them in its gardens. As a matter of fact, however, the plants were used as specimens rather than for experimental purposes.

This first attempt at introducing the teaching of agricultural science and field experimentation did not have much effect on farming, as might be expected, because of the limited scale and the lack of competent personnel. But the sericultural schools were an exception. They did succeed in introducing new Japanese methods to several provinces through their graduates, partly because silkworms could be raised at home and the work was much simpler and easier than field work for raising crops.

III

Agricultural Schools and Experiment Stations, 1912-1917

In the very first year of the Republican era in 1912, the Department of Agriculture of the Imperial Peking University was reorganized as an independent National Peking Agricultural College. The students were selected through competitive entrance examinations. All professors were Chinese who either had studied in Japan and the United States or were graduates of the Imperial Peking University. Those who had returned from Japan translated Japanese textbooks into Chinese to be used as lecture notes, and they used Japanese specimens of plants, animals, insects, and plant diseases as teaching aids. The students were given farm practices, including planting, cultivation, weeding, spraying of pesticides, and harvesting of crops.

During this period a few provinces also established agricultural high schools, of which the better ones were the First Kiangsu Agricultural School at Nanking, the Second Kiangsu Agricultural School at Soochow, and the Chekiang Agricultural High School at Hangchow. Most of the teachers in these schools had also studied in Japan; some were graduates of the Imperial Peking University. As was customary at this time, Japanese specimens were used as teaching aids. But a few teachers collected local Chinese materials for use in the classroom. For example, Chen Yung (陳嶸), who had a bachelor's degree from the Imperial Hokkaido University in Japan taught the students in the Chekiang Agricultural High School to identify local plants and trees. Hsu Hsuen (許璇), professor of agricultural policy in the National Agricultural College in Peking, who had a bachelor's degree from the Imperial Tokyo University, made use of Chinese materials on taxation, land, and population in his lectures. Similarly, Chang Tsu-shun (章祖純), professor of plant pathology with a Bachelor of Arts degree from the University of California, personally surveyed plant diseases in the vicinity of Peking and used the materials thus collected as part of his lecture notes. All these men had been better trained and were better qualified for their jobs than many other teachers of that period.

The Central Agricultural Experiment Station just outside the West Gate of Peking was improved in 1913 by recruiting a few well-trained agriculturists to serve on its staff. For the purpose of introducing American cotton into China, the Ministry of Agriculture and Commerce set up Cotton Experiment Stations in the cotton production provinces of Hopei, Kiangsu, Hupeh, and Honan in the years from 1915 to 1918. Their main function was to experiment with the growth of short and long staple cotton varieties to see how adaptable any given variety or varieties were adaptable to local conditions. In the end, Trice, a short staple cotton variety, was proved to be adaptable to North China. But owing to poor communications and lack of saw gins and a proper marketing system, not many farmers were able to grow this variety.

IV

Agricultural Colleges and Cotton Improvement, 1918-1928

The period from 1918 to 1926 was especially important in Chinese agriculture inasmuch as it was during those years that the idea of the American land grant college gained acceptance and that a close relationship was established between the agricultural colleges and the cotton and silk industries.

As mentioned earlier, John H. Reisner and Tsou Ping-wen were chiefly responsible for introducing the idea of the land grant college into China. The former succeeded Joseph Bailie as head of the Agricultural and Forestry Department of the University of Nanking in 1916 and later Reisner became dean of the Agricultural College. Some well-known American scholars came to China either to teach or to do research work in the University of Nanking. Among them were Dean L. H. Bailey of the New York College of Agriculture at Cornell University, Mr. W. T. Swingle, a botanist, and Mr. O. F. Cook, a cotton breeder, both of the

U. S. Department of Agriculture, who made on-the-spot studies of agricultural conditions in China with the University of Nanking as their headquarters. There were also prominent Chinese professors such as Tsou Ping-wen, Tsou Shu-wen (鄒樹文), Chien Tien-ho (錢天鶴), and K. S. Sie (謝家聲)—all of whom had studied at Cornell and later became leading agriculturists. They all taught for longer or shorter periods either in the Agricultural and Forestry Department or the College of Agriculture of the University of Nanking. Thus, the University became a center of Chinese agricultural studies for Americans as well as an early center for the training of Chinese agricultural students. Though the textbooks used were all written in English, the professors often went with their students to the countryside to observe farming methods and conditions and to collect specimens of insects and plant diseases for closer examination in the classroom. Hence the students at the University of Nanking were able to learn more about Chinese agriculture than those at the Peking Agricultural College.

Although the University of Nanking College of Agriculture, being a private missionary school, could not afford to have as many departments as the national colleges, it concentrated its attention on the development of a few of the more important departments. It had no departments of animal husbandry and veterinary. Its research was also confined to a few important projects promising practical results. Up to 1927 some noteworthy progress had been made along several lines. Dr. C. W. Woodworth and Professor Chien Tien-ho had succeeded in producing disease-free silkworm eggs; Professor J. B. Griffing in introducing two American cotton varieties, Trice and Acala, and developing the Chinese cotton variety (known as Million Dollars) by line selection; Dean Reisner in developing the wheat variety Nanking 26 by selection from farmers' fields; Professor R. H. Porter in selecting disease-resistant strains of wheat, barley, kaoliang, and millet also from farmers' fields; Professor John Lossing Buck in making agricultural economic studies; and Professor W. C. Lowdermilk in conducting studies on soil erosion in North China and formulating his well-known theory of soil conservation.

Unfortunately, the continued development and expansion of the University of Nanking was suddenly interrupted by the "Nanking Incident" of March 24, 1927, in which, in the confusion resulting from the routing of General Sun Chuang-fang's forces and the triumphant entry into the city of the revolutionary army, some foreign property was looted and a few foreigners, including Dr. J. E. Williams, Vice President of the University of Nanking, were killed. This most unfortunate episode led to the evacuation from Nanking of all staff members of foreign consulates and other foreign residents, including foreign members of the University faculty. With the departure of Dean Reisner in the general exodus, Co-Dean Ko Tan-hsien (過探先), Master of Arts in plant breeding from Cornell, took charge of the Agricultural College. As Ko was on the best of terms with officials of the newly set-up National Government, he rendered important services to the University during this critical period.

The Department of Agriculture of the Nanking Normal College was first set up in 1918. Headed by Tsou Ping-wen, it was later transformed into an agricultural college; and the Nanking Normal College itself also came to be known by a different name, first the National Southeast University, and, finally, the National Central University. By adopting the idea of the American land grant college, Dean Tsou worked with his colleagues to promote research and extension in addition to teaching. There were a large budget and more professors in their Department than the corresponding Department of the University of Nanking. Consequently, several research projects were successfully carried out by the professors of the National Central University, including zoological classification by Dr. Ping Chih (秉志); plant classification by Chien Chung-shu (錢崇澍), Hu Hsien-su (胡先驌), and Chen Huan-yung (陳煥鏞); cotton breeding, culture, and grading by Ko Tan-hsien, Wang Shan-chuan (王善銓), Sun En-lin (孫恩麐), and Yeh Yuan-ting (葉元鼎); rice and wheat breeding by Yuan Sung-chow (原頌周); plant pathology by Tai Fang-lan (戴芳瀾); economic entomology by Chang Chü-po (張巨伯); sericulture improvement by Koh Ching-chung (葛敬中); and rinderpest and hog cholera studies by Lo Ching-sheng (羅清生). With the exception of Koh who had studied sericulture in France, all the other professors had been trained in American colleges and universities and had earned Doctoral or Master's degrees.

During World War I Chinese cotton mills had made immense profits. But they were faced with a serious shortage of American cotton owing to shipping difficulties. Being anxious to increase the production of American cotton varieties in China, the Chinese Cotton Mill Owners Association requested the University of Nanking in 1919 to undertake experimental work on cotton improvement. As part of the University project, cotton seeds imported from the United States and representative of eight type varieties were planted in twenty-six different places in the provinces of Kiangsu, Chekiang, Anhwei, Honan, Hopei, Hupeh, Hunan, and Kiangsi.

When the cotton plants were approaching maturity and their bolls were opening in August of that year, Mr. O. F. Cook of the United States Department of Agriculture and Professor J. B. Griffing of the University of Nanking carefully observed and studied the behavior of the plantings. The information they gathered indicated to them that

Trice showed the greatest promise of adaptation in the experimental districts along the Yellow River, and Acala along the Yangtze. On the basis of these findings, the major work of acclimatization in China after 1920 was centered in the said two varieties, whose seeds were mass produced for distribution to Chinese cotton growers[2].

Owing to political instability and other factors, the export of silk from China had been gradually decreasing in the early years of the Republic. To cope with the situation, an International Commission for the Improvement of Sericulture in China supported by Chinese, British, French, Italian, American, and Japanese agencies was established in 1918 to improve the industry in Kiangsu, Chekiang, and Anhwei by the extension of first generation hybrid silkworm eggs. Though progress was slow, 184,000 sheets of such eggs were produced for extension through the joint efforts of the Commission, the University of Nanking, and the Kiangsu Sericulture Girls School at Soochow in 1924.

V

Crop Improvement and New Agricultural College, 1927-1933

To meet the food shortages in China resulting from the frequent droughts and floods in the 1915-1930 period, the colleges of agriculture began to place more and more emphasis on the breeding of rice, wheat, and other food crops in the late 1920's and early 1930's. Thus, the College of Agriculture and Forestry of the University of Nanking in cooperation with Cornell University undertook a program for the promotion of standard methods of crop breeding.

Cooperation Between Cornell and the University of Nanking

The Cooperative Crop Improvement Program between Cornell and the University of Nanking originated with a letter from Dean John H. Reisner, College of Agriculture of the latter university, dated February 4, 1924, in which he requested Professor H. H. Love of Cornell to recommend a plant breeder to help improve plant breeding in China. The request was made because the University of Nanking had received a considerable sum of money from a balance of leftover funds in the hands of the American Famine Relief Committee that had been raised in the United States for famine relief in China. Dean Reisner explained in his letter that the money thus given to the University of Nanking was for famine prevention and that the University was developing a project for the improvement of certain of the major crops with a view to increasing agricultural production and the food supply. The plant breeder Dean

Reisner wanted was a man interested in the practical applications of the principles of plant breeding and in obtaining practical results as quickly as possible.

Dean Reisner's letter was favorably received and thoroughly discussed at Cornell. But it was felt that a program of this nature could not be completely organized and placed on a permanent basis in one or two years. Professor Love and his associates drew up a program requiring five to ten years for its completion. With the approval of President Livingston Farrand, Cornell University, and Dean A. R. Mann, College of Agriculture, the plan was recommended to Dean Reisner of the University of Nanking for consideration.

This proposal made by Cornell was agreed to by the University of Nanking. But as it called for the services of more men than Cornell could provide through its system of sabbatical leaves, and as the University of Nanking did not have funds of its own to cover the additional expenses involved, a request for financial aid was submitted to the International Education Board of New York through Dean Mann, who was on leave from Cornell and serving as the Board's Director of Agriculture. The request was readily granted.

The program as originally recommended by Cornell was formally approved by the Cornell Board of Trustees, the University of Nanking, and the International Education Board late in 1924. As this was the earliest notable instance of international technical cooperation in agriculture and is not without value for reference purposes for those planning or implementing similar cooperative projects between advanced and developing countries, its essential features, as briefly summarized by Dr. H. H. Love and Dean John H. Reisner, who first conceived of the plan, may be quoted in full as follows:

1. The purpose of the program was two-fold, to organize and conduct a comprehensive crop improvement program, involving the principal food crops of the famine areas of central and northern China, and of equal importance, to train men in the principles, methods, application, and organization of crop improvement.

2. Each year, for a minimum period of five years beginning in 1925, a professor from the Department of Plant Breeding at Cornell would spend several months in Nanking, there to be associated with the Department of Agronomy of the College. Thus, he would have ample opportunity after his return to Cornell to discuss the program with the next visiting professor.

3. The University of Nanking assumed financial responsibility for the traveling expenses to and from China, and the maintenance and traveling expenses in China of the Cornell representative.

4. Cornell University agreed to grant sabbatical leaves, when possible, to members of the staff of the Department of Plant Breeding for work in China, and to grant such other special leaves, without pay, as might be found feasible and necessary in the development of the program.

5. The International Education Board assumed the responsibility of providing salaries for the Cornell representatives when on leaves, without pay, from the University, and to aid financially in other ways as might be agreed upon during the progress of the work.

From 1925 to 1931, three Cornell professors, Dr. Love, Dr. C. H. Myers, and Dr. R. G. Wiggans, took turns in coming to China for a few months every year to participate in the cooperative project at the University of Nanking. Dr. Love was a specialist in small grains and biological statistics, Dr. Myers in vegetable and forage crops, and Dr. Wiggans in both open-pollinated and forage crops.

Dr. Love made his first trip to China in April 1925 to have the program started, and he returned to Cornell in the following October. He began by getting acquainted with the faculty and facilities of the University of Nanking and its cooperating stations, most of which were attached to Christian missions. He held individual and group conferences with the staff and made a study of the available equipment. After reviewing the current projects in crop improvement, he rewrote some of them and drew up others covering new lines of work to be undertaken. This reorganization of the program at the Nanking station, and later at the cooperating stations, was a continuous educational process that went on in the fields and experimental plots, in the laboratory and the classroom.

In order to lay the groundwork for crop improvement, Dr. Love made thousands of individual head or plant selections each of wheat, barley, rice, kaoliang, corn, millet, and soybeans from farmers' fields in the vicinity of Nanking and at the cooperating stations to be used in field tests and selections in the following years.

Dr. Love also wrote two memoranda, "General Suggestions for Methods of Selecting and Testing to be Followed in Crop Improvement Work by the Department of Agronomy and Cooperating Organizations" and "Methods for Rod Row Testing," which were translated into Chinese and used as guidelines by the Nanking station and the cooperating stations. This marked the first efforts to standardize crop improvement methods in China.

The first conference with cooperators from the missionary stations of Shantung, Honan, and Anhwei was held in Nanking on September 25 and 26, 1925 and resulted in agreement on the following points: (1) each station would grow wheat as winter crop and kaoliang, soybean, and/or millet as summer crops; (2) the cooperating stations would join together in one large plan of cooperation rather than for each individual or station working separately; (3) the same plans for selecting and testing the various crops would be used at each station so that the results would be comparable; and (4) the improvement work would be closely associated with the diseases of the crops to be studied. Professor R. H. Porter, plant pathologist of the College of Agriculture and Forestry, University of Nanking, was in charge of the work relating to disease resistance of crops.

After the wheat experiments in Nanking had been sown, Dr. Love returned to Cornell and wrote a report on his work in China.

Personal Participation in the Program

After receiving my Master's degree at the University of Georgia, I went on to Cornell in September 1924 to work for a Doctor's degree in plant breeding and genetics under Professor H. H. Love. Before leaving Cornell to take up his assignment in Nanking, Dr. Love had talked with me to obtain information concerning crop production in China. Soon after arriving in Nanking in 1925, he suggested to Dr. C. H. Myers, who would succeed him the next year, that it would be extremely valuable if I could come back to China with him in 1926. The proposal, duly accepted by Dr. Myers, was submitted to the International Education Board which agreed to provide a fellowship and travel expenses. Thus, I was enabled to join Dr. Myers when it was his turn to go to Nanking in March, 1926, and to return to Cornell in the fall to continue my graduate studies.

On March 24, Dr. Myers arrived in Nanking, I preceding him by a few days. Dr. Myers supervised the crop breeding program and offered a course on plant breeding at the University of Nanking. I served as his assistant and taught a course on genetics. In May they visited the cooperating stations and helped them plant kaoliang experimental fields. They also carefully studied the 8,000 head rows of wheat, which had been selected from farmers' fields by Dr. Love and planted at the Nanking station and several cooperating stations in the previous year, and they selected 2,000 rows for further tests.

Since barley matures at about the same time as wheat, one of their tests focused on barley. There were 2,400 head rows of it, of which the seed had been inoculated with smut through the cooperation of Professor Porter. Out of these 2,400 head rows Dr. Myers selected 230 which did not show any trace of smut. He also assisted with the selection of the plant rows of soybeans at Nanking and started a cabbage breeding program there.

The First Summer Institute of Crop Improvement was held at Nanking under the direction of Dr. Myers from July 12 to August 4, 1926. Its purpose was to provide an intensive course of instruction in genetics, plant breeding, and plant pathology, mainly for the staff members of the cooperating stations. Participants included twenty-three students and experiment station associates and sixteen visitors representing the major crop improvement organizations in central and east China. Lectures with laboratory practice were given in genetics, plant breeding, and plant pathology. Dr. Myers lectured on plant breeding with the writer serving as his interpreter. Professor Porter lectured on plant pathology and the writer on gentics. There were also field observations. Discussion meetings were held with the participants about problems arising in connection with their work at their respective stations. At such meetings the techniques employed and the results obtained were also reported and followed by general discussion and comments. It was hoped that by such means unity, continuity, and coordination of work at Nanking and the cooperating stations would be maintained.

Dr. Myers returned to Cornell with the writer in December 1926. In a report on his work in China, he was kind enough to refer to my part as his assistant in these words: "This report would be incomplete without especial mention of the services of Mr. T. H. Shen. In a preliminary report sent to the International Education Board, the writer has already mentioned the excellent work done by Mr. Shen. As a matter of formal record, he desires to repeat here that any contribution he himself was able to make to this important work was due in no small measure to the very able assistance of Mr. Shen. His knowledge of China and his acquaintanceship with educational leaders everywhere made possible many contacts that would otherwise not have been made. It is gratifying to be able to state that before leaving Nanking, Mr. Shen was appointed to a professorship in the Department of Agronomy, to which he will return when he completes his graduate work."[4]

The fellowship granted to me by the International Education Board was continued until the completion of my graduate studies for a Ph. D. degree in October 1927. A grant to cover my return to China was also made by the Board, thus making it possible for me to take up my duties as professor at the University of Nanking, where I was in charge of wheat, kaoliang, and rice breeding up to the outbreak of the Sino-Japanese War in 1937.

Dr. R. G. Wiggans, the third Cornell professor to come to China, stayed in Shanghai for only one month and returned to the United States without having gone on to Nanking. This was because at the time of his arrival in the spring of 1927 the regrettable Nanking Incident had occurred, making it unsafe for foreigners. Consequently, Dr. Wiggans remained in Shanghai where he held conferences with the Chinese staff responsible for the crop improvement work. He discussed with them plans for crop improvement and outlined planting plans. As both sides continued to take a sustained interest in the success of the program in spite of the disturbing condition of the times, the Chinese staff carried on experiments at all the stations.

Though Dr. Wiggans' visit to China was cut short and rather disappointing to him personally, the encouragement he had given to the Chinese staff and the series of conferences he had held with them in Shanghai enabled the program to go on without interruption.

In view of the lack of sufficient general stability in China in 1928, the authorities of the University of Nanking continued to feel it unwise for a Cornell professor to go to Nanking. The planning for the crops to be planted in the fall of that year and the plans for 1929, nevertheless, were smoothly and successfully carried forward by the Chinese staff.

Continuation of the Project

When the political situation in China gradually stabilized in 1929, Cornell University decided to continue the cooperative project by sending Dr. Love to Nanking once again to supervise the plant breeding program that had been going on since 1925. He found with great satisfaction that the experimental work had been conducted with extreme care both at Nanking and the cooperating stations. Besides supervising the breeding work, he also conducted the Second Summer Institute of Crop Improvement at Nanking. The Institute was attended by fifty-two registered students, as well as by representatives of the same major crop improvement organizations which had taken part in the First Summer Institute in 1926. The same general program of instruction was followed. In addition, Dr. Love also offered a course in Biometrical Methods to advanced students and members of the faculty of the University of Nanking. I travelled with him during his visits to the Nanking station and the cooperating stations as he had done with Dr. Myers in 1926. But in 1929, I served as the Chinese counterpart on behalf of the University of Nanking.

Dr. Wiggans' second trip to Nanking was from March to October 1930. As he had worked with corn, sorghum, and soybeans at Cornell, he paid special attention to the breeding of the same three crops in China. He and the writer visited north China to study the needs for crop improvement there and to conduct the Third Summer Institute of Crop Improvement at Yenching University, Peking, so that a number of men who had been unable to attend the previous two Institutes in the south might take part in the third.

Dr. Myers again came to China in March, 1931, to strengthen the cooperation of the University of Nanking with the missionary stations, Yenching University, Peking, and the Oberlin in China School in Shansi Province. Dr. Myers and I visited all the cooperating stations and conducted the Fourth Summer Institute of Crop Improvement in Nanking from July 6 to 24. Ninety-one persons representing thirty-two institutions (seventeen governmental and fifteen private) from nine provinces mostly in north, central, and east China were registered participants of the institute, with twenty regular visitors from the staff of the College of Agriculture and Forestry, University of Nanking.

Beginning in 1931, several new improved wheat varieties obtained through pure line selection were being gradually extended to farmers and grown in large areas. These included Nanking No. 2905, Kaifeng No. 124, and Nanhsuchow No. 61, Tsinan No. 195 and Hsuchow No. 438. Similarly, there were extended new improved varieties of barley and soybean obtained through selection in Nanking and those of kaoliang in Kaifeng and Tsinan. The yields from all these varieties were from 15 to 30 per cent more than those from native varieties. The farmers who grew them took them to be miracle workers much as the IR8 rice variety developed by the International Rice Research Institute in recent years is regarded by the Philippine farmers today.

The Cornell-Nanking cooperative program was successfully concluded in September 1931, when Dr. Myers departed from China for home. It left behind far-reaching effects on Chinese agriculture, of which the most outstanding are three: (1) training of a group of Chinese plant breeders to carry on a national program of crop improvement; (2) development of better varieties of wheat, barley, kaoliang, millet, rice, and soybeans with yields 15 to 30 per cent more than those of native varieties; and (3) stimulation of the Chinese Government to establish in 1931 the National Agricultural Research Bureau under the Ministry of Industry, which, in later years, was to make important improvements in agricultural production in China through scientific research and agricultural extension services.

On looking back, one finds that this cooperative program between Cornell University and the University of Nanking was really the earliest pioneer project in the field of agriculture undertaken by a Chinese institution of higher learning with the technical assistance of American experts and the financial support of an American private organization. Important as the program was, it was carried out with a minimum expenditure of funds.

Other Researches

The College of Agriculture and Forestry of the University of Nanking also undertook other important researches. It received a grant from the Institute of Pacific Relations for the study of land use in China, which was conducted by Professor John Lossing Buck from 1929 to 1936 and resulted in the publication of his classic work, *Land Utilization in China*. In carrying out his study, Professor Buck consulted several visiting professors, and, incidentally, trained a number of Chinese agricultural economists. Other important work done by the faculty members of the College of Agriculture and Forestry included Professor Chen Yung's monumental *Classification of Trees in China* (written in Chinese), which was the result of several years of scientific expeditions to many parts of China to collect specimens of Chinese trees. The late 1920's and the early 1930's were, indeed, the golden age of the College of Agriculture and Forestry of the University of Nanking.

New Agricultural Colleges

A number of new agricultural colleges sprang up in the 1920's and 1930's. By the time of the outbreak of the Sino-Japanese War in 1937, there were altogether fourteen such colleges located in ten provinces. Most of their professors were graduates of Japanese, American, and French colleges and universities. The main emphasis was on instruction with research and extension service only on a very small scale. But the research work done by some of the professors was outstanding. Dr. Chao Lien-fang (趙連芳) of the National Central University, Nanking, conducted cytogenetic study and breeding of rice; Professor King Pao-shan (金寶善) of the same university collected and classified about 900 wheat varieties in China. Professor Ting Ying (丁穎) of the National Chungshan University discovered a kind of wild rice in Canton where the university was located, crossed it with cultivated rice varieties, and developed a new variety, Chungshan No. 1, which had the desirable characteristics of resistance to cold and acid soil and displayed vigorous growth. He also developed two new varieties through pure line selection.

Several graduates of the Kiangsu Girls Sericulture School, Soochow, working in cooperation with the silk industry, succeeded in making notable progress in raising first generation hybrid silkworms.

VI

National Agricultural Research and Extension Services, 1933-1937

The remarkable increase in crop yield achieved through the Cornell-Nanking crop breeding program aroused the interest of the Chinese government authorities. At the recommendation of two leading agriculturists, Tsou Ping-wen and Chien Tien-ho, and the writer, the Minister of Agriculture and Mining and the Governors of Kiangsu and Chekiang jointly invited Dr. H. H. Love to serve as director of crop improvement in the two provinces and as advisor to the Ministry in Nanking for a period of three years. With his office in the University of Nanking, Dr. Love travelled extensively in Kiangsu and Chekiang to collect and select rice, wheat, and cotton varieties for breeding tests. His services in China marked a new era in Chinese agriculture inasmuch as they began with a private university and expanded into a government co-operative program.

All the colleges of agriculture under the national universities in Peiping, Kwangtung, Honan, Kwangsi, Szechuan, and Shantung that came into being one after another in the period from 1927 to 1933 carried out crop improvement and other experimental work. A number of provincial governments established agricultural experiment stations largely for crop improvement. As there was an urgent need for coordinating their projects and for cooperation among them, it was thought that Dr. Love could serve much better in a national agricultural research agency than he could do in two provincial stations.

In a reorganization of the Cabinet early in 1931, the Ministry of Agriculture and Mining was abolished and its duties were transferred to the newly created Ministry of Industry, to which Dr. H. H. Kung was appointed Minister with Tsou Ping-wen as Director of the Commodity Inspection Bureau under the Ministry. Upon Tsou's recommendation, Dr. Kung appointed a committee of fourteen members to make a preliminary study for the establishment of a National Agricultural Research Bureau. The committee was headed by Vice Minister H. Y. Moh with Chien Tien-ho as deputy chairman and included among its members H. H. Love, Tsou Ping-wen, K. S. Sie, T. H. Shen, Chao Lien-fang, C. H. Myers, and John Lossing Buck. It spent several months in drawing up a program and working out an organization, as well as surveying a site for the proposed bureau. Upon the completion of its work in the fall of 1931, the committee was dissolved. Then Dr. Kung appointed Vice Minister Moh Interim Chief and Mr. Chien Deputy Interim Chief charged with the responsibility of negotiating for the purchase of land and building the offices and laboratories. With Dr. Love as advisor, the Bureau's program was to develop research in all the important phases of Chinese agriculture as rapidly as the availability of a trained staff and facilities would permit.

But the implementation of the original plan was obstructed by a reshuffling of the Cabinet in the winter of 1931 when Dr. Kung resigned as Minister of Industry and there was a change in the personnel of the National Agricultural Research Bureau. It was not until July, 1933, that the Bureau was again set on the right track with the appointment of Chien Tien-ho as Deputy Director and Dr. Love as Chief Technician.

Chien was given full authority with adequate funds by the Minister of Industry, who served concurrently as Director and delegated all powers to his deputy, to administer the Bureau and to buy 440 acres of land and build an experimental farm near Nanking. Eventually, office buildings, laboratories, greenhouses, cold storage rooms, a high temperature room, and dormitories were built so that the Bureau could carry on its research activities in earnest.

The Bureau consisted of an administrative office and technical departments in charge, respectively, of agronomy, soils and fertilizers, entomology and plant pathology, forestry, animal husbandry and veterinary, sericulture, and agricultural economics. The specialists of the Bureau were mostly professors of Chinese colleges who had studied in the United States, England, Germany, France, or Japan, or who were graduates of Chinese colleges with previous experience in the fields of their respective specialities.

Besides advising on organization and technical projects, Dr. Love collected a large number of wheat, rice, and cotton varieties from the provinces and also from the U. S. Department of Agriculture and other sources for nursery observation and regional tests. From Dr. Love's collection several outstanding varieties were finally selected for breeding and extension. In addition, Dr. Love conducted Winter Institute of Crop Improvement for the training of several hundred field workers of agricultural colleges and experimental stations. He lectured on plant breeding and field techniques, and the writer on genetics. It was due to Dr. Love's influence that his methods of cereal breeding were later widely adopted by the experimental stations. His book on biometry was translated into Chinese by the late Shen Li-yin (Mrs. T. H. Shen) and used as a college textbook. He was highly respected by his students as a great teacher and a great plant breeder.

New Blood and Foreign Consultant for NARB

When I was travelling in the United States and Europe in the summer of 1933, I was requested by Deputy Director Chien Tien-ho of the National Agricultural Research Bureau to contact Chinese students majoring in agriculture in foreign institutions of higher learning for service in the Bureau after the completion of their studies abroad.

As the political situation in China was quite stable and the salary scale for professors and research workers was fairly reasonable and adequate to provide for a comfortable living, and as it was rather difficult for Chinese to find suitable jobs in the United States in the early 1930's, I eventually succeeded in recruiting four holders of Ph.D. degrees from Cornell for the Bureau. I also negotiated with a few top professors of England and the United States for short-term consultations.

Upon the completion of Dr. Love's three-year service with the National Agricultural Research Bureau in the summer of 1934, I was asked by the Minister of Industry and Deputy Director Chien Tien-ho of the Bureau to succeed Dr. Love as Chief Technician. At first I hesitated to accept the offer because, in my view, the position might be subject to political fluctuations and, therefore, unstable, whereas stability and continuity of personnel were prerequisites for the successful implementation of crop breeding programs. But, on second thought, I was convinced that, in my capacity as Chief Technician, I would be able to carry out a national program of agricultural improvement and could do more for the country and the people than I could as a university professor. Moreover, I argued with myself that if I should do a really good job out of a spirit of service free from any political ambition, I might not be dismissed without grave reason and eventually succeed in making a stable job out of an unstable one. In any event, patriotic duty as a Christian inclined me to accept the offer in good faith and to leave the future to God. This decision later proved to have been well-founded, for in the course of the next seventeen years from 1934 to 1950, during which there were fourteen changes in ministry, I continued to work for the Bureau first as Chief Technician, later as Deputy Director, and finally as Director. This continuity of work was maintained not only in my case alone, but in that of other research personnel of the Bureau as well.

The first foreign professor to come to China at the invitation of the Bureau was Dr. John Wishart of Cambridge University, England, who was noted for his new design of random arrangement of experimental plots. Serving as consultant for six months in 1935, he designed field experiments and conducted a biometry class attended by about sixty professors and research workers. Next came Dr. H. K. Hayes of the University of Minnesota for ten-months of service in 1936. He specialized in breeding disease-resistant wheat varieties and was, along with Dr. Love, among the most outstanding plant breeders of that time. He and the writer took field trips to central and north China to visit the wheat and rice experimental stations. They also taught plant breeding and genetics at the Winter Institute of Crop Improvement in 1936.

Dr. H. L. Richardson, soil chemist of Rothamstead Experimental Station, England, was next invited by the Bureau to serve as consultant on soils and fertilizers. Unfortunately, when he arrived at Shanghai in the summer of 1937, the war with Japan had broken out. But he consented to go to West China; he worked in Chengtu, Szechuan, for three years. In spite of wartime conditions, he made important contributions to the Bureau's research work and conducted several seminars to train a large number of research and field workers in soils and fertilizers.

The Bureau spent only moderate sums of money for the payment of salaries and travelling expenses for these foreign consultants but the contributions they made to Chinese agriculture were of inestimable value. If the Sino-Japanese War had not intervened, other top foreign professors specializing in different subjects would have come to China to develop other lines of research and advanced training. The eight years of war with Japan resulted in the retardation of Chinese agricultural science by more than a decade. In retrospect, the period from 1933 to 1937 would seem to be the golden age of China's agricultural research and development.

The National Rice and Wheat Improvement Bureau

As China had been importing large quantities of rice, wheat, and cotton annually in the early 1930's, and as relations with Japan were worsening with the Japanese occupation of Manchuria at this time, China had to think of providing for her own needs for these products whether there should be peace or, if the Japanese continued to press hard, war. It was for this purpose that the Chinese National Government established the National Cotton Improvement Bureau in April, 1934, and the National Rice and Wheat Improvement Bureau in November, 1935. To avoid duplication of effort with the National Agricultural Research Bureau, the two newly created Bureaus were mostly headed by NARB personnel. Thus, NARB Director K. S. Sie and Deputy Director Chien Tien-ho were appointed concurrently director and Deputy Director, respectively, of the National Rice and Wheat Improvement Bureau; Dr. Feng Tzu-fang (馮澤芳), cotton specialist of NARB, concurrently Deputy Director of the National Cotton Improvement Bureau, and the writer, NARB Chief Technician, concurrently head of the wheat division of the National Rice and Wheat Improvement Bureau. All three Bureaus were located on the same campus on the outskirts of Nanking. They cooperated closely and developed rapidly without any duplication of effort. With an adequate budget for each, the three Bureaus had sufficient funds to carry out a national agricultural development program.

In addition to experimental work, the two new Bureaus put special emphasis on seed multiplication and extension of the new varieties of wheat (Nanking 2905), rice, and cotton that had been developed by the University of Nanking and the National Central University. The case of wheat may be cited as an example. A total of 36,000 acres was planted in 1936 to improve wheat varieties, which yielded on the average 15 per cent more than the farmers' varieties that yielded an average of

1.2 metric tons per acre. The total increased production of wheat result-ing from the use of improved varieties amounted to around 6,500 metric tons in that year, thus making a good beginning.

Studies were made by the authorities concerned of cotton, wheat, and rice production, and programs for the increase of production and im-provement of marketing of these crops were drawn up in 1933-1935. As part of the studies, the writer made a survey of the wheat mills at the seaports and along the Peking-Shanghai railway line. On the basis of his findings resulting from his exchange of views with the managers of flour mills on how to cut down the import of foreign wheat, he wrote a memorandum on "The Road to Self-Sufficiency of Wheat in China" and submitted it to the Premier in February, 1936. The memorandum con-tained the following observations:

> The import of foreign wheat began to show a significant increase in 1920, amounting as it did to 3.9 per cent of our own production. This has been caused mainly by the mushrooming of wheat mills in Shanghai which produce one half of our total flour production. Owing to the high cost and difficulties of transportation, the supply area of wheat for the Shanghai mills is confined to the lower Yangtze valley. The wheat produced there is not only of inferior quality but also barely enough to meet the demands of the mills for only seven months in a year. Therefore, the Shanghai mills, which consume over 80 per cent of our total wheat import, rather prefer to buy imported wheat because of its superior quality and reasonable prices.

> In order to achieve self-sufficiency in wheat, we should first of all improve our varieties, fertilizers, pest control, irrigation, and threshing machines. At the same time the production of miscellaneous crops such as corn, millet, kaoliang, barley, and potatoes should also be increased so that the farmers can consume more of them and save some wheat for sale. Secondly, all adulteration should be prohibited and grading strictly en-forced so as to meet the mills' needs. Thirdly, we should improve the tax and transportation systems so as to lower the cost of wheat flour produc-tion. Lastly, we should encourage the establishment of wheat mills in the wheat belt instead of at the seaports like Shanghai and Tientsin.

With the approval of the memorandum by the Cabinet, a national wheat program was inaugurated and successfully and effectively car-ried out in the following years.

In order to improve the quality of cotton, wheat, and rice, the Min-istry of Industry established a Cotton Inspection Bureau in 1934 and a Wheat Inspection Bureau and a Rice Inspection Bureau in 1936. It was the function of these newly created agencies to map out national regulations and systems of inspection for the three crops and to help the various provinces set up provincial inspection offices. In his capacity as Director of the Wheat Inspection Bureau to which he was appointed, the writer assisted Kiangsu, Anhwei, and Hupeh to establish their respective inspection offices in 1936 for the testing of moisture content, dust, and other foreign materials in wheat. This work was particularly important, because it was mainly from these three provinces that the Shanghai flour mills obtained their wheat for processing. It had been planned to establish similar inspection offices in Hopei, Shantung, and Honan, from which the flour mills in Tientsin obtained their wheat supply, but the plan was abandoned following the outbreak of the Sino-Japanese War in the summer of 1937.

Imports of Cotton, Rice, and Wheat

A national program was carried out by the Chinese Government in the 1933-1937 period for reducing the imports of cotton, wheat, and rice by increased production, better marketing, and the levying of import duties on foreign commodities. Though the time was short, the program produced noticeable effects as shown below in Table 1. In 1936 and 1937 the imports of rice were much reduced, those of wheat became insignificant, and cotton production was nearly self-sufficient for prewar consumption. As communications with the outside world were practically cut off during the eight years of war with Japan, no rice, wheat, and cotton were imported.

Table 1. *Imports of Rice, Wheat, and Cotton* (in metric tons)

	1933	1934	1935	1936	1937
Rice	1,295,400	771,053	1,296,448	310,349	345,725
Wheat and flour	1,353,062	550,656	594,416	161,421	86,767
Cotton (raw)	120,606	116,321	54,866	40,690	15,318

Source: T. H. Shen, *Agricultural Resources of China.* Appendix Table 15. Cornell University Press, 1951 p. 399.

It must be mentioned in this connection that non-agricultural developments such as the construction of the Huai River Conservancy project, improved irrigation in Shensi and North China, and the construction of the Chekiang-Kiangsi Railway and provincial highways were also factors contributing to the increased supply of cotton, wheat, and rice during the 1933-1937 period.

Research by NARB

Of the many research projects undertaken by the staff members of the National Agricultural Research Bureau, the following may be mentioned:

1) In 1919 Mr. O. F. Cook selected Trice and Acala out of eight American upland cotton varieties for extension in China. As more and better American cotton varieties became available by 1933, Dr. H. H. Love selected thirty-one American and Chinese varieties for regional tests in important cotton producing provinces in that year. After Dr. Love's departure from China in 1934, his good work was continued by Dr. Feng Tzu-fang, one of his students at Cornell. In 1936, Dr. Feng selected Stoneville No. 4 for planting in the Yellow River valley because it outyielded the native varieties by 34 per cent on an average and its staple was suitable for spinning yarn of more than thirty-two counts. He also selected Delfose No. 531 for extension in the Yangtze River valley because its average yield was 18 per cent higher than that of local varieties and its staple good for spinning yarn of sixty counts.

2) Based on the regional tests carried out from 1933 to 1935 of one hundred native varieties collected from important wheat production provinces, the writer classified China into six main wheat regions, which were described in a NARB bulletin published in 1937 and also in his book *Agricultural Resources of China*. In another NARB bulletin entitled "A Coordination Program of Wheat Breeding in China," he pointed out the urgent need for a well-coordinated program of wheat breeding. The same principle was of course equally applicable to rice, cotton, kaoliang, millet, corn, soybeans, sweet potatoes, and other crops.

3) The adulteration of wheat with water and foreign matter had been rather serious, especially in the Yangtze River valley. According to a survey made by the Rice and Wheat Improvement Bureau in 1936, the average moisture content of wheat was from 14.7 to 18.8 per cent and the average foreign matter content was from 4.3 to 5.9 per cent in the three provinces of Kiangsu, Anhwei, and Hupeh. The study also showed that wheat with a moisture content of over 17 per cent molds very easily and is most conducive to the growth and multiplication of grain moth and weevil, which do a great deal of damage to the grain. On the other hand, wheat with a moisture content of less than 14.5 per cent can be stored for a long period free from mold damage. Adulteration of wheat with water and foreign matter not only spoils its quality but also increases freight weight. To eliminate such malpractices, the Bureau established standards of wheat moisture and foreign matter content as a guide for the provincial wheat inspection offices.

4) The National Agricultural Research Bureau played a leading role in pushing a national rice breeding program under the direction of Dr. Chao Lien-fang, in cooperation with government agricultural stations in important rice-producing provinces in the years immediately preceding the Sino-Japanese War. To meet the urgent need for better seeds to increase rice production, the Bureau helped the provinces of

Kiangsu, Anhwei, and Hunan to test the farmers' varieties and to certify the better ones for seed distribution before the improved varieties developed by pure line selection became available.

5) The National Agricultural Research Institute was the first one to study the application of insecticides under the direction of Wu Fu-cheng (吳福楨) and succeeded in 1934 in controlling aphids and red spiders that infest cotton crops. As a result of the Bureau's efforts, both the acreage and the production of American cotton in north China was greatly increased.

6) Drs. Cheng Shao-chun (程紹迥) and Shou Piao (壽標) made a study of cattle rinderpest and hog cholera in different provinces and produced serums and vaccines in large amounts to meet the demands for the prevention of the two diseases. They also conducted classes to train field workers and teach them how to use the serums and vaccines.

7) Chang Nai-feng (張乃鳳) and his associates conducted 156 fertilizer trials with the results showing the relation between the requirements of three major plant nutrient elements (nitrogen, phosphorus and potash) and the great soil groups in various localities of China. Generally speaking, the soil of farm lands north of the Hwai River and the Tsinling Mountains needs nitrogen, that in the Yangtze Valley and the southwestern and southeastern provinces needs nitrogen and phosphorus, and the yellow earth prevailing in Kwangsi and Kweichow provinces needs not only nitrogen and phosphorus but also potash. The increase of crop yield per hectare in these areas demands an adequate application of chemical fertilizers.

The Yung-li Ammonia Plant near Nanking was established under the pioneership of Fan Hsü-tung (范旭東) to produce annually 50,000 metric tons of ammonia sulfate for crop production. Unfortunately, the plant was destroyed at the beginning of the war with Japan.

8) Sun Peng-chung (孫本忠) developed a first-generation yellow hybrid silkworm. The farmers were instructed to raise the first generation hybrids only. When the eggs of the Fl hybrids were hatched, the second-generation silkworms would be divided into two distinct kinds of white and yellow. This greatly simplified the task of identification for the inspectors. As the yellow hybrid silkworms yielded more and better silk than the native white silkworms, they were warmly welcomed by the farmers.

9) Tang Hui-sun (湯惠蓀) conducted a survey of 161 selected farms in Nanking and the provinces of Chekiang, Anhwei, and Hopei. He asked them to keep a detailed account of their incomes and expenses so that the material thus made available could be used to study their economic conditions and farm management.

(10) The National Agricultural Research Bureau conducted, under

the direction of Shen Hsien-yao (沈憲耀), crop reports, including annual production of crops and livestock and consumption.

Research by Agricultural Colleges and Institutes

A number of research projects and surveys was carried out by the professors and research workers of agricultual colleges and institutes in the thirties. Only some of the more important ones will be mentioned here by way of illustration. The National Geographical Survey of China started a soil survey program in 1930. James Thorp published in 1936 a work on the Geography of the Soils of China. Based on his studies made in the University of Nanking, the writer wrote four papers entitled "The Field Technic for Determining Comparative Yields in Wheat Under Different Environmental Conditions in China," "Direct-planting and Transplanting in Relation to the Breeding Test of Rice in China,"[5] "Studies on the Method of Kaoliang Breeding in China," and "Inheritance of Quantitative and Qualitative Characters in Wheat Crosses."[6]

Other University of Nanking professors engaged in agricultural research included Professors Yu Ta-fu (俞大紱) and Chen Hung-kwei (陳鴻逵) who selected a number of disease-resistant strains of wheat, barley, millet, kaoliang, and broad beans; Professor Kwan Chia-chi (管家驥) who improved cabbage varieties and multiplied their seeds for extension to different provinces, thereby making cabbage an important vegetable crop to the farmers; Professor Hu Chang-chih (胡昌熾) who surveyed and classified citrus in Kiangsu, Chekiang, Fukien, and Kwangtung provinces; and Professor Tai Fang-lan who published a *List of Fungi Hitherto Known From China*. Professor Teng Shu-chun (鄧叔羣) of the National Central University continued to work on his studies on the higher fungi of China and the diseases of rice and cotton. Shen Shou-chien (沈壽銓) of Yenching University bred a millet strain resistant to downy mildew. Professor Wu Keng-min (吳耕民) of the National Shantung University made a survey of Chinese cabbage in Shantung and developed some better strains for extension through pedigree selection. The Canton Christian College in Canton was famous for its research on tropical fruits under the direction of Dean G. W. Groff and the classification of bamboos in China under that of Professor F. A. McClure.

Important improvements were also made in sericulture at this time. There had been about thirty native varieties of silkworm before 1930. In order to obtain good, uniform quality of silk, the Joint Board of Sericultural Improvement of Kiangsu and Chekiang instructed the silkworm producers to use only four standard inbred strains for single crossing to produce first generation hybrid eggs. This led to a significant improvement in the silk industry.

Agricultural Survey in West China

At the request of the National Resources Commission, the writer served as head of an agricultural survey team to study agricultural conditions in northwest China in 1934. Starting from Sian, capital of Shensi Province, the team members traveled to Lanchow, capital of Kansu Province and to Kokonor Lake of Chinghai Province. They passed from winter wheat to spring wheat and then to grazing land. From Kokonor Lake, the team split into two groups, one taking the northern route and the other the southern, back to Nanking. A second survey team made a trip to the southwestern provinces of Szechuan, Kweichow, and Yunnan in the winter of 1935. Based on their observations and the materials the two teams had gathered on the spot, they made recommendations for the development of agricultural resources and the improvement of general conditions in the western provinces, which were more backward as compared with those along the seacoast. Three of their most important recommendations were land tenure improvement, soil conservation, and the strict prohibition of opium growing not only by the farmers but also by local warlords, who depended on opium as one of their main sources of revenue. All these recommendations were warmly received by high-ranking government leaders and put into execution.

The decade before the outbreak of the Sino-Janpanese War in 1937 was one of relative peace and prosperity. As the salary scale of government employees and teachers was reasonable and sufficient for a decent living, professors and research workers concentrated their efforts on teaching and research with the aid of adequate facilities and in a favorable atmosphere. Almost all the students of the time who had gone to the United States, Europe, and Japan for advanced studies returned home to take up teaching, research, or government service. A number of outstanding professors served in the government and acquitted themselves creditably. By relying entirely upon herself, China succeeded in making impressive progress in her economy, education, and governmental efficiency up to the summer of 1937 when the war with Japan started.

❋ ❋ ❋ ❋ ❋ ❋

A few months after the outbreak of war with Japan in 1937, the National Government was transferred to the wartime capital of Chungking in Szechuan on the upper reaches of the Yangtze. Following a reshuffling of the Cabinet in which the Ministry of Economic Affairs replaced the Ministry of Industry, the National Rice and Wheat Improvement Bureau, the National Cotton Improvement Bureau, and the National Sericultural Improvement Buerau were abolished and their duties were reassigned to the National Agricultural Research Bureau with K. S. Sie continuing to serve as Director and the writer as his deputy. Chien Tien-ho, who had been NARB Deputy Director for many years, was appointed to head the Agricultural Department of the newly created Ministry of Economic Affairs.

Following the reorganization of the National Agricultural Research Bureau, the Provincial Governments in West China also strengthened their respective provincial agricultural improvement bureaus by abolishing all the provincial agricultural stations and incorporating them into the provincial bureaus. Throughout the eight years of war, the National Agricultural Research Bureau maintained close relations with the provincial agricultural improvement bureaus and set up in each of them a field station to help their research and extension service.

As China was isolated from the outside world during the war years, she had to depend upon herself to provide food and clothing for her people and the armed forces. In order to insure economic self-sufficiency, the National Agricultural Research Bureau helped the provincial governments in planning and coordinating their food and cotton production programs. Its work was facilitated by the experience gained in boosting rice, wheat, and cotton production and marketing in the prewar years. In this way the National Agricultural Research Bureau was able to make some contributions to the war effort.

With the establishment of the Sino-American Joint Commission on Rural Reconstruction in Nanking in October 1948, the National Agricultural Research Bureau served as the prime source from which JCRR drew its initial supply of senior agricultural specialists. As I had by then become Director of NARB and was concurrently JCRR Commissioner, ten top specialists of the Bureau were enabled to join the JCRR staff. One of them was Dr. Y. S. Tsiang, who later became JCRR's Secretary General and, in more recent years, a Commissioner. Other NARB personnel who came to Taiwan after joining JCRR first became Division heads and then were either reassigned to be Dean of the Agricultural College, National Taiwan University, or appointed Commissioner of the Taiwan Provincial Department of Agriculture and Forestry. From the initial staff thus recruited and with the enlistment of new blood in Taiwan, JCRR has been able to implement its plans and projects for rural reconstruction in the last twenty years and help make it possible for the Republic of China to achieve an average 6 per cent annual growth rate of agriculture in Taiwan during the period from 1952 to 1968.

Comments:

BY FRANKLIN L. HO

THE SCOPE OF DR. SHEN's paper on the Transformation of Chinese Agriculture, 1927-1937, refers to modernization of agriculture through the application of science and capital to cultivation in order to attain the maximum production per unit of land and per unit of labor. In a proper treatment the topics to be included should be: (1) agricultural education; (2) research in crop improvement, insect and disease control, fertilizer, soil, animal husbandry, sericulture, and agricultural engineering; (3) agricultural extension; and (4) water control and irrigation.

As one who has devoted his whole life to Chinese agricultural education and research in crop improvement in which he has made notable contributions, Dr. Shen's paper is extremely revealing and enlightening in these two broad fields, with very interesting materials not easily available elsewhere. Regrettably, research on agricultural extension, water control and irrigation were outside the main thrust of his study.

It is true that during the period of nation-building in pre-communist modern China under the Nationalist Regime work on insect and disease control, fertilizer, soil, agricultural engineering, animal husbandry, and sericulture lagged behind in crop improvement. However, a start was made in some of these fields by the government. Studies by the National Bureau of Agricultural Research on the application of insecticides led to the development of practical measures for controlling some insect pests such as the migratory locust. In various localities, the practical control of insects attacking cotton and tobacco by using calcium arsenate, tobacco water extract and vegetable oil emulsion won the confidence of the farmers. Educational institutions became active in controlling plant disease through work on plant pathology in the early 1920's. This work was expanded after the organization of the Department of Entomology and Pathology in the National Bureau of Agricultural Research in 1933. It must be admitted, however, that these programs were not on a large enough scale, and the production of both insecticides and fungicides was far below the actual needs of the country. Equipment for the application of these materials was inadequate, and there were no laws in effect to enforce the control of insect pests and plant diseases.

Fertilizer field experiments were carried out with important crops in fourteen provinces by the National Bureau of Agricultural Research in the middle of the 1930's. Though there was a definite awareness of the increase in agricultural yields through the application of chemical fertilizers, China had no production of chemical fertilizers before 1935. In 1931, however, through the effort of Yung-li Chemical Works under the direction of Dr. T. P. Hou, China made a break-through in the techniques of its production; and in a short time the Yung-li Chemical Works began to erect a chemical fertilizer factory in Pukow. With the encouragement and help of the Ministry of Industries of the National government, the Yung-li Chemical Fertilizer Factory in Pukow was completed in 1935 and had a productive capacity of 50,000 tons per year. Fan Hsü-tung, President of Yung-li, made plans to have ten similar factories built in ten other regions in China with a total productive capacity of 500,000 tons per year.

A beginning in the study of soils was made in the early 1930's under the National Geological Survey in cooperation with the National Bureau of Agricultural Research. A reconnaissance soil survey which provided much useful information was made of most of the country. More detailed studies were undertaken in some individual areas. Unfortunately, no national program for conservation of soil was formulated.

As far as agricultural engineering is concerned, no work was done during the period. Animal husbandry was another field much neglected in China. Modern veterinary science was in its infancy. As an illustration of the inadequacy of the epizootic prevention service, the National Epizootic Prevention Service was established in 1932 with an annual budget of only CNC$ 40,000. The production of vaccine was far below the needs of the country. During the early 1930's, only five laboratories were devoted to such production; three of them were under national government, two under provincial governments of Kwantung and Kwangsi. Prior to 1937 it was estimated that 12 per cent to 15 per cent of the cattle and buffaloes, 20 per cent to 25 per cent of the swine, and 60 per cent of the poultry died annually of infectious diseases. Up-to-date training of veterinarians was negligible. The Northwestern Veterinary College was the only institution for the training of veterinarians and technicians.

The various programs dealing with sericulture in China before 1937 illustrate what can be done in research and experimentation. Prior to 1934, there were organizations both at the national level and the provincial level engaged in research and experimental work in sericulture. When the Sericulture Commission of the National Economic Council was established in 1934, the work on research and experimentation on sericulture was expanded in five directions: research, training of personnel, cultivation of improved mulberry trees, establishment of network of demonstration stations in Chekiang, Kiangsu, Anhwei, Hupeh, Shantung and Szechuan, and finally technical advice given freely to silk filatures and subsidies made available to them to modernize their equipment. These measures had a direct bearing on the improvement of the quantity and quality of silk production. The average production of workers engaged in spinning increased from eight or ten ounces to twenty-four or twenty-five ounces per day. Formerly it took five and one-half to seven catties on unsorted cocoons produced from local worms to yield one catty of silk. After the introduction of improved seeds, an average of four catties of unsorted cocoons yielded one catty of silk. In the case of sorted cocoons of a high grade it took a little over three catties to yield one catty of silk. The factory reeling costs per picul of silk were reduced from CNC$ 300-350 to an average of CNC$ 100 or less.

Agricultural extension was the weakest of agricultural development in China during the period under consideration. It lagged far behind the work on education, research, and experimentation. Some work on extension was started by educational institutions, such as the University of Nanking, Southeastern University, and by missionaries, but they were small in scope and symbolic in results. After the establishment of the Nationalist government, the first official regulation concerning agricultural extension was issued in 1929 and revised in 1933. In 1929, the first Agricultural Extension Conference was held, and a National Agricultural Extension Committee was organized to develop plans for extension throughout the country. However, due to lack of funds only a few demonstration hsiens were set up. In agricultural extension, in short, nothing went beyond the planning stage at the national level during the period from 1927 to 1937.

Water control was much neglected during the early Republican period in China because of the internal chaos and disunity in the country. The Nationalist government was made aware of the urgent need for water control by the great famines of 1920-1921 and 1928-1929 and the Yangtze Flood of 1931-1932, and undertook various public works for flood prevention and irrigation.

A significant development in water control under the Nationalist Regime was the unification of the various government hydraulic administrations in 1934. When the Nationalist government was first established in 1927, flood prevention was the responsibility of the Ministry of Communications and the hydraulic construction for power purposes was the responsibility of the National Commission for Reconstruction. The responsibility was so divided that nothing effective could be done. Thus, in 1933, when the National Economic Council started its work, the government moved to unify the various hydraulic administrations at three levels: the National Economic Council was the administrative organ at the national level, provincial departments of reconstruction directed the hydraulic work in their respective provinces, and *hsien* government controlled the work in the *hsien*. The provincial and *hsien* governments were under the direction of the National Economic Council.

There were four principal hydraulic commissions in four important regions, namely: The North China Hydraulic Commission, the Yellow River Hydraulic Commission, the Yangtze River Hydraulic Commission, and the Huai River Hydraulic Commission. All these Commissions worked under the close supervision of the National Economic Council. They did both fundamental work and palliative measures for purposes of flood prevention.

Irrigation development was emphasized during the period both by the national government and the provincial governments. Before 1937, a total of thirteen irrigation projects were completed, irrigating a total of more than six million *mou* of land. The projects were in the form of constructing canals, and the funds for the construction were mostly provided by the national government and the provincial governments. The most important canals constructed during the period were the Minsheng Canal in Suiyuan completed in 1932; the Kinghui Canal in Shensi completed in 1932; and the Lohui Canal in Shensi completed in 1935.

There were other irrigation works on a small scale sponsored by government at the local level during the period, especially in the digging of wells in North China. The value of such wells is demonstrated by the higher value of land and higher crop returns from the irrigated land than from non-irrigated land. In Tinghsien, Hopei province, for instance, the value per *mou* in the middle of the 1930s was CNC$ 75.00 for irrigated land by wells as compared with CNC$ 33.00 for non-irrigated; the value of annual crops per *mou* was CNC$ 13.00 on irrigated land by wells as compared with CNC$ 5.00 on non-irrigated land.

CHAPTER VII

Industrial Development and Economic Policy

BY YUAN-LI WU

ECENT STUDIES ON THE Chinese economy in the post-
1949 period have led to inquiries into China's
economic development during the republican period before 1949. This renewed interest in the
economic history of modern China, which was for a time totally overshadowed by popular interest in the contemporary Chinese scene, is a
healthy phenomenon. By stressing the continuity of time, it forcefully
reminds us of the fact that both the manner and the rate of a country's
economic development in a given historical period can never be completely divorced from what happened in the immediately preceding
period. In the Chinese case, there are several phases of modern economic history which deserve considerably more attention than has been
given to them heretofore, especially in recent years and in the context
of methods of contemporary economic analysis.

The most interesting periods after 1911 obviously would include (1)
the years of World War I and the immediately postwar years, (2) the
1927-1937 period, and (3) the period of wartime economic development (1937-1945), both in China proper and in Manchuria. This paper
will be concerned entirely with the 1927-1937 period, for it was during
this decade that concrete steps were taken to translate what had
previously been a body of inchoate ideas, aspirations, and slogans into an
emerging, purposeful approach to economic development. As shall be
shown, in a number of respects this emerging approach was rapidly
taking the form of a conscious policy, articulated with forethought and
structured in regard to its several interrelated component parts. The
principal policy components consisted of (1) the creation of certain
fundamental conditions independently of investments in the economic
infra structure, without which a large market economy could not be
expected to function; (2) introduction of new industries by the govern-

237

ment as pilot projects, often with the joint participation of private capital, in sectors which provided basic industrial raw materials; (3) encouragement of the establishment of private enterprises through the enactment of certain legislation and modifications of the import tariff; and (4) an effort to generate a national spirit and sense of participation in promoting domestic economic development through the "national economic construction" and "buy Chinese" movements, the latter implemented through a major marketing effort.

Neither the policy which was being gradually evolved in the last several years of the 1927-1937 period nor the philosophy and economic thinking underlying the policy constituted what one would describe as a comprehensive economic plan, and one can readily point to their shortcomings and missing links. Yet any pragmatic framers of a development strategy today would have to concede after study that some features of China's economic policy in 1927-1937 anticipated a number of the conclusions that many practitioners of foreign aid after World War II have arrived at only through painful personal experience. No less interesting is the fact that some of the ideas advanced then as appropriate to China's economic development have also found their way into some of Peking's economic plans since 1949. These coincidences —similarities, perhaps however, only serve to underline the real differences between the emerging Chinese economic policy of the mid- to late nineteen-thirties and that of post-1949.

I

Rate of Industrial Growth in 1927-1937

As of 1933, China's sector of modern industry (including modern manufacturing, modern mining, and utilities) was extremely small; it contributed no more than 3.4 per cent of the country's net domestic product of that year.[1] However, according to John K. Chang,[2] mainland China's modern industrial sector was growing rather vigorously from the late 1920's through 1936. At 1933 prices, Chang's industrial production series (based on fifteen commodities) rose from 240.2 million yuan in 1926 to 499.6 million yuan in 1936, which was also the prewar peak year.[3] The growth rates given for alternative periods are:

	Per cent annual growth rate[4]
1926-1936	7.6
1928-1936	8.4
1931-1936	9.3

From these and other figures, computed for periods of varying lengths, Chang concluded that there were periods before 1949 when China's industrial production spurted vigorously upward. An implication was that this record might have continued in the absence of the Sino-Japanese War and that the post-1949 accomplishments were heralded by those of earlier years.

The preceding remarks need to be examined further. In the first place, the industrial production series cited here includes all mainland China. While we can rightly regard the record of industrial growth on the entire Chinese mainland as forming the base for mainland China's future economic development, we cannot treat it as an appropriate measurement of the success of Chinese industrial and economic policy. The principal reason for this, of course, was the *de facto* separation of Manchuria from China proper in 1931, following the Huan-ku-t'un incident, and the establishment of "Manchukuo" under Japanese tutelage in 1932. The South Manchuria Railway (SMR) and the Japanese Kwantung Army through its special companies were instrumental in developing many manufacturing and mining enterprises, as well as railway transportation, in Manchuria, thus laying the groundwork for the first five-year plan of "Manchukuo" (1937-1941).[5] For an evaluation of China's own economic policy and industrial growth during 1927-1937, it is necessary, therefore, to look at the events in China proper.

A preliminary comparative review of industrial production in China proper versus that of Manchuria, based again on Chang's fifteen commodity series which has a heavy industry bias presents the following sets of figures for 1926, 1931, and 1936:

Index of Net Value-Added in Modern Industrial
Production at 1933 Prices

	China Proper	Manchuria
1926	100.0	100.0
1931	134.4	174.4
1936	186.1	378.0

These figures confirm the earlier supposition that for the entire 1926-1936 decade, Manchurian industry grew faster than that of China proper. As a matter of fact, for both the 1926-1931 and 1931-1936 periods, the rates of growth were considerably higher in Manchuria than in China proper.[6] However, it can be seen at the same time that the growth rate picked up considerably in China proper in the second half of the decade even though Manchuria registered a much higher rate of acceleration. Finally for 1931-1936, of the fifteen commodities, cotton yarn production constituted an exception to the rising trend in China proper: it fell by nearly 10 per cent. Thus, the differential rates of growth between China proper and Manchuria and within China proper alone should be considered from several points of view. In particular, differentials existed both in time and between industrial sectors.

Some further insight into these regional, sectoral, and time-phase differentials may be gained by examining a recently published study on Manchuria. For instance, Kungtu Sun's *overall* industrial production index for Manchuria presents a much lower rate of growth for the area for the entire 1926-1936 period than Chang's modern industry index for all China. The index for 1936 is 157.8 (1926 = 100), giving an annual growth rate of 4.7 per cent. For 1928-1936 and 1931-1936, the corresponding growth rates would be even lower. Sun's estimates, however, include certain figures for North Manchuria which showed rather sharp declines in 1931-1932, reflecting the decline (a) of flour milling and soybean processing at Harbin and (b) of coal production.[7] The food and beverage industry was, however, not included in Chang's series so that if the same exclusion had been made in Sun's series, the comparative result would be more favorable to Manchuria.

As a matter of fact, since Manchuria's *modern* industry was concentrated in the South, one could simply examine the record of the Kwantung Leased Territory and the South Manchuria Railway Zone. The index of industrial value added at 1926 prices computed by Sun for these two areas together, including mining, public utilities, and manufacturing (the last including the food, beverage and tobacco, textile, wood products, metal, machinery, ceramic, vegetable oil, and chemical industries), gives 110.7 for 1928, 117.6 for 1931, and 202.7 for 1936 (1926 = 100),[8] which are all lower than Chang's fifteen—commodity series at 1933 prices. On the other hand, on the basis of Sun's figures which give us the following annual growth rates:

	Per cent
1926-1936	7.3
1928-1936	7.9
1931-1936	11.5

the highest growth rates was for 1931-1936 after the establishment of "Manchukuo." They also give us higher growth rates in Manchuria for the 1926-1936 and 1931-1936 periods than the rates given by Chang for China proper.

Before proceeding, it will be useful to point out that much of Manchuria's industrial development in the 1926-1936 period occurred after Japan's seizure of the area, thus reflecting the major effort made by the SMR and the Kwantung Army and the large infusion of Japanese capital and technique as well as the return of order in Japanese controlled areas.[9] An examination of the industrial value added series for the SMR Zone and the Kwantung Leased Territory cited earlier brings this out plainly.

	Industrial Value added Index[10]
1926	100.0
1927	112.8
1928	110.7
1929	117.6
1930	122.4
1931	117.6
1932	112.0
1933	121.4
1934	142.2
1935	175.3
1936	202.7

Declines were observed in 1927-1928, 1930-1931, and 1931-1932. An uninterrupted sharp rise then took over after 1932. The increase was continued through 1937 and beyond. For specific industries, the rate of increase in 1933-1937 in Manchuria was very large indeed.[11]

This discussion of Manchuria's production statistics can be usefully combined with the data on all mainland China to cast light on developments in China proper. First, it enables us to derive a better appreciation of how modern industry must have fared in China proper during the 1926-1936 (or 1927-1937) period. If modern industry expanded faster in Manchuria than in *all* mainland China, it must have done so at a lower rate in China proper. This conclusion corroborates what has already been said in the earlier direct comparison of Chang's estimates for Manchuria and China proper. Since the development of heavy industry in China proper came later, its poorer showing must have been concentrated especially in the light industries.

II

The First Phases of the 1927-1937 Decade

Having established the quantitative aspect of the industrial development of China proper, we turn to a qualitative evaluation of the 1927-1937 period. In this connection, we come rapidly to the conclusion that a clear differentiation must be made between two stages, with approximately 1935 as the dividing line. There are some very good reasons why the first seven years of the decade really constituted a preparatory stage whereas the major spurt of development manifested in production statistics was concentrated in the last two to three years.

First, a most important development after the establishment of the new central government in Nanking in April 1927 was the adoption of the yuan to replace the *tael* as the unit of the national currency. This occurred in June 1928. In the following month, the National Financial Conference resolved to abolish the *likin*, a tariff on internal trade, by June 1929. Full implementation of this decision was not made immediately, however. In January 1929, the government again announced that *likin* would be abolished within two years, and "complete" abolition was reported in June 1931. Furthermore, interport duties on rice, wheat, and paddy were not abolished until February 1933. Thus, until 1933, the Chinese economy could hardly be regarded as a single national market, free from financial impediments to the movement of goods.

In addition, it made little sense to speak of China's *national* economic development in terms of the national economy as that of the entire geographical area of China proper, when transportation difficulties effectively prohibited large-scale goods traffic between major parts of the country. Since rail traffic was, and still is, the principal mode of bulk transportation over long distances, the national economy of China proper really consisted of those provinces that were served by the existing railway network plus those areas which are accessible by sea or via the few main rivers navigable by steamers.

Much of the difficulty that prevented the earlier resumption of railway building appeared to be financial. To raise new loans for investment in transportation or in any other form of social overhead capital was not possible as long as the existing debt was in default or the government's credit was not in high standing. By the same token, the abolition of *likin* was predicated upon its replacement by alternative sources of revenue. In brief, the economic unification of China proper was dependent upon the accomplishment of certain fiscal measures, but these could not be carried out right away. The political historian will have little difficulty in demonstrating that republican China did not achieve effective national unity in 1927. The same can be said of development in the economy. Thus, it was not until more than half of the decade of 1927-1937 was over that we could speak of China proper as moving toward a unified national market.

Secondly, and on a par with the removal of physical and fiscal obstacles to the movements of goods within a national market, the first half of the decade was marked by another unifying effort, the standardization of weights and measures. The new Ministry of Industry and Commerce first promulgated the adoption of the metric system in July 1929, to be accompanied by a "market," or *shih* system, which is scaled in convenient manner relative to the metric system, and which has since become the dominant system.[12] The new weights and measures law nominally came into effect in January 1930 when the National Bureau of Standards was established. Training of personnel to implement the law began in March 1930 while national implementation was scheduled to take three years (1931-1933). The new system came into use in general tax collection in 1933 and in the collection of customs revenue and the salt tax in the following year. Thus, the years between 1927 and 1933 can again be regarded as a preliminary phase during which certain basic prerequisites of development were acquired.

While the two preceding developments were prerequisites without which the development of a *national* market would be impossible, the third important undertaking during the first stage of the decade had to do with the expansion of knowledge about China's resources. As an illustration, consider the establishment of a large steel mill in China. Unless the weights and measures be standardized, it is not possible to purchase supplies from, or sell the mill's products to, areas where the standards employed may be different. Nor would it be feasible or economically worth while to do so if transportation cost is too high or further augmented by internal tariffs. But a no less basic problem must be resolved before one can decide whether a new steel mill can be established at all. One must know the location, amount, quality, accessibility, and other characteristics of the nation's physical resources.

Until 1926 Peking alone boasted of a Geological Survey Bureau. The organization was placed under the Ministry of Agriculture and Mining in 1928 when the latter was established. Two years later, in 1931, following the amalgamation of the Ministry of Agriculture and Mining with that of Industry and Commerce, the Bureau came under the jurisdiction of the new Ministry of Industry and was responsible for conducting geological and mineral surveys in the country. During 1927-1931, provincial geological survey offices were also established in such provinces as Hunan, Kiangsi, Kwangtung, Kwangsi, Honan, Shensi, and Kweichow. By the end of 1934, five survey reports covering different regions had been published. The seventh and most comprehensive report, also the last report issued in the republican period, covered the years 1935-36. There is little doubt that the work of the Geological Survey of China, like that of a few other research institutions such as the National Agricultural Research Bureau, was among the most important contributions to Chinese economic development both before and after 1949.

Chinese policy makers were preoccupied with fiscal reform in the first phase of the 1927-1937 decade. They were also engaged in the establishment of certain basic conditions for economic development as already mentioned. The need to perform these preliminary but essential tasks was complicated and adversely affected by several additional circumstances: the severance of Manchuria from China in intermittent civil wars with both warlords and Communist insurgents, 1931, a major flood in the same year, the competition of imported foreign manufactures, and monetary deflation brought about by the outflow of silver induced by United States purchase.

A Sino-American treaty restoring tariff autonomy to China was concluded in July 1928. While eleven European countries followed suit, Japan did not agree to China's tariff autonomy until May 1930. Certain favorable rates were even then stipulated for a period of one to three years. New rates on selected luxuries were introduced in the summer of 1932 and a more general rise took place in the spring of 1933. Under the pressure of Japan, a tariff revision in July 1934 again accorded the Japanese preferential treatment. Competition from Japan was further aggravated by rampant smuggling sponsored by the Japanese and aided by the East Hopei Autonomous Government, also a creature of the Japanese Military. The 1934 revised tariff was severely criticized at the time of its promulgation on the ground that it raised the costs of imported raw materials and equipment to Chinese manufacturers, especially cotton for the textile mills, and enhanced the competitiveness of Japanese products.

While tariff autonomy failed to afford protection to Chinese producers because of Japan's political dominance, United States silver purchases led to significant monetary deflation in China in 1934-1935 and the final abandonment of the silver standard in November 1935. The introduction of *fapi* and the exchange standard ushered in a new period of central banking and may therefore be conveniently regarded as signalling the end of the first phase of economic development in China proper during the decade of 1927-1937.

An examination of available production statistics would show that for China proper, the through of the downswing was reached by many industries at or immediately preceding the middle of the 1930's. The adverse economic factors mentioned above by themselves would perhaps have been sufficient to reduce demand for Chinese industry in the urban centers. When coupled with the severance of Manchuria, which reduced the export market of China proper, the disastrous flood of 1931, and the intermittent hostilities of the civil wars, both of which affected the rural sectors of the economy, little wonder that the years before 1935 were not years of uniform prosperity. What is surprising is that some of the minimal prerequisites of economic development were begun to be met during this phase.

III

Government-Sponsored Industrial Projects and Encouragement of Private Enterprise

The government-sponsored enterprises of the 1927-1937 decade were centered in industries producing certain basic industrial materials or producers' goods. They were relatively few in number and they were intended to be completed toward the end of our decade although planning in some cases had begun before 1935. In one or two instances, an effort was made to tap foreign funds as well as overseas Chinese capital, a special category of foreign capital that *a priori* might be expected to be somewhat more favorably disposed toward investment in China. The orientation toward producers' goods was also shared by private enterprises receiving special encouragement from the government. The concrete cases included:

(1) A machine manufacturing plant under the National Resources Commission.

(2) A steel mill under the National Resources Commission.

(3) An electrical appliances manufacturing plant under the National Resources Commission. Planning begun in 1932; operation expected in 1937.

(4) An industrial alcohol plant under the Ministry of Industry, joint ownership and operation with private overseas Chinese capital planned. Planning begun in 1933; plant construction completed in 1934.

(5) A newsprint plant also under joint operation between the Ministry of Industry and private capital. Planning begun in 1932; expected completion date uncertain.

(6) A vegetable oil processing plant to promote exports, also designed for joint operation between the Ministry of Industry and private capital. Planning begun in 1936; expected completion date uncertain.

Three of the above six cases possessed the common characteristic of joint public and private ownership and operation. The underlying contemporary thought was that such an arrangement would benefit from the greater ease of funding through government participation while more efficient operation could be provided by the private elements of the enterprise. This line of approach was in accord with the ideas shared by some members of the Chinese government in the mid-thirties which stressed the catalytic and leadership role of government intervention in industrial development, rather than its operating role.

A number of private industrial firms appeared on the scene during the latter half of the decade, notably the T'ien-li nitric acid plant in Shanghai (1934), two sulfuric acid plants (1932 and 1934) in Shanghai and Tientsin respectively; and the Yung-li Chemical Fertilizer Plant in Pukow, near Nanking (1935). Earlier, during 1927-1930, three hydrochloric acid plants had been established, two in Tientsin and one in Shanghai. With only minor exceptions the firms were exempted from taxes on transportation. Between 1932 and 1934, four private dyestuff manufacturers opened for business in Tientsin and Shanghai. Certain tax exemptions were also granted in these cases.

In general, government encouragement was given in the form of (1) exemption from export and raw material taxes, (2) reduction of freight rates by government-owned transport facilities (including notably the railways), (3) cash awards, and (4) monopoly privileges in specified geographical areas for a period of five years. These provisions were contained in the Encouragement of Industry Act of April 1934 (revised in June 1938) which was applicable to private firms falling into any one of the following three categories: (a) firms employing either machines or improved handicraft methods in production, (b) firms which were the first to adopt the latest imported techniques of production in specific domestic markets, and (c) manufacturers who had been awarded monopoly privileges for their inventions.

IV

Organization of Marketing Facilities for Chinese Products

Reinforcing the somewhat ineffectual attempt at establishing tariff protection, an effort was also made to encourage the demand for domestic products by making them better known and more accessible to potential buyers. Here again, certain preliminary steps were taken in the first part of the decade, followed by more active steps in 1936-1937. Chronologically, the initial measures included the establishment of (1) the Head Office (in Shanghai) for the Introduction of Chinese Products in March 1932, which was followed during the next seven months by the appearance of branch offices in Chungking, Swatow, Foochow, Canton, and Hankow, and by that of a joint national office in January 1933; (2) the Cooperative Association for the Production and Marketing of Chinese Products in September 1932, under the aegis of the Ministry of Industry, with the sole purpose of providing guidance for the completion of such a marketing network; (3) department stores specializing in distributing Chinese products, known as the *Chung-kuo Kuo-huo Kung-ssu*, in nineteen principal cities,[13] beginning with Shanghai in 1933. The above steps were supplemented by the holding of special short-term exhibitions or fairs of Chinese products in commercially less developed areas—Northwest China in January 1934 and Yunnan in April 1935. Following the inauguration of the National Economic Reconstruction Movement described below in the next section, a joint government-private enterprise was established to act as the sales agent of Chinese producers and the purchasing agent of the national product department stores that had already come into being. The firm was promoted by the Ministry of Industry in 1936. Officially established in April 1937, it began its operations July of the same year. The initial capital stock subscription amounted to one million yuan, with a third to be subscribed by the government. In spite of the outbreak of the war, total subscription exceeded 600,000 yuan by 1938 and four of the national product stores were among the initial seven subscribers. This particular development antedated the post-1949 effort to promote domestic trade through the organization of fairs and marketing cooperatives.

V

The National Economic Reconstruction Movement

We have noted thus far both attempts to establish pilot industrial plants by the Chinese government and the official encouragement of private enterprise through cost subsidy, promotion of marketing, and the granting of cash and other awards. In general, attention was focussed on these measures on broadening the market, on showing private enterprise the way to greater profitability, and on offering cost subsidy to selected industries which the government wished to encourage. The authorities apparently also believed that industrial producers' goods should be especially encouraged. These efforts were, however, only a part of the program to promote economic development. Another new measure was introduced during the last several years of the decade aimed at promoting what W. Arthur Lewis would have described as the "will to economize."

Students of Chinese affairs in the 1930's will recall the New Life Movement, an attempt to foster the spirit of modernization in everyday life in China. The "National Economic Reconstruction Movement" was officially launched in April 1935 in a press conference held by Chiang Kai-shek in Kweichow and was intended to be a successor to the New Life Movement, with the express purpose of promoting economic development. A national committee to give momentum to the movement was established in June 1936 within the Ministry of Industry, followed by the establishment of corresponding provincial and municipal committees. Unlike other earlier government commissions, such as the National Reconstruction Commission and the National Economic Council which were given operating functions they could not always carry out, the National Economic Reconstruction Movement's national and local committees were not intended to be another government bureau. Their principal functions were to conduct propaganda on the importance of economic development and the approaches to its problems, and to offer its aid to other government and private organizations on planning, collection of statistical information, training of technical personnel, and the matching of trained personnel with employment opportunities. The Committees were to be staffed largely by personnel from various government departments and were not to be paid separately for this particular assignment. In effect, therefore, the Movement represented the introduction of a new policy element aimed at evoking popular response without adding further to the burgeoning bureaucracy. This is worth especially noting.

Perhaps the best description of the Movement is to be found in the statement of one of its principal promoters: "The purpose of the National Economic Reconstruction Movement is to arouse the people to engage in the improvement of the national economy on their own initiative and to summon the collective efforts of the society and the organs of production for the development of a healthy economy. The government is to use all its power to remove the obstacles to economic development and to afford the latter every aid and facility it can."[14] The obstacles that should be removed were clearly delineated as (1) environmental obstacles to greater production, such as onerous taxation and regulation and poor capital-labor relations; (2) obstacles to greater production internal to the enterprise, such as incompetent management and technical personnel; (3) obstacles to the flow of goods present in the transportation, financing, and distribution systems; (4) psychological and behavioral obstacles to production, such as superstitious practices, undue conservatism, poor work habits, and lack of understanding for economic considerations. By helping eradicate these impediments the Movement was to contribute to increases in production, employment, export, and the security of investment. In connection with these positive goals, the Movement advocated thrift, institution of popular contributions to investment in terms of direct labor input, and promotion of popular purchase of Chinese products. As a fundamental effort to promote economic development, it would be hard to find a more far-reaching set of pragmatic and non-doctrinaire ideas which contemporary practioners of foreign aid and policy makers for economic development could use.

❖   ❖   ❖   ❖   ❖   ❖

The 1927-37 decade saw the unfolding of many other events of great importance to the development of the Chinese economy which cannot be dwelt upon in this paper. In particular, the movement toward financial and fiscal reform which culminated in the adoption of the exchange standard in 1935 and the tentative introduction of the income tax in the following year were landmarks in laying the foundation of a more vigorous effort to build modern industry. Moving in the same direction was the resumption of railway building of which the first important major accomplishment was the completion of the Chekiang-Kiangsi Railway. With the harvest of a bumper crop in 1936, the Chinese economy was unmistakably moving into a period of prosperity and rising expectations. As the National Economic Reconstruction Movement indicated, there was a strong body of opinion in China at the time which viewed further economic progress as a movement that had to be broadly based in a vigorous population and private entrepreneurship, with the government playing a vitally important but nontheless limited role.

In retrospect, one notices a rather significant lacuna. The economic policy makers of the time did not seem to have addressed themselves to the problem of whether the supply of new capital for industrial development would ever be adequate, nor how much the agricultural sector could be expected to bear the burden. The financial aspects of mobilizing rural savings was indeed a preoccupation of some modern bankers, but the problem did not seem to have been viewed in terms of the sufficiency of aggregate savings to provide for an investment demand that would be large enough for sustained economic growth. Indications were that the Chinese policy makers of the 1935-1937 period would eventually have come to grips with the problem and that their inclinations would have led them to a program encouraging the inflow of foreign capital. Had they been given this opportunity to experiment, the world we face today might be significantly different in many respects, not to mention the nature of the Chinese economy.

Comments:

BY CHI-MING HOU

SINCE I FIND MYSELF IN basic agreement with what Dr. Wu says in his highly informative and interesting paper, it may be useful for me to discuss briefly the course of economic, especially industrial development of Modern China in the hope that the economic performance in 1927-37 may be even better understood and evaluated.

As Dr. Wu noted, the Chinese economy in the 1930's was still predominantly traditional. Centuries-old indigenous technology was still widely used in farming, handicrafts, small mines, native banks, coolie carriers, trade, and other fields, though, in some instances—as is the case of the handweaving industry—modern technology had been introduced to modify or improve traditional technology. It is unmistakenly clear, however, that the Chinese economy in the 1930's was a dualistic one, consisting of a predominant traditional sector and a small modern sector. The latter was essentially based on Western technology, and with the exception of railways and modern mines, was located primarily in "treaty ports" on the coast or on rivers navigable by ocean-going steamers. In the 1930's, probably no more than 13 per cent of total national income originated from the modern sector.

Experiences indicate that the transformation from a traditional to a modern economy, if it takes place at all, is a matter of decades or centuries. In the Chinese case it can easily be argued that the process of economic modernization began after the Opium War, although some might prefer even to go back earlier. After China lost the Opium War she was forced to relax her trade restrictions by opening up more treaty ports, fixing tariff rates at five per cent *ad valorem* for all imported and exported articles, and granting extraterritorial rights to foreign nationals. As external trade grew, foreign merchants learned more about China and began to expand their economic activities from trade to manufacturing, especially in fields related to trade. But it was not until after the defeat of China by Japan in 1895 that foreigners obtained the right to manufacture in treaty ports, and thence began the "scramble for concessions" to build railroads and open up mines.

The fact that demands for expanding foreign trade and investment were imposed upon China by war and unequal treaties obviously outraged the Chinese. When this resentment was coupled with the fear that foreign enterprises would dominate the Chinese economy, it was natural for the Chinese to make special efforts to develop modern industries. First, the Manchu Government began to build arsenals and dockyards in the 1860's for the purpose of defending the country. In the 1870's it began to counter-balance foreign economic penetration by establishing state enterprises and by adopting the formula of *Kuan-tu shang-pan*, according to which the government was to exercise initiative. and supervision while private individuals were to supply capital, skill, and management. In the 1880's and thereafter (especially after 1895), the government made adjustments in laws and regulations, and encouraged modern enterprises. Monopoly rights or official ranks were granted to those who introduced modern technology, for example, and the burdensome inland transit tax was exempted from machine-produced articles. The Chinese populace responded to these government measures in the movement of "Recovering Economic Interests" in the 1890's and the 1900's.

Thus, the modern sector of the Chinese economy was initiated by a Western challenge which provoked the spirit of nationalism and provided the Chinese the will (and the "know how") to develop modern industries. Foreign capital was dominant in many fields of the modern sector, but the Chinese share remained remarkably stable before 1937. There was a co-existence of Chinese and foreign enterprise.

Chang's industrial production index, as cited by Dr. Wu and other economic indicators (quantity of external trade, railroad mileage, tonnage of steamers, etc.) invalidate the belief that there was economic stagnation in China before 1937. Modern industrial development did take place (especially since the 1890's) and perhaps at a rather rapid rate. Available data further suggest a rather constant long-term rate of growth, although there were periods of accelerated development, notably during 1912-1920 and the 1930's. (This statement, which is based on Chang's index, refers to all mainland China, including Manchuria, for the period 1912-1937. It is probably also applicable to China proper, though precise statistical verification is lacking. There is no doubt, however, that there was an accelerated development in China proper in 1931-1936, as noted by Dr. Wu.) The surge in 1912-1920 was probably largely due to import substitution, as China's leading trading partners were busily engaged in war. But what accounted for the acceleration in the 1930's?

The external economic relationship could hardly be said to be favorable to industrial development. For reasons too complicated to explain here (world-wide depression, the declining purchasing power of silver abroad), China's imports went up while her exports declined in the early 1930's. The import-export ratio (as measured in Haikwan *taels,* and with Manchuria included), increased by 26 per cent from 1928 to 1931. It probably continued to increase sharply until 1933 (the Chinese official trade statistics excluded Manchuria after 1931). For China proper, the annual growth rate of the import-export ratio did not begin to decline until after 1933, when the newly increased import duties probably began to take effect. But then the American silver-purchase policy of 1934 boosted the price of silver on the world markets. This in turn induced a heavy outflow of silver from China and finally forced her to abandon the silver standard in November 1935. In the process, the Chinese economy went through a deflationary slump, hardly conducive to industrial development.

Foreign investment, a driving force in China's earlier economic modernization as noted above, did not appear to contribute much either to the acceleration in the 1930's. Apart from whatever reinvestment there was of existing foreign enterprises in China, there was virtually no inflow of foreign capital to China until 1936 and 1937, when some substantial railroad loans were contracted. International capital movement virtually ceased in the 1930's for the world at large; for China, the National Government was particularly cautious in floating foreign loans partly for the purpose of improving Chinese credit position and partly to avoid loans with political implications.

On the domestic scene, likewise, the situation was no more conducive to rapid economic development. The nation was nominally unified after the founding of the National Government in 1927. But, both the internal (Communist) and external (Japanese) threats dictated a large share of the government budget for military and defense expenditures. They averaged 41 per cent of the total budget from 1928-29 to 1936-37. When another 33 per cent was allocated to service previous loans and indemnity payments, very little was left available for other uses. (The combined share of military expenditures and loan and indemnity service gradually declined, however, during the period from about 85 per cent in 1928-29 to about 57 per cent in 1935-36. It went up again in 1936-37 to 79 per cent.)

Thanks to the restoring of tariff autonomy, the introduction of consolidated (commodity) taxes and other fiscal measures, total government revenue (at the central level) rose substantially after 1929 (it had more than doubled from 1928-29 to 1936-37 as measured in 1936-37 prices), but it was still exceedingly small in comparison with GNP (less than 3 per cent in 1933). Thus, the National Government undoubtedly lacked funds to carry out its development programs. I hardly need to mention the adverse effects on the economy of China proper of the loss of

Manchuria, the precarious status of North China, and the disastrous flood in 1931.

Given this generally unfavorable internal and external environment, it is rather surprising that substantial industrial progress was made at all during the 1927-1937 period. Equally, it is in this unfavorable setting that the various measures adopted by the National Government to promote industrial development as outlined by Dr. Wu deserve close attention. The fact that development measures were taken by the government does not necessarily mean that they were primarily responsible for the industrial progress made; other factors might also have been at work. But unless such other factors are identified, these government measures must be duly accredited. It would be unreasonable to deny that the many measures adopted by the National Government were instrumental in providing a helpful environment and essential "pre-conditions" for industrial development, both in the 1930's and thereafter.

CHAPTER VIII

A Decade of
Chinese Railroad Construction
(1926—1936)

BY LING HUNG-HSUN

I

Early Period of Railroad Construction

HINA'S RAILROADS HAD AN EARLY START, although progress was rather slow. Even during the period preceding the T'ai-p'ing uprising (1850-1864), China had very little contact with the western world. Consequently, she had little knowledge of western science or its advantages. In 1864, Sir Macdonald Stephenson, a pioneer in railroad construction in India, came to China and offered his services to the Chinese Government. His offer, however, was rejected by the Government and people, although the first railroad had made its debut in Great Britain forty years earlier.

In 1865, a British merchant constructed a miniature railroad outside Peking largely for demonstration purposes. The people were so outraged by the monstrous contraption that the local government promptly ordered it dismantled. This happened to be the year that the first American trans-continental Union and Central Pacific trunklines were built with the help of thousands of Chinese laborers. Not until 1874, when Shanghai was showing signs of becoming one of the world's leading ports, did the British firm of Jardine Matheson and Company propose the building of a railroad from Kiangwan (江灣) in Shanghai to Wusung (吳松) to meet transportation requirements. This railroad, only nine miles in length, was completed forty years later in February 1876; and, primitive as it was, enjoys the distinction of being China's first railroad.

255

At that time, the Chinese people had yet to be exposed to new ideas and were less than enthusiastic about anything that was unfamiliar. Progress was further impeded when a man was struck by the train. The incident created such an outcry that the Chinese Government had no choice but to buy the railroad in order to dismantle it. It is interesting to note that the construction of this railroad preceded the construction of Japan's first railroad. If China's first railroad had not suffered this early setback, the history of railroad construction in China would have taken an entirely different turn.

China's first railroad truly worthy of the name is the seven-mile section between T'angshan (唐山) and Hsukochuang (胥各莊) in Hopei province used primarily for the transportation of coal. In 1880, the K'aiping Coal Mining Company was established when Li Hung-chang founded China's new navy and set up the China Merchants Steamship Navigation Company. This short railway was constructed primarily for the purpose of transporting coal from T'angshan to Hsukochuang from where it could be shipped to Tientsin, a major seaport in North China. This railway, completed in 1881, became the first section of the Peking-Mukden trunkline. The further extension of this trunkline was a slow process. It took more than thirteen years to reach Shanhaikwan (山海關), 174 miles from Tientsin. The work on this railroad was suspended at the outbreak of the first Sino-Japanese War.

Prior to the Sino-Japanese War, the slow progress of China's railroad development was due to two important factors. First, the Chinese people were inclined to be conservative, and the Manchu government was ultra-conservative. The section running from T'angshan to Hsukochuang is located in North China which is even more conservative than the South. Unlike Shanghai and Canton, which had commercial contacts with the West at a much earlier date, Tientsin, being closer to Peking in the north, was slow in accepting anything that was new. For instance, the construction of a railroad involved the appropriation of strips of farmland and the tearing down of houses. The speed of the trains was something which horrified the country folk.

The Chinese concept of the family was particularly strong and ancestors' graves were regarded as something sacred. The removal of graves necessitated that the construction of railways met with strong opposition. A high value was also placed on human life. Accidents and the loss of lives often created great problems. The incident of 1876 when a pedestrian was struck by a small train running from Shanghai to Wusung led to the dismantling of the entire railway, and Shanghai was comparatively more progressive than the rest of the country.

In addition to these factors, another impediment was the lack of capital. The Chinese Government did not have sufficient funds for railroad construction. The people were not used to investing in such enter-prises as public transportation. The raising of government bonds was something entirely new. Furthermore, China was not yet capable of producing such necessary equipment as steel rails, bridges, engines, and railway cars. Another serious problem was the lack of trained personnel and skilled workers, so that large numbers of foreigners had to be em-ployed. The influx of foreigners in turn created further problems.

In view of the vastness of China and the size of her population, the construction of railroads should have had a great future if it had not been for the opposition to borrowing outside capital, buying foreign materials, and employing foreign personnel. It was logical to use rail-road revenues to build new railroads. Unfortunately, the Western powers were at that time gradually encroaching on China, demanding spheres of influence and the right to construct railroads. In 1885, after the Sino-French War, for instance, France demanded that China should concede her priority in the construction of railways. This marked the beginning of the struggle for special privileges among the Western powers. In 1894, as a result of the Sino-Japanese War, China ceded Taiwan to Japan. At that time, Russia was in the process of constructing the Trans-Siberian Railroad. With a view to curbing Japan's territorial ambitions, China signed a secret Sino-Russian treaty granting Russia the right to build the Chinese Eastern Railroad (中東鐵路) across Manchuria. A scramble for the right to construct railroads in China by the Western powers had begun.

II

Period Following the First Sino-Japanese War

After China's tragic defeat in the Sino-Japanese War (1894-1895), the Manchu government began to appreciate the vital importance of railroads. In 1896, a Railroad Construction Company was set up in Shanghai with Sheng Hsuan-huai (盛宣懷) as Director-General and whose duty it was to raise foreign capital. The first big loan was con-tracted with a Belgian company named La Société Financiere et Indus-triale en Chine to construct the 728-mile Peking-Hankow Railroad, one of the most important north-south trunklines. The second big loan was concluded in 1898 between the Railroad Construction Company through the Chinese Minister to the United States and the American China Development Company. A contract was signed to construct the 660-mile Canton-Hankow Railroad (粵漢鐵路), the most important trunkline south of the Yangtze river. When completed, this mainline would serve to link North China and even Manchuria with Canton by rail. Moreover, this railroad could be further extended to Kowloon, a great seaport in the south of China. In 1902, after the outbreak of the Boxer Rebellion, the Director-General entered into a loan contract with Russia's La Banque Russo-Chinoise to collaborate in the building of the Chengtai Railroad (正太鐵路). This 142-mile railroad was to run eastward from the rich coal-producing area of Shansi and connect with the Peking-Hankow Railroad. Later, La Banque Russo-Chinoise turned over the contract to the Bank of Paris. In 1903, the Director-General entered into a contract with the British and Chinese Corporation to build the 190-mile Shanghai-Nanking Railroad (滬寧鐵路). In the same year, the Director-General also entered into a loan contract with La Compaigne Generale de Chemins de fer et de Tramways en Chine to build the 111-mile Pien-Lo Railroad (汴洛鐵路) which was a feeder of the Peking-Hankow Railroad (京漢鐵路). In 1905, another loan contract was signed with the British Peking Syndicate to build the ninety-eight-mile Taokow-Chinghua Railroad (道清鐵路), north of the Yellow River, another feeder to the Peking-Hankow Railroad.

It is clear that the ten years from 1896, when Sheng Hsuan-huai founded the Railroad Construction Company, to 1906, when it was liquidated, marked a turning point in the history of railroad construction in China. It is worthy of note that during this period other railroads were being built outside Sheng's jurisdiction.

In 1898, for instance, the Shanhaikwan Railroad Authorities entered into a loan contract with the British and Chinese Corporation to extend the Peking-Mukden Trunkline (京奉鐵路) from Tientsin to Shanhaikwan and thence to Mukden. The line from Peking to Mukden totalled 508 miles. The section of the T'angshan-Hsukochuang line which had been built earlier, constituted a part of this trunkline.

In return for helping China to curb Japanese territorial ambitions in the Liaotung Peninsula, Russia signed a secret agreement with Li Hungchang by which Russia acquired the right to shorten the Trans-Siberian Railroad by building a section through Manchuria directly to Vladivostok (海參威). This line not only shortened the route, but also passed through the richest parts of Manchuria. Later, China conceded to Russia's demand to build a branch line from Harbin to Changchun and then to Port Arthur and Dairen at the southern tip of Liaotung Peninsula. This was known as the Chinese Eastern Trunkline, running about 1500 miles across Chinese territory. In 1905, after the defeat of the Russians in the Russo-Japanese War, the line from Changchun to Port Arthur—about 570 miles—was ceded to the Japanese and came to be known as the South Manchuria Railroad. Russia had demanded the right to build the Chinese Eastern Railway without Chinese participation.

The Chinese Government was also deprived of the right to exercise her jurisdiction along the railroad. The Russians further insisted on the use of their own five-foot gauge so that the Chinese Eastern Trunkline could not be connected with the rest of China's railways. The building of this railroad offered Russia the right to exercise jurisdiction and to exploit the abundant natural resources along the southern section of the Chinese Eastern Railroad from Changchun to Dairen.

In the meantime, Japan built a line for military purposes from Mukden to Antung (安東), and also demanded the right to build the Kirin-Changchun (吉長鐵路) and other railroads. Great Britain, having already obtained commercial footholds in Tientsin and Shanghai, likewise "kept an eye" on the various provinces along the Yangtze.

Besides obtaining the right to build the Peking-Mukden Railroad in the north, Great Britain also demanded the right to take over the construction of five routes along the Yangtze. In 1903, the British entered into a loan contract with the Chinese Ministry of Foreign Affairs to build the eighty-eight-mile Canton-Kowloon Railroad (廣九鐵路). Capitalizing on their privileged position in Kowloon, the British extended this railroad to the southernmost port of Canton. In 1908, the British Chinese Corporation obtained the contract to build the 218-mile Shanghai-Hangchow Railroad (滬杭鐵路) so as to further strengthen England's position in the lower reaches of the Yangtze. While British influence was gaining ground in central and southern China, France demanded the right to build the Kunming-Indochina Railroad, as noted above. It was the intention of France, which was then in control of Indochina, or Vietnam as it is now known, to extend her railroads into the various southwestern provinces of China, especially the rich provinces of Szechuan and Yunnan.

In the midst of all this rivalry for railroad rights, China was not above playing one country off against another. In 1897, for one example, the Director-General of Railroads entered into a loan contract with a Belgian company to build the Peking-Hankow Railroad rather than with Russia or Great Britain, both of which had already acquired similar rights elsewhere in China. This decision was bolstered by the belief that Belgium, being a small country, entertained no ambitions in China other than the expansion of trade. Another example was the construction of the Canton-Hankow railroad, the most important and commercially lucrative north-south railroad south of the Yangtze. This railroad was scheduled to be built in 1898. At the time, the United States was the only country to which China could turn to for a loan. The relationship between China and the United States had always been amicable, and it was obvious that the United States had no territorial or other designs on China. A contract was therefore entered into with an American company, and construction work was begun in Canton. However, it was not long before internal dissension forced the American company to sell a major portion of its shares to the Belgian company. At that time Belgium was a close ally of France, which in turn was closely allied with Russia. Fearing that this trunkline might fall into the hands of the Belgians and the French, thus increasing Russia's already considerable influence, China decided to buy back the bonds from the American company and to finance the construction of the southern section of the railroad in Kwangtung province by selling bonds to the people of that province.

A third example of international power play occurred in 1907. The Chinese Ministry of Foreign Affairs entered into a loan contract with the Chinese Central Railways Limited and the Deutsch-Asiatsche Bank to build the Tientsin-Pukow Railroad (津浦鐵路), which was to stretch from Pukow opposite Nanking on the other side of the Yangtze to Tientsin in the north. The construction of this 607-mile trunkline was contracted with British and German companies. The northern section was financed by Germany and the southern section by the British. Thus German influence could not extend south of the Tsingtao-Tsinan Railroad (膠濟鐵路), and British influence was broken up by a section under German interest between the Yangtze and Tientsin. Such manipulations were indicative of the predicament confronting the Manchu government in the face of all these demands.

In 1911, the Manchu government also entered into a loan contract with a four-power (British, American, German, and French) consortium, namely the Deutsche-Asiatische Bank, the Hongkong and Shanghai Banking Corporation, the Banque de l'Indo-Chine, and Messrs. J. P. Morgan and Company, Kuhn Loeb and Co., First National Bank, and the National City Bank of New York to build the Hu-kwang Railroad (湖廣鐵路). The hub of this railroad was to be Hankow in the Yangtze valley. From Hankow, it would run southward to Canton and westward to Szechuan Province. The northern section of the Canton-Hankow line was financed by Britain and was put in charge of a British engineer-in-chief. The projected Szechuan-Hankow line was to run from Hankow to Ichang and thence to Kweichow (夔 州) and further westward. This line was to be financed and built by a three-bank consortium of American, French and German interests. The rationale behind this arrangement lay in the fact that it would be under the control of four powers which could be counted on to furnish the capital.

In 1912, the Ministry of Communications and the Belgian Compaigne Generale de Chemins de fer et de Tramways en Chine concluded a loan contract to build the Lunghai Railroad (隴海鐵路). This was to be an extension of the Pien-Lo Railroad to the port of Lienyun (連雲港) in the east and Lanchow in the west. At 1050 miles, this railroad, running across the central plain, was the longest trunkline to be built with a foreign loan. When finished, it could be further extended westward all the way to Europe.

The rapid acquisition of railroad rights by the Western powers greatly alarmed the Chinese government and her people who gradually began to understand the vital importance of railways. Unable to raise all of the necessary capital, the Chinese people came to the view that Chinese capital should be used to build railways section by section. In 1903, the 26-mile Chaochow-Swatow Railroad (潮汕鐵路) was financed and built by overseas Chinese merchants in Southeast Asia. In 1906, the people of Kwangtung Province, instead of using foreign loans to build the Canton-Hankow Railroad, raised the necessary capital to build the 136-mile section from Canton to Shaochow. This represented an early private enterprise on a fairly large scale. In 1906, an overseas Chinese from the United States started to build the 60-mile Hsin-ning (新寧鐵路) railroad with local funds. In 1907, other overseas Chinese built the 21-mile Changchow-Amoy Railroad (漳廈鐵路) in Fukien Province. The same year, the local authorities in Honan Province built the 244-mile Lo-t'ung Railroad (洛潼鐵路). With the exception of the southern section of the Canton-Hankow railroad, which was later developed into a trunkline, all these short-distance railroads were financed by the local people without any plans to develop them any farther into a national network. Naturally, these short railroads proved difficult to maintain in the long run.

During this period, however, China began to build one of her important railroads by using her own funds and her own engineers. When Yuan Shih-k'ai was in power, he realized the importance of developing the vast territory of the Northwestern provinces. Thus, he decided to build the Peking-Kalgan railroad as the first leg of the great Northwest trunkline by using surplus funds from the lucrative Peking-Mukden Railroad. At first, objection was raised by the Russians who maintained that the region north of the Great Wall was under their sphere of influence, and that if any railroad was to be built, a Russian engineer-in-chief should be employed. Yuan Shih-k'ai rejected the Russian protest and appointed as chief engineer of this line Jeme Tien Yu, a Yale graduate of engineering who had already had considerable experience as division engineer of the Peking-Mukden Railroad. Jeme, with the assistance of a competent staff, completed this difficult line in less than four years. The railroad was later extended from Kalgan to Suiyuan (綏遠)

and Paotu (包頭), a distance of 372 miles, clearly proving that, given the necessary capital, Chinese engineers were equal to the task of railroad construction.

Quite a few contracts for the construction of railroads were in the process of negotiation towards the end of the Manchu dynasty. The central government had decided to exercise control over all the main routes so that provincial governments would be prevented from negotiating with local or foreign firms. After the establishment of the Republic, the government continued the policy of placing railroads under state control. The Ministry of Communications took over local lines in the various provinces in order to ensure uniform planning and management.

In 1912, a foreign loan was signed with the Belgian La Compaigne Generale de Chemins de fer et de Tramways en China to build the Lunghai Railroad. In 1913, Dr. Sun Yat-sen, in his capacity as Director-General of Railroads, entered into a contract with British Pauling and Company to build the Canton-Chungking railroad. In the same year, the Ministry of Communications signed a loan contract with representatives of the Franco-Belgian Company Representant des Societes Belge et Francaise to build a railroad from Tatung to Chengtu (同成鐵路). The Ministry also entered into a loan contract with the China Central Railways, Ltd. of London to build the 208-mile Pukow-Sinyang Railroad (浦信鐵路). In 1914, the same ministry and the Ministry of Finance jointly signed a loan contract with the La Bangue d'Industrielle de Chine to build the Chin-yü Railroad (欽渝鐵路). They also made a loan contract with a Sino-British company, namely, the British and Chinese Corporation, to build the Nanking-Hunan Railroad (寧湘鐵路). The trunk and branch lines would be altogether 643 miles long. If it had not been for the outbreak of World War I in 1914, the above trunklines would have been built and would have greatly facilitated transportation in China.

When the war broke out, countries having railroad interests in China, such as Belgium, France, Great Britain, and Germany were immediately involved. The old loan certificates of the Lunghai Railroad, as well as other railroads, took a sharp plunge in the European market. Without the means to raise further bonds, railway construction came to a standstill. The 220-mile northern section of the Canton-Hankow railroad, however, still had certain funds from the British loan which made it possible to complete the section from Wuchang to Changsha. Work on the rest of the railroad line was completely suspended. The line from Szechuan to Hankow could not even get started because neither the United States, Britain, nor Germany would come forward with the loan. Nor was progress made on other railroads, such as the T'ung-ch'eng, Pu-hsin, Ning-hsiang, and Chin-yu (同成,浦信,寧湘,欽渝).

In 1916, before the United States entered the Great War, an American firm by the name of Siems and Carey Company indicated interest in investing in the building of railroads in the Chu-ch'in area (株欽). After the United States entered the war, however, construction work could not be started. As for the southern part of the Canton-Hankow railroad, which was built by the people of Kwangtung, it could not be extended beyond Shaochow (詔州) as an indirect result of the war.

In 1912, the Manchu dynasty fell. Although many factors contributed to its collapse, there was no doubt that it was triggered by its policy of nationalizing its railroads. The Manchu regime cannot, however, be faulted for its policy, because the lack of uniformity in the construction would obviously lead to complete chaos. Hence, after the Republic was established, the policy of railroad nationalization was further implemented. Furthermore, all those railroads which had been started by the local groups were bought back by the government. This policy gained the complete acceptance of the people. Dr. Sun Yat-sen, founder of the Republic, had won the confidence not only of the Chinese people, but the international community as well. Unfortunately, the Republic was soon involved in a power struggle, so that Dr. Sun Yat-sen was unable to carry out his ideas. The outbreak of World War I also made it possible for Japan to renew her demands on China, so that the construction of many railroads had to be suspended.

Although the construction of railroads was virtually at a standstill, the Chinese government nevertheless adopted many administrative measures relating to railroad operations. Among these were the setting up of a system of uniform accounting, the standardization of railroad techniques, and the designing of a national network of railways and branch lines.

III

Period Following the Establishment of the Republic of China

The first fifteen years following the founding of ·the Republic were adversely affected by World War I and internal struggles as well. Consequently, there was little progress in the construction of railroads other than in Manchuria. After the Sino-Japanese and Russo-Japanese Wars, Japan and Russia acquired their respective spheres of influence in southern and northern Manchuria through railroad construction. After World War I, Russian influence receded somewhat while Japanese influence was on the ascendancy. At that time, China was making a serious attempt to regain her rights from foreign powers. The government at the time had to contend with a new wave of nationalism in the Northeast, which became a bone of contention between Japan and Russia. The local governments and people were quite interested in building railroads. They were anxious to link up local railroads with railroads in Manchuria, so as to break up the monopoly of the Chinese Eastern Railway owned by Russia and the Southern Manchurian Railway owned by Japan.

In 1921, the Manchurian authorities established the Manchurian Communications Commission in Mukden to deal with the problem. Its major policy was to prevent the expansion of encroaching Japanese influence and the further extension of the Southern Manchurian Railroad. The Commission decided, therefore, to use its own resources to build railroads from Mukden directly to the capitals of the two provinces of Kirin and Heilungkiang. Thus, two connecting lines, one running east of the South Manchuria Line and the other west of it, were built to form a system. In the course of ten years, Manchuria was able to build with its own resources no less than 800 miles of railroads. The progress made in Manchuria aroused the envy of Japan and led to the Japanese occupation of Manchuria in September 1931. The result was that more than 3720 miles of railroads in Manchuria fell into the hands of the Japanese.

In 1927, China was united by the revolutionary army under Generalissimo Chiang Kai-shek. Dr. Sun Yat-sen's Three People's Principles were adopted as the guiding principles of the country, especially the Principle of People's Livelihood. In 1928, the Ministry of Railways was established by the Republic of China. Dr. Sun Fo, the son of Dr. Sun Yat-sen, was appointed the first Minister of Railways to carry out the railroad policy of his father.

Four major problems had to be tackled by the Ministry. The first was to restore all existing railroads and to improve the system of administration. All of the railroads which had been damaged by war were restored, and parts of those railroads whose construction had been suspended were resumed with financial support of the national treasury and surplus from other lines. The second was to readjust debts incurred by the old roads. Outstanding debts to the various foreign loan consortiums were renegotiated either for a lower rate of interest or a longer term basis. This measure was intended to build confidence on the part of the loan consortiums in China's railroads and to open the door to further foreign investment. The third was the increase of financial sources for the construction of new railroads according to schedule. The fourth was the extensive investigation of national resources, especially regarding the concentration and wealth of agriculture and the mining industries as a basis for the construction of new routes.

The first, second and fourth problems need not be elaborated upon.

The third, however, was of great importance. In 1929, the Ministry of Railways proposed to the government that the surplus from customs and the returned Boxer Indemnity Fund should be used for the railway building. The surplus from the customs consisted of what remained after foreign loans had been paid from what was collected by the customs. Later on, the surplus collected from the customs was turned over to the national treasury. The Boxer Indemnity Fund had for many years imposed a heavy burden upon the Chinese people. The United States was the first foreign power to advocate returning the unpaid amount of the fund to China for educational projects. The Russian portion was cancelled as a result of the revolution. The German portion was suspended when diplomatic relations with Germany were severed during the war. Agreement was also reached that the unpaid amount owed to Belgium and Great Britain should be used for the building of railroads and the purchase of railroad materials.

According to the 1927 agreement between China and Belgium regarding the disposal of the returned Boxer Indemnity, the unpaid amount was to be used as basic capital to float a bond of US$5 million, 25 per cent of which was to be used for cultural and charitable projects, 40 per cent (i.e. US$1,750,000) to purchase materials from Belgium for the building of other railroads. The Lunghai Railroad was originally scheduled to be finished in four years; because of various circumstances, not even half of it was completed in ten years. At that time, the western terminus of the Lunghai Railroad was Lingpao (靈寶) in the western part of Honan province. From Lingpao to Tungkuan (潼關) on the border between Honan and Shensi provinces, the distance is forty-five miles and the construction work was quite difficult. With the help of the returned Boxer Indemnity Fund from Belgium, this section was completed in 1932. After 1932, when the Belgium Indemnity Fund was depleted, the continuation of the railroad was financed from the national treasury, supplemented by surpluses from other railroads. In 1934, there was through rail traffic from Tungkuan to Sian, a distance of about eighty-one miles. The section from Sian to Paochi (寶鷄), about 105 miles, was extended and completed in 1937. Following the outbreak of the Sino-Japanese war, construction work from Paochi to Tienshui (天水) and then to Lanchow was very slow. From 1932 on, the repair of old railroads and the building of new ones had been done by the Chinese without a single foreign engineer or foreman.

The amount of the Boxer Indemnity which China owed Great Britain came to more than 5,000,000 taels. In 1922, the British government announced its agreement to use the unpaid amount of the indemnity towards enterprises which were mutually beneficial. After the Chinese Republic was established, the Chinese government negotiated with

Great Britain to use all of the unpaid amount on education projects to be administered by a commission made up of representatives from the two countries. It was also decided that a large portion of the basic capital be invested in the building of China's railroads and other productive enterprises, especially those which were beneficial to British industries. According to the terms of the agreement, all those materials which had to be purchased from abroad, such as steel rails, engines, bridges and other equipment, must be purchased from England. Thus, the Boxer Indemnity owed to Great Britain became an important source of revenue in the building and improvement of China's railroads, especially the Canton-Hankow railroad.

The Completion of the Canton-Hankow Railroad

The length of the Canton-Hankow railroad totalled 660 miles. It was an investment which most interested the British government and British merchants in China, as Hankow and Canton were centers of British commercial activities. Early in 1911, the Canton-Kowloon railroad was completed with a British loan. The British wanted to carry British commercial activities from Hongkong to the interior of China and to make the most of British shipping along the Yangtze. The British had used up the Hukwang loan for the section of 222 miles between Hankow and Changsha, and so the 28-mile section from Changsha to Chuchow in Hunan province was built by the Chinese themselves. Altogether only 250 miles of line were completed. There was no fund for the extension northward of the section within Kwangtung province. This resulted in a complete halt in the construction of the gap from Chuchow to Shaochow (株韶段), a distance of 275 miles. The suspension of the construction of this section not only affected potential economic value of the whole route, but also made it impossible for the two unconnected north-south sections to maintain themselves. After the setting up of the Ministry of Railways, this situation was immediately investigated. At this time, negotiations were taking place with Great Britain with regard to the Boxer Indemnity. The Ministry of Railways suggested to the Sino-British Indemnity Commission that the section between Chuchow and Shaochow should be completed at a cost of some £4,700,000. With this as the guarantee, a 6 per cent British Boxer Indemnity Bond of £1,500,000 was issued, thus making it possible for the construction to start. In July 1933, a contract was signed for the completion of the Canton-Hankow railroad, a distance of some 275 miles, within a period of four years.

The building of this railroad started two years after the Japanese occupation of the whole of Manchuria. Japan not only established illegal organizations there but also expanded her power gradually into China proper. This led to constant conflicts with China, forcing China to accept Japan's endless demands. Because of this, the Ministry of Railways realized that the completion of the Canton-Hankow railroad had great bearing on the whole situation, and that it had to be finished ahead of schedule. With the help of other national funds from the ministry, the railroad constructed entirely by Chinese engineers was completed in 1936, a year ahead of schedule.

The Chinese government was aware of the fact that some of the railroads which had been built previously had somewhat lower technical standards because of a shortage of funds. Often the rails were light, the bridges weak, and loading capacity limited. In 1922, the Ministry of Communications set up various new standards and requirements for the building of new railroads. The old railroads were also to be improved to meet new standards over a period of time. Traffic was expected to be extremely heavy on the Canton-Hankow railroad, so that the Chuchow-Shaochow section had to meet the requirements of new standards. For example, steel rails were eighty-five pounds per yard instead of forty to sixty, and bridges were designed to take 50,000 pounds axil load instead of 35,000 pounds of the old locomotives.

The completion of the Canton-Hankow railroad had a bearing on the overall China situation in three ways. First, the southeastern part of Kiangsi province was originally the home base of the Communist armed forces. Unless they could get away from the Chuchou-Shaochow area, the rebels knew that they would be encircled. So a year before this section was completed, the Communist army bolted and moved its home base to northern Shensi in the so-called "long march". Second, after the unification of China, political differences still existed between the central government and two southern provinces. There was no uniform currency, and there was a language barrier. After this road was completed, the political factions in the south were unified by the central government. The people were able to live in harmony. Third, during the period of Japanese encroachment, if this road had not been completed, China would not have been able to offer any defense in case of war. That was why the Japanese rushed into action, knowing that the completion of this railroad would lead to the unification of the north and the south and that China would then be greatly strengthened. Fortunately, when the Japanese began fighting in the north, this railroad had already been completed for a whole year. Before Canton fell into Japanese hands, more than 2,000,000 troops had been transported and more than 540,000 tons of military supplies had been carried, enabling Hankow to hold out for more than a year.

Related to the completion of the Canton-Hankow railroad was the connecting link with the Canton-Kowloon railroad. In Canton, there was a terminal for each railroad, one in the eastern part and one in the western part of the city with no connecting link between them. There was no plan to link up the two terminals when the loan for the building of the Canton-Kowloon railroad was under negotiation and even when the Canton-Hankow railroad was about to be completed. The idea was strongly objected to by the people in Canton who feared that their commercial interests would be jeopardized if Canton were to serve as merely a passing station. But in 1936, after the completion of the Canton-Hankow railroad, Japan was launching a massive and coordinated attack on China. The objections of the local people were overruled. On July 7, 1937, at the outbreak of the Sino-Japanese War, the importance of linking up these railroads became obvious. The two railroads were finally connected on August 19. Connection of the two railroads served to enable Hankow to hold out for more than a year since it became possible to ship to Hankow military materials and construction materials from abroad via Kowloon.

While a large portion of the indemnity funds owed to England was used for the completion of the Canton-Hankow railroad, a smaller portion was used to purchase cars for the northern and southern sections of the railroad, as well as for the Tientsin-Pukow railroad, the Tsingtao-Tsinan railroad and the Hang-Kiang railroad (杭江鐵路), the Shanghai-Hangchow railroad and the Nanking-Kiangsi railroad (京贛鐵路). A small portion was also used for engines and equipment for the Nanking-Pukow Ferry across the Yangtze.

The Building of the Chekiang-Kiangsi Railroad

Upon the completion of the Canton-Hankow railroad, the Chekiang-Kiangsi railroad was started. In 1930, the Chekiang provincial authorities started raising funds for the building of the Hang-Kiang railroad from Hangchow to Kiangshan (江山) on the provincial boundary, a distance of about 206 miles. At that time, the new foreign loan consortium had not yet begun investing in China's railroads and a large portion of the British indemnity funds was used for other purposes. The Chekiang provincial government, therefore, issued its own loan bonds along with the guarantee of the Hangchow power plant to make a loan of 2,700,000 silver dollars from the Bank of China for building expenses. In 1932, the 104-mile trunkline from Hangchow to Chinhua (金華) was completed as well as the 14-mile branch line from Chinhua to Lanchi (蘭谿). Because of limited funds, expenditures had to be closely watched, a lower standard had to be adopted and a narrower roadway constructed. The loan from the Bank of China opened a new future to other banks in the country in railroad investment. There was a new concept towards the future of railroads on the part of the government, the people, and the community.

After the connecting line to Chinhua was completed, a hundred more miles had to be built in order to reach Kiangshan. The provincial government of Chekiang therefore sold the Hangchow power plant and asked for a loan of 1,900,000 silver dollars from the Bank of China and 1,200,000 silver dollars from four banks in Hangchow. The provincial government also asked the Sino-British Indemnity Commission for a loan of 140,000 British pounds to purchase materials and cars from abroad. In 1934, the Hang-Kiang Railroad, as it was known, was connected to Yushan (玉山).

Completion of the Hang-Kiang railroad gave railroad planners some new ideas. The idea was current that if this railroad was extended to the neighboring province of Kiangsi, connecting Kiangsi province with Nanchang (南昌), cutting across the central part of Kiangsi province and thence westward to connect with the Canton-Hankow railroad, it would not only open up the northern part of Kiangsi, but would also serve as a connecting link between Canton and Nanking and Shanghai. At this time, German commercial interests were planning to resume their commercial activities in the East after the war. Representatives were sent to China to investigate opportunities for investment. In proposing to extend the Hang-Kiang railroad to become the Kiangsi-Chekiang railroad, China decided to cooperate with a German steel company, which proposed joint investments from the Bank of China consortium as one of the conditions. The funds in cash were provided by the various banks in China, while material was supplied by the German company. Thus, a new form of international cooperation was initiated. Moreover, to facilitate overall planning, the central government invited the local governments to participate in the Chekiang-Kiangsi Railroad Company. In 1934, the Ministry of Railways issued loan bonds in the amount of 12,000,000 silver dollars, using the surplus from the various state-owned railroads as collateral. The Kiangsi provincial government issued the same amount of bonds, using an increased salt tax as collateral. The various banks in China then agreed to loan in cash the amount of 8,000,000 silver dollars. Furthermore, the Bank of China entered into a contract with the German firm of Otto Wolf for a loan of 8,000,000 silver dollars worth of materials. With sufficient funds and materials, the 176-mile section from Yushan to Nanchang was completed in 1936.

When the Yushan-Nanchang section was almost completed, the Ministry of Railways in January 1936, again issued the second portion of loan bonds in the amount of 27,000,000 silver dollars at an annual interest rate of 6 per cent, using the surplus from the various state-owned railroads as guarantee. The 169-mile section from Nanchang to P'inghsiang (萍鄉) was built by using the second portion of loan bonds. From P'inghsiang, a small section to Chuchow on the Canton-Hankow railroad had already been built. The Chekiang-Kiangsi Line was connected to the trunkline of the Canton-Hankow railroad in October 1937. The Chientang River Bridge (錢塘江橋) had already been completed at the outbreak of the Sino-Japanese war. These trunklines played a vital role in the movement of men and materials during the early war period.

The Building of the Tung-Pu Railroad in Shansi

Shansi province in North China is rich in coal reserves. Plans for railroads to be built by the province itself were proposed quite early, although their execution came rather late. In 1930, when the overall situation in North China was fairly settled, the Shansi provincial government established an Administrative Office responsible for developing locally-owned enterprises. In 1932, the administration decided to build the north-south trunkline between Taiyuan (太原) and Tatung in the north, connecting with Puchow (蒲州) in the south. Taiyuan already had railroads connecting with Shihchiachuang (石家莊) on the Peking-Hankow railroad in the east. Now that the Tung-pu railroad (同蒲鐵路) had been built, it could reach the Peking-Suiyuan Railroad in the north.

Eventually, it was to reach Tungkwan on the Lunghai railroad in the south, once a bridge had been built across the Yellow River at Fengling (風陵). Its significance and economic value would be tremendous. The Shansi provincial authorities used men in the military service to build this railroad. The embankment and ballast were the sole work of the military. The building of tunnels and bridges was sublet to contractors, with portions of the work given to the military. The construction was originally planned for a section between Taiyuan and Chiehshiu (介休), about ninety miles long. Subsequently, in order to facilitate the completion of the entire railroad route, work was begun on both the northern and southern ends in 1933. The 310-mile southern section ran from Taiyuan to Puchow, extending to Fengling on the north shore of the Yellow River. It was completed in 1935. The Yellow River bridge was planned in 1937 by the Ministry of Railways, but its construction was delayed because of the outbreak of the war. The northern section from Taiyuan to Tatung was completed in June 1937 when the Sino-Japanese War had already begun.

In 1927, there were many plans for the building of railroads. Those provinces whose financial resources were not greatly affected by the war became the leading ones in the construction of railroads with Chinese capital. In the south, the provinces of Chekiang and Kiangsi were responsible for building the Chekiang-Kiangsi railroad. In the north, Shansi was responsible for building the Tung-pu railroad. These two railroads exerted great influence on future construction.

New Railroads North and South of the Yangtze

While the Chekiang-Kiangsi railroad was under construction, shorter lines were constructed north and south of the Yangtze. These include: (1) *Huai-nan Railroad.* In 1930, the Huai-nan Mining Administration started coal mining in the area of T'ienchiaan (田家庵) on the southern bank of the Huai Ho (淮河). To facilitate the transportation of coal, the administration built the Huai-nan Railroad (淮南鐵路) which ran south from T'ienchiaan to Yuchikow (裕溪口) on the northern bank of the Yangtze to connect with water transport. Its total length was about 130 miles. Begun in 1934, it was completed in June 1935. (2) *The Kiang-nan Railroad* (江南鐵路). In 1933, leading railroad builders jointly made investment for the building of a railroad from Nanking along the south bank of the Yangtze to Anhwei province. The Kiang-nan railway company was thus established with a large portion of its capital from individual stocks. Tracks were laid from Wuhu (蕪湖) to Hsuanch'eng (宣城), a distance of more than forty miles and was completed in November 1934. The 67-mile section from Wuhu to Nanking was completed in May 1935. It was then connected with the Shanghai-Nanking railroad. Although this line was rather short, it was well-built and managed and set a good example for private railroads. (3) *The Soo-chia Railroad* (蘇嘉鐵路). In 1932, Japan attacked Shanghai, obstructing transportation from Nanking to Hangchow via Shanghai. The Ministry of Railways decided to bypass Shanghai by building a line linking Soochow on the Shanghai-Nanking railroad to Chia-hsing (嘉興) on the Shanghai-Hangchow railroad. This was the Soo-chia railroad and ran about forty-five miles. Begun in 1935, it was completed in July 1936. Although relatively short, the above railroads proved extremely useful in connecting the two trunklines.

The Construction of Connecting Trunklines

In addition to the above mentioned long and short trunklines, several others built by local interests had great importance in the entire railroad system. The following were finished under the management of the Ministry of Railways:

The Nanking-Pukow Ferry. Since there were through-trains on the Shanghai-Nanking and Tientsin-Pukow railroads, Nanking became an important transportation center. Nanking was separated from the terminal of the Tientsin-Pukow railroad by the Yangtze, a distance of about 3600 feet. Trans-shipment of passengers and freight involved considerable danger and delay. After the national capital was moved to Nanking, transport connections with the north became more important. At first, it was proposed that a long bridge should be built across the Yangtze. The Yangtze River is more than 170 feet deep at high tide and only twenty-four feet deep at low tide. The river not only had to provide access to the sea by large vessels, it also had to be navigated by the navy vessels. If a bridge was to be built, it either had to provide a wide opening (or a drawbridge) or it had to rise high above the water. The expense would be enormous. Therefore, the decision was made to start a ferry service across the Yangtze.

Building of the ferry involved construction of two approaches for the vessels. The ferry boats were 360 feet long. Three tracks of rails were laid on the deck, capable of accommodating twenty-one cars. Funds were provided by the Ministry of Railways in the form of a loan of £256,000 from the Sino-British Indemnity Commission. All the equipment was purchased from England. Local construction expenses were also paid partly by a loan from the indemnity funds amounting to £40,000. The rest of the funds were raised by the Ministry of Railways. In 1930, work began on both banks and was completed in 1933. Ferry service across the river greatly facilitated the movement of goods and passengers from north to south.

Chientang Bridge. In 1929, Chekiang province began the construction of a railroad to cut across the northern part of the province. Its starting point in Hangchow was situated at the south bank of Chientang River. It was separated from the already completed Shanghai-Hangchow railroad, so that the two roads did not meet. After the completion of the Hangkiang railroad, the Chinese government decided to extend it to the Chekiang-Kiangsi trunkline, thus connecting it with the Canton-Hankow railroad. This allowed direct connection between the big ports of the south with Shanghai and Nanking. The Chientang Bridge therefore was of great importance. Although the building of public roads in Chekiang province was going on apace, the Chientang River constituted a gap in the road system. In 1933, the Ministry of Railways joined forces with the Chekiang provincial government to build a combination highway and railroad bridge across the Chientang. The estimated construction expenses were 5,000,000 silver dollars to be equally borne by the central government and the provincial government. The planning and construction were undertaken entirely by Chinese engineers.

The main bridge across the Chientang had sixteen spans of 220 feet each. The approach to the bridge on the northern bank was 740 feet long, while the southern approach was 300 feet long. The total length of the bridge was 4,550 feet. The main bridge had two decks. The lower deck had a single track railway; the upper deck was of concrete. It provided for two-lane highway traffic, with a five foot wide pedestrian walkway on both sides. The construction of this bridge began in September 1934 and was completed in October 1937. At that time, the Japanese army was approaching Hangchow from Shanghai. Before the bridge was destroyed by the Chinese defenders, all the locomotives and rolling stock from the various railroads in the north as well as industrial materials and equipment had been moved to the rear in the southwest across this bridge by way of the Chekiang-Kiangsi, Canton-Hankow, and other railroads.

Lienyun Port. The Lunghai Railroad which went from east to west across the central plains of China, and which penetrated into the potentially rich northwest, occupied a very important economic position. Priority, however, was given to the extension of the line westward rather than the development of a seaport on the east coast. In 1925, as the eastern section of this railroad approached the sea coast, port facilities came under great pressure. Lienyun, requiring considerable construction work, was not an ideal seaport. The initial part of the construction work was carried out by a Dutch company. It included the building of a portion of the bank and two piers. In 1934, a 2,000 foot long break-water, two piers, and a 400-ton electrically-operated coal loading machine were built. All these large-scale constructions were under the administration of the Lunghai Railroad. Situated as it was between the two large ports of Tsingtso and Shanghai, Lienyun occupied a very important position.

Economic and Geological Aspects of Railroad Lines

After the founding of the Ministry of Railways, the planning of railroads on a national scale was a matter of great importance. The construction of railroads in the early period was concentrated in the north to facilitate the transportation to and from the then capital city of Peking. There were only several short lines south of the Yangtze River. There were no trunklines and no railroad system in this area. It was therefore decided that the Canton-Hankow, the Nanking-Hunan, the Nanking-Canton, the Foochow-Nanchang, the Canton-Kunming, and the Hunan-Kunming railroads should first be completed. These railroads were mainly to the south of the Yangtze and were connected with the capital at Nanking.

In order to understand the physical conditions of each route, survey teams for each of the above railroad lines were formed. In addition to undertaking surveys on various possible routes, each team was equipped with personnel who undertook an economic survey along the route of productivity, relationship between water and land transportation, and other related problems. These surveys served as a basis for estimating transportation requirements. Some of the surveys made disclosed several rich coal mines in provinces in the southwest. Prior attention, therefore, was given to rail lines in the southwest. The rationale behind all this planning, such as the opening up of a port in the south, Kwangchowwan, for example, so that one end of the railroad would run from the port and the other end to the productive and densely populated interior of Szechuan province, was to provide railroad lines of greatest economic value. The surveys involved a lot of work, but they proved beneficial even before the outbreak of the Sino-Japanese War.

The Readjustment of Old Railroad Debts and the Contracting of New Loans

The raising of loans to build railroads could be a sound practice if handled properly. The chief obstacle to the raising of loans in the early period arose from the fact that a large portion of the principal and interest could not be paid on time. This led to the depreciation of railway bonds (loan certificates) in the international market. From 1931 to 1932, bonds for the Lunghai Railroad depreciated as much as 95 per cent. Bonds issued by the United States for the Hu-kwang railroad were not even listed on the stock market. Other railroad bonds also depreciated by 50 per cent or more. Furthermore, funds for purchasing materials were not forthcoming on time. Since old debts could not be settled, it was almost impossible to issue new bonds to build new roads. By the end of 1935, the total amount of debt for the construction of railroads came to more than 265,000,000 U. S. dollars. If bigger programs for the construction of railroads were to be carried out, then more cash and materials would have to come from abroad. The first problem was the restoration of confidence, so that new loans could be contracted. Only then would foreign capital be forthcoming. Soon after its establishment, the Ministry of Railways negotiated with the various loan consortiums on such issues as financial resources and the readjustment of old debts. As a result of these efforts, the various bonds rose above 70 per cent in the spring of 1937. The bonds for the Shanghai-Nanking railroad rose even to 90 per cent. Subsequently, the British and China Corporation decided to begin issuing Chinese railroad bonds in the London market; and, in 1937, the 280-mile Kwang-Mei railroad from Canton to Mei Hsien was started.

As for the readjustment of old loans, the Tientsin-Pukow railroad served as an eminent example. Up to 1935, China owed the British firm

£1,150,000 for that railroad. Another loan of £880,000 was made. The unpaid interest accumulated and came close to £1,000,000 over the years. China was unable to clear this debt on her own. Accordingly, the two countries negotiated the following terms: (1) the rate of interest to be paid every three years from 1936 onwards was reduced to 2½ per cent after which time the rate was to be restored to the original rate of 5 per cent; (2) the principal was to be paid from 1940 onwards from the gross cash income of the railroad. One per cent of its yearly income was to be paid. Later, a higher percentage was to be paid until the debt was cleared; (3) The creditor was to write off four-fifths of the hitherto unpaid interest; (4) all the principal and interest were to be paid with the income from the railroads. If the income was not enough, then the payment was to be subsidized by the custom's revenues. The above method enabled the creditors to obtain their principal over an extended period of time, giving the railroads a breathing spell. Other main routes, such as the Lunghai Railroad and the Hu-kwang Railroad, and even shorter ones, such as the Tao-ching Railroad and the Canton-Kowloon Railroad, also used similar methods of payment of loans. It was estimated that the amount of principal of the various railroads thus readjusted amounted to £40,360,000.

After the unification of China in 1927, several European countries gradually encouraged the export trade and established a system of government guarantees for exports. Export merchants could rely on the government to bear a large portion of any risk. Otto Wolf of Germany, who loaned money and materials to China for the building of the Chekiang-Kiangsi railroad, was a prime example. In addition to imported materials, the Ministry of Railways also had to raise cash for domestic construction work. Although, by that time, there was increased interest among Chinese banks and business concerns to invest in railroads, available funds were limited. Guarantees were not easy to obtain. Foreign firms, in considering whether or not to furnish materials and equipment on a loan basis, wanted to see whether Chinese banks were willing tc provide local expenses. The China Development and Finance Corporation took the lead in this regard, and, with the participation of the various Chinese commercial banks in Shanghai, asserted a great influence on the future construction of railroads. Further assistance was provided by the provincial governments and businessmen. For instance, assistance was furnished in the building of the Chekiang-Kiangsi and the Szechuan-Kweichow railroads. With this assistance, the Ministry of Railways was able to issue bonds amounting to 12,000,000 silver dollars for the first period of railroad construction in 1934 and 27,000,000 silver dollars for the second period in 1936.

Several Uncompleted New Routes

(1) *The Hunan-Kwangsi Railroad.* When the Canton-Hankow railroad was completed in 1936, the Kwangsi provincial government proposed to the central government that the newly completed railroad be extended to link up Kwangsi province with Hankow and the area around Nanking and Shanghai. In 1937, the raising of funds was completed and work was begun. It was originally planned that the line should run from Hengyang (衡陽) to Kweilin in Kwangsi province, a distance of about 218 miles. Soon after construction was begun, the Japanese army began to attack China in the north. This railroad served a great purpose during the war. Subsequently, it was extended to Liuchow (柳州) and thence into the hitherto rather inaccessible Kweichow province. The Hunan-Kwangsi railroad was built with the aim of connecting with Kweilin. But after the outbreak of the war, plans were made to connect the whole line with railroads in Indochina and to use Haiphong as an outlet. Construction was begun to connect the Nanning Chen-nan-Kwan (鎮南關) section with the Indochina Railroad at Langson, but it had to be suspended when the Japanese army entered Kwangsi province.

(2) *The Hunan-Kweichow Railroad.* After the Japanese invasion and occupation of the Northeast, the entire northern part of China came under Japanese threat. The Ministry of Railways made emergency plans for the construction of railroads from central China to each province in the Southwest. When the Canton-Hankow railroad was completed and linked up with the Chekiang-Kiangsi railroad, the Ministry of Railways decided to build the Hunan-Kweichow railroad to develop the rich coal mines of western Hunan and to connect Shanghai, Nanking, and Wuhan with Kweichow province in the Southwest. To this end, the third stage of bonds were issued. The Ministry also entered into a contract in January, 1936, with representatives of German interests for the loan of materials and funds amounting to 19,000,000 silver dollars. A small portion was used for the rehabilitation of the Peking-Hankow railroad, while a larger portion was used to build the Hunan-Kweichow railroad. This railroad ran westward from Chuchow (株洲) on the Canton-Hankow railroad, passed through the rich coal region of western Hunan and terminated in Kweiyang (貴陽). The total length was about 600 miles. Work was begun at the eastern end of the railroad in 1937, but soon had to be suspended when Japan invaded North China. Consequently, some imported materials were used on other roads.

(3) *The Chungking-Chengtu Railroad* (成渝鐵路). Between 1934 and 1935, when construction of the Canton-Hankow and the Chekiang-Kiangsi railroads was going on south of the Yangtze River, the whole country seemed to undergo a construction boom. In 1935, the China Develop-

ment and Finance Corporation undertook to develop the vast natural resources of Szechuan province. The area from Chungking to Chengtu was particularly rich in natural resources, and Chungking became the economic center of the Southwest. The Corporation proposed to form the Szechuan-Kweichow Railroad Company and to build the section from Chengtu to Chungking as a first step. The next step was to connect the provinces of Szechuan and Kweichow by rail. The Corporation decided that the initial capital should be $20,000,000 silver dollars. Since the French banks and French industrial circles had shown considerable interest towards developing the southwest provinces of China, the Corporation invited the French banking consortium to invest in the form of a loan for all of the materials and part of the construction expenses. Since this road was to become the only national trunkline reaching into Szechuan province, and in order to facilitate its progress, the Corporation invited the Ministry of Railways and the Szechuan provincial government to invest 4,500,000 silver dollars each. The remaining funds were to be provided by the Corporation itself. Negotiations with the French banking consortium for a loan of 27,500,000 silver dollars were completed at the end of 1936. Another loan of 7,000,000 silver dollars was made at 7 per cent interest guaranteed by the Ministry of Railways to be paid within 15 years.

This rather circuitous railroad started from Chungking and proceeded westward along the Yangtze river. It was about 320 miles long. Work was begun in 1936, and materials from France had already been purchased. But in 1937, Japan invaded China. Although this area was not immediately affected by the war, river transport on the Yangtze was obstructed so that very little of the materials could reach the construction site. The materials which reached Hong Kong could not be transported by the Canton-Hankow railroad because Canton had fallen into Japanese hands. Hence all purchasing and shipping of materials were stopped, and construction work had to be suspended. By this time, the roadbed of the eastern section and a large portion of the tunnels had been completed.

(4) *The Nanking-Kiangsi Railroad* (京贛鐵路). As the war situation became more serious, the Chinese government wanted to extend the section on the Kiang-nan Railroad from Nanking, the capital, to the southern part of Anhwei province and into Kiangsi province to link up with Kweichi (貴谿) station of the Chekiang-Kiangsi railroad. This would provide a more direct connection between Nanking, the capital, and the various provinces south of the Yangtze. Moreover, there were such products as timber, paper, pottery, and coal available along this route; hence, its economic value was very high. This Nanking-Kiangsi railroad was 290 miles in length. At that time, it was estimated that

imported materials would cost about £900,000, and construction expenses would cost about 34,000,000 silver dollars. The funds for materials were borrowed from the Sino-British Indemnity Fund Commission while construction expenses were jointly provided by seven domestic banks in the amount of 14,000,000 silver dollars. The various contracts were signed in 1936.

Work was to begin at both ends, in Anhwei and in Kiangsi. In November, 1936, construction began in Anhwei. About 100 miles of rails had been laid when the Sino-Japanese War broke out. Construction was delayed at the Kiangsi section until December 1937 when the rails were laid from Kweichi heading northward, a distance of about thirty-six miles. Work had to be suspended because of the war.

Contracts For Projected New Railroads

The years preceding the Sino-Japanese War was a period marked by intensive construction work by the joint efforts of the Chinese government and the people. At that time, the government had a Five-Year Plan for the construction of 4,800 miles of railroads. The Japanese knew that the invasion of China would be made more difficult once China had been united and her communications developed. That was why Japan struck in 1937. The war brought railroad construction to a complete standstill. In addition, the following railroads for which loans had been negotiated could not be started because of the Japanese invasion:

1) *The Paochi-Chengtu Railroad* (寶成鐵路). The proposal to build a north-south trunkline west of the Peking-Hankow railroad to connect the upper course of the Yellow River with the upper course of the Yangtze was made in 1913. At the time, the Chinese government was negotiating for a loan from a French banking consortium to build the so-called Pao-ch'eng railroad. It was to run from Paochi on the Lunghai railroad southward through Kwangyuen (廣元) to Chengtu in Szechuan Province. The subsequent outbreak of the European War made it impossible to proceed. Furthermore, the westward extension of the Lunghai Railroad was very slow. Until the Lunghai Railroad was able to extend westward at a greater speed, the Ministry of Railways started clearing up the old debts for this railroad. The Belgium banking consortium was willing to continue negotiating with China for more loans. Thus, in August 1936, the Ministry of Railways signed a contract with two Belgian banking corporations for a loan of 450,000,000 Belgian francs for materials and cash to be made available in four annual installments. After the completion of the railroad, the loan was to be paid off in seven years at the rate of 6 per cent interest per year. The outbreak

of the Marco Polo Bridge Incident in the following year made this an abortive attempt.

(2) *The Canton-Meihsien Railroad* (廣梅鐵路). In 1936, after the unification of Kwangtung by the central government, the Ministry of Railways decided to build a Canton-Meihsien railroad from Shihtan (石灘) station on the Canton-Kowloon railroad to Meihsien. It was decided later on to extend it to Kiangsi to connect with the Chekiang-Kiangsi Railroad. The Ministry initially decided to issue bonds for the construction of the Canton-Meihsien Railroad. Materials had to be purchased from abroad and loans had to be negotiated from the Hong Kong and Shanghai Banking Corporation and the China Development and Finance Corporation. In July 1937, a contract was signed in London by the representatives of the Ministry and the China Development and Finance Corporation. The loan was in the amount of £3,000,000, at the rate of 5 per cent interest per year. The interest during the construction was to be provided from the salt tax. The loan period was to be thirty years, and the principal was to be repaid after five years. A railroad company was established after the signing of the contract. The trunk and branch lines of this railroad ran about 280 miles. According to plans, it was to be completed in two years, but while the contract was being signed in London, the Marco Polo Bridge Incident broke out and construction was suspended.

(3) *The Pukow-Hsiangyang Railroad* (浦襄鐵路). In 1936, when Great Britain accepted China's invitation to help in the Chinese currency reform, she was inclined to invest in China in the amout of £10,000,000, a portion of which was to be used for the construction of railroads. Thus, when China negotiated with the British banking consortium for a loan for the building of the Canton-Meihsien Railroad, she proposed to modify the old contract for the building of the Pu-sin (Pukow-Sinyang) Railroad (　　浦信鐵路　) which had been delayed. This was to be changed to a loan for the building of the Pukow-Hsiangyang Railroad. The terminal was to be changed from Sinyang to Hsiangyang on the upper course of the Yangtze. The total length was about 250 miles. In 1937, after the signing of the loan contract for the Canton-Meihsien Railroad, the Chinese Minister of Finance proceeded to London and signed the contract for the Pukow-Hsiangyang Railroad on the 4th of August. The amount of the loan was £4,000,000, at 5 per cent interest per year. The rest of the contract was similar to that of the Canton-Meihsien Railroad. After the signing of this contract, the war was already spreading southward, making it impossible to proceed.

(4) *The Kueichi-Meihsien and The Sanshui-Wuchow Railroads* (貴谿—梅縣，三水—梧州). The projected loan from England in the amount of £10,000,000 was to be used for the building of two

lines: £3,000,000 for the Canton-Meihsien railroad, and £4,000,000 for the Pukow-Hsiangyang railroad, leaving a surplus of £3,000,000. The Ministry of Railways was of the opinion that if the Canton-Meihsien railroad could be connected with the Chekiang-Kiangsi railroad and the Nanking-Kiangsi railroad, then the three provinces of Kiangsi, Chekiang and Kwangtung could be connected, and the development of the natural resources of Kwangtung and Kiangsi would be greatly facilitated. It was therefore decided that a line be built from Meihsien passing through the southern part of Fukien to Kueichi in Kiangsi, and thence connecting with the Nanking-Kiangsi railroad, and then to the Chekiang-Kiangsi railroad. The total length was to be 450 miles. The Ministry also decided to extend westward a branch line of the Canton-Hankow railroad at its terminal in Sanshui along the West River to Wuchow, a length of 137 miles. These two lines needed about £8,000,000. In May, 1937, the representatives of the British banking consortium agreed to provide capital for the building of the Canton-Meihsien railroad. The rest of the loan was to be raised in the form of bonds at a later date. This period was marked by tremendous British interest in China's railroads. Unfortunately, the Marco Polo Bridge Incident prevented the completion of the formal contracts for these two roads.

(5) *The Kweiyang-Kunming Railroad* (貴昆鐵路). After the construction of the Hunan-Kweichow railroad had begun, the Ministry of Railways started planning to extend the line from Kweiyang to reach Kunming in Yunnan. This was to connect with the Yunnan-Indochina railroad, and then to proceed to the Indochinese seaport of Haiphong. The French banking consortium and the China Development and Finance Corporation which had contracted for the Chungking-Chengtu railroad also had an interest in this railroad. Negotiations were initiated to contract for 50,000,000 silver dollars for materials and 50,000,000 silver dollars for labor and local materials. Before the completion of negotiations, however, the outbreak of the Marco Polo Bridge Incident made further discussions impossible.

On the whole, the period between 1926 and 1936 was a very active decade for the construction of railroads in China. During this period, China had built altogether 2,900 miles of trunklines, including 804 miles in the Northeast and 2,080 miles within the Great Wall. In July 1937, when Japan first started invading China, there were about 1,110 miles of railroads under construction. Due to the Japanese invasion, loan contracts for more than 2,240 miles of railroads could not be finalized. At 'this time, the re-adjustment of old debts was estimated to be in the amount of £40,360,000. If it had not been for the Japanese invasion, the history of China's railroads would have been entirely different.

IV

Policy Changes Resulting from a Decade of Building Railroads

The policy of the national government in its ten years of railroad construction program from 1926 to 1936 was to complete the various trunklines which had not been completed. The next step was to build several important connecting trunklines. This was to be followed by an intensive investigation of natural resources and physical feasibility for the planning of future railroads in those areas. The aim was to construct a system of railroads which were economically feasible. In 1921, Dr. Sun Yat-sen announced his plan for building 100,000 miles of railroads throughout China within ten years. He also proposed a blue-print for the entire railroad system. But at that time, China was lacking in information concerning natural resources in the remote areas so that it was difficult to determine the economic value of the proposed lines. Moreover, between 1921 and 1927, only a few railroads had been built, and the internal situation in China was undergoing changes. Thus, after the republican government was established, the matter of priority in building railroads was reexamined. To Dr. Sun Yat-sen's plan was added a Five-Year Plan for the building of 4,800 more miles of railways.

Changed Conception towards the Building of Railroads
The early period of construction of railroads and the selection of lines were lacking in overall planning. Many decisions were influenced by foreign powers which had no overall conception of China's needs. The most obvious examples were the railroads from north and central China which ran west or northwest, more or less along parallel lines. The Peking-Suiyuan railroad in the north, for one, ran northwestward to Paotou. The Lunghai railroad in central China, extending to Shensi and Kansu, serves as another example. A third example is the Hunan-Kwangsi railroad in the southwest. The terminals of these three lines were far apart. From the point of view of through transportation, it was obvious that the situation was both uneconomical and inefficient. Thus, when the Chekiang-Kiangsi and the Nanking-Kiangsi railroads were built, plans were made to connect Paocheng, Paoning, Lanning, Hsiangch'ien, Ch'uanch'ien (寶成,包寧,蘭寧,湘黔,川黔) railroads with the main trunklines. The building of the Nanking ferry, the Chientang Bridge, as well as the Wuhan-Yangtze Bridge and the bridge from Tungkwan to Fengling, were built with this end in view.

Standardization of Railroad Techniques

A nation's railroad network must have a uniform standard of construction to facilitate through traffic. In the early periods of construction in China, funds for the building of railroads were borrowed from foreign powers, and foreign standards in engineering were adopted. The result was a hodge-podge standard of railroads in China. A railroad such as the Chinese Eastern Railroad used a broad gauge, while the Chengtai (正太) railroad used a narrow gauge. Other matters, such as heavy or easy grades, gradual or sharp curvatures, high or low platforms, heavy or light rails or bridges, as well as different dimensions for locomotives and passenger and freight cars are all different for different lines. The result was that trains from one line could not run on another line. Locomotives of one line were not allowed to cross the bridges of another line, resulting in utter confusion. Although the Ministry of Communications in the early period of the Republic had already started to prepare for the standardization of railroads, the actual implementation of the plan was mainly the work of the national government. Railroad administrations began to understand the importance of uniformity, so that the construction of railroads henceforth was entirely in the hands of Chinese engineers, regardless of the source of funds and materials. This led to a gradual standardization of construction techniques.

During the early periods of railroad construction in China, lightweight rails were often used to save costs. The result was that only light locomotives and cars could run on them. The rapid increase of passenger and freight traffic after the opening of the railroads was not anticipated. Thus, after 1927, the various trunklines had to increase the weight of the rails from sixty pounds to eighty-five pounds per yard, and bridges had to be reinforced to accommodate larger locomotives. Moreover, the capacity of freight cars had to be increased from twenty tons to fifty tons to meet transportation needs. Steam locomotives were the order of the day. However, the supply of coal in China was not adequate, and the effectiveness of steam locomotion was low and uneconomical. Thus, consideration was given quite early to experimenting with diesel locomotives in potential oil-producing areas, along with research in the electrification of railroads in the southwestern mountainous areas.

Organization and Development

The organization of railroads in China was largely based upon the old British system. In the administration of railroads, a Traffic Department was established, which had to handle business affairs as well. This was due to the fact that in the early period, railroads belonged solely to the state and their business was in effect a monopoly. Furthermore, there were no public highways to compete with them. After the unification of the Republic, the need for the expansion of railroad business became painfully obvious. Therefore, the old Traffic Department was divided into an Operating Department and a Business Department. This system was first adopted by the Peking-Mukden Railroad. In 1936, the just-completed Canton-Hankow Railroad also adopted this system. However, state-owned railroads came directly under the control of the Ministry in the Cabinet. Their organization was inevitably bureaucratic and suffered from the lack of private enterprise. Even before the Sino-Japanese War, the Ministry of Railways had begun to adopt modern methods for the operating of new railroads. For instance, the Hunan-Kwangsi Railroad and the Szechuan-Kweichow Railroad formed their own railroad companies. Each company was able to manage its own business affairs, subject only to supervision by the Ministry of Railways. Although this system could not be widely adopted after the start of the war, the basic principle of adopting sound business methods for the operation of railroads had already taken root. This system made it possible for business to generate further business.

International Cooperation with Local Interests

The early periods of negotiating for loans for the building of railroads with the various European countries and Japan were marked not so much by international commercial competition as by competition for economic and political privileges in China. This was contradictory to the so-called "Open Door" policy. After the Republic was united, the political and financial situation began to stabilize. The European capitalists began to look at China from another angle. Chinese banking circles also showed more interest in investing in railroads. Therefore, with the combined resources of Chinese and foreign capital, the building of railroads began to take on a new face. The greatest difference was that the loans were made on a commercial rather than a political basis. One result was that the construction and operation of the railroads were solely in Chinese hands. Although the various countries had an historical interest in China, the idea of spheres of influence was dead and gone. The guarantees for loans were not solely confined to the railroads themselves, so that during the period of construction, the creditors only had the right to audit expenditures, while management and construction were completely under the control of the Chinese. More skilled construction personnel began to appear after the Republic was set up, capable of handling all the difficult tasks. The choice of materials and the question of techniques were up to the Chinese. This marked a new period of international cooperation.

At the time, the various provinces regarded the central government as chiefly responsible for the construction of railroads because the provinces themselves were unable to shoulder the responsibility. After 1929, however, when Chekiang Province built its Hang-kiang railroad on its own, the various provinces began to take an interest in the building of railroads. Kiangsi, Hunan, Kwangsi, Szechuan, and other provinces, for instance, began to cooperate with the central government. This arrangement was ideal, because the provinces were then financially incapable of offering the guarantees for loans for building their railroads without assistance from the central government and the banking circles. Although the financial resources of the provinces were limited, they were able to supply the labor. This cooperation between the central and provincial governments was largely responsible for the rapid construction of railroads prior to the Sino-Japanese War.

Comments:

BY CHIAO-MIN HSIEH

ROFESSOR H. H. LING'S PAPER is invaluable because of the qualifications and experience of the author. Professor Ling received a Chinese classical education, as well as American technical training. During his early career, he was president of Chiaotung University in Shanghai, a noted engineering institution, and later served as Vice-minister of the Ministry of Communication from 1945 to 1949. He began his railroad career in 1918, and played an active role in railroad construction in China from 1929 to 1945. As a railroad engineer-in-chief, he took charge of the surveying, construction, and management of several trunklines in China. Obviously, therefore, Professor Ling is well qualified to write on railroad construction in China.

The importance of railroads in China is revealed by the fact that for 1950 it is reported that railroads carried 93.2 per cent of transported cargo in China, inland waterways, 3.9 per cent; maritime, 2 per cent; and highways, 2.9 per cent. In 1958, railroads still accounted for 78.5 per cent and highways for 2.9 per cent, while the combined percentage for inland waterways and maritime was 18.6 per cent.

Professor Ling has concentrated upon the history of railroad construction, including its early beginnings, policy changes, technical complexity, and standardization problems. Hopefully, my remarks will complement Ling's work, especially with respect to the characteristics of China's railroads, as well as their network pattern. My remarks conclude with a brief discussion of railroads in mainland China today and the problems confronting them.

The most striking characteristic of early Chinese railroad construction is its north-south pattern. This is closely related to the direction in which China's major rivers flow.

The Amur, the Yellow, and the Yangtze rivers are among the longest in the world. The Yangtze, with its tributaries, helps to bind the country into a unit. Since the major rivers in China run from west to east, the Chinese have little trouble carrying goods in that direction. For example, the agricultural goods from the producing province of Szechuan can easily be shipped eastward to the lower part of the Yangtze. But China needed a means of transportation between the north and the south. Since the direction of a river's flow is predetermined by nature, the Chinese used artificial means to change its direction. In ancient times the Chinese built the Grand Canal from Hangchow to Peking which became the main thoroughfare for transporting rice from south to north. In modern times, one of the earliest railroads constructed in China was the one that connects Peking in the north with Canton in the south.

It is interesting to compare the orientation of China's railroads with that of railroads in the Soviet Union. The Ob, Yenisey, and Lena rivers in the Soviet Union flow northward, and empty into the frozen Arctic Ocean in an area that is sparsely populated and has no important ports. By contrast, the Yellow, Yangtze, and West rivers flow, in their lower sections, through the most densely populated areas of China. Peking and Tientsin are located near the Yellow River delta, Nanking and Shanghai near the mouth of the Yangtze, while Canton is located on the West River delta.

The major Soviet rivers flow from south to north; however, the main routes of trade and communication, such as the Trans-Siberian Railway, run from west to east. As a result, there are important cities where the railways cross the rivers. Examples of such cities are Omsk on the Irtysh River, Tomsk on the Ob, Krasnoyarsk on the Yenisey, and Khabarovsk on the Amur. In China, as noted above, the most important rivers flow from west to east while the great communication routes, such as the Grand Canal from Hangchow to Peking and the railways between Canton and Peking and between Nanking and Tientsin, run north and south. As in the Soviet Union, important cities have arisen at the junctions of the railways with the rivers. Such cities are Hankow and Nanking on the Yangtze River, Chengchow and Kaifeng on the Yellow River.

A second characteristic of China's railroads is their uneven distribution.

A map of the railroad network of China prior to 1949 shows that the major railroads were largely concentrated in *two* distinct areas, the north-eastern provinces, or Manchuria, and North China, which together accounted for more than three-fourths of the total length. South of the Yangtze River there were only a few railroads, and west of a line extending from 100 longitude there were practically no railroads. This resulted from the interplay of a number of factors. By far the most important was the scramble for concessions by the great powers at the end of the nineteenth century.

Raliroads provided the most effective access to the interior of the country and soon led to the establishment of spheres of influence. Manchuria fell within the Russian sphere when the Chinese Eastern Railway was completed. Germany obtained the concession to build the

Tsingtao-Tsinan Railway and a section of the Tientsin-Pukow line, enabling it to exploit the minerals of Shantung Province. The British attempted to open up a corridor across China from Burma to Shanghai. France built the Kunming-Haiphong Railway and attempted to construct a railroad in the Luichou Penninsula. Southwest China was thus to serve French interests. Japan gained concessions in Fukien Province and the adjacent area. Belgium undertook construction of the Peking-Hankow Railway, while American capital was used to build the southern section of this railroad, the Canton-Hankow line. Many lines were built with foreign loans and were managed by Chinese.

The most active period of railroad construction, as Ling notes, was between 1926 and 1936. During this period, China constructed 2900 miles of trunklines, of which 2080 miles were located in China proper and 804 miles in the Northeast (Manchuria).

Professor Ling observes quite correctly that the completion of the Canton-Hankow Railroad in 1936 had important economic and political consequences. Thus, after the railroad was completed, the various political factions in China were unified, a standardized currency was adopted, and the Chinese people gained a sense of national unity. Most importantly, the completion of the railroad enabled the National Government to hold out the Hankow area against the Japanese attack for more than a year. More than 540,000 tons of military supplies had been carried by this railroad from abroad via Kowloon to this area.

For the sake of political coherence and the furtherance of economic development, the Communist government in China has paid great attention to the building of railroad systems. The length of the main line built since 1949 is 12,500 miles. Of the many completed systems of railroads, two have geopolitical significance and are worth noting.

1. Along the east coast five ports, Yentai, Ningpo, Foochow, Amoy, and Chiankiang, have been linked to the interior by short lines. The military intention of the railroads built in the areas around Foochow and Amoy apparently is that of confronting Taiwan.

2. Two long railroads have been built for the purpose of connecting China with the Soviet Union. One, which was built in 1954, runs from Tsining through Ulan Bator in Outer Mongolia, then on to the Soviet Union. With the completion of this railroad, the mainland was joined to the so-called Mongolian People's Republic. The other one, which is 1,400 miles long, runs between Lanchow and Urumchi via Hami in Sinkiang. The Communist government obviously feels that the political importance of these railroads is greater than their economic value. Since the great bulk of China's population, markets, and production, lies east of Lanchow and south of the Great Wall, many railroads are urgently needed in that part of China. One must wonder whether the two rail-

roads built in the desert for the main purpose of connecting China with the Soviet Union were so necessary and their construction so urgent. Moreover, there is at the moment a sand-dune problem confronting the operation of the railroad in these desert areas. This seems to be insoluble by use of present techniques and makes the value of the whole project even more questionable.

The Communist government has given industrialization top priority in its planning and building the massive railway a first rather than an accompanying step. Communist government disregard normal economic consideration, but the shortage of capital nevertheless imposes limits. The logical direction of transport flow in China is, in broad outline, to and from the coast, and secondly between north and south. This is the trade pattern which best reflects the complementary function of regional and international transport connections, and which is fortunately already served by the great river systems and the coastal sea routes. The great bulk of China's population, markets, and production lies east of Lanchow or Chengtu and south of Great Wall. For obvious political reasons, the present regime is attempting to change this orientation, to build up the northwest and its trade at the expense of the coast. The shortage of high cost of fuel and equipment and the inherent limitation of truck transport will not make of it a major solution to a transport problem of China's dimensions. Land distance in China is great. Truck transport is thus doubly unsuited to act as a low-cost volume mover. China should pay attention to waterway instead of railroad and highway. For example, the Rhine, which still carries more traffic than the combined railways through its basin (and at lower coast) should be suggestive to China, where the Yangtze system is larger and at least equally well placed to serve a majority of the domestic and export flows. The manifold disappointments and heavy unprofitable investment in railway building in the past in China should provide a warning even to Communist economic planners.

CHAPTER IX

Education in China, 1927–1937

BY THEODORE H. E. CHEN

Early beginnings

HINESE EDUCATION IS AS OLD as China's long history, but modern schools were not introduced until the latter part of the nineteenth century and the establishment of a modern school system is essentially a development of the twentieth century. The fragmentary efforts of the last century were made in response to external threat. Humiliated by military defeats, China saw the need of introducing the new knowledge that accounted for the superior power of the West. Schools were accordingly established to teach military science and other areas of Western knowledge. These early schools were not coordinated to form an organized system.

The first system of schools, proposed in 1902, was modelled after the Japanese, since Japan furnished a shining example of successful modernization. With the establishment of the Republic in 1912, the Japanese system, which bore the earmarks of the Prussian school system, was considered unsuitable, and China turned to the United States for guidance. A new school system patterned after the American was then introduced. Another revision made in 1922 was again influenced by American ideas and provided for two levels of secondary education consisting of three years each. In basic features, this 1922 organization of schools remained effective throughout the period under study in this paper.

Period of ferment

The years following the birth of the Republic in 1912 witnessed a deep interest on the part of China's educated people in the intellectual currents of the world and an eagerness to infuse new ideas into the old traditional culture. World War I and the declaration of lofty ideas by such world leaders as Woodrow Wilson further stimulated the search for new patterns of thinking and living more in harmony with modern times. The influx of new ideas and the release of creative energies resulted in a vigorous intellectual movement which became known as the Chinese Renaissance. It had many manifestations. The Chinese term for it is the New Thought Movement. China opened its doors to new ideas and proponents of different schools of thought from abroad. A wide range of publications appeared; books and periodicals translated the writings of European as well as American philosophers, and discussed the concepts of individualism, self-realization, freedom, science, and democracy. It was at this time that Marxism was introduced into China.

Marxism was studied with interest along with other thought systems from abroad. No school of thought was barred; the New Thought Movement thrived in an atmosphere of free inquiry and intellectual curiosity. Out of this movement arose two important developments which greatly influenced the course of Chinese education in the ensuing decades: the Literary Revolution and the May Fourth Student Movement.

The Pai-hua Movement

The Literary Revolution was launched in 1917 by scholars who rebelled against the classical style of writing and advocated its replacement by a vernacular written language. Traditional Chinese education had taught and perpetuated the classical style and disapproved the vernacular as crude and devoid of literary refinement. The classical language was so different from the spoken language that a pupil could learn to read the written characters without understanding their meaning; it was necessary for him to learn the written characters first and then translate them into the spoken tongue before their meaning could be understood. Teachers and scholars would not condescend to write as they spoke; instead, they perpetuated a stylistic form of writing whose meaning was not directly recognizable to one who knew only the spoken language.

The classical style persevered through the centuries. Scholars were afraid to depart from the accepted forms. No respectable scholar dared write as he spoke. A few brave souls yielded to their inner impulse and wrote novels in the vernacular; their works gained popularity but they avoided censure by the use of pseudonyms.

The freedom and creativity of the New Thought Movement provided a fresh stimulus to write as one would speak—in other words, to write in the vernacular language. Two outstanding scholars—Hu Shih and Ch'en Tu-hsiu—initiated a Literary Revolution by openly declaring that the classical language had outlived its usefulness. They began to write articles and publicize profound ideas by using the simple words and style of the spoken tongue. This vernacular writing became known as the *pai-hua* (literally, "plain speech"). A new *pai-hua* literature came into existence and quickly gained popularity and respectability.

With the old vernacular novels as models of living language, Chinese scholars now write prose and poetry in *pai-hua*, and anyone with a modicum of schooling was able to express ideas in the vernacular without the confinement of a formalistic style. "Expression," said Hu Shih, "soon became a passion of the new generation, who found in the *pai-hua* an effective vehicle for giving vent to their feelings and aspirations."[1]

The *pai-hua* movement spread so fast that the schools responded by teaching pupils to read *pai-hua* books and to write *pai-hua* essays. The educational effect of this movement was considerable and will be discussed in later sections of this paper.

The student movement

The second by-product of the New Thought Movement was the Student Movement. It was known as the May Fourth Movement because of the explosive reactions of students to disappointing political events on May 4, 1919. Japanese aggression combined with Wilsonian promises of self determination during World War I had greatly raised the hopes of the Chinese nation for a just peace that would right the wrongs of aggression and restore to China what she had under duress been compelled to concede to Japan. Power politics at the Paris Peace Conference in April 1919, however, aroused the fears of the Chinese and produced a deep frustration especially felt by students. Rising nationalism and profound disillusionment erupted in violent action on the part of the students when news came from Paris that the great powers had sustained the demands of Japan and ignored the hopes and aspirations of the Chinese nation. Enraged by the incompetence of their government and its delegates at the Paris Conference, students from various colleges and universities in Peking, the national capital, led mass demonstrations on May 4 to voice their opposition to the action of the Paris Conference and to awaken the nation to the peril confronting Chinese sovereignty. After marching to the foreign legations, where they were stopped by police, the more militant students sought out leading government officials and gave them a severe beating. Clashes between students and police further flamed the emotions and produced reverberations all over the country.

The significance of the May Fourth Movement lies not so much in what happened in the first week of May 1919, but more in the events preceding and following the spectacular eruption of student protests against the Paris peace treaty. The explosion in the first week of May was the result of blasted hopes, keen disillusionment, and deepened frustration. The aspirations as well as the frustration were in large part an outgrowth of the New Thought Movement, which had created an atmosphere of rebellion against the past, skepticism in regard to the old order, and assertion of the right to challenge and oppose. These were new forces released by the New Thought Movement; without them, the student actions of 1919 would not have had such a great impact on Chinese life.

The purpose of this brief review of the May Fourth Movement is to recall the historical background of the youth problems that confronted the Nationalist government in the decade under consideration. By 1927, student activities had become a serious educational problem. Student demonstrations and strikes frequently disrupted school work, sometimes compelling the closure of schools for weeks or months. Strikes were called to protest against government and schools policies. Students demanded the removal of unpopular teachers and administrators; the more aggressive ones did not hesitate to beat teachers and school administrators they disliked. Thus arose serious problems of student discipline and educational stability that the Nationalist government later struggled to solve.

At the time of the May Fourth Movement, however, the students were, in the main, motivated by patriotism and high idealism. They demanded a new way of life characterized by more freedom, independence, and more active participation in social and political affairs. In international politics, they demanded the end of foreign aggression. In national politics, they opposed the selfishness and corruption of the warlords. In social affairs, they declared their concern for the common man and the welfare of the masses. In the family, they rebelled against the old system of patriarchal authority and parental control, insisting on the right to choose their own mates as well as their individual careers. In the school, they demanded a voice in school affairs and refused to be confined to quiet study in the classroom. They wanted activity instead of passivity, individualism instead of unquestioning acceptance of authority, freedom from the restriction of traditions, and independence in the conduct of personal life. Girls were as assertive as boys and demanded equality in education and social life. Co-education, hitherto permitted only in elementary schools, was now introduced into higher education.[2]

Unfulfilled promises

If there had been a stable government and competent political leadership, the ideals of the New Thought Movement and its offshoots might have found expression in positive educational advance and intellectual growth. Unfortunately, the hopes and aspirations aroused by the Movement were smothered in a depressive political climate. The warlords who dominated the Chinese scene prevented the rise of a united nation. A divided nation embroiled in internal strife not only neglected the tasks of domestic reconstruction but was unable to take a positive position in defense of its elementary rights against predatory external aggressors. Hopes ended in despair and ideals were submerged under deep frustration.

Education received scant attention from the ruling warlords. A characteristic of the warlord period prior to 1927 is that no warlord could be sure how long he could remain in power. Since his control was usually temporary, he was hardly inclined to make any long-range plans. There was no educational planning, no thought-out policy for the development of education, and no assured support for schools that were already in existence. Teachers in public schools were not only poorly paid and inadequately prepared, but their salaries were frequently months in arrears with no definite prospect of funds being made available. Buildings fell into disrepair and there was no money for equipment. Needless to say, academic standards were low.

This, then, was the educational situation at the time the Nationalist government was established. The intellectual fermentation of the Renaissance had produced a wealth of fresh ideas and revealed the distant and faint outlines of possible educational vistas, but these remained as vague hopes and unfulfilled promises.

Nationalism and education

Unlike the transient warlords, the Nationalist government conceived and pursued a plan of nation-building, and its leaders were aware of the crucial importance of education as an instrument of nation-building. The Nationalist Party, i.e., the Kuomintang, had risen to power on the crest of ascending nationalism. This nationalism was spearheaded by the students and intellectuals and was in large part the product of modern education. Students were among the most active supporters of the Kuomintang, which was then recognized as a revolutionary party and the champion of nationalism.

A positive educational policy combined with the upsurge of nationalism means an educational program imbued with the spirit of nationalism. It may be said that in the initial period of the decade under consideration, the major characteristic of education was nationalism, while in subsequent years the painstaking efforts of nation-building assumed a more prominent role.

Chinese nationalism that reached an apex of development in the 1920's consisted of two major phases: the establishment of a unified government to replace the divided nation dominated by the warlords, and the abrogation of "unequal treaties" and other vestiges of nineteenth century imperialism in order to attain independence and equality among the nations of the world. In education, there was also a twofold objective: to build up a national system of schools, and to terminate the control of education by foreigners.

Aim of education

An initial step in the formulation of a positive educational program after 1927 was a clear statement of aim which reflected the nationalism of that time and the ideology of the Kuomintang, the Three People's Principles. Such a statement was officially issued in 1929. It read as follows:

> The aim of education in the Republic of China is to enrich the life of the people, to maintain and develop social life, to promote the livelihood of the citizens, and to foster national life, in accordance with the Three People's Principles, ultimately aspiring to the independence of the nation, the universal assertion of the people's rights, the development of the people's livelihood, and the realization of world peace.

In the implementation of the general aim, three points of emphasis came into evidence: (1) education for national regeneration, (2) education for production and practical use, and (3) education in the Three People's Principles. To achieve national regeneration, it was held that education should strive to develop national consciousness and national self-confidence. It should foster a positive pride in the national culture and create an awareness of cultural unity among the people. The study of the national culture became a central subject of the curriculum.

State control

To set up a national system of schools and see to it that the officially declared educational aim was heeded in all the schools, a system of state control was instituted. A centralized administration was considered the quickest way of ending the chaos that resulted from the laissez-faire educational policy of the warlords. At the top of the administrative machinery was the Ministry of Education, which controlled all levels of education, from the kindergarten and the elementary schools to the university and research institutes. The Ministry prescribed minimum standards of curriculum, equipment, finance, teacher qualifications, and many other details. Elementary and secondary education were under the direct control of local authorities, but all local authorities were subject to the direction of the Ministry of Education and merely carried out the orders from above.

All schools were required to make periodic reports to the authorities, giving detailed information about courses of study, distribution of hours in the weekly schedule, qualifications of teachers, achievement of students, a complete list of students, faculty and administrative personnel, and such matters as budget provisions for equipment, for maintenance of buildings, and for various phases of the instructional program. Standardization of curricula meant the abolition of electives. All students were required to study the same subjects. There were different types of secondary education—vocational, normal, and college preparatory—and differentiation of departments in higher education, but for each course of study the government issued prescribed subjects to be studied and the amount of time given to each subject.

An effective means of insuring compliance was to require students from all schools to take, before graduation, common final examinations administered by the state. Since diplomas were issued only with the approval of the government, no student and no school could evade the centrally administered examinations. These examinations served as a powerful standardizing agency and quickly weeded out inferior schools that had operated without reference to what other schools were doing.

Prior to 1927, there were many schools which were loosely managed with inadequate funds for equipment and for teachers' salaries. Now, it was no longer possible for such schools to continue. Besides prescribing minimum standards, the government provided grants to schools for the specific purpose of increasing library and laboratory facilities. Teachers of the lower schools were required to take examinations and meet minimum standards of certification. Laws were enacted to specify the ratio of budgetary distribution. For example, primary schools were directed to use 70 per cent of current expenses for salaries, 15 per cent for equipment, 9 per cent for running expenses, 3 per cent for travel and other specified expenses, and 3 per cent for a standing fund to be used only with the approval of the educational authorities.[3] Regulations of similar nature were in effect for secondary and higher schools.

Private education

Private education was allowed, even encouraged. During the laissez-faire period, private education was not subject to any control or inspection. Many private schools played a key role in the development of modern education, and they were recognized as among the leading educational institutions of the country. At the same time, there were also private schools which were operated as commercial enterprises and were little concerned with the quality of instruction. Under the Nationalist regime, private education was subject to state control no less than public education.

All private schools were required to register with the government. To achieve registration, they had to comply with all government regulations concerning curriculum, textbooks, teachers, admission and graduation requirements, finance, physical plant, equipment, and other details. In addition, there were government regulations that applied especially to private schools. Schools which did not fully meet the specifications were ordered to close. The academic standing of the students of unregistered private schools would not be recognized, which meant that they would not be accepted for transfer or promotion to other schools.

State control of private education was intended to serve the dual purpose of insuring educational quality and of promoting nationalism. A large number of private schools were established by Christian missionaries; in the main, they were among the better private schools, and some had even won recognition as the outstanding schools of the nation. Nevertheless, with rising nationalism demanding the end of foreign domination, the operation of schools by foreigners, free from government control or inspection, was considered a vestige of imperialism. In an emotionally charged propaganda campaign for the "Recovery of Educational Authority,"[4] the missionary schools were attacked as tools of cultural imperialism. The government never advocated the abolition of the missionary schools, but it did insist that they be treated like all other private schools and that they must obey the government directives for all private education.

The government took the position that except for the source of support and responsibility for management, there should be no difference between private and public schools. All must be guided by the spirit of Chinese nationalism and the aim of the Three People's Principles.

The regulations for private schools stipulated that foreign citizens were allowed to establish higher schools according to regulations, but not elementary schools. The school principal must devote his full time and was not permitted to hold another job. Religion must not be a required subject for study, and compulsory attendance at religious ceremonies was forbidden. Responsibility for the school rested on the Board of Directors, who appointed the principal. The principal must be a Chinese citizen; the Board of Directors, likewise, must have a Chinese citizen as chairman, and foreigners must not exceed one-third of its membership.

Missionary schools for a time resisted registration with the government. They not only hesitated to accept the limitation on religious instruction and religious services, but they were also apprehensive of political interference with their work. But they had no alternative than to fall in line. Other private schools, in the main, accepted the new regulations, though often with reluctance. The closing of sub-standard schools resulted in the elimination of "diploma mills." Three colleges and a medical school were ordered closed in Shanghai; others in Peiping, Nanking, Canton, and other cities met the same fate.[5]

Despite restrictions, private schools still played a large role in Chinese education. It was reported in 1935 that one-fourth of the primary schools in the country were maintained by private individuals or organizations, one-third of the second schools were private, and 52 per cent of the students admitted into higher institutions came from private middle schools.[6] In higher education, private institutions played an even more prominent role. Their importance in the national system is attested by the fact that the government appropriated funds for subsidies to private colleges and universities. Some grants were designated for professional chairs, others for the development of practical studies in science and technology.[7]

Language reform

One of the noteworthy accomplishments in the field of education during this period is the unification of the spoken language and the popularization of the vernacular style of writing. Mention was made above of the promotion of *pai-hua* writing during the Literary Revolution in the second decade of the century. The *pai-hua* movement gained headway rapidly under the Nationalist regime. In 1928, the Nationalist government ordered that all textbooks in the lower secondary as well as primary schools should be written in *pai-hua*.[8] Even for textbooks adopted in the higher institutions, *pai-hua* was used far more than the classical language. The *pai-hua* was used exclusively in adult education.

A related reform was the unification of the spoken language. The drive for national unity stimulated an intensive effort to overcome the difficulties arising from the multiplicity of dialects. The *pai-hua* writing was based on the spoken tongue common to most areas of China, especially the north. Despite local variations and accents, this spoken tongue could be understood by most people, except those in the dialect-ridden areas. This northern spoken tongue, with the Peiping pronunciation as the norm, was accepted as the National Tongue (*Kuo Yü*) to be used in all parts of the country. While radio broadcasting and *pai-hua* literature helped to bring about the change, the school was made a major agency for unifying the spoken language of the country. The national tongue, the *Kuo Yü*, was used as the medium of instruction on all levels of schools, and a new generation of young people appeared who could all speak the common tongue of the newly unified country.

To aid in the standardization of pronunciation, a system of phonetic symbols was adopted. The symbols, printed alongside the written characters, enabled pupils to learn the pronunciation of the characters in the National Tongue. These phonetic symbols are still in general use in the schools in Taiwan today. Thus, the legacy of the earlier Literary Revolution was expanded, enriched, and turned into an instrument for making education easier and more popular.

Educational planning

Centralized administration made it possible to make plans for educational growth in the light of the over-all needs of the entire nation. Planning sought to correct the inbalance that resulted from the uncoordinated efforts of the past: top heavy at the level of higher education but weak in the foundation of primary education; too many secondary schools offering academic courses but few providing vocational training; over-supply of college graduates in the arts, law, and commerce but a scarcity of persons competent in science and technology. The government adopted measures to shift emphasis to the neglected areas and to avoid wasteful duplication as well as uneven development.

Inbalance in development was also reflected in the geographical location of educational facilities. Of the 103 institutions of higher learning reported in the *First Yearbook of Education,* published by the Ministry of Education in 1934, twenty-two were located in Shanghai and ten in Peiping; in other words, one-third of the total were found in two cities, while no higher education of any kind was available in the entire province of Shensi or of Kweichow. Some of the so-called higher institutions in Shanghai and Peiping were academically weak and unworthy of independent existence; yet they were struggling along in cities where they were not needed.

In secondary education, the Yearbook reported that 213 out of every 10,000 people in Shanghai had the opportunity of second education, but in such provinces as Shensi, Kweichow, and Kansu it was available for fewer than four out of every 10,000. On the primary level, schools were available for seventy out of 1,000 people in the province of Shansi, but for only seven out of every 1,000 in Hupeh, and five out of 1,000 in Kweichow. This situation was also found in the types of schools established on each level. In other words the provision of education was left to chance and no endeavor had been made to plan a program with the needs of the nation in view.

Mention may be made in this connection of an important influence on the evolution of Chinese educational policy during this period. In May, 1931, in response to a request of the Chinese government, the International Institute on Intellectual Co-operation of the League of Nations appointed a mission of experts to visit China to make a study of the educational situation. The mission was originally composed of four educators,[9] but they were later joined by three other persons connected with the League of Nations in different capacities. After three months' travel and study, the mission submitted a report, later published by the League of Nations' Institute of Intellectual Co-operation in Paris, in 1932, under the title *The Reorganization of Education in China.*

The report of the mission criticized the lack of systematic planning which allowed schools to grow by chance rather than by careful consideration. It found "that schools and institutions are developing rather as independent organisms modelled on the forms and ideology of private education instead of being included in an organized system of public eduction related to immediate social problems."[10] It criticized "the creation and development in China of schools and educational institutions not conducted on a strict system and not suitable to the needs and conditions of the country.[11] It deplored "the haphazard distribution of Chinese universities" and the "disadvantages of the multiplicity of separate academic institutions within a small number of cities."[12]

Using its authority of centralized control, the Ministry of Education tried to avoid wasteful proliferation in the big cities by ordering weak institutions to merge and strengthen their resources. It was obviously easier to reduce wasteful effort in the large coastal cities than to establish new schools and universities in interior and financially poorer provinces. The latter called for vast sums of money which were not readily available, and consequently unequal educational opportunity must continue to exist for some time. It was, however, significant that the National Government was aware of the need and that it had the machinery of centralized administration to effect the change if and when needed funds became available.

The League of Nations' Mission of Educational Experts made many specific recommendations for educational reform. To carry out the various phases of reform, it proposed a powerful Ministry of Education which appointed the personnel responsible for education in the provinces. Such a proposal lent strong support to the trend of centralized administration of the Nationalist government.

Practical Studies

National reconstruction and the improvement of the people's livelihood called for the application of knowledge and scholarship to the solution of practical problems. In meeting this need, many Chinese leaders felt that the old tradition of literary culture had impeded the advancement of scientific and technological studies. The traditional literary education had tended to produce scholars who were versed in ideas and clever with the pen, but lacked the skills and abilities to enable them to come to grips with the practical problems of production and material reconstruction. The modern world, it was argued, was the world of science and technology, and it behooved Chinese education to effect a transition from a literary culture to a scientific culture.[13]

The findings of the League of Nations' Mission fully supported this point of view. The Mission recommended that "education should be more practical and in particular more professional and technical,"[14] and that "manual work and training by actual practice" should begin in the elementry schools. In secondary education, the importance of vocational education was stressed. In higher education, the Mission deplored "the atrophy of Natural Science and Technology, and the hypertrophy of legal, political, and literary studies" and the production of "a somewhat excessive number of men with the intellectual equipment and outlook of the journalist or rhetorician."[15]

To rectify this situation, the Ministry ordered the primary schools to pay more attention to "education for production," secondary education to make more provision for vocational training, and higher education to promote the study of science and technology. Labor and the use of hands were given a new emphasis in the primary schools in order to overcome at the early stage of schooling the traditional reluctance of the literati to use their hands and to engage in physical work. To spur the development of vocational education, the Ministry of Education decreed that provinces and cities should assign no less than 35 per cent of their current budget to vocational schools, with 25 per cent for normal schools and not more than 40 per cent for academic middle schools. Comparing this ratio with the figures for 1930, as found in the First Yearbook of Education, viz., 72.59 per cent of the total budget used for middle schools, 17.28 per cent for normal schools, and only 10.18 per cent for vocational schools, one realizes the extent of the shift of emphasis. The Ministry further directed the local authorities not to approve new private middle schools but to urge the use of funds for agricultural and technological schools instead.

In higher education, the government policy was to discourage the study of literature, arts, law, social science, education, and commerce and to lay emphasis on "practical courses," namely, science, technology, agriculture, and medicine. The shift of emphasis from the former to the latter was achieved by a variety of methods. The regulations for higher education stipulated that to qualify as a university, an institution must have three "schools" or "colleges," one of which must be in the second group of "practical courses." New technical schools would be approved only if they were in the "practical courses." Provincial authorities were instructed not to spend money on technical schools for the first group, and weak schools in these "non-practical" fields were ordered either to close or to shift to the practical studies. Besides, grants were available for the establishment or the strengthening of practical courses of study in technical schools, colleges, and universities. In 1934, the government began to provide annual grants to aid private universities, and it was stipulated that 70 per cent of the money must be used for science, technology, medicine, and agriculture.[16]

For many years the ratio of students enrolled in the two groups of courses stood at approximately three to one in favor of the first, the non-science group. To correct this inbalance, the Ministry limited the number of students to be admitted into the non-science courses; in some cases, departments or schools of arts, education, law, etc. were ordered to suspend the admission of new students for a temporary period. As a result of such measures, and influenced at the same time by the fact that graduates of practical courses were more likely to find employment, enrollment in the practical courses increased steadily. In 1931, 69.3 per cent of students in higher education were enrolled in the non-science courses, but by 1935, enrollment in the practical courses had risen from 30.7 per cent to 51.2 per cent.[17] By the end of the period under discussion, the science and technology departments of universities had definitely overshadowed the liberal arts departments in enrollment as well as in budget expenditures.

The schools

Within the school system, primary education consisted of the kindergarten between four to six, and the elementary school was subdivided into the four-year primary schools and the two-year higher primary. There were primary schools with only the first four grades and there were abbreviated schools with one or two grades serving the purpose of compulsory education. All schools followed a time-table with weekly hours and minutes devoted to each subject prescribed by the Ministry of Education. About one-third of the time was given to the Chinese language, with emphasis on the National Tongue and the *pai-hua;* other subjects were arithmetic, hand work (including art), civics, social and nature study, athletics and music.

The problem of compulsory education was largely that of finance. Theoretically, the government was committed to the goal of four-year compulsory education, but shortage of teachers and schools made this only a hope for the future. In 1935, the Ministry of Education drew up a plan of gradual advance in three stages. In the first stage, 1935-1940, provincial and municipal governments were directed to establish one-year primary schools in the hope that 80 per cent of children between nine and twelve would at the end of the period have one year of schooling. In the next period, 1940-1944, the plan was to establish two-year primary schools for 80 per cent of children between eight and twelve; and in the third stage, the hope was to expand all abbreviated schools into four-year primary schools to meet the goal of four years of compulsory education for all. Noteworthy progress was made in 1935-1937, but after the outbreak of war and the devastation that followed, the projected schedule became another paper plan.

Secondary education consisted of two levels of three years each, as in the United States. There were three types of secondary schools: the academic middle school, the vocational school, and the normal school. The vocational schools and the normal schools took graduates of the elementary school as well as those of the junior middle school. The junior middle school, however, was essentially academic in character and preparatory to the senior high school, which in turn prepared students for higher education. English was a required subject through the junior and senior middle school.

Government policy in secondary education sought to achieve three objectives: (1) to seek a more balanced development in the three types of schools by paying more attention to vocational and normal schools, (2) to promote the qualitative, not the quantitative, growth of middle schools, and (3) to improve the teaching of science. In all schools, there was an effort to stress the practical values of education and to supplement classroom study with work in shops, gardens, farms, foundry, blacksmithery, and carpentry.

Institutions of higher learning included the universities, the colleges, and the two-year technical (or specialized) schools. Their total number was seventy-four in 1928 and 108 in 1937. Those established by the National Government were, as a rule, stronger institutions than those established by the provincial governments. Private colleges and universities slightly exceeded the public in number, but there were more public technical schools than private. Eight kinds of colleges were recognized: arts, law, education, commerce, science, agriculture, technology, and medicine. The first four were generally referred to as "arts" courses, and the last four "practical" courses. A college could be in any of the eight fields, but "arts" colleges were definitely discouraged. With the exception of medicine, which required five years for graduation, all the other colleges required four years. Most of the technical schools were of the practical kind.[18]

The curricula of higher institutions were also rigidly prescribed. The credit system was used. The number of units required in the major field exceeded the maximum usually stipulated for an undergraduate major in an American college, thus leaving little room for electives. The undergraduate program of study, therefore, tended to be more specialized, with more concentration on the major field. A thesis was required for graduation.

The lecture was the dominant method of classroom instruction. Its abuses constituted a major source of weakness of higher education. The students were too often engrossed in unquestioning note-taking in the classroom and in the memorization of knowledge which they seldom attempted to apply to practical problems. Teachers just as often considered the ritualistic rendition of lectures as their sole duty and did little to stimulate independent or creative thinking on the part of students. An evil that grew out of this abuse of the lecture system was the large number of college teachers holding concurrent positions in several institutions, hurrying from one to another to repeat their lectures to different audiences. This practice was especially common among the second rate institutions which the Ministry tried to eliminate, but the better-known universities were not free from it either. The concentration of superflous institutions in a few large cities tended to encourage the practice. To curb this abuse, the regulations stipulated that the faculties of higher institutions should be full-time teachers, as a rule, and that holders of concurrent positions should not exceed one-third of the total. They also limited additional work to six hours a week. But as long as salaries were low, popular lecturers could not resist the opportunity of supplementing their income, and it was difficult to enforce the regulations.

Beginnings in post-graduate education were made in selected universities. The Academia Sinica was authorized by the National Government in 1927 and organized the following year as the highest body of scholarly research "to promote scientific research and to direct, coordinate, and encourage scholarly research." Under this Academia were established a number of institutes for research in mathematics, physics, astronomy, meteorology, geology, chemistry, botany, zoology, materia medica, philosophy, ethnology, history, social sciences, and other fields. The National Institute of Compilation and Translation was established in 1932 to translate foreign publications, to standardize scientific and technical terms, to approve text books and teaching equipment of elementary and secondary schools, and to publish college textbooks.

Social education

An aspect of education that was given much attention was the education of adults, not only in schools but also through a variety of media outside the schools. Public libraries, museums, adult education centers, reading rooms, recreational facilities, music, sports and athletics, radio broadcasting, and a broad range of out-of-school agencies that carried on educational as well as other functions were all included in the category of social education.

To assure attention to this heretofore neglected phase of education, the Ministry of Education ordered that local authorities must set aside 10 to 20 per cent of their education budget for the promotion of social education. As a result of this order, expenditures for social education increased sixfold within five years from $3,632,466 in 1928 to $20,979,026 in 1932.[19] In the view of some educationists, social education was among the most noteworthy aspects of Chinese education in this period. It brought education to the masses and underscored the importance of enlightening the entire population in order to lay a firm foundation for the popular nationalism, democracy, and improvement of mass welfare as envisioned in the Three People's Principles. From the standpoint of educational innovations, it was untrammeled by the rigid traditions and lockstep methods that characterized the established schools and was therefore more inclined to try new ways shunned by the schools. The use of audio-visual media and the development of reading materials more closely related to life activities opened up possibilities of making education more vital and more meaningful.

An important objective of social education was the reduction of adult illiteracy. A vigorous effort was made to popularize the phonetic script (mentioned previously in connection with language reform) as an aid to learning and reading. Scientific study of the most commonly used vocabulary produced a list which was made the basis of new textbooks for adult classes. It was claimed that within a few months' time an illiterate adult could learn about 1,000 most useful characters sufficient for the practical purposes of reading simple material and writing simple letters. In adult education centers, pai-hua newspapers using the simple vocabulary of "1,000 characters" enabled the new literates to have the satisfaction of reading about the big events of the nation and the world. The significance of such a development is obvious.

Since the majority of China's masses resided in rural areas, the mass education movement and the rural betterment movement became closely related and practically merged into one. Each of these movements resulted from the confluence of several currents that had been gaining momentum for a number of years. The New Thought Movement had inspired a concern for the lot of the common man and after the May Four Movement more and more of the young and the educated found appeal in the call to "go to the people." The people meant the villages and the small towns. The rural betterment program went farther than literacy, but the teaching of reading, writing, and the rudiments of knowledge was certainly a basic step.

The integration of adult education into the rural betterment program found expression in a number of pilot projects sponsored by universities as well as the National Mass Education Association. One of the best known was the project at Tinghsien, a rural county in North China where, under the Leadership of renowned Dr. James Y. C. Yen, a comprehensive program combining literacy with civic participation and agricultural improvement showed how it was possible to transform an illiterate population into intelligent and self-reliant members of a growing community. Designed to combat the evils of illiteracy, poverty, disease, and misgovernment, the program promoted education, economic livelihood, public health, and good local government.[20]

No praise is too lavish for the pioneering spirit and accomplishments of Dr. James Y. C. Yen, first with the Chinese labor corps in France during the first World War, and later with the mass education movement in China. At the same time, it is to be noted that besides the project at Tinghsien there were other centers carrying on experimental programs of mass education and rural betterment. Among them were a rural center in Tsouping under the aegis of the Shantung College of Rural Reconstruction, and a Center at Ch'ingho, under the auspices of Yenching University.

Party education

The official statement of the aim of education stipulated that education must be carried on within the framework of the Three People's Principles. Specifically, education was to foster nationalism, the exercise of civic rights, and the economic livelihood of the people. Though clear and understandable, these objectives still had to be translated into curricular provisions, courses of study, and practical matters of educational administration and planning. This was not a simple task. The Three People's Principles were subject to diverse interpretations. In what concrete ways the schools should promote nationalism, rights, and livelihood was not a question that teachers and school administrators could readily answer.

Since the Three People's Principles was the ideology of the Kuomintang, it seemed simpler to make the Kuomintang ideology the central theme of education. The Three People's Principles were also known as Party Principles. The curriculum of all schools, from the primary school through the university, contained a required subject of study titled civic education or Three People's Principles or just Party Principles. The teacher as well as the content of this subject must be approved by the Kuomintang; as a rule, only members of the Kuomintang could obtain certification as a qualified teacher of the Three People's Principles. To underscore the importance of Party control, the term Party Education—*tang hua chiao yü*—was used to remind teachers and students that the Kuomintang was the watchdog of all educational activities.

Party education was not confined to a single course of study devoted to the study of Kuomintang ideology. Kuomintang functionaries inspected the schools and demanded that school life in general should reflect the revolutionary cause then espoused by the Party. All schools and government offices were required to hold a Sun Yat-sen Memorial Service every Monday morning. The ritual for the service was prescribed by the Kuomintang and punctiliously observed in all schools. At the call of the master of ceremonies, the audience stood and bowed to the portrait of Dr. Sun Yat-sen, which was hung at the center of the stage, visible to all. Then followed a moment of silence in tribute to the late founder of the Kuomintang and the Republic, after which the chairman read aloud the will of Dr. Sun, consisting of two short paragraphs prominently displayed along with the portrait, and exhorting continued struggle to achieve the final success of the revolution. At the conclusion of the ritual, the chairman, who was usually the school principal or dean, would proceed to use the remainder of the hour for a regular school assembly, and the theme of the assembly might or might not bear any relation to the ritual or the Party ideology.

The term "Party Education" was frequently heard in the earlier years of the Nationalist regime, but seemed to have waned as a topic of discussion in the latter part of this period, either because the concept was already generally accepted and required no further affirmation, or because more attention was given to the contributions of education to the program of national reconstruction and material progress which became the major concern of the government after 1932. Even in the earlier years, there was no general agreement on the meaning of the term. Did it only mean that education should be revolutionary and patriotic in spirit? Did it simply mean that education should instruct the people to understand the meaning of nationalism, people's rights, and people's livelihood, and equip them with the skills and knowledge and abilities to achieve these objectives? Or did it mean more specifically that education should be controlled by the Kuomintang and try to indoctrinate the ideology of the Kuomintang?

Since the Party controlled the state, it claimed the right to control education. The question was how that control should be exercised. Should all educational authority be channeled through the Ministry of Education and the provincial and local educational authorities, or should the Party through its central and local organizations directly assert their authority over the schools, the teachers, and the students? Throughout this period, there was no change in the curricular requirement for the study of Three People's Principles or Party Principles, and in the ritualistic requirement of the weekly Memorial Service. The Party kept a close watch on the observance of these requirements. The Party also exercised direct control over military training in schools and programs for the training of youth. To what extent Party control actually accomplished the purpose of insuring education in the spirit of the Three People's Principles is open to question. Whether or not the required study of the Principles and attendance at the weekly rituals actually won the support of young people for the Kuomintang or created enthusiasm for the Kuomintang program is also a moot question.

The youth problem

The youth problem of this period was a legacy of the May Fourth Movement and the warlord regime. The high ideals and impassioned aspirations of the May Fourth Movement could find no expression in constructive channels during the years of political instability, when government was corrupt and unconcerned about national welfare, and when there was no acceptable leadership to give the nation a sense of direction and purpose. Unprincipled politicians and unscrupulous power-seekers wormed their way into student organizations and exploited them for selfish purposes. At the same time, frustration led to undisciplined outbursts and rebellious actions which seriously disrupted their study and the work of the schools.

Before it came to power, the Kuomintang had considerable success in enlisting the support of the students. Its campaign against the warlords was a popular cause that appealed to the entire nation. Its espousal of nationalism and opposition to imperialism marked it as a revolutionary party that challenged the status quo. Students rallied to the Nationalist cause and engaged in patriotic activities under Kuomintang leadership. After the establishment of the government, the official policies seemed to have lost their appeal to youth. Faced with the need of imposing order and stability, the government began to stress student discipline rather than active participation in politics. Restlessness and frustration once more prevailed. Students had enthusiastically plunged into such campaigns as the Recovery of Educational Authority and the

Abolition of Unequal Treaties. After the Japanese occupation of Manchuria in 1931, student nationalism was manifested in a demand for stopping Japanese aggression and in mounting dissatisfaction with the cautious no-war policy of the government. Thus the Nationalist government lost its hold on the student activists and student disturbances again posed difficulties for the educational authorities.

Unfortunate circumstances combined to worsen the situation. First, at the time of the May Fourth Movement, the Chinese public respected the idealistic motives of the students and supported their demands for a stiff government policy against the unsympathetic Big Powers. In later years, the student movement was weakened by internal dissensions, while the abuse of power and indiscriminate indulgence in strikes and disruptive activities alienated the goodwill of the public.

Secondly, in order to bring a quick end to the chaotic conditions, the government had to adopt immediate measures such as the prohibition of student strikes, the restriction of outside activities, and the enforcement of strict discipline within the schools. Positive guidance was attempted to direct student interest into orderly self-government and such forms of service as the health campaign, afforestation, and the New Life Movement; but these failed to arouse student enthusiasm, and the repressive measures seemed to overshadow the more positive ones.

Thirdly, a new factor entered to complicate the already difficult situation—that is, the propaganda appeal of the Communists. While the government cautiously avoided a military confrontation with Japan, the Communist Party hoisted the banner of anti-aggression and declared its readiness to lead the nation in fighting against the Japanese invaders. While the government talked about the slow process of political tutelage to prepare the nation for eventual constitutional government, the Communists proposed an immediate program of rural reform to improve the livelihood of the peasants. To many young people, the Kuomintang had lost its revolutionary character and had become a conservative force, while the Communists challenged the status quo and promised a bold social revolution. A part of the government effort now had to be directed to refuting and counteracting Communist propaganda, and to adopt stern measures to prevent the infiltration of Communist propagandists and agitators. Radicalism was suppressed; students disobeying orders to refrain from demonstrations and unauthorized organizations were subject to suspension or expulsion; those believed to be Communist agents were either expelled or arrested.

The government program for student discipline stressed order and stability. It underscored the importance of restraint and the observance of law and regulations. The training of youth was supposed to inculcate moral values such as the New Life Movement tried to popularize. A move of potentially high educational significance was an attempt to integrate teaching with counselling. The Ministry ordered that while every school must have an officer in charge of discipline, teachers must share the responsibility of counselling. Each teacher was supposed to serve as counsellor to a specified number of students with whom he was able to make close and frequent personal contacts outside the classroom. It was emphasized that the duties of a teacher were not confined to classroom instruction, that he must take responsibility for guiding his students in the solution of their personal problems and in the formation of good habits and wholesome attitudes.

With thoughtful implementation and conscientious cooperation of teachers, this could prove to be a reform of major significance. It could have driven home to teachers and students alike the viewpoint that education was more than the acquisition of knowledge. It could have revived the personal, even life-long, relationship between teacher and pupil that characterized old Chinese education before the advent of modern schools. It could also have helped to correct the evils of "commercialized" institutions[21] where travelling lecturers disappeared from the campus as soon as they had delivered their class lectures.

Unfortunately, the educational climate of those years was not favorable for the fruition of this proposed reform. Political events and foreign aggression continued to flame student emotions and it was not easy to put a stop to the demonstrations and disturbances. At the same time, Communist propaganda and agitation continued to exacerbate student restlessness and sense of frustration. As far as teachers were concerned, even if they had wished to accept the responsibility, many of them were at a loss as to how they could best offer counsel to youth caught in the ideological and political turbulence of the period. The proposed system of counselling could at best provide the machinery for guidance, but unless counselling could reach the hearts and minds of the young by suggesting outlets for their emotions and possible or partial solutions of the problems that disturbed them, the counselling system would remain an empty shell.

More exhortation would not do. Lecturing and moralizing would only further alienate youth. The government required military training in the schools in order to develop habits of discipline and orderly group life. To what extent the objectives were achieved is debatable.

Government leaders were not unaware of the need of more positive measures for guidance and for the constructive release of patriotic and idealistic emotions. While prohibiting disruption of classes and disturbances that upset peace and order, they encouraged student participation in health campaigns and various forms of community service. Official sponsorship, however, tended to stress formality at the expense of spontaneity, and formally structured programs did not make a strong appeal to youth eager to assert their freedom and independence.

Christian education

No story of education in China from the first appearance of modern schools to the disappearance of all private education under the Communists would be complete without mention of the role of Christian schools and colleges established by missionaries. They were truly pioneers in modern education in China. They were the first to stress the education of the common man and the education of women. They were the first to make music and athletics an integral part of the educational program. They did a superb job in the teaching of English. They were deeply concerned with character education before the other schools began to grapple with the problem of discipline. Academically, they were the oustanding private schools of the land and ranked among the leading institutions of the whole country.

During and immediately after the Nationalist revolution, Christian education underwent a critical period of adjustment. Its critics charged that the schools were primarily proselytizing, rather than educational agencies, and that compulsory Bible study and compulsory chapel attendance violated the principle of freedom of religion. Even more serious was the charge that preoccupation with the study of foreign language and of foreign history and culture entailed a woeful neglect of Chinese language and culture, and the result was a process of "denationalization" in conflict with the new spirit of national education.

Some of the government regulations in regard to private schools were specifically directed against these vulnerable aspects of Christian education. They proscribed compulsory religion in any form and required more attention to Chinese language and culture as subjects of a standardized curriculum uniform for all private as well as public schools. Some Christian leaders had serious reservations about secularizing their schools, but after much careful thought and deep soul-searching, most Christian leaders came to see that within the framework of government regulations there was still much they could do to perpetuate the intrinsic values of Christian education. They found ways and means of fostering the Christian spirit in the lives of young people without the appurtenances of compulsory religious exercises and religious study.

Credit is due the foreign administrators, willing to relinquish their authority and to transfer their responsibilities to Chinese administrators, and to missionary teachers who adjusted well to the new situation of working under Chinese leadership. Headed by Chinese principals and presidents applying their usual vigor and thoroughness to the study of

Chinese culture, Christian schools and colleges after registration rose
to answer the new challenge of the day, and they continued their contributions as among the most highly respected institutions of the country. In conferences on Christian higher education during those years,
Christian educators often heard the summons to make their institutions
more Chinese, more Christian, and higher in standards. Certainly, within
this framework there was plenty of room for solid contributions to
Chinese national education as well as to Christianity as a way of life.

Summary and critique

In conclusion, Chinese education in the decade preceding the outbreak of the Sino-Japanese war was marked by growth, expansion,
greater government effort, and better co-ordination. For the first time
since the introduction of modern schools, China had a stable government
committed to long-range educational planning. For the first time, public
schools were assured of financial support and were enabled to provide
educational programs equal, or even better, in quality than those of the
best private schools.

A national system of schools was being evolved, with schools of all
levels and in different parts of the country working toward common
goals. A common aim guided private as well as public education. The
unification of the spoken tongue served the cause of cultural and national
unity. Definite provisions for compulsory education, adult education, and
education of the masses helped to broaden the base of the educational
structure, while emphasis on higher standards in higher education
strengthened its top. Long-range planning from the standpoint of
national needs made it possible to take promising first steps in the
achievement of a more balanced development of different types of education on different levels for different parts of the country. Boys and
girls were given the same educational opportunity; the removal of barriers to women's education must be considered one of the major achievements of the period.

The decade of reconstruction and progress did not actually get under
way until after 1930, for in the first few years the new government was
busy with stabilizing and consolidating its own position. In the early
years, education was infused with the new spirit of nationalism, which
provided the setting for the establishment of a national system of education. The negative aspects of nationalistic education were during those
years more evident than the positive efforts of reconstruction. By and
large, the concrete tasks and specific problems of educational reform did
not receive serious attention until after 1930. The statement of educational aim in terms of the Three People's Principles, however, was issued
in 1929. The Law on University Organization was promulgated in the

same year, but regulations spelling out details of organization and curricula were not completely formulated until 1934. Basic laws and regulations for secondary education were adopted in 1932 and 1933, and those for elementary education appeared at approximately the same time.

Especially impressive was the growth in higher education. The national universities were now recognized as among the best of the country and were able to attract the most capable students. Private colleges and universities joined the public institutions in producing the personnel needed in the manifold phases of national reconstruction. Educated persons, products of modern education, were attracted to public service and found satisfaction in applying their knowledge and their talents to the positive tasks of nation-building. The League Mission observed as follows:

> In the last twenty years university education in China has advanced with extraordinary rapidity. The most superficial observer must be struck by the influence which it has exercised upon the life and thought of important strata of the population. Distinguished scholars have received part, or all, of their higher education in Chinese universities, and, in their turn, have taught in them; the personnel of Civil Service, central and local, and of teachers in secondary schools—both key professions—is largely recruited from them. Their contribution to the advancement of knowledge has, in certain fields of study, been of genuine significance. It is not an exaggeration to say that modern China is, to a large and increasing extent, the creation of her universities.[22]

No one could fail to appreciate the substantial progress during this decade. At the same time, it would not be inappropriate to mention some of the puzzling problems that remained unsolved or questions that remained unanswered. A major question concerned the pitfalls of centralized control. It is easy to see how control was important to the establishment of a national system and how centralized administration could achieve reforms in the shortest time possible. The question is whether centralized administration in time reaches a point of diminishing returns when its disadvantages become more and more conspicuous.

Centralized state control served its purpose well when the urgent need was to establish common standards for all schools. After years of licence and confusion, some degree of uniformity was no doubt desirable. All schools and universities, private as well as public, were subject to public inspection. Inspectors sent by the Ministry of Education and the local education authorities visited the schools to ascertain whether official requirements in regard to curricula, equipment, finance, and personnel had been complied with.

The tendency of the inspectors and the administrators was to interpret the laws and regulations rigidly and exactly. Any deviations were likely to incur censure. A premium was put on uniformity. There was little room for flexibility of interpretation, still less for variety. The laws and regulations offered few options, and the administrators seemed to see little need for adaptations to local conditions. The result was a dull mechanical uniformity which tended to kill the spirit of education. Minimum standards became maximum standards. After the evils of loose administration had been corrected, further advance in education were dependent on the enthusiasm and creative spirit of the teaching profession. To encourage this enthusiasm and creativity, some liberalization of centralized control seemed necessary.

Related to the question of uniformity and variety is the role of private education in a national system of education. The Nationalist government laid down specific conditions for the establishment of private schools and required all private schools to observe the same regulations as public schools. That the government recognized the need for private education was attested by the fact that the Ministry of Education made annual as well as special grants to private schools and universities to strengthen their programs. The question here raised is whether private education should be the replica of public education in content, methods, and form of organization, or whether it may be given the opportunity, or even the responsibility, of trying out new ideas and new programs without violating the spirit of national education.

Was private education permitted and encouraged primarily because the state was not financially able to provide enough schools to meet the needs of the nation? If so, would the need for private education decrease with the growth in the resources of the state until it would not be needed any more? Or, would there be always room for private education, and, if so, what kind of role would it play?

All schools, must, of course, meet the minimum standards established by the government. The question is whether and how private education, while obeying all laws and regulations, might maximize its contributions by exploring new methods and programs and thus enrich national education by creative innovations and constructive experimentation. It may be said in retort that the government was not opposed to experimentation under proper authorization, and that education under the National government was not so rigidly regimented. This may be true. What is suggested here is that an explicit clarification of the role of private education could give more positive encouragement to constructive innovation, that after the attainment of order and stability the government could well afford to stimulate and encourage private schools and universities to explore possibilities of contributions different from those of state-supported institutions.

Other questions may be raised in regard to a national system of education in China. One may ask, for example, whether in the promotion of science and technology it was wise to discourage the liberal arts courses, and whether in trying to correct the inbalance of the past there was not a danger that the pendulum might swing too far in the other direction, thus producing an inbalance of another kind. One high official seriously proposed in 1932 that no new students be admitted into higher institutions to study arts, law, and other non-science studies for a period of ten years. Although this proposal was not adopted, this line of thinking did indirectly influence official policy. An atmosphere was created in which capable ambitious students avoided the humanities and social sciences. This state of affairs, though temporarily justifiable, obviously should not have continued over an indefinite period of time.

Questions may also be asked about positive versus negative methods of dealing with the problem of student unrest, about the political control of education giving scholars and educators little voice in the determination of basic policies, about the effects or effectiveness of Party education, and other phases of official policy during these years. It should be said in conclusion, however, that these questions are raised from the standpoint of long-range educational planning and do not imply disapproval of the measures needed in the initial years of the regime to forge national unity and to establish a stable system of schools. An over-all review of education during this decade must conclude with genuine gratification over the substantial progress made within a few years, and with high praise for the positive policy of the government to support education, to broaden its scope, to equalize educational opportunity, and to make education an effective instrument of nation-building.

Comments:

BY CHI-PAO CHENG

O NE EPISODE IN THIS PERIOD which was meant to have far-reaching effects on education but was never given due attention because of the turmoil of events arising out of international situation at the time was the exchange of educational missions between the now defunct League of Nations and the Chinese Government. Dr. Theodore Chen in his excellent paper focused only on the Educational Mission composed of five European educators sent out by the League of Nations to China, but neglected to point out that the Chinese Government also dispatched a return mission composed of five Chinese educators to study educational conditions in Europe.

This Chinese Mission was organized upon the recommendation of the League of Nations. It travelled widely in Europe and made extensive observations on educational conditions in over ten countries, including Soviet Russia. This mission, upon its return to China, presented to the Government a lengthy report and also a series of recommendations for educational reforms in China. It was emphasized that in the period of 1927-1933, and in fact many years prior to that, Chinese education in both spirit and substance, was essentially American in character. This was understandable. In the early twenties, a large number of young scholars were sent to the United States for their higher education. Many of them studied education under such great teachers as Dewey and Thorndike and were strongly influenced by them. When these scholars returned to China, they were at the helm of Chinese educational development, and, consequently, exerted a tremendous influence on education at the time.

The League of Nations Mission strongly criticized this development and urged that China with her ancient culture was more akin to European than to American culture. She could profit more by following European educational systems than the American system alone.

The Chinese Education Mission was sent to Europe in that spirit and its report and recommendations were drafted in that context.

Its report was well-received and its recommendations were seriously discussed. Had these recommendations been even partially adopted, Chinese education might have undergone even more drastic changes. Unfortunately, the rapid development of political situations in China, especially war with Japan, forced the consideration of these new recommendations into oblivion with the result that the Education Mission to Europe came to naught.

NOTES TO CHAPTER I

INTERNATIONAL SETTINGS

[1] Hu Shih, *The Chinese Renaissance,* University of Chicago Press, 1933, p. 66.

[2] Cf. *United States Relations with China,* Department of State Publication 3573, Far Eastern Series 30, released 1949, pp. 2,3.

[3] Cf Crowley, James B., *Japan's Quest for Autonomy,* Princeton University Press, pp. 4, 5.

[4] Cf. *United States Relations with China, op. cit.,* pp. 7,8.

[5] *Ibid.,* pp. 8,9.

[6] *Ibid.,* pp. 9,10.

[7] Hu Shih, "China in Stalin's Grand Strategy," *Foreign Affairs,* October 1950 issue, Vol. 29, pp. 16-17.

[8] Cheng Tien-fong, *A History of Sino-Russian Relations,* Public Affairs Press, 1957, pp. 124-125.

[9] "China in Stalin's Grand Strategy," *op. cit.,* p. 12,13.

[10] Cf. Liang Chin-tun, *The Sinister Face of the Mukden Incident,* St. John's University Press, 1969, pp. 113,114.

[11] Cf. *United States Relations with China, op. cit.,* pp. 12,13.

[12] *Ibid.,* p. 13.

[13] *Ibid.,* p. 14.

[14] Cf. Stimson, Henry, *The Far Eastern Crisis,* Harper and Brothers, 1936, Summary only, pp. 109-183.

[15] *Foreign Relations of the United States (Japan), 1931-1941,* The U.S. Government Printing Office, 1943 (Department of State Publication 2008), Vol. 1, p. 207.

[16] *Ibid.,* Vol. 1, pp. 197,198.

[17] "China in Stalin's Grand Strategy," *op. cit.,* p. 23.

[18] *United States Relations with China, op. cit.,* pp. 15,16.

[19] *Ibid.,* p. 17.

[20] "China in Stalin's Grand Strategy," *op. cit.,* pp. 28-33.

[21] *Foreign Relations of the United States,* Diplomatic Papers, 1935, Vol. 3, *The Far East,* p. 385.

[22] *Ibid.,* pp. 386-389.

NOTES TO COMMENTS

(a) U.S. Senate, Committee on the Judiciary, *Hearings on the Institute of Pacific Relations,* 82nd Congress, p. 801.

(b) President Chiang's *Collected Work,* Volume 2, p. 2106.

(c) Mamoru Shigemitsu, *Japan and Her Destiny,* 1958, p. 117.

NOTES TO CHAPTER II

POLITICAL RECONSTRUCTION, 1927-1937

[1] Sun Yat-sen, San-min Chu-i, "The People's Power, Lecture 1" (*The Teachings of the Republic Founder: Summary Collection of Works on San-min Chu-i*°, ed. by Hsu Wen-shan & pub. by the Chung Hwa Series Publication Committee, Taipei, 1960—hereafter referred to as *The Teachings*), p. 196. Here and hereafter

the asterisk denotes that the work is written in Chinese. Wherever available I have mainly but not exclusively followed the translations by Frank W. Price. This applies, too, to the English version of Chinese documents in the *China Year Book* and the works of other scholars.

2 For enumerated reasons supporting this statement, see my *Essays on Government and Politics** (Taiwan: Cheng Chung Book Co., 1955), pp. 44-46.

3 This theme is elaborated in my monograph *Political Power: Composition and Preservation**, first printed in *National Chengchi University's Thirtieth Anniversary Memorial Volume* (Taiwan, 1958).

4 The five-element approach in the study of politics is initially presented in my *Modern Western Political Theories** (1st printing in 2 volumes, 1939; 5th printing in 4 volumes, The Cultural Press, Taipei, 1965), Vol. 1, pp 2-7, and also in my *Essays on Government and Politics**, pp. 43-59.

5 As the storm was gathering that early summer the Chinese Political Association happened to be holding its three-day annual conference at Nanking. Generalissimo Chiang invited its attending members to a luncheon party, and I was designated beforehand by the Association leadership to speak out if the host should —as normally he would—ask for some opinion from university professors. Generalissimo Chiang did. I stood up and spoke very briefly on one point, without naming anything in particular: that any thorny political problem is best solved through negotiation and compromise because the use of force, like surgical operation, is the last resort, to be avoided if at all possible. The host smilingly nodded, adding "Good, good." The day after, at a noon reception party by Wang Ching-wei, the then President of the Executive Yuan, the late Dr. Wang Hua-cheng, my colleague at Tsing Hua University, responding to the host's solicitation for opinion, raised this sharp question: "*What* and *where* is our last stand at which there would be no further retreat in the face of Japan's advance—diplomatically as well as militarily?" These two occasions, still in my memory, testify to the existence at one and the same time of "internal worries" and "external threats."

6 Article on modern China during this period, *Encyclopedia Britannica* (1969 edition), Vol. V, p. 592.

7 Pan Kung-chan, "China's Unification Movement," in *China of the Present Decade**, first pub. by the Chinese Cultural Reconstruction League (Nanking, 1937), now reprinted with a changed title, *China of the Pre-War Decade**, by the Lung Men Bookstore (Hong Kong), pp. 11-16.

8 Arthur N. Holcombe, *The Chinese Revolution* (1929), p. 351.

9 This English translation is by Tu Ting-hsiu. See *China Yearbook, 1967-68*, opposite page i.

10 Several articles on education during this period by Chiang Chien-pai and others in *China of the Pre-War Period**, esp. pp. 585-590.

11 Chiang Kai-shek, *China's Destiny* (English trans. by Wang Chung-hui), p. 10.

12 Chiang Monlin, *Tides from the West* (Yale University Press, 1947), p. 154.

13 *Ibid.*, pp. 158-159.

14 F. F. Liu, *A Military History of Modern China* (Princeton University Press, 1956), p. 72.

15 *Ibid.*, pp. 72-73.

16 *The Collected Wartime Messages of Generalissimo Chiang Kai-shek* (John Day, N. Y., 1946), pp. 1-2.

17 *Fundamentals of National Reconstruction*. The English translation of this document may be found in Ch'ien Tuan-sheng, *The Government and Politics of China* (Harvard University Press, 1950), Appendix E.

[18] Chiang Kai-shek, "On the Essentials of the Republic's Founder's Teachings," *Collected Writings and Speeches of President Chiang** (Taiwan: National War College, 1960), pp. 8-9.

[19] *The China Yearbook, 1931-1932;* also William L. Tung, *The Political Institutions of Modern China* (Martinus Nijhoff, the Hague, 1964), pp. 115-116.

[20] *The China Year Book, 1931-1932,* pp. 528-530.

[21] There seems to be a trend of late to show less appreciation of Dr. Sun as a political thinker. For instance, Harold Z. Schffrin remarks in his *Sun Yat-sen and the Chinese Revolution* (University of California Press, 1968): "The search for Sun Yat-sen's true doctrine is the less rewarding because he was not a great thinker." To my mind, Dr. Sun's defining politics as management of common affairs; taking life and livelihood as the central force in all human history; discerning the true need and deed of political tutelage, whether desired or not, and whether called as such or not; regarding local self-government as the basis of workable democracy; pointing out the impossibility of practising one uniform type of socialism for all countries; and teaching the Chinese people to preserve certain Confucian virtues of a universalistic nature; these are either penetrating observations or genuine abiding principles. See my *Essays on Government and Politics**, pp. 44-46, 80.

[22] Sun Yat-sen, *Five-Power Constitution, The Teachings**, p. 772. The English translation of this address is contained in Leonard S. Hsu, *Sun Yat-sen: His Social and Political Ideals* (University of Southern California Press, 1937).

[23] *Five-Power Constitution (The Teachings) op. cit.,* p. 114.

[24] Paul M. A. Linebarger, *The Political Doctrines of Sun Yat-sen* (The John Hopkins Press, 1937), pp. 221-222.

[25] *Ibid.,* p. 223.

[26] Sun Yat-sen, *San-min Chu-i,* "The People's Power, Lecture 3" (*The Teachings*), p. 246.

[27] Paul M. A. Linebarger, *op. cit.,* p. 223-224.

[28] Wang Chung-hui, "The Theory and Practice of the Five-Power Constitution (1956)," in his *Selected Writings from the Hard-Learning Study**, ed. by Hsieh Ying-chou & pub. by the Chung Hwa Series Publication Committee (Taipei, 1957), pp. 114-116.

[29] *Five-Power Constitution (The Teachings), op. cit.,* p. 778.

[30] Wang Chung-hui, *op. cit.* p. 115.

[31] *Pao-chia* was a local security scheme under which a fixed number of households constituted a *chia,* the head of which was known as *chia-chang,* and usually every ten *chia* formed a *pao,* which was placed under the care of a *pao-chang.* The function of the *pao-chia* was the registration of the households and inhabitants in the neighborhoods for the purpose of keeping track of all the villagers. The second and perhaps principal function was the detection and reporting of crimes.

[32] *President Chiang's Writings and Speeches**, *op. cit.* Vol. 1, p. 7.

[33] Chang Chun, "The Role of Local Self-government in Resistance-War and Nation-building," in *Chang Chun's Speeches and Writings in Szechwan** (ed & pub. by the Szechuan Compatriots Association, and the Chungking Compatriots Association, Taipei, 1968—in honor of the author's 80th birthday), p. 111.

[34] There are two informative articles—one, "Reforms in Chinese Laws and Institutions," by Sun Fo, and the other, "The Chinese Judicial Field," by Chu Cheng—in *China of the Pre-War Decade** (pp. 58-67 & 70-89).

[35] *Ibid.,* pp. 58-60.

[36] Chang Chi-yun et al, *Collected Essays on the Fifty Years of History of the Republic of China,* Vol. 1. See related articles.

[37] *Ibid.*

NOTES 319

38 This is the second article of the *Fundamentals*.

39 *San-min Chu-i* "The People's Livelihood, Lectures 1 & 2" (*The Teachings*) pp. 333 & 342.

40 *San-min Chu-i,* "The People's Livelihood, Lecture 2" (*The Teachings*), p. 359. Dr. Sun's arguments against the materialist philosophy and class war of Marx remind us of Jeremy Bentham's clear-cut opposition to revolutionary communism. Bentham offers five reasons: (1) Individuals differ in their sensitivity; (2) Even for two persons with the same sensitivity there is no identical ratio between one's amount of property and amount of happiness; (3) Society is nowhere a sort of *tabula rasa,* to begin with; (4) Periodic redistribution of property would eventually lead to no more property to distribute; (5) A communist system could be maintained only through political and religious slavery. These arguments are found in Bentham's *Theory of Legislation* (1802 edition), pp. 124, 135, 143, 158, 160. See my *Modern Western Political Theories**, Vol. IV, p. 739.

41 See my *Contemporary Political Theories of the West** (Taipei: Cheng Chung Book Co., 1962), pp. 283-414.

42 These two quotations within quotation are from *San-min Chu-i* (*The Teachings*), p. 345 and from *Complete Works of the Republic Founder** (National War College, Taiwan), p. 265.

43 This quotation within is taken from Two Supplementary Chapters in *San-min Chu-i by Dr. Sun Yat-sen with Two Supplementary Chapters by President Chiang Kai-shek** (China Publishing Co., Taiwan), pp. 213-214.

44 The whole passage is from my *Contemporary Political Theories of the West**, pp. 414-415.

45 *The China Year Book, 1931-1932,* p. 532.

46 Chen Cheng, *Land Reform in Taiwan* (China Publishing Co., Taiwan, 1961), p. 18.

47 *Ibid.,* p. 19.

48 *San-min Chu-i,* "The People's Livelihood, Lecture 2" *(The Teachings),* pp. 357-359.

49 *The Teachings, op. cit.,* p. 792.

50 Chen Kuo-fu, "Chinese Cooperative Movement," in *China of the Pre-War Decade**, p. 457.

51 *Contemporary Political Theories of the West**, *op. cit.*, p. 158.

52 S. K. Bailey & H. D. Samuel, *Congress at Work* (1953), pp. 231-236.

53 *Essays on Government and Politics**, *op. cit.*, pp. 231-234.

54 *Contemporary Political Theories of the West**, *op. cit.*, pp. 135-141.

55 James Bryce, "Relations of Political Science to History and Practice," *American Political Science Review,* Vol. III, p. 18. See also his *Modern Democracies,* Vol. II, concluding chapter.

56 Arthur N. Holcombe, *The Foundations of the Modern Commonwealth* (1923), p. 30.

57 Dison H. F. Poe, "An Analysis of the Party-and-Government Relationship in 63 Countries" (first printed in *The Tsing Hua Political Science Journal,* June, 1932), *Essays on Government and Politics**, pp. 235-248.

58 S. P. Huntington, *Political Order in Changing Societies* (Yale University Press, 1968). See the various tabulated charts.

59 *The Chinese Revolution, op. cit.,* pp. 312, 319.

60 *Ibid.,* p. 319.

61 F. F. Liu, *op. cit.,* p. 93.

62 Edgar Snow, *Red Star over China* (rev. ed., 1968), p. 387.

63 *China's Destiny, op. cit.,* p. 109.

64 Tsiang Ting-fu, "Revolution and Absolutism," in *Independent Review*, No. 80, Dec., 1933. This quotation is taken from Wm. Theodore de Bary et al, *Sources of Chinese Tradition*, pp. 792-793.

65 Kung-chuan Hsiao, *Rural China, Imperial Control in the Nineteenth Century* (University of Washington Press, 2nd printing, 1967), pp, 510-511.

66 Chang Chun, *op. cit.*, Most of the writings and speeches are illustrative of the continued efforts made by the local governments in sustaining the long war of resistance. The two volumes of Wu Ting-ch'ang, *Desultory Notes by the Blossom-Creek** (Kweichow, 1940-1943) are also worth reading.

67 *China's Destiny, op. cit.*, p. 104.

68 The initial step of such a role could be discerned in its way and spirit displayed at the drafting and adoption of the United Nations Charter during the days of the Dunbarton Oaks Conference and the San Francisco Conference. "As a participant of these two Conferences, . . . I recall with vividness that . . . there was altogether too much realism, too little idealism. The United States and Great Britain, apprehensive lest differences with Soviet Russia over fundamental issues should defeat the timely setting up of a new security system, readily and repeatedly compromised with or yielded to the latter's stand which was always stubborn, haughty, and apparently—at least apparently to us already—with some ulterior motive. This compromising and yielding encouraged Soviet Russia all the more to insist on having its own ways in framing up the world organization: ways designed to allow sufficient room and excuse for its future action. Those of us who had inklings of the inside story questioned from the very start the workability and effectiveness of the new collective security system—particularly in coping with future aggression, in dealing with the would-be aggressor." See Additional Note to the reprint of my "Freedom from Fear: on Post-War Peace Organization" (originally a paper published by the Chinese I.P.R., and presented to the I.P.R. Conference at Silver Springs, Maryland, Dec., 1944) by the Chinese Association for the United Nations, Taiwan, 1954.

NOTES TO CHAPTER III

CHINA'S FISCAL TRANSFORMATION, 1927-1937

1 H.B. Morse, *The Trade and Administration of China* (London, 1920), p. 93.

2 *Ibid.*, p. 130. The symbol C$ is herein used to represent the Chinese dollar or *yuan*, and US$ to designate American dollars. The Chinese dollar's value in 1925-1928 averaged a little less than US$0.50. It fluctuated widely thereafter, falling to about US$0.20 during the world wide depression and rising with the upward movement of silver from 1932 to over US$0.40, until stabilized at about US$0.30 by the currency reform of November 1935.

3 *China Year Book, 1928*, pp. 540-542. The Commission for the Readjustment of Finance compiled a provisional budget for 1925 based upon data from the ministries, together with estimates from the 1919 budget for the southwestern provinces which were in revolt and made no reports. That provisional budget showed revenues of C$284 million, including C$120 million from customs, C$99 million from salt, and C$41 million from wine and tobacco tax. Expenditures were stated as C$310 million, including C$101 million for armed forces and C$166 million for debt service *ibid.*, pp. 551-552).

4 *Foreign Relations of the United States, 1923*, v. 1, pp. 551-579, and 1924, v. 1, pp. 409-416.

5 *China Year Book, 1928, op. cit.*, pp. 543-547.

6 *The China Year Book, 1929-30*, pp. 629-633, contains a full report of these conferences.

7 Quoted in Akira Iriye, *After Imperialism: The Search for a New Order in the Far East, 1921-31* (Cambridge, Massachusetts, 1965), p. 41.

8 The figures in this paper are from data of the Finance Ministry unless otherwise stated.

9 Finance Ministry, *Annual Report*, 1929-1930, p. 5.

10 Address reprinted in *St. John's Echo*, St. John's University, Shanghai, January 1929, pp. 58-61.

11 *North China Daily News*, May 5, 1936.

12 *North China Daily News*, November 9, 1933.

13 See *Foreign Relations of the United States, 1937*, v. IV, pp. 605-606, 619-620.

14 F. A. Cleveland: *Digest of . . . Statistical Review of the Work of the Inspectorate of Salt Revenue from 1913 to 1933 Inclusive* (Shanghai, 1934), p. 29.

15 Finance Ministry, *Annual Report, 1928-1929*, p. 4.

16 Salt Inspectorate: *Advance Annual Report for 1937*, p. 3.

17 Including C$3 million from Manchuria, where collections immediately preceding 1932 were about C$25 million yearly.

18 See Arthur N. Young: *China and the Helping Hand, 1937-1945* (Cambridge, 1963), pp. 42-48, 96-99.

19 Despatch of January 12, 1931, from American Legation, Nanking (State Department file 893.00PR/41).

20 Despatch of January 24, 1934, from American Legation, Nanking (State Department file 893.512/1312).

21 See Directorate General of Budgets, Accounts, and Statistics: *Statistical Abstract* (Chung-hua Min-kuo t'ung-chi t'i-yao, Chungking, 1940, p. 144); and Finance Ministry: *Public Finance Yearbook, Supplement* (Ts'ai-cheng nien-chien, hsu-pien, Chungking, 1943, pp. 107-111).

22 D. S. Paauw, "Chinese National Expenditures During the Nanking Period," *Far Eastern Quarterly*, November 1952, pp. 1-26.

23 See Chang Kia-ngau, *The Inflationary Spiral: The Experience in China, 1939-1950* (MIT Press, 1958), p. 16; and Shun-hsin Chou, *The Chinese Inflation, 1937-1949* (New York, 1963), p. 72.

24 See Ch'ien Tuan-sheng, *The Government and Politics of China* (Cambridge, 1950), p. 213.

25 See *China Handbook, 1943*, p. 199, for a summary of the budget law of 1932, revised in 1937.

26 Figures of yield are from the index of the Sinhua Bank, *Chinese Economic and Statistical Review*, October 1937, p. 20.

27 *Report for the 19th and 20th Fiscal Years, July 1930 to June 1932*, p. 1.

28 Kurt Bloch, *German Interests and Policies in the Far East* (New York, 1940), p. 29.

29 For particulars of the debt as of 1937 see Arthur N. Young, *China's Wartime Finance and Inflation* (Cambridge, 1965), pp. 337-342.

30 These are the most reliable figures available. The subject of economic growth including available sources of data is treated more fully in my book in course of publication by the Hoover Institution, Stanford University: *China's Nation-Building Effort, 1927-1937: the Financial and Economic Record*.

31 In June 1937 Ambassador Bullitt in Paris thus reported a talk with Minister Kung concerning the projected British loan of £20 million: "He was prepared to

promise that the money would not be taken out of England. So long as he should have such a credit in England he could issue notes which would serve the same purpose as cash" (*Foreign Relations of the United States, 1937*, v. IV, p. 604). As to his views during the war on significance of external reserves, see Arthur N. Young, *China and the Helping Hand, 1937-1945* (Cambridge, 1963), pp. 287, 287n, 320-321.

NOTES TO TABLES PAGES 122-124

Source: Data through 1935 are from the published reports of the Finance Ministry, and for 1936 and 1937 from Ministry data currently supplied and stated to be final. Blanks in the table indicate either zero or a sum less than C$0.5 million.

a) Prior to fiscal 1935 costs of revenue collection were stated as deductions from revenue, and thereafter as expenditures, as explained in the *Report for the 23rd Fiscal Year, July 1934 to June 1935*, Ministry of Finance, Nanking, p. 16n. Here these costs are treated as expenditures.

b) Includes revenue from kerosene, the tax on which was thereafter collected as import duty.

c) Includes C$62 million of "National revenue collected by provinces and directly disbursed for military expenses."

d) Most of "Government enterprise receipts" is from railways, including the value of transport services for the military. A corresponding amount is included under military expenditure. These were not cash transactions. Most of "Profit on government business enterprises" is from the Central Bank.

e) This item, according to a letter of July 23, 1937, to me from the Accountant General of the Finance Ministry comprises (millions of C$): refund from loan service fund, 10; refund of principal and interest on bonds and treasury notes held by the Treasury, 14; proceeds of sale of bonds and treasury notes issued in previous years, 12; balances carried forward from various accounts of the Salt Inspectorate, 19; other, 23; total, 78.

f) The Finance Ministry's published report for fiscal 1935 lists C$83 million from bank loans and C$55 million from overdrafts, and subtracts C$102 million for "Repayment of bank overdraft from last year," leaving net proceeds of C$36 million under those heads.

g) The accounts do not show for either the beginning or end of fiscal 1937 any separate item of cash balances of the Customs and Salt administrations, which were shown for previous periods. Much the larger part of such balances was with Customs.

NOTES TO COMMENTS

a. The GNP deflator is given in footnote 1 to Table 1.

b. Since government receipts from taxation were never more than 3 per cent of the gross national product during this period.

NOTES TO CHAPTER IV

TOWARD MODERNIZATION OF CHINA'S CURRENCY AND BANKING, 1927-1937

[1] *The Bankers' Weekly*, Shanghai, Vol. 10, No. 478, p. 25.

[2] The vice-governor of the Bank of China.

[3] Kato Joshihiko; *Japan's Banking History*, Tokyo University Press, 1957, p. 227.

[4] *Ibid.*, p. 198.

[5] C$=1 CNC.

6 Chang Kia-ngau, *The Inflationary Spiral—The Experience in China, 1939-1950* (MIT Press, 1958), p. 8.

7 This is a partial total based on figures for provincial banks which are available. Kiangsu Farmers Bank, 1935 statement:

Total loans CNC $10 million. No meaningful breakdown given. It is assumed that the half was loaned to co-operatives or small peasants.

14 Chekiang County Farmers Banks 1935 estimate:

Average $100,000

Chekiang Provincial Bank	$ 489,000	(1936)
Anhwei Provincial Bank	1,568,000	(1936)
Yunnan Provincial Bank	4,960,000	(1936)
Shantung Provincial Bank	7,883,000	(1935)
Fukien Provincial Bank	210,000	(1936)
Shansi Provincial Bank	550,000	(1936)
Total	$15,660,000	

NOTES TO CHAPTER V

THE AGRICULTURAL ECONOMY OF CHINA, 1927-1937

1 Buck, J. Lossing, *An Economic and Social Survey of 102 Farms near Wuhu, Anhwei, China,* volume one, number seven, Part I and Part II, University of Nanking, Agriculture and Forestry Series, December 1923, pp. 20, and July 1924, pp. 28, with acknowledgment to the student, Tao Yuen-chiao, for collecting the original data.

2 Buck, J. Lossing, *An Economic and Social Survey of 150 Farms Yenshan County, Chihli Province, China.* The University of Nanking College of Agriculture and Forestry, Nanking, China, Bul. No. 13, June 1926, pp. 110.

3 Buck, J. Lossing, *Chinese Farm Economy—A Study of 2866 Farms in Seventeen Localities and Seven Provinces,* China, published for the University of Nanking and the China Council of the Institute of Pacific Relations by the Commercial Press, Shanghai for China and Japan and by the University of Chicago Press, Chicago, 1930, 476 pp. (now out of print). Also a translation in Chinese by L. L. Chang.

4 Shanghai: *Chinese Economic Journal,* Vol II, No. 3, March 1928, pp. 219-235.

5 A summary in the *Annual Report of the College of Agriculture and Forestry,* University of Nanking, Bulletin volume seven, No. nine, pp. 1926-27, pp. 30-32.

6 *Ibid,* pp. 21-23; and Shanghai: *Chinese Economic Journal,* Vol III, No. 3, 1929, pp. 22.

7 *Annual Report of the College of Agriculture and Forestry,* University of Nanking, Bulletin, volume seven, number four.

8 Lien-ken Yin, "Twenty-two Years of Agricultural Economics," Department of Agricultural Economics, University of Nanking, (1920-42), December 1942.

9 Swen, W. Y., *Report on the 25th Anniversary of the Department of Agricultural Economics,* College of Agriculture and Forestry, University of Nanking, 1946 (chiefly in Chinese). Students are listed by name and year of graduation.

10 *Cooperative Statistics,* Central Cooperative Administration, Nanking, China, December 31, 1945.

11 Tseng Hsiao, *The Theory and Practice of Land Reform in the Republic of China,* 2nd edition July 1968, Land Reform Museum, Taipei, Taiwan, Republic of China, p. 142.

12 Complete sets are available in the National Agricultural Library, Washington, D.C. and in the Horace Mann Library, Cornell University, Ithaca, New York.

[13] *Annual Reports of the College of Agriculture and Forestry, op. cit.,* volume seven, number ten, p. 50.

[14] Buck, Dawson and Wu, *Food and Agriculture in Communist China,* New York: Praeger Publishers, pp. 9-14.

[15] Wu, Y. L., ed., *Handbook on Communist China,* New York: Praeger Publishers, to be published.

[16] Ardon B. Lewis and Chang Lu-luan, *Silver and the Chinese Price Level.* College of Agriculture and Forestry, University of Nanking, Bulletin No. 11 (New Series), December 1933.

[17] Ministry of Industries, *Silver and Prices in China.* "Report of the Committee for the Study of Silver Values and Commodity Prices." Shanghai: The Commercial Press, pp. xxi, 245, 1935.

[18] *The 1931 Flood in China—An Economic Survey,* Department of Agricultural Economics, College of Agriculture and Forestry, University of Nanking, in cooperation with the National Flood Relief Commission, Bulletin No. 1 (New Series) April 1932, p. 74.

[19] The following list is compiled from a manuscript "Development of Agricultural Economics at the University of Nanking" in process of publication by the Department of Agricultural Economics, Cornell University. For further information contact Professor G. W. Hedlund, Warren Hall, Cornell University, Ithaca, N.Y. 14850.

NEW PERSONNEL OF THE DEPARTMENT OF AGRICULTURAL ECONOMICS UNIVERSITY OF NANKING, AUGUST 1927-1937

Aug. 1927-summer 1930; 1931-Aug. 1932: Chang Sing-I (C.C. Chang), B.S. Iowa; M.S. Cornell 1926. Agricultural Statistics, developed Crop Reporting (first initiated by Buck in 1926), which was transferred in 1928 or 1929, to the Bureau of Statistics, Legislative Yuan, Nanking, but still under direction of C.C. Chang, resigned for position with Bureau of Statistics, Legislative Yuan, Nanking in 1930, but released as Land Utilization Regional Investigator for part of 1931 and 1932. Author of "An Estimate of China's Farms and Crops," December 1932, University of Nanking and in *The Statistical Monthly,* Combined Issue of January and February, 1932, The Directorate of Statistics, Nanking.

Sept. 1930-Jan. 1931, Li Hsuen-chin (Hoon-K, Lee), Korea, Ph.D. Wisconsin, Professor of Agricultural Economics.

Feb. 1928-Mar. 1934: Shen Hsien-yao, B.S. Nanking 1928; B.S. Cornell 1938. Business Manager (resigned to head the Dept of Agricultural Economics, National Agricultural Research Bureau).

Feb. 1929-Dec. 1937: Chang Lu-luan, B.S. Nanking 1929. Agricultural Economics and Prices.

July 1930-May 1940: Yang Wei (Yank, W. Y.), B.S. Nanking 1927; Ph.D. Cornell 1935. Instruction and research in Prices and Statistics.

July 1930-Mar. 1934: Yien Meo, B.S. Nanking 1930. Regional Investigator and Assistant Statistician.

July 1930-1946: Liu Rwen-tao, B.S. Nanking 1925; M.S. Cornell 1937, Marketing, resigned in 1946, position with Ministry of Agriculture and Forestry.

July 1930-1947: Pan Hong-shen, B.S. Nanking 1930; M.A. in Agricultural Economics, Washington State 1949. Farm Management and Economics of Farm Implements.

1931-1943: Chen Tsai-chang, B.S. Shanghai, Associate.

1931-1936: Yang Ming-tsong, B.S. Nanking 1928, Associate, Assistant Statistician.

Sept. 1931-Aug. 1932: Stanley S. Warren, B.S. 1927 and Ph.D. 1931, Cornell. Agricultural Economist, Training staff in Land Utilization and Statistical Analysis.

Sept. 1932-Dec. 1933: Wan Kwoh-ting, B.S. Nanking, 1920. Research in Chinese Agricultural History, resigned for Government position.

Aug. 1932-1950: Chen Tsu-kwei, B.S. Nanking 1924. Associate Research in Chinese Agricultural History (transferred from University Nanking Library).

Feb. 1933-1941: Eo-Yang Ping, B.S. Nanking, Feb. 1933. Associate, Instruction in Extension and Rural Credit.

Oct. 1933-June 1936: Ardron B. Lewis, B.S. University of Maine 1928; Ph.D. Cornell 1933. Analysis of Land Utilization Data, Research on "Silver and the Chinese Price Level," teaching Elementary Statistics and Prices.

Oct. 1933-Dec. 1937: Brian Low, M.S. Canterbury College, New Zealand. Classification of data to determine Agricultural Regions and Areas, Atlas and Proof Reading, Author of Chapter on "Standard of Living" in Land Utilization in China.

Dec. 1933-1935: Yang Wen-chao, B.S. Peiping, Associate.

Apr. 1934: Leonard A. Maynard, Ph.D. Nutrition. On leave of absence in cooperation with Cornell University, assisted in analysis of Food Data, Instruction in Nutrition and Author with Collaboration of Chiao Chi-ming of the chapter on "Nutrition" in Land Utilization in China.

Feb. 1934-Jan. 1935: Nan Ping-fang, B.A. Park College, M.A. Chicago, Instruction in Agricultural Economics.

Feb. 2, 1934-Dec. 1950: Li Hwei-chien, B.S. Nanking, Feb. 1932, organization of Rural Credit Cooperatives and Farmers' Associations.

Sept. 1934-May 1935: C. F. Strickland, (England) Instruction and Extension in Rural Cooperatives, formerly with extension experience in India.

Sept. 1934-June 1936: Dr. Wayne M. Stevens, B.S. Illinois 1917, M.B.A Northwestern University 1924, Ph.D. American University 1926, Instruction in Cooperatives, compilation of instruction material on Cooperatives and Research on "Seasonal Prices of Farm Products."

1935-1942: Chen Hong-ken, B.S. Nanking 1935, Agricultural Economics.

July 1935-Dec. 1950: Hu Kwoh-hwa, B.S. Nanking, 1936, Associate, Prices.

Sept. 1936-Dec. 1937: John R. Raeburn, (England), B.S. College of Agriculture, Edinburgh, M.S. Cornell 1934, Ph.D. Cornell 1936, Agricultural Economist, Instruction in Prices, Statistics and Advanced Statistics, Research in Prices with many articles in Economic Facts of which he also became Editor, a publication by the Department of Agricultural Economics.

Sept. 1936-June 1937: Glenn W. Hedlund, B.S. University of Nebraska 1930, Ph.D. Cornell 1936, Agricultural Economist, Advisor and Instruction in Cooperatives, Farm Management and Economics.

July 1936-Dec. 1950: Ko Fuh-ting, B.S. Nanking 1936, Research in Prices and Statistics with articles in Economic Facts.

Sept. 1937-July 1938: W. Marshal Curtiss, B.S. University of Illinois 1927; Ph.D. Cornell 1936, Agricultural Economist, indexing Land Utilization in China, preparation of Farm Management text book for Chinese students in simplied English with John Lossing Buck. Also translated into Chinese by F. T. Ko, and Y. Y. Yang.

Sept. 1937-Apr. 1950: Wang Yin-Yuen, B.S. Nanking 1937, Research and Instruction in Prices.

[20] A detailed list of publications of the Department of Agricultural Economics by subject matter under thirteen broad subjects as recorded in appendix IV of the manuscript "The Development of Agricultural Economics, The University of Nanking at Nanking, China, 1920-1944" (in process of publication by the Department of Agricultural Economics, Cornell University).

NOTES TO CHAPTER VI

First Attempts to Transform China's Agriculture, 1927-1937

[1] Arthur W. Hummel: *Eminent Chinese of the Ch'ing Period* (*1644-1912*). U. S. Government Office, Washington, 1943. pp. 102, 318.

[2] T. H. Shen: *Some Suggestions About Cotton Breeding in China* (Proceedings of the Third Pan-Pacific Science Congress, Tokyo, Japan, 1926. pp. 1191-1196). The writer has first-hand knowledge of the experimental work and its later developments because he took part in growing American cotton varieties at a field station sponsored by the Chinese Cotton Mill Owners Association at Chengteh, Hunan province, in 1920, and also growing rice in the vicinity of Peking in 1921 and 1922.

[3] H. H. Love and John H. Reisner: *The Cornell-Nanking Story*, Cornell International Agricultural Development Bulletin 4, 1964, p. 7.

[4] *Ibid.*, p. 13.

[5] T. H. Shen: "The Field Technic for Determining Comparative Yields in Wheat under Different Environmental Conditions in China." *Journal of the American Society of Agronomy*, Vol. 22, No. 3 March 1930. T. H. Shen: "Direct-planting and Transplanting in Relation to the Breeding Test of Rice in China." *Journal of the American Society of Agronomy*, Vol. 26, No. 6, June 1934.

[6] T. H. Shen: *Studies on the Method of Kaoliang Breeding in China*: Part 1, Effect of Selfing; Part II, The Method of Kaoliang Treshing and Relation of Total Weight of Kaoliang Head with the Weight of Grain. T. H. Shen: *Inheritance of Quantitative and Qualitative Characters in Wheat Crosses* (Proceedings of the Fifth Pacific Science Congress, Vancouver, Canada, 1933).

NOTES TO CHAPTER VII

Industrial Development and Economic Policy in 1927-1937

[1] Liu and Yeh, *The Economy of the Chinese Mainland: National Income and Economic Development, 1933-1959*, Princeton University Press, 1945, p. 66.

[2] John K. Chang, "Industrial Development of Mainland China, 1912-1949," in *The Journal of Economic History*, Vol. XXVII, March 1967.

[3] Chang, *op. cit.*, p. 66.

[4] Chang, *op. cit.*, p. 68.

[5] Kungtu C. Sun (assisted by Ralph W. Huenemann), *The Economic Development of Manchuria in the First Half of the Twentieth Century*, Cambridge, Mass.: Harvard University Press, Harvard East Asian Monographs, 1969.

[6] The average annual growth rates were 6.5 per cent for China proper and 14.2 per cent for Manchuria.

[7] Kungtu C. Sun, *op. cit.*, p. 98, Table 23. It should be noted that Sun's original data were reconstructed without his being able to check over them.

[8] Sun, *op. cit.*, p. 96, Table 22.

[9] The fact that the order was imposed by harsh rule and against the popular sentiments of anti-Japanese nationalism only serves to stress all the more the importance of order to economic activities as long as the motivation of the decision-makers—the Japanese in this case—is not adversely affected by the need to use coercion in maintaining order or nullified by resistance.

[10] Sun, *op. cit.*, p. 96.

[11] With 1933=100, Manchuria's output in 1937 was 2600 for steel, 319 for flour, 294 for cigarettes, 281 for jute bags, 198 for cotton yarn, 187 for pig iron, 158 for cement, 155 for power, and 132 for coal. See Yen Chung-p'ing et al, *Chung-kuo Ching-tai Ching-chi-Shih T'ung-chi Tsu-liao Hsuen-chi* (*Selected Economic Historical Statistics of Modern China*), Peking, K'o-hsueh Ch'u-pan-she, 1955, p. 146.

These high rates help explain why Chang's estimates which are weighted in favor of heavy industry show a higher over-all growth.

[12] The relationship between the metric and the *shih* systems can be clearly illustrated by the following easily remembered ratios:

1 meter equals 3 *shih-ch'ih*, the standard lineal "foot."

1 kilogram equals 2 *shih-chin*. I litre equals I *shih-sheng*.

[13] The nineteen cities were Shanghai, Nanking, Canton, Hankow, Changsha, Chungking, Chengtu, Kunming, Kweilin, Kweiyang, Wenchow, Tsinan, Foochow, Tsingtao, Sian, Chengchow, Hsuchow, Chinkiang, and Hong Kong. For the data cited here, see *Chung-kuo Kuo-huo Kung-ssu Fa-chan Ching-kuo (Development of the National Product Companies)*, Shanghai, 1939, pp. 1-48.

[14] D. C. Wu, "The Significance of the National Economic Reconstruction Movement," *Kuo-min Ching-chi Chien-she Yun-tung (The National Economic Reconstruction Movement)*, Shanghai, China, *Chung-kuo Wen-t'i Yen-chiu hui*, 1937, p. 127.

NOTES TO CHAPTER IX

EDUCATION IN CHINA, 1927-37

[1] Hu Shih, "The Literary Renaissance," in *Symposium on Chinese Culture*, edited by Sophia H. Chen Zen (Shanghai, 1931), p. 131.

[2] K. Chu, "Education," in Sophia H. Chen Zen, *op. cit.*, p. 212.

[3] Wang Shih-chieh, *Education in China* (Shanghai: China United Press, 1935), p. 14.

[4] Also translated as "Recovery of Educational Rights."

[5] Huang Chien-chung, "Shih Nien Lai Ti Chung Kuo Kao Teng Chiao Yu," in *K'ang Chan Ch'ien Shih Nien Chih Chung Kuo*, compiled by Lung Men Bookstore, Hong Kong, 1965, p. 511.

[6] Wang Shih-chieh, *op. cit.*, pp. 10,12.

[7] *Ibid.*, p. 29; also Huang Chien-chung, *op. cit.*, p. 515.

[8] Hu Shih, *op. cit.*, p. 131.

[9] Carl H. Becker, once Prussian Minister of Education; M. Falski, Director of Primary Education Department at the Polish Ministry of Education, Warsaw; P. Langevin, Professor of the College de France, Paris; R. H. Tawney, Professor in the University of London.

[10] P. 14 of *Report*.

[11] P. 21 of *Report*.

[12] Pp. 147,149 of *Report*.

[13] Wang Shih-chieh, *op. cit.*, p. 16.

[14] P. 128 of *Report*.

[15] *Ibid.*, pp. 151,152.

[16] Wang Shih-chieh, *op. cit.*, p. 29.

[17] Huang Chien-chung, *op. cit.*, p. 523. Also see Appendix A.

[18] See Appendices B, C, and D for statistical data on elementary, secondary and higher education.

[19] Chiang Chien-pai, "Shih Nien Lai Ti Chung Kuo She Hui Chaio Yu," in *K'ang Chan Ch'ien Shih Nien Chih Chung Kuo* (Hong Kong, Lung Men Bookstore, 1965), p. 593. Also see Appendix E.

[20] Space does not permit elaboration on Dr. Yen's eminent contributions. Readers are referred to his story as told to Pearl Buck in her little book, *Tell the People* (John Day, 1945).

[21] The term was used in Chinese to indicate schools and colleges operated to satisfy the profit motive.

[22] P. 145 of Report.

APPENDIX (A)

Ratio of new students admitted into "arts" departments and
"practical studies" in higher institutions*

Year	"Arts" or non-science studies	Science and practical studies
1931	69.3%	30.7%
1932	63.4%	36.6%
1933	60.2%	39.8%
1934	54.0%	46.0%
1935	48.8%	51.2%

*Huang Chien-chung, op. cit., p. 523

APPENDIX (B)

Enrollment in elementary schools and kindergarten*

Year	Enrollment	Percentage of school age-children
1929	8,882,077	17.10
1930	10,948,979	22.07
1931	11,720,596	22.16
1932	12,223,066	24.79
1933	12,383,479	24.97
1934	13,188,133	26.27
1935	17,742,887	35.91
1936	21,454,165	43.42

*K'ang Chan Ch'ien Shih Nien Chih Chung Kuo, p. 564

APPENDIX (C)

Growth in Secondary Education*

Year	Middle Schools	Normal Schools	Vocalist Schools	Total Enrollment
1928	954	236	149	234.811
1929	1,225	667	219	341,022
1930	1,874	846	272	514,609
1937	2,042	1,211	370	547,207

*Figures for 1928-31 from the First Educational Yearbook of the Ministry of Education (1934); those for 1937 from K'ang Chan Ch'ien Shih Nein Chih Chung Kuo, p. 554.

APPENDIX (D)

Growth in Higher Education[*]

Year	Institutions	Students	Faculty	Expenditures
1928	74	35,198	5,214	$17,909,810
1929	76	29,123	6,218	25,533,343
1930	86	37,566	6,985	29,867.474
1931	103	44,167	7,053	33,619,237
1932	104	42,710		33,203,821
1933	111	46,758	7,075	34,643,000

[*] Figures for 1928-31 are from the *First Yearbook of Education of the Ministry of Education;* those for 1932 and 1933 are from the *Chinese Yearbook, 1935-1936.*

APPENDIX (E)

Growth of Social Education[*]

Year	Expenses	Number of Schools, Centers, etc.	Students	Teachers
1928	$ 3,632,466	16,723	219,828	10,495
1929	13,030,337	60,232	1,036,160	101,203
1930	14,028,461	70,166	1,104,187	110,178
1931	13,440,634	78,278	1,252,475	131,605
1932	20,979,062	80,212	1,298,487	136,206

[*] Chiang Chien-pai, *op. cit.,* p. 38

CONTRIBUTORS TO THIS VOLUME

Joseph W. Ballantine, LL.D. 巴蘭亭

American diplomat and statesman; Special Assistant to the Secretary of State, 1945-1947; Assistant Chief, Far Eastern Division, Department of State, 1937-1942, with a special assignment in 1941 as Aide to the Secretary of State in the pre-Pearl Harbor conversations with the Japanese Ambassador; Chief of the Far Eastern Division, 1943; B.A. *cum laude*, Amherst College, 1909; LL.D., Roanoke College, 1947; served with American Foreign Service since 1909 as Japanese Secretary, American Embassy in Tokyo (1917-1921); Consul in Dairen, Manchuria (1921-1923), Yokohama (1923), Tokyo (1924-1928); Japan desk officer, Far Eastern Division, Department of State (1928-1930); First Secretary, American Embassy, Tokyo (1936); participated as a member of the American Delegation to the London Naval Conference (1930), the Dunbarton Oaks Conference (1944), and the San Francisco United Nations Conference (1945); Senior staff member of Brookings Institution (1947); Visiting Professor, Department of Government, University of Miami, Florida (1956-1961); lectures at various institutions of higher learning including New York University, Columbia University, New School for Social Research, Hunter College, Fordham University, St. John's University; author of *Japanese as It is Spoken* (1945, 1949); *Formosa* (1952); co-author of *Search for Peace Settlements* (1951) and *Major Problems of United States Foreign Policy, Annual Issues*, from 1947-1954; author of numerous articles published in *Foreign Affairs*, the 1950 edition of *Encyclopedia Americana* and other learned journals.

John Lossing Buck, Ph.D. 卜凱

Agricultural Economist; B.S., 1914; M.S., 1925; Ph.D., 1933, Cornell University; Head of Department of Agricultural Economics, University of Nanking, 1920-1934; Monetary Adviser to the United States Secretary of Treasury, November 1934 to May 1935 and Treasury Representative in China, June 1935 to April 1939; Adviser, Ministry of Finance, Republic of China, May 1939 to September 1940; Professor, Department of Agricultural Economics, University of Nanking, October 1940 to March 1944; Chief Economist, National Agricultural Engineering Corporation of Chungking, August 1944 to March 1946; Agricultural Economist, Office of Foreign Agricultural Relations, United States Department of Agriculture, July 1945 to June 1946; Member, China-United States Agricultural Mission, June to December 1946; Head of Land and Water Use Branch, Food and Agriculture Organization of United Nations, February 1947 to August 1954; Director for Agricultural Economics, Council on Economics and Cultural Affairs, New York, September 1954 to August 1957; American Specialist to Far East, United States State Department, October to December 1964; author of *Land Utilization in China* (three volumes, 1937); *Chinese Farm Economy* (1930); co-author of *Food and Agriculture in Communist China* (1966); *Farm Management in China* (1942); and author of numerous monographs, papers, and articles, including "Fact and Theory About China's Land" (*Foreign Affairs*, October 1949); "Farm Tenancy in China" (1944); "An Agricultural Survey of Szechuan Province, China" (1942); "The 1931 Flood in China: An Economic Survey" (1932).

Chang Kia-ngau, L.H.D. 張嘉璈

Senior Research Fellow, Hoover Institution, Stanford University, 1965–; economist; honorary doctorate, St. John's University; Professor of Economics, Loyola University, Los Angeles, 1953-60; Visiting Professor of Economics, Nanyang University, 1968-69; served China's banking institutions since 1913, first as Vice-Manager, Shanghai Branch, Bank of China; Vice President, Bank of China, 1929-1936; and government of China as Minister, Ministry of Railways, 1936-1938; Minister, Ministry of Communications in wartime China, 1938-1943; Chairman, Economic Commission of Northeastern Provinces and concurrently Chairman, Board of Directors, Changchun Railroad in Manchuria, 1945-1947; Governor, Central Bank of China, 1947-1949; author of *China's Struggle for Railway Development* (1943); *The Inflationary Spiral: The Experience in China, 1939-1950* (1958); and many other articles in professional journals.

Theodore Hsi-en Chen, Ph.D., LL.D. 陳錫恩

Director, East Asia Studies Center and Professor of Education and Asian Studies, University of Southern California since 1938; B.A., Fukien Christian University; M.A., Columbia University; Ph.D., LL.D., University of Southern California; Dean, Fukien Christian University, 1927-1937; President, Fukien Christian University, 1946-1947; Academic Dean, Summer Institute on Chinese Civilization for American College Professors in Taiwan, 1962; Director, Summer Institute for American High School Teachers in Taiwan, 1968; author of seven books, including *Thought Reform of Chinese Intellectuals* (1960); *Teacher Training in Communist China* (1960); *Chinese Communist Regime* (1967); and of more than one hundred articles and of chapters in nine other books; articles in *Encyclopedia Britannica, Encyclopedia Americana, World Book Encyclopedia, Encyclopedia of Education* and others.

Chi-pao Cheng, Ph.D. LL.D. 程其保

Acting President, Institute of Chinese Culture since 1967; A.B., Hamline University, 1920; A.M., Chicago University, 1922; Ph.D., Columbia University, 1923; LL.D., Hamline University, 1958; Dean of Instruction, National Southeastern University, Nanking, 1925; Acting President, Shanghai College of Commerce, 1926; Professor of Education, Cheloo University, Tsinan, 1929-1931; Dean, College of Education, National Central University, Nanking, 1931-1933; Commissioner of Education, Hupeh Province, 1933; Professor of Education, National Cheng Chi University, Nanking and Chungking, 1938-1943; Commissioner of Education, Sikang Province, 1943-1945; elected sometime member of the Legislative Yuan, 1946; Deputy-head and Acting-head, Department of Education, UNESCO, Paris, 1947-1950; Visiting Professor, Hanover College, Indiana, 1950; Research Professor in Philosophy, Long Island University, 1951-1952; Director of Cultural Projects, China Institute in America, 1953-1967; served as Chairman of the Government Education Mission to Europe (1932); Delegate of China to UNESCO General Conference (1954, Montevideo; 1960 and 1962, Paris); author of *Education in China* (1924), *Principles of Education* (1929), *Studies of Teaching of Social Science* (1936); and of numerous articles and papers in professional journals.

Franklin L. Ho, Ph.D. 何　廉

Professor Emeritus of Economics, Columbia University, 1962–; B.A., Pomona College, 1922; Ph.D., Yale University, 1926; Professor of Economics, Nankai University, 1926-1929; Director, Nankai Institute of Economics, 1929-1936; Director of the Department of Political Affairs, Executive Yuan (Cabinet),

Republic of China, 1936-1938; Vice-Minister, Ministry of Economic Affairs, 1938-1939, 1944-1946; Acting Chancellor, Nankai University, 1948; Professor of Economics, Graduate Faculty of Political Science, Columbia University, 1949-1962; author of *A Treatise on Public Finance; Whole Prices and Price Index Numbers in North China; Index Numbers of the Quantities and Prices of Imports and Exports and of the Barter Terms of Trade in China, 1867-1928; Extent and Effects of Industrialization in China; Population Movement to the Northeastern Frontier in China; Rural Economic Reconstruction in China;* etc.

Chi-ming Hou, Ph.D. 侯繼明

Charles A. Dana Professor of Economics, Colgate University, 1956—; LL.B. (Economics), Fu Jen University of Peiping, 1945; M.A. (Economics), University of Oregon, 1949; Ph.D. (Economics), Columbia University, 1954; Kazanjian Economics Foundation Scholar, Columbia University, 1950-1951; Faculty Research Seminar Fellowship, Ford Foundation, Summer 1958 (at Yale University); Research Fellow in Chinese Economic Studies, Harvard University, various periods from 1959-1963; Brookings Research Professorship, 1965-1966 (at University of California, Berkeley); author of *Foreign Investment and Economic Development of China, 1840-1937* (1965); and of articles in various professional journals, including "Manpower, Employment, and Unemployment" (Alexander Eckstein, Walter Galenson and Ta-chung Liu, eds., *Economic Trends in Communist China,* 1968); "Sources of Agricultural Growth in Communist China" (*Journal of Asian Studies,* August 1968).

Chiao-min Hsieh, Ph.D. 謝覺民

Professor, Department of Geography, University of Pittsburgh, 1967—; B.A. (Geography), National Chekiang University, 1941; M.A. (Geography), 1950; Ph.D. (Geography), 1953, Syracuse University; Research Consultant, Institute of Geography, Academia Sinica, China, 1941-1946; Assistant Professor in Geography, Taiwan Normal University, 1946-1947; Instructor, Department of Geography, Dartmouth College, 1953-1954; Research Associate, Center for International Studies, M.I.T., Cambridge, Massachusetts, 1954-1956; Assistant Professor, 1956-1959, Associate Professor, 1959-1964, Ordinary Professor, 1964-1967, Department of Geography, Catholic University of America, Washington, D.C.; Visiting Lecturer, Department of Geography, University of Leeds, England (sabbatical year from Catholic University); served as vice-chairman in the section of population geography at the 12th International Geographical Congress (New Delhi, 1968) and the first External Examiner in geography, Chinese University, Hong Kong; author of *Taiwan—Ilha Formosa (1964); China—Ageless Land and Countless People* (1967); and of chapters in two books and of numerous monographs, papers, and articles published in professional and learned journals.

Chin-tung Liang, LL.B., Litt.D. 梁敬錞

Research Professor, Center of Asian Studies, St. John's University, 1964—; LL.B., National University of Peking, China, 1917; M.A., London School of Economics, University of London, 1921; Litt.D., The China Academy, Taiwan, 1968; Professor, National University of Peking, 1922-1926; Justice, Supreme Court, China, 1930-34; Secretary General, Chinese Supply Commission, Washington, D.C., 1943-1945; author of *A History of the First World War* (1921), *Extraterritoriality in China* (1931), *The Chinese Revolution of 1911* (1962), *The Cairo Conference and China* (1962), *A Historical Study of the Mukden Incident* (1964, 4th printing, 1968), *The Sinister Face of the Mukden Incident* (1969).

Ling Hung-hsun, B.S. 淩鴻勛

B.S. (Civil Engineering), National Chiao Tung University, 1915; started railroad career in 1918 as junior engineer, engineer, and senior engineer in various Government-operated railroads; President, National Chiao Tung University, Shanghai, 1924-1927; Director and Engineer-in-Chief of the extension of Lunghai Railroad; and in the completion of Canton-Hankow Railroad; in charge of building Hunan-Kwangsi Railroad and developing the transport of railroads and highways in Northwestern provinces of China in wartime China; Vice-Minister, Ministry of Communications, 1945-1949, responsible for resumption of several trunk railroads in north and central China crippled first by the Japanese and then by the Communists; Elected Member, Academia Sinica, 1948; Professor of Railroad Engineering, National Taiwan University, 1951-1955; Chairman of the Board of Directors of the Chinese Petroleum Corporation since 1951; author of several books, including *The History of Chinese Railroads* (1954); *The Chronological Studies of Dr. Jeme Tien Yu* (1960); and *The Chinese Eastern Railways* (1965).

Ta-chung Liu, Ph.D. 劉大中

Goldwin Smith Professor of Economics since 1964, and Director, Program on Comparative Economic Development since 1966, Cornell University; Chairman, Commission on Taxation Reform, the Executive Yuan (Cabinet), Republic of China, since 1968; Member, Academia Sinica, Republic of China since 1959; Jacob Ziskind Visiting Professor of Economics, Brandeis University, 1966-1967; Professor of Economics, Cornell University, 1958-1964; Economist, International Monetary Fund, 1948-1958; Visiting Lecturer, Johns Hopkins University, 1949-1958; Professor of Economics, National Tsing Hua University, 1946-1948; Assistant Commercial Counselor, Chinese Embassy, Washington, D.C., 1941-1946; Research Fellow, the Brookings Institution, 1940-1941; B.E., National Chiao Tung University,; Ph.D., Cornell University; author of *China's National Income, 1931-1936* (1946); *Production of Food Crops on the Chinese Mainland: Prewar and Postwar* (1964); *The Economy of the Chinese Mainland: National Income and Economic Development, 1933-1959* (1965); *Manufacturing Production Function of the United States* (1965); *Economic Trends in Communist China* (1968); and of numerous papers and articles.

Franz Michael, Ph.D. 梅 谷

Director and Professor of International Affairs, Institute for Sino-Soviet Studies, The George Washington University; Chairman, Research Colloquium on Modern China; studied at the Universities of Freiburg (Ph.D., 1933), Hamburg, and Berlin, and Orientalisches Seminar, Berlin; pre-Hitler attaché, Foreign Service, Berlin; professional member, faculty of National Chekiang University, Hangchow, and "on the march" into interior after Japanese invasion, 1934-1938; Research Associate and Lathrope Fellow, Walter Hines Page School, Johns Hopkins University, 1939-1942; Associate Professor and Acting Chairman, Far Eastern Department, Professor of Chinese History and Government, University of Washington, Seattle, 1942-1964; author of *Der Streit um die Manschurei* (1933); *The Origin of Manchu Rule in China* (1942); *Our Peace With Japan* (1945); *The Role of Communist China in International Affairs, 1965-1970* (1958); *The Taiping Rebellion: Volume I: History* (1966); co-author of *The Far East in the Modern World* (1955, 1964); and of numerous articles.

Dison Hsueh-feng Poe, LL.D. 浦薛鳳

Distinguished Professor of Philosophy and Political Science, University of Bridgeport, 1963–; graduate, Tsing Hua (Junior) College, Peking, China, 1921; B.A., Hamline University, 1923; M.A. Harvard University, 1925; LL.D., Hamline University, 1944; Assistant Professor, Tung Lu University, Yunnan, China, 1926-1927; Associate Professor, Chekiang University, Hangchow, 1927-1928; Professor and Chairman, Department of Political Science, National Tsing Hua University, Peiping, 1929-1939; Professor, National Central University, Chungking, 1941-1944; Professor and Dean, concurrently Director of the Graduate School of Political Science, Chengchi University, 1954-1962; John Hay Whitney Visiting Professor, Hanover College, Hanover, Indiana, and University of Bridgeport Bridgeport, Connecticut, 1962-1963; served with the Government of the Republic of China as Counselor, Supreme National Defense Council, 1939-45; Technical Expert, Chinese Delegation to the San Francisco Conference, 1945; Deputy Director-General, CNRRA (Chinese National Relief and Rehabilitation Administration), 1945-1946; Deputy Secretary-General, Executive Yuan (Cabinet) Republic of China, 1947-1948; Secretary General and Council Member, Taiwan Provincial Government, 1948-1954; Vice-Ministry of Education, 1958-1960; author of *Modern Western Political Theories,* (1939, 5th printing, 1965), *Freedom from Fear: On Post-War Peace Organization,* (1944, reprint with additional note, 1954), *Essays on Government and Politics* (1955), *Political Power: Composition and Preservation* (1958), *Law and Politics,* (1959), *Contemporary Political Theories of the West* (1962). For a brief sketch, cf. *Who's Who in the East, 1968-69,* p. 383; *American Men of Science,* 11th ed., L-Z, p. 1267.

T. H. Shen (Shen Tsung-han), Ph.D. 沈宗瀚

Chairman, Joint Commission on Rural Reconstruction, Republic of China; B.S., National Agricultural College, China, 1918; M.S., State University of Georgia, 1924; Ph.D., Cornell University, 1927; Professor of Plant Breeding, University of Nanking, 1927-1937; Chief Technician, Vice-Director and then Director of National Agricultural Research Bureau, 1934-1950; Director, National Tobacco Improvement Bureau, 1947-1949; Deputy Head, China Section, Joint China-United States Agricultural Mission, 1946; Member, the Planning Committee of National Defense, 1931-1933; Member, Natural Resources Commission, 1934-1946; Head, Agricultural Division, Central Planning Board, 1943-1946; author of *Agricultural Resources of China* (1951); *Agricultural Development on Taiwan Since World War II* (1964); *The Sino-American Joint Commission on Rural Reconstruction: Twenty Years of Cooperation for Agricultural Development* (1970); and of numerous monographs, papers, and articles relating to Chinese agriculture.

Paul K. T. Sih, Ph.D., LL.D. 薛光前

Professor of History, Director of the Center of Asian Studies, St. John's University, New York, 1959–; Consultant to the National Science Foundation, Washington, D.C., 1961–; LL.B., Soochow University, Shanghai, China, 1933; Ph.D., University of Rome, Italy, 1935; LL.D., Carroll College, Montana, 1953, and University of Portland, Oregon, 1956; served with the National Government, Republic of China, as Director, Deputy Director-General in the Ministry of Railways and the Ministry of Communications, 1936-1943; Technical Counselor of the Ministry of Foreign Affairs; Minister Plenipotentiary of the Chinese Embassy in Rome, Italy; Adviser of the Chinese Delegation to Five Ministers' Council, London, 1945; Peace Conference, Paris, 1946; U.N. General Assembly, Paris, 1948; Chief of the Chinese Delegation to the U.N. Special Committee on the Balkans, 1947-1949; Chinese Delegate to UNESCO Conference in 1956, New Delhi; 1958, 1960, Paris; recipient of the Knight of St. Gregory from Pope Pius XII, 1956, and Knight Commander of St. Gregory from Pope Paul VI, 1967; the Gold Medal Award of Meritorious Recognition from the Chinese Government, 1968, author of *From Confusius to Christ* (1952); *Democracy in East Asia* (ed., 1957); *Chinese Culture and Christian Spirituality* (1957); *Decision for China* (1959).

Sho-chieh Tsiang, Ph.D. 蔣碩傑

Professor of Economics, Cornell University, 1969–; Member, Commission on Reconstruction, the National Security Council, Republic of China since 1967; Member, Commission on Taxation Reform, the Executive Yuan (Cabinet), Republic of China, 1968–; B.Sc. (Economics), 1941; Ph.D. (Economics), 1945; and Hutchinson Silver Medal Award, 1944-1945, London School of Economics, University of London; Professor of Economics, National University of Peking, China, 1946-1948; Professor of Economics, National University of Taiwan, 1948-1949; Economist, Research and Statistics Department, International Monetary Fund, 1949-1961; Visiting Lecturer, Johns Hopkins University, 1958-1959; Visiting Professor of Economics, 1960-1961; Professor of Economics, 1961-1969, University of Rochester; Visiting Senior Research Fellow, Jesus College, Oxford University, 1966-1967; sometime Consultant to the United Nations, 1963-1964; served as British Council Fellow, 1943-1945; Fellow of Academia Sinica, Republic of China, 1957–; John Simon Guggenheim Fellow, 1966-1967; author of *Variations of Real Wages and Profit Margins in Relation to Trade Cycles*, Pitman, London; "Liquidity Preference and Loanable Funds Theories, Multiplier and Velocity Analysis: A Synthesis," *American Economic Review*, September 1956; "The Role of Money in Trade Balance Stability: Synthesis of Elasticity and Absorption Approaches," *American Economic Review*, December 1961; "A Model of Economic Growth in Rostovian Stages," *Econometrica*, October 1964; "The Precautionary Demand for Money, An Inventory Theoretical Approach," *Journal of Political Economy*, January/February 1969; and numerous other articles in professional journals.

William L. Tung, Ph.D. 董霖

Professor of Political Science, Queens College of the City University of New York, 1962–; Professor and Chairman of the Department of Political Science, St. John's University, New York, 1957-1962; Professorial Lecturer, Fuh Tan University, China, 1945-1947; Professor of Political Science, Hangchow University, China, 1940-1942; Lecturer of Government, Northwestern University, China, 1928-1930; B.A., Fuh Tan University, Shanghai, 1928; M.A., University of Illinois, 1937; Ph.D., University of Illinois, 1939; Postdoctorate Research Fellow, Yale University, 1939-1940; served with the Government of the Republic of China as Counselor, Peiping Headquarters of the National Military Council, 1932-1935; Secretary, Central Political Council, Nanking, 1935; Counselor, Supreme National Defense Council, 1942-1943; Secretary-General, Ministry of Information in wartime China, 1943-1944; Member of the Legislative Yuan (corresponding to United States Senator), 1943-1945; joined the Chinese Diplomatic Service from 1943-1950, as

Director of the Department of American Affairs of the Ministry of Foreign Affairs; Ambassador to the Netherlands, and Vice-Minister, Ministry of Foreign Affairs, Republic of China; editor, *Cases and Other Readings in International Law* (1940); author of *China and Some Phases of International Law* (1940); *The Political Institutions of Modern China* (1964); *International Law in an Organizing World* (1968); *International Organization Under the United Nations System* (1969); *China and the Foreign Powers: The Impact of and Reaction to Unequal Treaties* (*New York*, 1970).

Yuan-li Wu, Ph.D. 吳元黎

Professor of Economics (on leave), University of San Francisco; Deputy Assistant Secretary of the U. S. Department of Defense for Policy Plans and NSC Affairs, International Security Affairs, 1969—; sometime student at Berlin University, Germany, B.Sc. (Economics) London School of Economics and Political Science, University of London, 1942; Ph.D., London School of Economics, University of London, 1946; Assistant Professor of Economics, Hofstra College, 1950-1951; Lecturer in Economics, Stanford University, Summer 1954 and Spring 1952; co-ordinator of Research, HRAF project, Stanford University, 1955-1956; Associate Professor of Economics, Marquette University, 1956-1958; Professor of Economics and Director of the Institute for Asian Studies, Marquette University, 1958-1960; Consultant, Hoover Institution, Stanford University, 1960-1968; Professor of International Business, University of San Francisco, 1960-1968; author of *Economic Warfare* (1952); *An Economic Survey of Communist China* (1956); *Economic Development and the Use of Energy Resources* (1963); *The Economy of Communist China, An Introduction* (1965); *The Steel Industry in Communist China* (1965); *The Spatial Economy of Communist China* (1967); and of numerous papers, studies and articles.

Arthur N. Young, LL.D. 楊 格

Financial Adviser to China, 1929-1947; aided the National Government to carry through monetary and fiscal reforms before the war, and stayed during the war to aid with problems of war finance, including procurement of American aid; served either as financial adviser or on a mission for the American Government in some fifteen countries of the Far East, Middle East, and Latin America; recipient of advanced degrees in economics from Princeton and in law from George Washington University; LL.D., Occidental College, California; author of *China and the Helping Hand, 1937-1945* (1963); *China's Wartime Finance and Inflation, 1937-1945* (1965); and of numerous reports, papers, and articles.

CHRONOLOGY OF 1927-1937*

Date	Achievements of the National Government and Important Economic Events	Internal Difficulties	External Trouble
1927 February	Rendition of British Concessions in Hankow and Kiukiang.		Dispatch of British Navy to Shanghai.
March	Provinces of Shensi, Chekiang, Anhwei, and the cities of Shanghai and Nanking brought under the National Forces.	Publication of Mao Tse-tung's report on the peasant movement.	The Nanking Incident, causing bombardment by American and British warships.
April	Establishment of the National Government in Nanking.	Purge from the Kuomintang of its Communist elements. The Nanking-Hankow split.	Japanese landing of Marines in Hankow, causing national indignation. Conflict of a British gunboat and National Forces near Chinkiang.
May	First Nationalist loan of C$30 million issued at Shanghai.	Communist abortive uprising at Changsha, known as the Ma-jih Incident. Earthquakes at Liangchow, Kansu.	Japanese dispatch of troops to Shantung, further intensifying Sino-Japanese tensions.
June	Provinces of Honan, Shansi, Suiyuan, and the Huai Valley brought under the rule of the National Government.	Stalin's instruction to the Chinese Communists to tighten their grip on the Wuhan regime.	First Eastern Conference of Japan presided over by Tanaka, planning to prevent Nationalist control of Manchuria.
July	Reconciliations between the left and right factions of the Kuomintang. Commitment of the National Government to abolish *likin*. Adherence of Yunnan to the National Government.	Departure of Borodin and Russian aides from Hankow.	Dispatch of Japanese troops from Tsingtao to Tsinan.

August	Agreement of the Russo-Chinese Board of Directors of the Chinese Eastern Railway to transfer to the custody of the National Government $16,000,000, one half of the operating fund of the railway. Measures taken for judicial reforms.	Communist uprising at Nanchang, instigated by Besso Lomindse. Resignation of Chiang Kai-shek as Commander-in-Chief of the National Army. Defeat of Sun Chuang-feng's forces of 70,000 men which had crossed the Yangtze at Nanking and Chinkiang.	Second Eastern Conference of Japan at Dairen presided over by Mori. Meeting of Yoshizawa Kenkichi with Chang Tso-lin, ruler of Manchuria, relating to Manchurian-Mongolian problem.
September	Measures taken for enforcing the 25% land rent reduction in Kwangtung. Completion of the 35-kilowatt Chinese International Broadcasting Station in Nanking.	Communist uprising at Changsha. Penetration of defeated Communist forces led by Ho Lung and Yeh Ting into Fukien and Kwangtung for continued uprisings.	Warning of Yoshizawa to Chang Tso-lin to suppress anti-Japanese activities in Manchuria.
October		Arrival of Mao Tse-tung at Chinkiangshan in Kiangsi. Tang Sheng-chih insurrection.	Secret agreement of Chang Tso-lin with Japan relating to the Ki-hui Railroad.
November	Inauguration of the Supreme Court of Justice.	Communist uprisings at Haifeng and Lufeng in Kwangtung.	
December	Re-establishment of the Salt Inspectorate at Shanghai to develop and improve salt administration.	Communist uprising at Canton directed by Heinz Neumen and Gerhart Eisler.	Breaking of Soviet Russia diplomatic relations for her subversive activities in China. Outbreak of anti-Chinese movement in Korea.
1928 January	Restoration of Chiang Kai-shek to office as Commander-in-Chief of the National Army. Arrangements initiated for foreign tobacco and oil companies to pay taxes despite extraterritoriality.	Revolt of peasants against over-taxation at Tohua and Linkiang in Manchuria.	Chinese protest against Japan for sending troops to Shantung.

CHRONOLOGY OF 1927-1937*

Date	Achievements of the National Government and Important Economic Events	Internal Difficulties	External Trouble
February	Establishment of the National Reconstruction Commission in charge of economic and industrial development.	Flood of the Yellow River at Litsin, Shantung, affecting 20,000 people.	Japanese opposition to bringing the Han-Yeh-Ping Iron and Mining Company under the control of the Chinese Government.
April	Continued Northern Expedition toward Peking led by Generalissimo Chiang.	Joining of Chu Teh with Mao Tse-tung at Chinkiangshan.	Serious consideration by Japanese Cabinet for a more aggressive policy toward Manchuria and Mongolia.
May	First National Educational Conference for reforms.	Nation-wide protest against Japanese atrocities in Tsinan.	The Tsinan Incident—clashes of the National Army with Japanese troops. Japanese demand for the right of building five railroads in Manchuria.
June	Peking and Tientsin brought under the rule of the National Government. Peking re-named Peiping. National Economic Conference at Shanghai to discuss programs for reduction of Army and for national reconstruction. Adherence of Sinkiang Province to the National Government.	Resignation of Chiang-Kai-shek as Commander-in-Chief of the National Revolutionary Army.	Assassination of Chang Tso-lin by the Japanese.
July	Conclusion of Sino-American Treaty, restoring tariff autonomy to China, with eleven nations following suit before the end of 1928 except Japan. National Financial Conference at Nanking.	Formation of the National Anti-Japanese organization at Shanghai. Civil war between military groups in Szechuan.	Japanese warning to Chang Hsueh-liang, ruler of Manchuria, not to pledge allegiance to the National Government. Japanese bombing of Chowtsun in Shantung.

August	National Conference of Communications at Nanking. Completion of the Ki-tun Railroad.	Abortive Communist uprisings at Hangchow and Chuchi in Chekiang. Flood of the Wen and Mi Rivers in Shantung, leaving more than 30,000 homeless.	Conference of Japanese consuls in Manchuria to map out aggressive plans.
September	Rehabilitation of salt revenue and salt-secured loans begun.	Communist uprising at Pingkiang and Liuyang in Hunan.	Military maneuvers of Japanese at Tsinan.
October	Promulgation of Organic Law of National Government. Promulgation of regulations creating Central Bank of China.	Communist uprising at Liyang in Kiangsu.	
November	Chang Hsueh-liang's pledge of allegiance to the National Government at Nanking. Establishment of the Academia Sinica as the highest body of scholarly research. Promulgation of law governing allocation of revenue and expenditures between National and Provincial Governments.	Formation of the Manchurian Committee by the Chinese Communists, advocating independence of Manchuria.	
1929 January	Military Reorganization and Disbandment Conference, aiming at unifying military system and reducing military expenditures. Establishment of National Highway Commission.	Fleeing of the military forces of Mao Tse-tung and Chu Teh from Chinkiangshan toward the border region of Fukien, Kwangtung, and Kiangsi.	Conference of Japanese Consuls in Manchuria resolving to settle the "Manchurian-Mongolian problem," by force if need be.
February	Promulgation of the Law Governing Weights and Measures thus standardizing weights and measures. New tariff effective after Japan's agreement completed the needed assents.		Break-up of Chinese-Japanese negotiations relating to the Tsinan Incident.

CHRONOLOGY OF 1927-1937*

Date	Achievements of the National Government and Important Economic Events	Internal Difficulties	External Trouble
March		Revolt of Kwangsi faction. Communist attack on Tingchow in Fukien.	
April	Agreements for air service by China National Aviation Corporation.		Maneuvers of Japanese Navy in East China Sea for one month. Japanese demand for suppression of all anti-Japanese activities in China.
May	Adherence of Ningsia Province to the National Government. Promulgation of Civil Code.		Exposure of a secret meeting at Russian Consulate at Harbin for Communist activities.
June	Burial of Sun Yat-sen at Nanking. Establishment of the Huai River Hydraulic Commission and the Commission for the Reconstruction of the Nation's capital.	Stepping up of Communist activities in Kiangsi and Fukien.	Close of the Chinese Consulate at Khabarovsk by Soviet Russia in retaliation for Chinese action at Harbin.
July	Promulgation of the Opium-Suppression Law.	Establishment of a Soviet regime at Si-chung and Hochuang in Szechuan by irregular military elements with Communist assistance.	Russia breaks off diplomatic relations with China.
August	Promulgation of the Law of Examination for civil service.	More extensive disturbances in western Fukien by the Communists.	Russian attack on Manchuli. Protest of the National Government against British plan to construct railroads in Tibet.

September	National Conference on Forestry. Announcement of plan to pay arrears of salt-secured loans.	Rebellion of the Chang Fa-kwei army at I-Chang.	
October	Abolition of capital punishment by be-heading. Promulgation of the law for the organization of district governments.	Rebellion of the Sung She-yuan and Shih Chin-ding armies.	Loss of San-kiang-kuo in Manchuria to the Russian troops after bloody battles.
November	Reports of Kemmerer Commission on fiscal and monetary matters. Declaration of the Mexican Government denouncing her consular jurisdiction in China. Rendition of British Concession in Chinkiang.	Occupation of Shanghang, Fukien, by the Communists.	Russian occupation of Manchuli.
December	Enactment of regulations concerning religious temples. Promulgation of the Factory Law, the Maritime Law, and the Insurance Law. Creation of the Ministry of Agriculture and Mining, and the Central Field Health Station.	Insurrection of the Shih Yu-shan army at Pukow. Insurrection of the Tang Sheng-chih army at Chengchow and the Chang Fa-kwei army in Kwangtung.	Establishment of the "Solan Republic" at Hailar in Manchuria by Inner and Outer Mongolian Youth under Russian military direction.
1930 January	Adoption of customs gold unit and collection of import duties on gold basis.	Fleeing of the Chang Fa-kwei insurrectionary army to Western Hunan.	Withdrawal of Mongolian Army from Hailar.
February	Promulgation of budget-making regulations. Signing of the agreement concerning the reorganization of the Provisional Court of the International Settlement of Shanghai.	Communist occupation of nine districts in Kiangsi.	Attempts of Nepal to invade Tibet.
April	Creation of the Shanghai Mint.	Communist attack on Nansiung in eastern Kwangtung.	

CHRONOLOGY OF 1927-1937*

Date	Achievements of the National Government and Important Economic Events	Internal Difficulties	External Trouble
May	Conclusion of Sino-Japanese Treaty restoring Chinas right to tariff autonomy. Creation of the Comptroller-General Office.	Feng-Yen separatist movement resulting in a war for four months. Tientsin Customs seized by Yin Hsi-shan until September.	
June	Promulgation of the Land Law.	Adoption of the Li Li-san line by the Chinese Communist Party.	Reinforcement of Japanese troops at Toumen in Manchuria.
July	Construction of the port of Hu-lu-tao.	Communist seizure of Changsha in Hunan for ten days. Communist attack on Chintehcheng in Kiangsi.	Protest against Russia's building railroad along the border of Tungning in Kirin, Manchuria.
September	Restoration of the British Concession in Amoy to China.		
October	Restoration of Weihaiwei to China after thirty-two years of British rule.	Leaving of Li Li-san for Moscow. Communist occupation of Kian in Kiangsi.	Riots in Chientao on the border between China and Korea, with participation of Chinese, Korean, and Russian Communists.
November	National Conference on Industry and Commerce at Nanking. Conference on settlement of debts in arrears.	Penetration of the Communist forces led by Ho Lung into Tsinli, Kiangsi.	Japanese attack on the aboriginies in Formosa.
December	Promulgation of the Farmers' Organization Law.	Launching of the First Encirclement Campaign against the Communists.	Outbreak of anti-Japanese activities in Korea.

1931		
January	Abolition of *likin*; "native customs" beyond 50 *li* (16 2/3 miles) from treaty ports, coast trade duty, and transit dues; import duties raised to compensate for revenue loss. Arrival of League of Nations experts to aid China. Restoration of the Belgian Concessions at Tientsin to China. National Conference of Internal Affairs, planning for earlier realization of local autonomy.	Penetration of defeated Communist forces led by Ho Lung in western Hupeh into western Hunan in guerrilla formation.
February	Establishment of the International Tele-Communications Bureau. Introduction of excise taxes on cigarettes, cotton yarn, matches, cement and wheat flour. Establishment of the Eurasia Aviation Corporation.	Launching of the Second Encirclement Campaign against the Communists. Sterling exchange reached low of under 10c per C$1.
March	Adoption of the law to reform salt revenue, followed by administrative reforms.	
April	Establishment of the Directorate General of Budgets, Accounting and Statistics.	Launching of the Third Encirclement Campaign against the Communists. Fighting among military groups in northern Szechuan.
May	Adoption of a provisional constitution by the National Government. Election of Chiang Kai-shek as President of the National Government.	Attempt of the Canton group to establish a rival regime in guise of advocating war on Japan.

CHRONOLOGY OF 1927-1937*

Date	Achievements of the National Government and Important Economic Events	Internal Difficulties	External Trouble
June	Completion of the Ming-Shen Dam in Suiyuan, capable of irrigating an area 2.5 million *mou*. Completion of the abolition of "native customs."	Seizure of South China Customs by dissidents until October.	
July		Insurrection of the Shih Yu-shan army at Shunteh. Great Flood of Yangtze and Huai Rivers, affecting many millions.	The Wanpaoshan Incident.
August	Establishment of the National Flood Relief Commission to deal with major flood in central China.	Shanghai wholesale price index reached peak of 130.3 (1926=100).	
September	Institution of Cornell-Nanking (Universities) Cooperative Program for Agricultural Development. Arrival of League of Nations Mission of Educational Experts for a three-month study of China's problems. Loan of U.S. $9 million to buy American wheat for flood relief.	Nation-wide movement of students demanding war on Japan, continuing until December.	The Mukden Incident followed by Japanese invasion of Manchuria.
November	Establishment of the National Economic Council as co-ordinating body for national economic policies. Increase in higher customs rates to triple national revenue.	Setting up of the Central Soviet Government by Chinese Communists at Juichin, Kiangsi, with an increase of armed forces to 60,000 men.	Japanese occupation of Lungkiang, capital of Heilungkiang.

Month			
December		Resignation of Chiang Kai-shek to let the Canton group try to govern.	Japanese occupation of Chinchow in Manchuria. Japanese attack on Shanghai.
1932 January		Failure of the Canton group to govern.	Establishment of "Manchukuo" by the Japanese.
February	Appointment of Chiang Kai-shek as Chairman of the Military Affairs Commission. Reorganization of internal debt saving about C$100 million yearly in debt charges, and enabling budget balancing in calendar year 1932.	Communist occupation of Shang Hang and Wu Ping in Fukien and expansion of Communist controlled area of some 100,000 square kilometers, covering parts of seven provinces of Hunan, Kiangsi, Chekiang, Fukien, Hupeh, Honan, and Anhwei.	
March	Concentration of Government revenues in Central Bank instead of foreign banks. Simplification of Salt Administration by amalgamating offices of District Inspectors and Commissioners.		Seizure of Manchurian Customs, salt and other revenues by Japan.
April	Inauguration of the conservancy work on the Huai River.	Communist occupation of Chichun in Hupeh.	
May			Signing of the Shanghai truce. Bombing of Heilun by Japanese airplanes.
June	Establishment of the National Bureau of Compilation and Translation.	Communist occupation of Chikunshan in Hupeh. Launching of the Fourth Encirclement against the Communists.	Japanese occupation of Heilun.

CHRONOLOGY OF 1927-1937*

Date	Achievements of the National Government and Important Economic Events	Internal Difficulties	External Trouble
July	Resumption of office by Chiang Kai-shek to confront national crisis.	Communist occupation of Nanhsiung in Kwangtung. Defeat of the Communist forces in Kwangsi and Kwangtung.	Japanese further advance toward Jehol.
August	Tariff revision raising rates especially on luxuries.		
September	Adoption of General Budget Law and the Forestry Law.		Japanese recognition of "Manchuko."
October		Civil wars among military groups in Szechuan. Attack of Outer Mongolia on Inner Mongolia instigated by Japan.	Publication of the Lytton Report which failed to provide any concrete measures by which Japan could be expelled from Manchuria.
November	Creation of the National Defense Planning Commission. Conference of Seven Provinces on Public Highways, planning to construct eleven trunk lines.		
December	Inauguration of nation-wide Opium-Suppression movement. Completion of the Hangkiang Railroad from Hangchow to Chinhua. Completion of Kinghui Canal in Shensi.	More fighting among military groups in Szechuan. Return of defeated forces led by Mao Tse-tung to Juichin in Kiangsi. Dollar exchange reached low of US$0.19 per C$1.	Bombing of Chaoyang by the Japanese for invading Jehol.

1933			
January		Halt of the Fourth Encirclement Campaign against the Communists with decisive victory in sight because of Japanese attack on Shanhaikuan.	Japanese occupation of Shanhaikuan.
February	Promulgation of the Cooperative Societies Law. Abolition of interport duties on rice, paddy wheat.	Penetration of defeated Communist forces into the border region of Fukien and Kiangsi close to the border of Chekiang.	Adoption by the League Assembly of a report by the Special Committee with suggestions of adopting the Lytton Report, followed by Japanese notice of withdrawal from the League on March 27.
March	Enactment of the Silver Standard Dollar Coinage Law and Abolition of the *tael*.	Attack on Tsinghai by Tibetan troops. Penetration of the Communists in Kiangsi into the Kan River region.	Japanese occupation of Jehol. Fighting at the various passes along the Great Wall.
April	Formation of the Four Provinces Agricultural Bank to relieve peasants in areas overrun by Communists.	Fighting among military groups in Sinkiang.	Russian instigation of political troubles in Sinkiang. Advance of Japanese forces into Hopei, only twelve miles distance from Peiping.
May	Establishment of the Rural Rehabilitation Commission dealing with urgent economic problems. Conclusion of the Sino-American Agreement for $50,000,000 Wheat Loan.	More fighting among military groups in Szechuan.	Russian proposal to sell to Japan the Chinese Eastern Railway, a *de facto* recognition of "Manchukuo." Signing of the Tangku Agreement, setting up a demilitarized zone in Hopei Province.
June	Enactment of the Conscription Law.	Communist occupation of Kwangyuan in Szechuan.	Meeting of the representatives of Russia, Japan, and "Manchukuo" at Tokyo for the sale of the Chinese Eastern Railway.

CHRONOLOGY OF 1927-1937*

Date	Achievements of the National Government and Important Economic Events	Internal Difficulties	External Trouble
July	Adoption of a three-year plan for the reconstruction of Air Force.	Flood of the Yellow River in Yungchi.	Occupation of Tolun by the Japanese.
August	Enactment of regulations to relieve the people overrun by the Communists.	Communist attack on Leinchen in northern Fukien.	
September		Earthquakes in Szechuan.	
October	Acceleration of constructing highways linking the provinces of Kiangsi, Chekiang, Hupeh, Hunan, Fukien and Kwangtung.	Launching of the Fifth Encirclement Campaign against the Communists.	
November		Revolt of Fukien against the National Government.	
December	Completion of the Nanking-Pukow Train Ferry. Inauguration of Peiping as the first municipality with an elected assembly of thirty-seven members.	Penetration of Communist forces led by Peng Teh-huai into eastern Kwangtung.	Creation of the "Inner Mongolian Autonomous Area" in Tolun by Japan.
1934 January	Completion of some 2,900 "strategic forts" in addition to those along the highways in Kiangsi, thus completing the blockade of the Communist forces in the area.	Suppression of the insurrectionary elements in Fukien.	Japanese attack on Chahar.

February	Inauguration of the New Life Movement at Nanchang for a moral revival of the nation.	Election of Mao Tse-tung as Chairman of the National Soviet Government at the Second National Soviet Congress.	Protest against opening of mines by the British at P'ien-ma in Yunnan.
March	Ratification of the London Silver Agreement reserving freedom of action if value of silver raised contrary to spirit of agreement.	Fighting between the army in Szechuan and Tibetan troops.	Creation of the "Great Union of China-Japan-Manchukuo" in Chinhuangtao by Japanese and Korean *ronin*.
April	Creation of the National Cotton Improvement Bureau.	Communist attack on Yungan in Fukien.	Amou Statement claiming Japanese primacy in China affairs and opposing foreign financial and technical aid except by Japan.
May	Inauguration of a vigorous six-year campaign for the suppression of opium. Enactment of the Law of Census to become effective July 1. Second Financial Conference held in Nanking.	Communist attack on Chengpa in Szechuan with intention of moving toward southern Shansi. Adoption of guerrilla tactics by the Communists in Kiangsi.	Bombing of Kirin by Japanese airplanes killing a large number of Chinese. Recognition of "Manchukuo" by El Salvador.
June	Adoption of American silver purchase law. Creation of China Development Finance Corporation.	Communist attack led by Ho Lung on Wuchuan in Kweichow.	Self-imposed disappearance of Eimei Kuramoto, a Japanese vice consul, in Nanking, but discovered five days later, a plot to further increase tensions between China and Japan.
July	Revision of import tariff with more favorable treatment of Japanese goods.	Serious drought in Chekiang, Honan, and Kiangsi Provinces.	

CHRONOLOGY OF 1927-1937*

Date	Achievements of the National Government and Important Economic Events	Internal Difficulties	External Trouble
October	United States refusal of China's proposal to swap silver for gold; flexible export duty on silver adopted to check rise of exchange rates.	Success of the Fifth Encirclement Campaign against the Communists in Hupeh, Hunan, Kiangsi and Fukien, resulting in the "long march" with Communists cornered in northern Shensi.	
November	Completion of the Hang-kiang Railway from Chinhua to Yushan. Construction of the Lienyuan Port.		Military maneuvers of Japanese troops for three days at Tangshan and Luanhsien along Peiping-Mukden Railroad.
1935 January	Promulgation of the Criminal Code.	Election of Mao Tse-tung as Chairman of the Communist Political Bureau at Tsungyi in Kweichow.	Dispatch of Japanese troops in Jehol to Tulun and Japanese attack on Tungshantze in eastern Chahar. Sale of Russian interests in Manchuria, including the Chinese Eastern Railway, to Japan.
March	Government control of Bank of China and Bank of Communications. British proposal to join with the United States, Greece and Japan to help China with currency reform.		

April	Inauguration of the National Economic Reconstruction Movement. Extension of government's fiscal and monetary authority to Szechuan Province. Dollar exchange reached high of over US$ 0.42 per C$1.		
May		Assassination of Yang Yin-pu and Pai Yu-heng, two journalists in Tientsin.	The Ho-Umezu Agreement which forced China to evacuate her troops from Hopei.
June	Completion of the Szechuan and Kweichow Highway. Creation of Farmers Bank of China. British announcement of the visit to China of Sir Frederick Leith-Ross in connection with financial problems. Approval of coinage reform, with nickel 20-, 10-, and 5-cent and copper 1- and ½- cent coins.		Abortive uprising of irregular elements led by Pai Chien-wu and supported by Japan at Fengtai near Peiping.
July	Integration of Szechuan currency into national system.	Great flood covering four provinces of Hupeh, Hunan, Kiangsi and Anhwei, affecting 14,000,000 people with property losses aggregating C$500,000,000.	Conclusion of the "Economic Agreement" between Japan and "Manchukuo."
August	Extension of operations of Internal Revenue Administration to Szechuan Province.	Appeal of Mao Tse-tung at Maoerhkai for "United Front" against Japan in a policy corresponding to the resolution made at the Seventh World Congress of the Communists at Moscow.	Japanese-sponsored smuggling through its puppet establishment in north China.
October	Inauguration of Central Trust in Shanghai.	Settling down of the Communists in northern Shensi.	Japanese military meetings in Dairen and Shanghai.

CHRONOLOGY OF 1927-1937*

Date	Achievements of the National Government and Important Economic Events	Internal Difficulties	External Trouble
November	Change from the Silver Standard to a foreign exchange standard. Termination of the note-issuing rights of provincial and private banks and establishment of a single note-issuing authority. Sale of 50 million ounces of silver to American Treasury. Establishment of the National Rice and Wheat Improvement Bureau.	Unsuccessful assassination attempt on Wang Ching-wei, President of the Executive Yuan.	Reinforcement of 12,000 Japanese troops at Shanhaikuan.
December	Completion of the Lohui Canal in Shensi. Completion of the Yung-li Chemical Fertilizer Plant at Pukow. Attempts made for four-year compulsory education. American Treasury limited price paid for foreign silver causing fall from US$ 0.45 by January.	Attack on the Mongolian-Suiyuan border region by "Manchukuo" military units. Disturbances created by the Liu Kwei-tang bandits in Nankuo with Japanese assistance.	Establishment of the puppet North China Autonomous Regime in East Hopei under Japanese protection.
1936 January	Completion of the Huai-nan Railroad. Consolidation of thirty-three issues of internal loans into five issues, saving about C$85 million yearly. Agreement of foreign banks except Japanese to hand over silver to Central Bank.	Clashes between Chinese and Japanese troops at Chaoyangmen in Peiping. Proclamation of the establishment of the "Provisional Military Government" at Changpei by the "Manchukuo" units led by Li Shou-sin.	Occupation of five districts in Chahar by the "Manchukuo" military units with Japanese assistance. Hirota's three demands leaving China with no choice between war and capitulation.

February	Announcement of the Settlement of Tientsin-Pukow Railway loans. Issuance of subsidiary nickel and copper coins.		Close of Russion Consulate General in Mukden.
March		Clashes of university students with police at Shanghai and Peiping.	Declaration of Russia on the signing of the "Mutual Assistance Agreement with Outer Mongolia."
May	Promulgation of the draft of permanent constitution. Second sale of 75 million ounces of silver to American Treasury and credit of US $20 million against further 50 million. Agreement to issuing fiduciary silver coins of C$1 and C$ 0.50 at American insistence.	Establishment of the Communist-sponsored "Chinese Students' National Salvation Union" in Shanghai.	Further reinforcement of Japanese troops in north China on pretext of self-protection.
June	Integration of South China currency and revenues into national system after the collapse of South China revolt.	Large scale students' demonstrations in Peiping and Canton. Revolt of Kwangtung and Kiangsi groups in the guise of fighting against Japan.	Creation of the puppet Inner-Mongolian autonomous regime under Japanese auspices.
July	Completion of the Soo-chia Railroad. Adoption of revised salt law and income tax law.	Clashes between the 29th Army and Japanese troops at Taku in Hopei.	
August	Settlement of various publicly issued railway loans.	Attack of "Manchukuo" military units on Taolin in eastern Suiyuan.	Japanese invasion of northern Chahar from Chengteh.
September	Completion of the Canton-Hankow Railroad.	Clashes between Chinese and Japanese troops at Fengtai near Peiping.	Landing of Japanese Marines at Hankow.
October	Enforcement of the Income Tax Law.		

CHRONOLOGY OF 1927-1937*

Date	Achievements of the National Government and Important Economic Events	Internal Difficulties	External Trouble
November	Completion of the Hangkiang Railroad from Yushan to Nanchang.	Repelling of "Manchukuo" irregulars directed by Japanese Kwangtung Army from northern Suiyuan by Chinese National forces at Paolingmiao.	Extensive military maneuvers of Japanese units in Tientsin and Peiping. Recognition of "Manchukuo" by Italy.
December	Adoption of an organic law for the salt administration terminating the prerogatives of foreign personnel. Rise of industrial production from 240.2 million *yuan* in 1926 to 499.6 million *yuan* in 1936. Founding of 26,244 cooperative enterprises, 12,517 of which had been set up in 1935 alone. Completion of a total of 2,900 miles of railroad trunk lines from 1926 to 1936, with another 1,100 miles under construction and 2,240 miles in planning. Readjustment of old debts amounting to 40,360,000 pounds sterling.	The Sian Incident, with Generalissimo Chiang Kai-shek being seized by Communists-inspired generals for two weeks.	Landing of 1,000 Japanese Marines at Tsingtao.
1937 January	Agreement of Japanese banks to hand over silver to Central Bank.	Elimination of the irregular military units involved in the Sian Incident. Exposure of attempted riots of Japanese *ronins* at Chengchow.	

Month			
March			Reaffirmation of Hirota's three demands on Chinese by Japanese Foreign Minister Sato in the Diet.
April	Announcement of Hukuang and Chicago Bank loan settlements.	Invasion of Suiyuan by "Manchukuo" military units with Japanese assistance.	Military maneuvers of Japanese troops in North China. Success of moderate elements in Japanese elections, which proved abortive. Trumping up of "incidents" by Japanese *ronin* at Swatow.
May	Providing of £1.1 million loan by British and Chinese interests for Shanghai-Hangchow-Ningpo Railway; agreement of American Export-Import Bank to finance half the cost of purchase of US$3 million of locomotives.		
June	Completion of the northern section of the Taiyuan-Tatung Railroad. Reserves of foreign currency, gold and silver reached U.S. $379 million as of June 30. Recovery of Shanghai wholesale index to 126.1 (1926=100), the approximate level of 1931, from low of 90.5 in July 1935.		"Dairen Conference" of Japanese military leaders in Manchuria and North China for a more aggressive policy.
July	Agreement of American Treasury to buy 62 million ounces of silver.		The Marco Polo Bridge Incident.
August	Linking of the Canton-Kowloon Railroad with the Canton-Hankow Railroad.	Setting up of a "Shensi-Kansu-Ningsia Soviet Government" by the Communists for self-expansion under the guise of national resistance against Japan.	Japanese attack on Shanghai.

CHRONOLOGY OF 1927-1937*

Date	Achievements of the National Government and Important Economic Events	Internal Difficulties	External Trouble
October	Completion of the Chientang River Bridge.		
November	Completion of thirteen irrigation projects, irrigating a total of more than six million *mou* of land.	Move of the site of the National Government from Nanking to Hankow.	Fall of Shanghai to the Japanese.
December			Fall of Nanking to the Japanese.

*Based primarily on: (1) papers included in this volume; (2) the chronology of the *Eastern Miscellany*, a bi-weekly published by the Commerce Press, Limited, Shanghai; (3) *A Record of Major Events of the Republic of China* (Chung-hua Min-kuo Ta-chih Chi) by Kao Yin-tsu (Taipei: World Society, 1957); (4) "Chronology of Major Economic Events," 1912-1946 (pp. 507-521, from 1927-1937), compiled by Li Yung-ting, which constitutes Part II of a Chinese volume on *The Economic History of the Republic of China* compiled and issued by the Bankers' Association, Shanghai, in commemoration of the 30th anniversary of the *Bankers' Weekly*, and reprinted by Hua-wen Press in August, 1967, Taipei.

Acknowledgment

The General Editor desires to record here his sincere appreciation of the splendid cooperation he has received from the Staff of the St. John's University Press in the editing of the manuscript and the making of this book. In particular, he is indebted to Dr. Frank L. Kunkel, Editorial Director, and Mrs. Julia Barone, Production Director of the Press; to Mrs. Virginia McEntee for editorial assistance in every part of the volume; and to Mrs. Dorothy Canner, Secretary to the Center of Asian Studies, for accurate and painstaking typing and secretarial work.

Index